T0305047

BRAND NEW NATION

RAVINDER KAUR

BRAND NEW NATION

*Capitalist Dreams and Nationalist Designs
in Twenty-First-Century India*

STANFORD UNIVERSITY PRESS

STANFORD, CALIFORNIA

Stanford University Press
Stanford, California

Printed in the United States of America on acid-free, archival-quality paper

Library of Congress Cataloging-in-Publication Data

Names: Kaur, Ravinder (Professor of South Asian studies), author.
Title: Brand new nation : capitalist dreams and nationalist designs in twenty-first
    century India / Ravinder Kaur.
Other titles: South Asia in motion.
Description: Stanford, California : Stanford University Press, 2020. | Series: South
    Asia in motion | Includes bibliographical references and index.
Identifiers: LCCN 2020009907 | ISBN 9781503612242 (cloth) | ISBN 9781503612594
    (paperback) | ISBN 9781503612600 (epub)
Subjects: LCSH: Investments, Foreign—India. | Branding (Marketing)—Political
    aspects—India. | National characteristics, East Indian. | Nationalism—
    Economic aspects—India. | Capitalism—India. | India—Economic
    conditions—1991– | India—Economic policy—1991–2016. | India—Economic
    policy—2016–
Classification: LCC HG5732 .K384 2020 | DDC 330.954—dc23
LC record available at https://lccn.loc.gov/2020009907

Cover design: Rob Ehle
Typeset by Motto Publishing Services in 11/15 Adobe Caslon Pro

For Anton and Noor

CONTENTS

BRAND NEW NATION

CHAPTER 1

FUTURES MARKET

FOR ONE WEEK every year, the main street in Davos, the Promenade, turns into an unusual marketplace. As the annual meeting of the
World Economic Forum (WEF) commences in this upscale Swiss ski
town each January, many of its posh hotels, cafes, and even museums
turn into sites of an extraordinary kind of exchange. The colorful billboards displayed on the buildings have messages such as "India: Land
of Limitless Opportunities," "Make in India," "Malaysia: Doing Business, Building Friendships," "Brazil: A Country of Opportunity, Innovation, Sustainability, Creativity," "Mexico: Seize the Day," "Egypt:
Invest in the Future," and "Proudly South Africa: Imagine New Ways."
First-time visitors may find these advertisements puzzling. What kind
of commodity is being showcased, and who might be the intended consumers? But for regular visitors, the spectacle of nations jostling for attention is a familiar sight during WEF week. These sites are the verita-
ble front offices of "nation brands": nations packaged and advertised as
"attractive investment destinations" in global markets. During the past
decade and a half, they have become popular landmarks on the global
investment trail, well-known stopovers in the packed itinerary of investors forever in search of new profitable opportunities.

This exclusive world of nation brands is a strange, heady mix of
optimism and anxiety, and it is seemingly forever on the move. On

FIGURE 1.1. *India Adda publicity poster featuring technofriendly young Indians invites global conversations on India. Kirchner Museum, Promenade, Davos, 2012. Taken by author.*

my first visit to Davos in 2012, I found myself seated next to two men dressed in smart business suits at Brand India's lounge, India Adda—marketed as a "quintessential Indian hangout" representing India's culture of commerce—at Café Schneider. I recalled seeing them the previous day on Brand South Africa's premises in the Kirchner Museum, where an exhibition on the African growth story had been inaugurated. We exchanged our business cards, the first ritual of networking, and over cups of masala chai sponsored by the Tea Board of India, they expressed their love for India and all things Indian. They were both investment bankers at a major global investment-management firm specializing in emerging markets. As I glanced at their business cards, the one in the purple tie jovially explained his job as an explorer who

FIGURE 1.2. *A street view of the India Adda/Make in India Lounge. Winter Garden, Café Schneider, Davos, 2015. Taken by author.*

FIGURE 1.3. *Hotel Belvedere featuring Brand Egypt. 2015. Taken by author.*

discovers new investment hotspots in the world. "So where are those new hotspots?" I asked. He replied promptly, "In the emerging markets": the bright rays of hope in Asia, Africa, and Latin America cutting through the dark clouds of recession in the Euro zone. "Mexico is coming up, Brazil is an attractive bet, and even Egypt is promising for those looking for alternatives," his companion chimed in. "India is a long-term investment," he said in a reassuring tone. But the emerging markets can be risky; "they heat up and cool down," and therefore one had to be "ready to seize new opportunities," the man in the purple tie added with a broad smile as they prepared to leave. In this futures market, it seemed, the investors were forever in search of new investment hotspots across the world, just as the nations hoped to be discovered and loved as attractive investment destinations. Due thanks and pleasantries done, they stepped out in the fresh snow that had covered the Promenade in the meantime. They were headed to the Mexico pavilion in Hotel Panorama, where a festive evening celebrating Mexico's potential as an investment destination was about to begin.

This flash-in-the-pan encounter, polite and even charming, peppered with speculations and forecasts of risks and opportunities, is typical of how conversations unfolded in these settings. The affective language of hope and optimism—the compulsory good news the business world thrives on—that the two bankers had used to describe the futures market of nation brands was familiar to me. I had been drawn into this world at a particularly dramatic moment when India's emergence and rise as a world player, propelled by its high economic growth performance and future potential, was being celebrated across the world. India was said to have "arrived on the global stage," the primus motor of the Asian century that together with China was expected to eclipse Western hegemony in world affairs. It was as if the pace of history had accelerated in anticipation of a new time when India could finally be rescued from the "waiting room of history" and reoriented toward a limitless future.[1] The early twenty-first century, we were told, was that of ascendance of the South, especially BRICS—Brazil, Russia, India, China, and South Africa—the so-called big five. These countries were the leading stars of the many capitalist growth stories

FIGURE 1.4. *"Malaysia: More Opportunities" at Hotel Panorama. 2015. Taken by author.*

unfolding in the postcolonial and postcommunist nations. Envisioned afresh as an investment opportunity, the old third world was no longer a dark container of deprivation and overpopulation but a rich reservoir of resources and raw talent bolstered by its youthful demographic dividend waiting to be tapped by innovative entrepreneurs. The established hierarchies of north/south, rich/poor, core/periphery, developed/developing, and empire/colony seemed superfluous in the large-scale transformations redrawing the twentieth-century world map. The familiar world appeared to be upside down. In this unsettling capitalist geography, India's emergence as a prominent nerve center of unbridled capitalism was a critical event in more ways than one.

FIGURE 1.5. *Brand Brazil bus in Davos. 2012. Taken by author.*

FIGURE 1.6. *Make in India campaign in Davos. 2015. Taken by author.*

Recall here India's established moral-political legacy as the prime mover of the third-world movement: the anticolonial coalition comprising newly liberated nations across Asia, Africa, and Latin America.[2] Built on the shared experience of colonialism, the third world was more than a utopian dream of political liberation. Its cornerstone was economic independence seeking a fair redistribution of the world's resources,[3] the very opposite of the nineteenth-century free-trade imperialism that had created rich economic centers in the north and poor peripheries in the south. This move to fashion an independent third way beyond capitalism and communism in the mid-twentieth-century bipolar world underpinned India's postcolonial nation-building efforts too. The sphere of economy itself was shaped as a "mixed economy"—an experimental hybrid of free-market enterprise and a planned economy—to realize the modernist dream of development.[4] The Indian state was the key actor that planned large-scale development schemes and experimented in industrialization and import substitution in what came to be known as the tightly controlled License Raj, or a closed national economy. Against this background, India's embrace of liberal economic reforms in the early 1990s was not merely an instance of liberal triumphalism sweeping the globe. It also signified an end of the third-world vision that India had helped shape in the heady years of independence. Given its sheer size and complexity, India's shift toward capitalism was a momentous event in the organization of the world economy and the nature of global politics about to unfold. The official lounge of Brand India where I was seated was precisely a microcosm of these manifold shifts, a theater in which "New India"—the popular name for the postreform, technofriendly, high-consumption entrepreneurial nation—encountered the elite that governed the world. I was surrounded by cheerful images of the India growth story that foretold success and the unlimited potential of the nation to investors and policy makers. The publicity posters, glossy brochures, videos, and blogs were all geared to project India's image in the language of desire: aspirations, promise, potential, talent, and limitless opportunities and growth. Dressed up as a branded commodity in Davos, the sign of India was called on to perform hope and promise for global capital, its nationalist dreams fully harnessed to the ever-enchanting project of capitalism.

The spectacle of the impending capitalist transformation of the nation-form has been in the public domain for a long time. An apt example of this hiding-in-plain-sight phenomenon is an Incredible India advertisement issued about a decade into the opening up of the Indian economy (fig. 1.7). The image features simple bold text reading "Open for Business!" against a rich crimson background. A common sign hung on shop fronts, "Open for Business" signals a commercial space accessible to potential consumers.[5] Brought into the image frame of India, it is assigned a heavier task: to publicize the nation as a commercial enclosure, a space of limitless exchange and capital investment, now accessible in the global markets. That India is "open for business" is not just a witty turn of phrase; it is also an unambiguous description of the large-scale capitalist transformations—dubbed as the 1990s "new economic policy"—that deregulated the state control of the economy. Perhaps more significantly, the image is a disclosure of the making of the twenty-first-century nation-as-investment-destination phenomenon occurring in many parts of the world. The investment-destination model entails a full capitalization (transformation) of the nation into an income-generating asset: a new imaginary of the national territory as an infrastructure-ready enclosure for capital investment, its cultural identity distilled into a competitive global brand and its inhabitants— designated as demographic dividend—income-generating human capital that can be plowed back to generate more economic growth. In this logic, the injection of capital from outside is the vital force that fertilizes the earth of the investment-ready nation.[6]

This internalization of the market logic reconfiguring the nation-state into an enclosed commercial-cultural zone is what I call the *brand new nation*: the nation revitalized and renewed as a profitable business enterprise with claims to ownership over cultural property within its territory. Erected upon a double scaffolding of austere structural adjustment programs and lavish dreamworlds of long-awaited good times, the brand new nation form increasingly mimics an income-generating asset that can be branded, valued, and ranked according to its

FIGURE 1.7. *"Open for Business" poster. ITB Berlin, 2007. Courtesy of V. Sunil.*

capacity to yield profits. In turn, its profitability is seen as the fast track to utopic futures. This phenomenon is especially visible in the old third world, now dubbed "emerging markets." Once deemed out of sync with "world time"—the temporal rhythm of transoceanic trade and capitalist modernity—these new frontiers of capitalism are now said to be the unstoppable forerunners in the march to the future.[7] What fuels this relentless capitalization of the nation-form, the urgent calls for ever-more economic reforms, is not just the nationalist dream of getting ahead of the first world but also the fear of being stopped, of being permanently left behind by global capital. The postcolonial anxiety of never making it always lurks beneath the spectacle of hope and optimism.

The counterintuitive logic at work, then, in the rational, profit-oriented world of investors is this: what is beyond economy is that which truly animates the economy. The *affective investments*—hope and optimism, love and devotion, and even anxiety and nationalist fervor—that at first appear superfluous or as distractions to the business of economic investments are in fact crucial to its workings. The noneconomic elements are always at work in what seems to be purely the domain of economy—the affective force that energizes the project of capitalist transformation and helps unlock the potential of economic investments. Witness here too a particular inflection of "millennial capitalism"[8] taking shape especially in the Global South. The infusion of capital here is not only a magical moment that promises progress and prosperity but also the promise of effacing the shame of colonial subjugation and violence. Capital appears as a curative force that can even redeem the nation's lost glory via economic growth. It is not just the infusion of capital that is critical in the making of the brand new nation; equally critical is the recognition of the nation's growth story by global capital. Thus, twentieth-century *nation building* is increasingly being replaced by twenty-first-century *nation branding*. What is dubbed a growth story in policy-business circles is essentially an enchanting fairy tale of capitalist dreamworlds, a fairy-tale blueprint of economic reforms along with calls for a strong political leader to implement it. This transaction clearly exceeds the sphere of economy and liberal politics and cannot be explained in purely materialist terms. Instead, it reveals how twenty-first-century capitalism and cultures of hypernationalism are fully locked in embrace. It is hardly a coincidence that the era of liberal economic reforms has given way to populist strong leaders of the muscular variety. After all, capital has always rooted for strong, decisive leaders and centralized governance that can ensure its swift mobility and put the nation's resources at the disposal of investors (see chapter 5, "The Magical Market").

In many ways, this is an unprecedented shift in the history of the nation-state. The state has indeed always been an active economic agent, but what is different is the unabashed spectacle of alliance between economy, politics, and publicity through which the brand new nation takes shape. To make sense of this emerging phenomenon, we need to take the enhanced visibility of economy in politics not as a sideshow but as a signal of how the logic of the capitalist growth story has seeped into popular politics as the harbinger of good times. Across the third world turned emerging markets, the promise of the growth story is affectively entangled with the collective dreamworlds visualized and illuminated in the great spectacle of mass-publicity campaigns, the tantalizing blueprints of mass utopias by which the material condition of free markets comes alive.[9] This book is about how the brand new nation came to be and about the kind of future that awaits the nation-state in the twenty-first century.

BRAND NEW NATION

The spectacular appearance of the brand new nation might seem off-script or even plain ironic to those familiar with the story of globalization—like a late-twentieth-century shorthand for the unhindered movement of capital, labor, goods, and people—and the opening up of the world. Weren't we once told that the nation-state had been made "obsolete," a superfluous political artifact in the age of globalization? And that the nation-state was standing on "its last legs," faced as it was with "crisis" and potential demise?[10] Recall how the euphoric triumph in the 1990s of liberalism at the "end of history" had ushered in the seemingly unstoppable force of globalization and in the process brought world areas previously closed to global capital into the fold of free markets.[11] The global nature of this capitalist transformation was produced in the language of accelerated mobility—of flows, movement, interconnections, fluidity, networks, transnationalism, deterritorialization, and cosmopolitanism—and the infrastructures of cheaper air travel, ever-new media technologies, new modes of consumption, and digital connectivity. In this moment of interconnectedness, the bounded enclosure of the nation-state increasingly stood out as an anomaly. The world in motion was moving toward denationalization in search of a postnational world order,[12] and whatever was left of the nation-state was the mere skin or the cracked casing of its former self, a vestige of an earlier age that was surplus to the age of unbridled capitalism.[13]

But there's a twist and then a turn in this story. Defying all predictions, the nation-form was refusing to disappear, even going in the exact opposite direction of the one that proponents of globalization would have had us believe it would go. The moment the nation-state was being written out of the script of world politics was also the moment it was preparing to make a spectacular, highly choreographed comeback. Simply put, the very thing that was supposed to have been effaced in the borderless, flat world of free markets was morphing into a lucrative resource in the capitalist transformation of the old third world. The nation-form was ready to make a fresh debut in the circuits of global economy, having been decked out in the new garb of an "attractive investment destination" and its cracked skin or casing having been tailored into a distinct corporate brand. It wasn't just India, Brazil, Mexico, Egypt, or South Africa creating unique brand identities—the nation brands were everywhere. From Cool Japan; Creative Korea; Amazing Thailand; Wonderful Indonesia; Malaysia: Truly Asia; Russia: The Whole World Within; Azerbaijan: Land of Magical Colors; Australia Unlimited; 100% Pure: New Zealand; Brand Kenya: Make it Here; Remarkable Rwanda; Ghana: Uniquely Welcoming; and Turkey: Discover the Potential, to Miraculous China and Commercial Yiwu, the list is endless—and growing.

The second turn in the life of the nation-state is still unfolding. It is this: the age of globalization is said to be on retreat. The structures of globalization built on neoliberal economic interdependence appear to have reached their expiration date. Once celebrated as the harbinger of the world of flows sans barrier, globalization is now the object of political backlash in Europe and America. The ongoing nationalist challenge to borderless territories and free-trade blocks that enable the easy flow of capital and labor is a case in point. The double pressure of widening social inequality and northward immigration has created ground for populist measures to reclaim the nation-state and to erect a variety of barriers.

But what if we posit that the folding up of globalization does not mean a collapse of capitalism as such? That the popular move toward neonationalism, or nation-first politics, does not weaken but instead strengthens the nation-state as a dominant player in global capital? And what if we suggest that the twenty-first-century nation-state is not a mere rerun of the original that unfolded in previous centuries but has undergone an altogether new makeover in the age of capital? Put differently, we need to revert to an old (and overmined) question: What is a nation? Or more concretely, what kind of nation-form is emerging from the embers of late-twentieth-century globalization, which saw the implosion of millennial capitalism amid volatile boom and busts, the return of identity politics, and the attendant dramatic flux rearranging the liberal world order?

I propose that the brand new nation—recrafted and repackaged as a branded enclosure for capital in the twenty-first century—has emerged from within the structures of unbridled free markets and centralized state governance and of the spectacular imagination of utopian dream-worlds in capitalist design. This form emerged from an ongoing historical shift—the capitalist transformation of the nation-state wherein the logic of capital is the glue holding the nation and state together. The *nation* in this scheme is imagined as a vast enclosure of production, its territory a reserve of untapped natural resources, its population potential producers/consumers of goods and services, and its cultural essence a unique nation brand that distinguishes it from other investment destinations. All of these can be capitalized (transformed) into income-generating assets. The *state* is the authority that manages the income-generating capacity of the national enclosure and holds the power to visualize, brand, legislate, and spatially rearrange the national enclosure as a market-ready investment destination.[14] The process of capitalization—the packaging of the nation and its identity by the state as an exclusive commercial brand—is what binds the nation to the state. This process unfolds along a visual *reterritorialization* of the national enclosure as a distinct economic zone and as a unified cultural-political identity.

The transformative work of the branding project lies not just in selling the nation to potential investors but also in the consecration of a particular form of state sovereignty—the visual power to celebrate the revitalized homeland and to *see* and *show* the national territory and its population as valuable factors of production available to global capital.

The critical point in the making of the visual territory of nation brands is this: to be featured in the visual frame of the nation brand and to be shown (or shown off) to the world is to be affirmed as an organic part of the nation. The questions of economy, politics, and publicity remain deeply entangled in this visual reterritorialization. Who are the chosen people who inhabit the visual surface of the nation brand? Which cultural practices and ideas are left out of the frame, concealed from the eyes of the world? Who owns the nation and its natural and cultural possessions, and who has the power to capitalize these possessions? The visual frame of the nation brand is a form of public recognition of the nation's cultural essence, the unique difference that acquires legitimacy precisely by being chosen for illumination by the state. Put differently, the state asserts its power by claiming proprietary control over the material and cultural possessions of the nation and, more importantly, the power to market them. The brand new nation reveals the close kinship between *identity economy* and *identity politics* and between *publicity* and *populism* at the heart of the ongoing rearrangement of the liberal political order.

I do not mean to suggest that capitalization of the nation is a smooth, uncontested operation. In fact, it opens space for political contestations, albeit of a specific kind.[15] Witness here a field of politics that emerges through the brand—a volatile enactment of (neo)liberal statecraft and illiberal nationalism that feeds off of and further authenticates populist notions of an organic nation and the blood-and-soil purity of its inhabitants. The brand boosts the populist entanglements between corporeal and affective matters as a solution to *economic* problems faced by the people even as it generates *extraeconomic* reification of hypernationalist pride. What aggravates political volatility is the populist competitiveness between the state and its opponents—inasmuch as the state seeks legitimacy as an efficient brand manager of the nation and its opponents accuse it of not having performed that function well enough, of having failed the people. The economic success of the brand is what potentially enables extraeconomic agendas to be implemented. That the brand itself is inherently unstable, forever shaped by the excess of meaning it produces and even by counterfeit versions, means that such politics is almost always vulnerable to contingency.[16] Nevertheless, the logic of the brand has by now filtered through the structures of power and governance—the nation is not just branded but actually turned into a territorial container of branded regions, provinces, and cities that compete to attract investments.[17] Termed *competitive federalism*, this form of governance lives off a system of constant auditing and rankings that rewards and humiliates regions on the ease-of-doing-business criterion and the size of capital flows to boost economic growth. The capitalization of the nation brand is the magical formula that promises to unleash the authentic national spirit and, in the case of the old third world, even cleanse the shame of colonial subjugation that has long defined its place in the world. In short, to be discovered as an attractive investment destination in the world economy is to be affirmed as a proper nation in the early-twenty-first-century world order.

THE GREAT SPECTACLE

The making of the brand new nation cannot be explained only as the triumph of human greed and crass utilitarianism or even as the bland blueprint of structural adjustments that policy experts hand out. What gives it lifeblood is something else—its affective translation into popular politics via the great spectacle of the growth story—shorthand for the promise of economic reforms, dreamworlds of good times, and even a full sense of being-in-the-world—immediated through enchanting mass-publicity campaigns. To be sure, this translation of economic policy into popular politics is not seamless. The prevailing accounts of the great transformation of the postcolonial world—through structural adjustments and reform packages—move between two poles that hold the market formula either as an external imposition on reluctant nations or as a necessary utilitarian measure to lift people out of poverty and create development.[18] What is often glossed over in such accounts is the human capacity and desire to *draw* futures, a desire that has always been a critical force in the project of transformation. I intend the verb *draw* to have a double meaning here—as the act of etching an image or a model and as the force that moves, that pulls something in the desired direction in order to rearrange the world. Once harnessed to the technologies of mass media via murals, photographs, films, posters, advertisements, billboards, events, and, now, social media trends, the art of drawing futures has been turned into the art of public persuasion. The vastly amplified circulation of symbols and messages is more than a public notice offering information. It is designed not just to inform but "to seduce, to exhort, to sell, to educate, to convince, to appeal," to grab the attention of the general populace (or consumers or spectators), and to mass market a given commodity or worldview.[19] The work of mass-publicity campaigns is to invite or even provoke the public to partake in the project of drawing forth the futures.[20]

This spectacular drawing of futures is what I call the *great spectacle*: the zone of contact between the speculative dreamworlds of the future and the material conditions of the present, the encounter between what *is* and what *could be* in the new time. In this theatre of persuasion, cold statistics and expert recommendations are transformed into populist politics dressed up as "good times": visions of economic growth tied to hypernationalist dreams of a glorious ancient-modern future. This affective mediation is what gives nourishment to the enterprise of the nation brand, a kind of intimate yet impersonal "immediate" engagement that intensifies its mass appeal and circulation.[21] The mass-publicity campaigns transform complex policy interventions into desirable blueprints of hope and possibility, producing a tantalizing vision that is the very opposite of the lacks, failures, and stagnations that have otherwise defined the old third world. Put differently, the spectacle of hope requires the "lacking" third world to be produced as a constitutive anteriority. Dressed up as attention-grabbing campaigns, the spectacle seeks to draw the attention of the different publics—from foreign investors, policy makers, and financial experts to citizens, local businesses, and consumers—to boost the global image of the nation as an investment destination, to draw foreign capital, to garner favorable trade agreements, and to sell economic reforms to its own citizens as pathways to progress and prosperity. The great spectacle, I suggest, is the drawing board of futures on which individual and collective dreamworlds can be speculated endlessly, the affective production of an avalanche of images that seek to overrun all other competing visions. In an image-saturated world, the work of the great spectacle is not just to produce images of the future but to modify and repurpose the flow of images in the desired direction.

The great spectacle produced through publicity campaigns has at best remained overlooked and at worst been dismissed as propaganda. Yet it is here that we find a rich visual archive that allows us to trace the complex social world within which the contemporary renewal of the nation is taking shape. The term *propaganda* comes with heavy baggage that tends to obscure more than reveal the complex processes at work. Any information labeled as propaganda, more so in the time of post-truth and fake news, is either viewed anxiously as a dark art of deception practiced via rumors and untruths to conceal reality or dismissed as meaningless noise that occupies the public sphere. In both cases, this tainted appellation means that propaganda material is often discarded in the junkyard of archival knowledge, and its potential remains un-utilized. To be sure, the original use of *propaganda* was to indicate re-production, but by the mid-sixteenth century the term came to be deployed in a religious sense to mean "propagation of the doctrine of faith among nonbelievers."[22] Perhaps it is this older etymological association with faith and indoctrination rather than with reason that gave *propaganda* its contemporary common usage: a recursive loop of dis/information designed to alter ideas and belief. But this recursive quality is what makes propaganda a rich archive of knowledge, albeit of a performative variety that aims to reproduce the self-contained worlds. Its value lies in activating an abundant repository of collective dreams, the mimetic archive, that sought to sneak into the lived worlds and transform those into their own image.[23] I gather this abandoned archive, the scattered bits and pieces of images, from the junkyard of propaganda and recycle it as an invaluable resource to write the history of the brand new nation.

This neglected archive discloses how the growth story has been laminated onto the old postcolonial nationalist dream of freedom, but this time freedom has been harnessed to the economic prowess of the nation-state. The possibility of a "second liberation" via economic growth not only taps into the collective insecurities and humiliation of the colonial past but also holds out the chance to finally overcome them on the global stage. The capitalization of the nation as a branded investment destination is an opportunity to at once *add value* to the nation by generating capital and, in doing so, gain prestige and influence in the world. The global celebration of the nation brand is even taken as an expression of national pride, fueling hypernationalist movements in many parts of the postcolonial world. The colorful display of the nation as an investment destination, a very twenty-first-century mode of arriving or making it in the world, grows out of these complexities— the desire to unhinge the nation from its colonial past and the impatience to inhabit the long-promised future. The enhanced visibility of the nation serves a dual function—it makes visible the potential and availability of the national enclosure in the global markets and simultaneously manufactures images of mass utopia that imagine personal aspirations and restoration of the authentic self in alliance with the national growth story.

This latest turn in the history of the nation requires that we engage with the modern enchantment with nation and nationalism, a form of intimate affiliation that at first appears at odds with commodification and market transactions.[24] In fact, thinking of the nation-form as a commodity seems to be an aberration, even a sacrilege. After all, weren't we once told that "nations are not just political units but *organic* beings, living personalities"[25] or that nations are not founded "on mere consent or law but on the passions implanted by nature and history"?[26] Yet I suggest that this very imagination of the nation as a unique eternal person is what opens ontological possibilities for the emergence of the brand new nation. Recall how nineteenth-century cultural nationalism evolved around the presumption that "the essence of a nation is its distinctive civilization, which is the product of its unique history, culture and geographical profile."[27] For Johann Gottfried Herder, the father of cultural nationalism, nations were natural solidarities, living organisms endowed with individuality that could not be replicated across the global terrain.[28] And nearly a century after Herder, Ernst Renan, in his famous essay "What Is a Nation?," proposed that "a nation is a soul, a spiritual principle."[29] While Renan emphasized the question of consent and the dynamic nature of nation making—the everyday plebiscite—he saw the nation as a distinct moral-spiritual project that entailed a common history of love and suffering as an essential condition for being a nation.

This love, or national romance, embraced the *geist* (spirit) of the *volk* (people) and is a well-woven theme through more than two centuries, when national identity was carved in literary and artistic forms of natural landscapes and its ethnic inhabitants.[30] Sumathi Ramaswamy has shown how the nation has long been a sacred object of worship, its territory personified and pictured as sacred, the mother goddess placed at the sacrificial altar of patriotic devotion.[31] This passion of nationalism has always demanded a "special kind of love" that exceeds all others and whose ultimate expression is martyrdom for its cause.[32] For Benedict Anderson, it was precisely the question of death in the service of the "imagined political community" called nation that made him ask, "What makes the shrunken imaginings of recent history (scarcely more than two centuries) generate such colossal sacrifices?" This question tugs at tensions that are at the heart of the idea of the modern nation—the secular transformation of the sacred, the ideas of suffering and salvation poured into the form of nation that "always loom(s) out of an immemorial past, and still more important, glide(s) into a limitless future."[33] The "cultural roots" of the imaginings of the nation and its variants, nationality and nationalism, grew from these tensions. What was fashioned was the modern nation: a political artifact of a particular kind, a virtual person who has long claimed origins in a timeless past and a wholly inalienable essence and whose nurturing required routine performance of love and complete devotion.

In the ongoing shift to capitalism, it is precisely these premodern expressions of love and devotion for the nation that strengthen the project of economic growth, albeit in a new form. The old cultural nationalist imagination of the nation as a living organism, a singularity, is what renders it transcendental and open to exchange in the market. To love and be devoted to one's nation now means to work to enhance the economic value and potential of the nation. Put differently, what makes the project of promoting the economy is the noneconomic affective investments: love and devotion. This special kind of love for the brand new nation requires channeling positive, uplifting images of the nation in the global public sphere and overlooking and countering negative images that might harm its brand value in the world. As John and Jean Comaroff have argued, what abets the projection of the nation form into the broader plane are the "primitive" features of the nation, a project that they have dubbed Nationality, Inc.—the making of the nation-state into a business enterprise.[34] What was once held as an inalienable cultural essence of the nation is now an alienable property, and national identity is distilled into corporate brand identity. This is the distinctly contemporary version of the familiar nation-form—the virtual person rendered into a unique corporate brand in global markets. This shift is not entirely unexpected given that modernist nations "always have been brands-under-construction, always immanent, imminently corporate."[35] The corporate form invokes both the economic form of the corporation and the *corporeal* dimension of the social that returns, affectively, in nationalism.

What Nationality, Inc. has enabled is the assertion of this corporate nationhood—economic and affective—or more specifically, the corporeal embodiment of national identity and heritage under the arch of the nation brand. Far from corroding the celebrated spirit (*geist*) of the nation, the nation's market value as a profit-generating commercial enclosure becomes a mode of affirming the worthiness of the people (*volk*) as a great nation. The more the brand new nation attracts and generates capital, the more it legitimizes its aura, claims of civilizational essence, identity as the chosen people, and natural ties with the landscape. The infusion of capital continually generates something that exceeds capital—the aura/spirit or the nonextractable difference that is plowed back to generate brand capital. In short, the cultural difference distilled into a corporate brand is put to work to generate capital, and capital in return enhances the cultural brand. With culture and commerce locked in embrace, the glory and the corpus of the nation are themselves now tied to speculative cycles of economic boom and bust. The futures of the brand new nation, at this point, appear to be open-ended, messy entanglements of tantalizing dreams of the future that economic growth promises to bring. These dreams in turn are harnessed to speculative trade in the nation's future capacity to generate capital.

I do not mean to suggest that the capitalist transformation of the nation-form was inevitable. These material and ideological shifts were shaped as much from long genealogies as from contingencies, the anticipated and the unanticipated events of the twentieth century. In what follows, I trace the past and present lineages of the brand new nation.

THE PROMISE OF BRANDING

In the world of advertising, a profession that lives off of marketing cultural identities and difference, the nation has long been recognized as a corporate brand built on coherent and unified identity. In the 1990s, this vital insight was duly turned into a commercial opportunity to build corporate brands for nations, to channel its soft power to generate financial value. The logic of Nationality, Inc. at this point, began filtering into policy recommendations to enhance the competitiveness of national economies, especially those just opening up across the old third world. The promise of branding was offered up as the "transformative magic of ritual"[36] that could infuse new life into the body of the nation and even reincarnate its identity as commodity-image in the global economy. What truly animated the economy was "beyond economy"— the sublime brand could function both as an object of investment and a medium of exchange and thereby corral the nonextractable element into a system of extraction.[37] Once branded and transformed into an attractive investment destination, the newly opened nation could hope to realize its true potential and place in the capitalist world order. In what follows, then, I lay out the new and old ancestral lines of the idea of branding national territories that continue to shape the twenty-first-century world.

The project of branding national territories as investment destinations began evolving into a governmental practice in the 1990s on the premise that companies and nations share similar corporate features and can be imagined, branded, and capitalized likewise. A key voice in this enterprise was Wally Olins, a historian turned branding guru in London, who provocatively and perceptively drew on Hobsbawm and Anderson to point out that the constant reinvention of the nation and of national identity was akin to how corporations continuously "change, merge, divest, invest and rebrand and reinvent themselves."[38] He disputed the prevalent idea that nations were sacred, immutable, and in possession of "a nature and a substance other than that of a corporation. A corporation can be re-branded, not a state. . . . One can take a product, a washing powder for instance, and then change the name which is actually done very regularly, . . . [whereas] a country carries specific dignity unlike a marketed product."[39] Instead, he argued, nations have always been reinventing their images by creating "self-sustaining myths to build coherent identities," a process that in the world of advertising is known by another name—branding. The techniques for branding the nation and company were similar, he reasoned, because "people are people whether they work in a company or live in a nation, and that means they can be motivated and inspired and manipulated in the same way, using the same techniques."[40] In a 1999 policy paper commissioned by a British neoliberal think tank entitled "Trading Identities: Why Countries and Companies Are Becoming More Alike," Olins had argued for nation branding to be recognized as a contemporary form of nation building in a rapidly changing world, "partly by combining regional integration with devolution, a bit like the decentralized management of mega-merged corporations—but also by developing national brands."[41] The argument that country-is-company—forever in the transformative mode of mergers and closures, territorial expansions and secessions—should take shape in the 1990s is hardly surprising. That was when the global map was being dramatically redrawn—the Soviet Union had dissolved and reemerged instead as the Commonwealth of Independent States (CIS), including Russia and eleven central Asian nations; the two Germanys had unified; and the European Union was turning into a concrete entity. The postcommunist and postcolonial nations were also being reinvented and rebranded as open economies and investment destinations in the global free markets. In this heady moment of open economies and structural reforms, Olins appeared as a leading proponent of the new policy prescriptions and vocabulary of nation branding. What set him apart from his peers was that he assertively took the debate outside the narrow confines of business and marketing to tap into the shared, albeit camouflaged, genealogy of modern nation and company. In doing so, he at once exposed and capitalized the shape-shifting corporate form of the nation. At the heart of this country/company entanglement is the older idea of the corporation, a central actor in the story of branding nations, as we will find out later.

Corporation simply means persons joined together for a common purpose to assume a single, unified body.[42] Such a structure composed of joined parts came to be duly recognized as a "legally authorized entity, artificial person created by law from a group or succession of persons" in order to serve a variety of economic, religious, and political causes.[43] The fictional person qua corporation could exist continuously and potentially live forever—its powers and liabilities distinct from those of its human members, who could be replaced, dismissed, or incorporated as the need arose. To incorporate, then, was to fashion a new body that ultimately was more than the sum of its parts: the capitalist iteration of the medieval doctrine of the king's two bodies—the mortal human body and the immortal sacred body that never ceases to exist.[44] By the late sixteenth century, however, the corporation had taken the form of a for-profit enterprise that would act both in the national interest and in the interests of its stockholders. This is when we began seeing the peculiar modern alliance between capital and state, the making of the public-private formula that has become an enduring feature of millennial capitalism.[45] The appearance of the corporation in the form of a joint-stock company indeed coincided with an acceleration in transcontinental and transoceanic world trade, an occurrence that by the nineteenth century both generated and required vast stocks of capital investment and in many ways reshaped the world.[46] This long history of the nineteenth century has by now been dubbed "the transformation of the world," a global transition marked by commerce, communication, industrial manufacturing, technological inventions, faster transport, and colonization of vast overseas territories that puts vast natural resources at the disposal of colonial powers.[47] A capsule version of this world-in-transformation can be witnessed in the spectacular nineteenth-century world exhibitions that for the first time ever assembled commodities from all over the world. Walter Benjamin called these glittering exhibitions "the places of pilgrimage to the fetish commodity" or even the "phantasmagoria" of the "capitalist culture" that had come to define this age.[48] This assembly of commodities from all over the world, especially the overseas colonial territories, meant that the world itself could now be measured and seen in terms of its commodity value, abundance of raw material, industrial skill, and consumer desires.[49] It is in this unbridled nineteenth-century imperial world of free trade and its conflicts that we can trace the forgotten roots of Nationality, Inc., the evolution of trademarks and intellectual property rights, and the practice of branding places. What is critical, at this point, is the emergence of geographical indicators or "Made in" stamps disclosing the source of origin of commodities. Places came to be incorporated into the brand identity of commodities and eventually turned into commodities in their own right.

The story begins with the accelerated pace of global trade and commodity culture represented in the 1851 exhibition, following which the question of patents and trademark, or "the natural right of everyone to enjoy . . . an exclusive profit on the results of his power of invention," became a pressing issue.[50] The right to enjoy exclusive profit inevitably entailed measures against forgery, imitation, and counterfeit marks that threatened to siphon off or, at the very least, disperse profits. The early regulations, then, were created specifically "for the purpose of preventing the forgery of trademarks and the false marking of merchandise,"[51] and a trademark—the right to the specific application of symbols on "vendable commodities"—itself was recognized as quasi property that could be valued as an asset in the individual or in corporate stock.[52] This move to regulate trademark-as-property set the stage in the late nineteenth century for the emergence of a geographical indicator—the "Made in" mark—in response to the "rise" of Germany as a major manufacturing center in Europe. It was drawn as a legal weapon in the bitter trade wars that followed, a move that had mostly unanticipated consequences. In the late nineteenth century, Germany was

accused of flooding British (and European) markets with "cheap and
nasty goods," outcompeting local manufacturers.[53] Shades of contemporary discourse against cheap Chinese goods in Euro-America can be
witnessed here, albeit with a difference—the British trademark rules
were held responsible for indirectly branding and publicizing German
manufacturing amid anxieties of Britain's industrial decline. In 1896,
E. E. Williams published a widely circulated book called *Made in Germany* on the specter of the rising power of German manufacturing and
the concurrent decline of "the industrial supremacy of Great Britain."
Or as he ominously put it, "The industrial glory of England is depart-
ing, and England does not know it." In a chapter entitled "Why Germany Beats Us," he made a counterintuitive case that German manufacturers were profiting not just because of cheaper labor or better
products but because of "negative" trademark practices pursued in Britain. In 1887, the Merchandise Marks Act had been revised to include
a new provision for "the addition of a definite indication of the place
or country in which the goods were produced. . . . [And to this effect],
a definite statement should be added, such as 'manufactured in Germany,' to indicate the origin of goods."[54] The act called for a full "trade
description" of commodities, including information about the country
of origin, so as not to deceive customers about the source. The "Made
in" mark was meant as a supportive measure for British manufacturers so that foreign goods could be not be deceptively marked and sold
under a "false trade description" in the British market.[55] To this end,
however, the British effort to obstruct the circulation of German-made
goods via trademark laws had little impact. But what began as a le-
gal-bureaucratic measure to sort out and *expose* inferior foreign goods
by branding them—in the literal sense of burning the mark on the
body—with a "Made in" stamp had by the turn of the century become
an established commercial branding practice, in terms of advertising.
This move to mark and market cultural uniqueness as a national brand
became rampant in the intensification of world trade and the flow of
commodities: Swiss knives, Dutch cheese, French champagne, Danish design, Italian grappa, Scotch whiskey, Chinese porcelain, Indian
muslin, Egyptian cotton, English tea blends grown in India, and so on.

The brand value of geographical indicators in trademarks began to be recognized and was duly incorporated into what became the 1891 Madrid Agreement Concerning the International Registration of Marks.[56]

What is noteworthy is how the language of branding was less that of business and more that of moral values, a reiteration of a consistent theme that it is the noneconomic, the nonexchangeable elements that ground economic exchange. For example, the Madrid Agreement offered legal protection to trade names not only to ensure commercial profits but to serve "the interest of the consumer and commercial morality."[57] The legal arguments to capture cultural or national uniqueness and transform it into branded commercial property were constructed as moral measures against falsehood, unfair competition, counterfeits, theft, and forgery. The branding of "Made in" stamps, too, was articulated as an indignant moral response to the suppression of truth about the original source of commodities. These are the legal-political antecedents of trademarked geographical indicators and the contemporary phenomenon of nation branding that has evolved into an established global practice.

The idea of nation branding appears simple, but its implications are radical, even uncertain. The basic assumption at the heart of this project is that the nation *is* a brand par excellence. Its territory, people, natural resources, and cultural identity can be capitalized to enhance its competitiveness in the global economy. This assumption runs through the entire project of restructuring and transforming the nation into an investment destination, an enclosure than can be marketed to investors, tourists, and governments. This is the building block on which, in the past two decades, an entire discipline of destination marketing and reputation management, supported by a community of experts, has been constructed. It has its own body of knowledge, epistemic logics, and policy prescriptions that nation-states can draw on. The exponential expansion of this field resulted in the establishment of the International Place Branding Association in 2015, which aims to provide a forum for scholars and practitioners "to exchange . . . ideas around [the] theory and practice of place branding."[58] The new scholarship in the field is presented on a quarterly basis in two specialized academic journals—*Place Branding and Public Diplomacy* and *Journal of Destination Marketing and Management*—with a dedicated readership.[59] A nation-brand index launched in 2005 even measures and ranks the brand equity of nations in terms of global image and reputation. In the field of publicity, a specialized cross between old-fashioned advertising and new age personal development has emerged, such as the London-based Institute for Identity, that promises to help "places define, live and communicate their purpose." The functional language of advertising is replaced here by a near-therapeutic vocabulary of helping and giving—an updated version of a "special kind of love," the salvific discourse of the old nationalism that the brand new nation demands. Consider their tagline, "We help attract attention, foster loyalty, and earn respect" by seeking to "amplify the core of [the place/destination]. Give it a modern meaning and a modern use. Make it available to experience by others. Make it attractive to join in and follow. Numbers (inflow, profit, and loyalty score) will grow." [60] In short, destinations are like people with personalities, whose attractiveness can be augmented and updated via strategic sculpting, nips, and tucks—all with the tantalizing promise of profits and capital inflows.

Across the world, then, especially in the past two decades, many national governments have embarked on these nation-branding exercises as part of public diplomacy and as an essential tool in the pursuit of national interest, especially as economic diplomacy has become an area of specialization on its own. Although there is nothing new in the idea of economic diplomacy, the sectors of trade and investment have become increasingly prominent in the arena of foreign relations. Consider the proliferation of "Invest in" departments across the world that specifically push the agenda of drawing in capital to the national territories. Each of these departments has a prominent role as a strategic branch of government, supported by overt or covert branding programs that have become an essential part of this enterprise. Unlike the more humble soft-power diplomacy of the post–Cold War era that always appeared to cling to the coattails of hard power,[61] branding pitched itself more assertively on the forefront, arguably with a "deep responsibility in this changing world . . . , (for) promoting the nation-state."[62]

This presumption of "deep responsibility" with which advocates of nation branding imbued their project accrues from a deep-seated belief that branding is an "all pervasive and ubiquitous" condition of a globalized early twenty-first century and that "anybody who lives in today's world is involved in branding."[63] In other words, all branding did was to extract and enhance value, to capitalize what was deemed to be an inescapable condition of the present. Or perhaps nation branding attends to a more contemporary existential anxiety: that the nation does not exist if it does not possess a brand identity.

This argument of inevitability has often framed the utilitarian idea of honing a competitive identity for nations. Simon Anholt, a brand consultant, pitched competitive identity making as "a necessary part of modern statecraft" in a world in which "all countries must compete with each other."[64] In this enterprise, he suggested, "a nation's brand image is its most valuable asset: it is national identity made robust, tangible, communicable, and—at its best—made useful." [65] The underlying rationale was that the brand value of commodities could increase (or decrease) if compounded with the brand value of the places they are manufactured in. In marketing management parlance, this is called the country-of-origin (COO) effect, and it encompasses the "emotional value resulting from consumers' association of a brand with a country."[66] The legacy of the late-nineteenth-century geographical indicators—the "Made in" marks—is made visible here, this time abetted and transformed into the early-twenty-first-century project of nation branding. The COO effect has since evolved beyond the idea of territories/places as mere sites of commodity production to territories-as-commodities, the conspicuously branded investment destinations that can be put at the disposal of investors. The idea of enhancing competitive identity—branding—has become a commonplace feature as governments seek to attract investments into their national territories. But just as branding national territories started becoming a matter of common sense across the world—an exciting recipe for reinventing nations—doubts began to be raised from the most unlikely quarters about the efficacy of branding programs to actually change perceptions or the fortunes of the nation. A telling example is the recent volte-face by Anholt, who has expressed worries that nations risked "becoming mere brands" and that nation branding was ineffective "because countries and cities aren't for sale, [therefore] the marketing communications campaigns associated with them can only be empty propaganda."[67]

What is palpable here is not just the old anxiety that commodification of the nation corrodes its essence but also the theological dimension of the nation as an inherently sacred entity located outside the realm of trade and commerce.[68] If at all, the fear of nations "becoming mere brands" reveals the strange ambivalence that actually shapes the nation-branding project, wherein the commodity (nation) being branded is deemed to be above commodification. It is therefore that many nation-branding experts speak of their work as a "service to the nation," motivated by their devotional love for the nation rather than by mere profits. This strange ambivalence also reveals how the nation-branding experts have not always completely grasped the full implications of the phenomenon they were deeply implicated in and the nature and effects of capitalist transformations that underpinned the reimagination of the nation as a branded territorial enclosure. The project of branding via global publicity has always been the proverbial tip of the iceberg, the most spectacular aspect of massive structural transformations that refashion the nation into a commercial enclosure.

To make full sense of this phenomenon, then, I finally turn to an older conceptual bloodline of *enclosures*, from which the contemporary idea of *investment destination* has evolved.

ENCLOSURES OF CAPITAL

I begin by drawing attention to a "terms of use and disclaimer" note that prefaces the World Economic Forum's annual report on global competitiveness. This brief note measures and ranks productivity and the long-term economic growth prospects of nations. It states that "the terms *country* and *nation* as used in this Report do not in all cases refer to a territorial entity that is a state as understood by international law and practice. The terms cover well-defined, geographically self-contained economic areas that may not be states" (italics in the original).[69] This idea of the nation as a "self-contained economic area," although what precisely is self-contained is never fully defined, offers keen insights into how nations are increasingly imagined as enclosed spaces of wealth generation in the world of commerce. To be sure, the language and practice of enclosing territories as vast reservoirs of natural resources to be tapped for commercial use is not new. In many ways, the WEF's definition of the nation as an enclosed space of economic activity and surplus merely reiterates the older idea of territorial enclosures that began taking shape in the early modern era. Yet its twenty-first-century incarnation as an investment destination—one that can also *enclose ideas* and claim ownership of intellectual property—has evolved its own form and logic in which nations are arranged and ranked primarily as means of production and consumption. What is critical is how nations as investment destinations are valued not merely for their current economic size but also for their *potential* to generate wealth in the future (see chapter 2, "Economy of Hope"). In a strange way, the nation's place in the world, its destiny, is precariously tied to its assessment as an attractive investment destination. To make sense of the idea of the investment destination, I trace the making of territorial enclosures and the shifts therein.

The story of enclosures usually begins with the social upheavals in the English countryside in the sixteenth and seventeenth centuries, when open farmland was turned into fenced units of commodity production.[70] I want to address the idea of the enclosure of the countryside together with a parallel development that is often overlooked—the enclosure of overseas territories via the expansion of long-distance commercial trade through sea routes and the attendant colonization of the newly "discovered" lands (see also chapter 2). The late fifteenth century began the age of exploration, when European merchants, armed with royal charters and the blessings of the church, began financing profitable overseas trade in the New World. The old enterprise of trading commodities took a new turn around this time as entire overseas territories came to be seen as potential enclosures of commodity production. It has been argued that the practices of territory making, the parceling of land, did not logically extend from the settled Old World to the chaotic New World. Instead the old and the new worlds constituted a single space of imperial formations and territory making, and both were faced with questions of proprietary right to land at the same time.[71] In fact, the transformation of the commons into commercial enclosures unfolded almost simultaneously in the European country-side and in the overseas colonies.[72] What is critical in this shift is how the two connected ideas of the discovery and improvement of land became a prime claim of possession in overseas territories—the right to harvest fruit, cut timber, and cultivate the land, and the river rights to travel and trade, among others. Central to this politics of possession was the imagination of newly discovered territory as the great frontier. The idea of frontier at once signified an "empty space," a "vacancy," a "vast body of wealth without proprietors," and, to top them all, a "vast property which had suddenly been bestowed on the Metropolis (Europe)" that was up for grabs, to be turned into civilized productive colonies.[73] The frontier was seen as having reserves of unlimited wealth, where "you can get everything of a material nature you want, more than you ever dreamed of having, from gold and silver to fur and foods, and in any quantity you want, provided only that you [are] willing to venture and work."[74] That proprietary rights were tied to human labor was a frequent theme in the making of enclosures. Cultivation was deemed a patriotic act through which land was brought under the plow and thereby converted to a valuable income-generating asset. This careful distinction meant that the native populations, classified as primitive inhabitants, were deemed to have no property rights and therefore could be lawfully dispossessed. The question of improvement of land, however, was more than that of mere cultivation or bringing it under the plow. It was about *efficient* utilization of land that was deemed essential for economic prosperity. The ability to extract maximum yield or economic value from the enclosure became a claim of possession in itself.[75] The economic boom accrued from the ever-widening enclosure of frontiers in the hinterland and overseas territories, an event that entered some of the Enlightenment debates on national sovereignty, property rights, citizenship, and progress in unlikely ways.

Of particular significance here is the idea of the closed commercial state that emerged in this nineteenth-century free-trade era and that counterintuitively can be considered a preliminary blueprint of the early twenty-first-century investment-destination phenomenon. I suggest a counterintuitive reading, because the idea of closure is usually interpreted as a move toward antiglobalization and national self-sufficiency. What is critical for our present purposes, though, is how Johannes Gottlieb Fichte conceptualized the nation as a unified economic and cultural unit—an enclosed arena of production and exchange.[76] Somewhat radically, Fichte conceived the nation as "a closed whole, a totality" of economic relations controlled and optimized by the state. The multitudes inhabiting the closed nation were imagined as income-generating human estates—producers, artisans, and traders—whose activities had to be carefully managed so as to "eliminate the anarchy of trade" and achieve the greatest state of prosperity.[77] Yet this vision was cracked, mired in contradictions regarding the central question of closure itself. What kind of territory—fertile arable land, mines, woodlands, and that with a variety of natural resources—should be enclosed in order to achieve economic prosperity? After all, not everything could be produced in an enclosure, given differences in the kinds of resources and raw materials available. Fichte's answer to this problem was that "a state about to close off as a commercial state must assume first its natural borders," through violent means if necessary.[78] It is worth noting that while the closed commercial state forbade its individual inhabitants from trading with foreigners, it did not give up on foreign trade as such. All the state did was to seize trading privileges and powers from individuals and vest them in itself so it could trade with foreign entities on behalf of the collective.[79] What we witness here, then, is a nineteenth-century rough draft of the nation as commercial enclosure, stripped of the trappings of national romance and steered efficiently by a centralized state power into the realm of prosperity.

The key to this transition was the distillation of the territory and its population into primary factors of production, rearranged and optimized by a panoptic authority into a profitable enterprise. The nineteenth-century blueprint in some ways both reflected the contemporary ideas of land as profit-yielding commodity and presaged the investment-destination model yet to come. But what it didn't forecast was that the act of closure would always be temporary and flexible so as to continuously absorb surplus territory into the ever-demanding capitalist machine of economic growth. The contemporary idea of emerging markets works precisely on this principle of the continuous rediscovery and absorption of new, untapped territories that can be incorporated into the cycles of production and consumption (see chapter 2, "Economy of Hope"). The foundations of such expandable enclosures of production had long been laid in the process of the colonization of overseas territories by European powers. By the early nineteenth century, the vast territorial enclosures across Asia, Africa, and Latin America were absorbed into the sphere of the global market, a process accelerated through a different mode: infrastructure development. This was the beginning of massive investment in infrastructures of trade and mobility in the colonized enclosure to make the "undeveloped resources" into profitable propositions.[80] A prime example of this nineteenth-century infrastructural boom was the British imperial investments in a railway network in India intended to bridge the "tantalizing gap between potentialities and the actualities" of Britain's greatest overseas possession.[81] The growing demand for raw materials—for example, cotton—to feed the industrial revolution in Britain as well as the promise of a large consumer market for British products strengthened the calls for investing in both railways and steamship connections to "overcome the impediments of distance."[82] These transport networks were meant to connect the landlocked hinterlands to oceans—railway lines connected agrarian centers with ports that in turn connected the colonial markets to the metropolitan economic center through faster steamships. These new lines of mobility not only transformed the colony into a unified enclosure of economic production but also connected the enclosure to the potential global investors in multiple ways.[83] The investments in transport coincided with investments in large-scale agrarian infrastructure—for example, irrigation networks—to improve land productivity for commercial purposes.[84]

Let's turn now to the twenty-first century, in which terms such as *infrastructures*, *investment*, and *innovation* continue to pepper conversations in business and policy circuits. In many ways, the recipe to make land profitable and productive by creating infrastructures of extraction remains the same. What has changed is the scale, size, and mode of this enterprise. Consider the move to undertake large-scale infrastructure projects—material and virtual—in order to transform territories into fully networked commercial enclosures, a trend-in-acceleration that remains pivotal in the making of nations into investment destinations in the twenty-first century. The seed investments in infrastructure development such as roads, railways, ports, special economic zones, and smart cities that facilitate trade and commerce are prerequisites for nations aspiring to attract foreign capital. In fact, the need for infrastructure development itself is an opportunity that attracts capital as well as the promise of recurring returns in future. And capital is more likely to flow into national enclosures that are fully infrastructure ready. In short, the never-ending cycles of capitalist growth are predicated on a constant availability of enclosures, infrastructures, and investments. The contemporary global phenomenon of investment destinations unfolds on this logic, which has permeated the inner workings of national politics in unanticipated ways. Unlike the nineteenth-century free-trade imperialism or the twentieth-century globalization that sought to overcome borders, the twenty-first-century phenomenon thrives precisely on borders that enclose the national territory, its natural and cultural resources, and its people into exclusive branded units. Here we witness how the nationalist logic is not necessarily opposed to global capital. Instead, in its branded form, it coheres with capitalist designs—the nation-state is assured a share of profits (the promised well-being of its people) as well as a glorious place in the world. If anything, the state-capital relationship and the division of labor have become more transparent than ever in the present moment.

The emergence of this phenomenon has been in the making for the past quarter century. I turn now to the people who imagine the brand new nation and bring it alive in a concrete form.

THE NATION BRANDERS

Who are the makers of the modern nation? Posed in the twentieth century, this question would have inevitably led us to the domain of politics. The agents credited with spearheading the transformations of the twentieth century were mostly political leaders, thinkers, social reformers, and activists.[85] They were engaged not only in anticolonial struggles to gain political freedom from empires but also in laying the foundations of a possible sovereign nation-state. The blueprint of nation making, in this era, came to be associated with the high politics—the establishment of modernist developmental schemes and institutions of governance—heralded by charismatic visionaries. Dubbed the founding fathers of the modern nation, these leaders were widely seen as the creators of postcolonial futures.[86]

The makers of the brand new nation of the twenty-first century, in contrast, appear to primarily inhabit the domain of antipolitics. By antipolitics, I mean the domain of professional experts who mostly identify themselves as apolitical, that is, unaligned or opposed to political interests where the sphere of politics is inherently perceived as dirty and corrupt.[87] What brings this community of nation branders—policy experts, image specialists, advertising professionals, corporate lobbyists, bureaucrats, business executives, and social influencers—together is the sincere and deep-seated belief in the power of branding, and capitalism as such, to renew the nation. A number of experts I met in this field seemed to genuinely regard the branding operation as a way to enhance the economic and cultural value of the nation in the global economy.

The primacy of professional brand experts on the forefront of nation making in the twenty-first century is hardly surprising. Consider how the sphere of economy—especially the nation-as-investment-destination model—has emerged as the prime sphere of nation making and how *nation branding* has eclipsed the old project of *nation building* in the past quarter century.[88] In this shifting worldview, the sphere of politics is what curbs the potential growth of businesses, and government is a barrier that stands between the nation and its promised glory. The old refrains that say "the government has no business being in business" and that say the nation is growing "not because of government but despite the government" are frequently rehearsed in these circles. Put differently, the sphere of economy is deemed too critical to be entrusted entirely to the established political class. The political class is not absent in this script—it is subordinate to the capitalist futures designed by experts. The makers of the brand new nation encompass and even transcend the older public-private divisions. And in doing so, they reassemble the public as well as the private even as outward distinctions remain unaltered. In this hybrid apparatus, we meet state officials in an investor-friendly corporate makeover and corporate executives as public service–minded nonprofit nationalists. These public-private mutations in the making of the brand new nation are still evolving, but some trends can already be traced.

First is the makeover of public-sector officials in the image of high-flying business executives. In Delhi and Davos, I was often introduced, with a hint of admiration, to government officials—politicians or bureaucrats—as CEOs, especially the ones seen as key players in the India growth story. Eventually, I discovered that in the community of nation branders, the term *CEO* (chief executive officer) did not always refer to an actual function or designation in an organization. It was an honorific title bestowed as a mark of respect on politicians or government officials seen as the go-getters—the efficient, enterprising people. The CEOs were those who meant business in the affairs of governance. This informal practice of addressing political executives as CEOs gained currency with Prime Minister Manmohan Singh, considered the main architect of India's economic reforms, a mantle that the current prime minister, Narendra Modi, has enthusiastically assumed.[89] To be addressed as CEO was as much an honor conferred by the business world as a cheerful reminder that the prime task of the political leadership was to capitalize the nation's resources. The prime minister turned CEO was responsible not just for the welfare of the citizens but, first and foremost, for selling India in the global economy. This practice has filtered downward through the apparatus of bureaucracy. The honorific CEO is now a form of recognition, even fulsome praise, of those who bring corporate style—as men of action— to the work of state administration.[90] The term *corporate-style* itself is used as shorthand for the capacity to make swift decisions and execute them with an iron hand. It also suggests the capacity to circumvent or

override cumbersome democratic processes that involve lengthy deliberations, objections, and negotiations. The ability to act decisively in
the face of opposition is deemed the hallmark of a successful corporate
leader, a distinction coveted by politicians and bureaucrats who seek to
turn the nation into a profitable enterprise. Palpable in this ongoing
corporate revamping is the recurring fetish for the strong leaders—the
ones who can deliver—preferred in business circles. Unlike ordinary
CEOs, however, the emerging class of honorary CEOs combines old-
fashioned political strongmen skills with corporate suave. These agents
of the brand new nation are market-friendly executives who are equally
at ease with the global policy elite and the rough-and-tumble politics
at home.

Second is the repositioning of private-sector executives as non-
profit nationalists. The branding experts—including policy experts,
image specialists, advertising professionals, corporate lobbyists, business executives, and social influencers—I met over the years mostly,
and no doubt sincerely, positioned their work as a service to the nation
rather than as a mere professional assignment. A number of professionals would emphasize how nation-branding projects were different from
their regular projects of branding commodities. This distinction appeared to be critical in how they perceived and presented nation branding as a cut above their routine work. The refrain "We don't do this
for money" was echoed frequently. The nation-branding project seemed
to have acquired a higher purpose—you could pay homage to the nation by illuminating its beauty and wonders that others had failed to
see. In doing so, you could also help market the nation and its cultural
heritage to the world in a way that the state seemed unable to. In fact,
among the professional branding experts, the official publicity apparatus dubbed "government-type ads" was seen as not just ineffective but
outright counterproductive. The professionals pitching their services to
Brand India often presented their work as remedial—a visual correction of substandard government-type images. The motivation to brand
the nation, I was often told, was to make the world see its economic potential and its beauty and culture the way these professionals see it. The
production of beautiful images was a selfless service, a task that could

never be fully compensated monetarily. By emphasizing service as the prime motivation ahead of financial gain, the nation branders sought to locate their labor beyond the sphere of exchange and reciprocity, and this noneconomic element is what made their work especially valuable. In the community of nation branders, nation branding was deemed more than a business transaction, and its intended effect was beyond economic growth. What drew them to nation branding was especially affective gains—recognition of the nation's cultural essence—that could potentially be generated from the nation's economic growth.[91]

That these unresolved economic and noneconomic tensions continued to shape the nation-branding project became clear in my personal interactions with the nation branders. I often heard ad executives tell their personal stories as explanations for their professional engagement with nation branding. The stories were usually about their personal struggles, ambitions, and achievements—about having "made it" in the world. Many saw themselves as unlikely candidates for the success and social mobility they had managed to achieve. A highly successful Delhi adman told me his own story of lower-middle-class origins, of his childhood defined by the absence of material comforts that middle-class kids took for granted. He remembered his early years as difficult, as a time when opportunities were few and the future looked bleak. What secured his future were two factors—a good-quality high-school education that he received in a state-run school and his ability to draw and design. He was hired straight out of school by an advertising agency as an apprentice visual designer. These were the early years of India's reforms, the prelude to the economic boom to follow in the new millennium.[92] He entered the business of advertising and publicity just as it was being boosted by foreign investments. In our conversations, he would emphasize the special character of the advertising industry, in which the skills of drawing and dreaming were more important than formal education. He could not imagine being so successful in any other field given his social background. His lucky break came when he moved to Delhi to work in the Indian subsidiary of a global advertising firm. He made a name for himself by creating high-impact brand campaigns, moved through the company ranks, and ultimately established his own advertising company. It was his solid professional reputation and networks within the government agencies that earned him the opportunity to brand India. Over the years, he created a range of iconic campaigns for Brand India that brought professional accolades and recognition. What is especially significant is how he drew a distinction between his Brand India assignments and routine advertising projects. Brand India campaigns were always presented as a form of personal and professional homage to the nation.

Although the attempts to elevate Brand India campaigns above the sphere of commercial advertising could be dismissed as the smooth talking of silver-tongued admen, there appeared to be something more at work. It seemed as if the personal stories of struggle were being projected on to the nation's postcolonial history. The nation branders, especially the ones who came from lower-middle-class backgrounds, clearly identified with the setbacks and failures the postcolonial nation was faced with. The underlying logic seemed to be that India could make it too if it persisted like they had. The event of economic reforms in this script was a precious chance—for individuals as well as for the nation—to fulfill their dreams of prosperity and upward mobility. In a way, then, the trajectories of the nation and its branders seemed entwined. The themes of mobility and pride formed these entangled narratives of Brand India in which the personal and professional were not always clearly separated. Consider the following stories, often told in these circles, about airport encounters.

The airport in these narratives is not just an infrastructure for mobility but also a critical point of encounter with the world. The Delhi adman drew a distinction between the before and after of India's economic rise by explaining how Indians were received at international airports. During our very first meeting in 2009, he told me that "when Indians traveled, say, to London, before the economic reforms, they were treated shabbily. The immigration officers would ask if your intention was to stay here. The Indian passport had no value. Now when you are at Heathrow, the immigration [office] treats you with respect. They know that you are not here to stay. There are opportunities at home. The Indian passport has become valuable. This is the power of

Brand India."[93] This notion of the changed status of the Indian passport bore the imprint of optimism prevalent in the boom years. The foreign investors, in the parlance of financial speculation, were bullish on India; that is, they had put their money on India's potential to deliver profitable returns on investment. The good news about India's imminent rise had seemingly spread throughout the world. Yet not all Indian citizens experienced this shift in India's fortunes; many continued to look elsewhere for opportunities.[94] And this was a sore spot for the nation branders who were sometimes especially scornful of educated Indians who migrated abroad. They were dismissed as risk-averse first-generation professionals—greenhorns who had newly entered the world of the global elite but lacked the sophistication required to shine in that world. As the Delhi adman remarked, those other Indians at Heathrow, most likely on their way to the United States, presented a picture of embarrassment for India. They could be spotted from afar, he said. They huddled together at the airports, ate the food brought in tiffin from home, and didn't dare to spend money even on a cup of coffee. They represented an India, in his eyes, that was less confident, less proud of its culture and heritage, and therefore marginal on the world stage. This was the very image the nation branders had to set out to change. Their goal was to design an image of India in which Indians weren't timid or rendered invisible in global spaces. The citizens of this brand new India faced the world with confidence and were welcomed by the world with open arms.

What we have witnessed here is the circulation of the logic of nation branding far beyond the confines of organizations and corporate strategy making. This logic enfolds citizens who are encouraged, even expected, to do their patriotic bit to help brand their nation. Thus, the ideal citizens are those who assume personal responsibility for helping to spread the good news about the nation and thereby enhance its reputation in the world. At an individual level, nation branding necessitates fine-tuning one's personal behavior so that it is in lockstep with the idealized imaginary of the nation. It means embodying the desired look of the nation—of citizens who are supremely confident, speak positively of the nation's past and present, and remain optimistic about its future. At the very minimum, this fine-tuning requires that one does not speak ill of the nation and overlooks the negatives that make the less salubrious sides of the nation visible (see chapter 2, "Economy of Hope"). Clearly, the brand new nation continues to evolve—from having limited utilitarian goals of projecting the nation as an investment destination in the global economy into enjoying the popular mobilization of its citizens toward the brand new nationalist imaginaries. In brand new India, this mobilization imagines its citizens as inhabitants of an economic superpower whose ancient civilizational culture remains par excellence in the world.

NOTES ON GATE-CRASHING

I sometimes thought of my presence in this elite world of nation branding as that of a gate-crasher. It was not gate-crashing in the formal sense of being an uninvited guest. After all, many of the events I attended were public, designed to actively court attention and create publicity buzz for India. The personal meetings, sometimes billed as "bilaterals" in these settings, were mostly longer follow-ups of conversations started at public events but continued elsewhere. The vast majority of people I came across in this field were welcoming and forthright, willing to give their time despite their hectic schedules that involved a lot of international travel.

If sometimes I had the sense of being a stranger even amid pleasant surroundings, it was due to the very category of *public* at work—a very specific kind of people were being courted whose attention was deemed desirable and valuable in the project of nation branding. The rarified nature of this public became especially apparent in places such as Davos, where the global elite assembled during the annual meeting of the WEF.[95] Encompassing the world's billionaires, hedge-fund managers, lobbyists, political leaders, newspaper editors, social entrepreneurs—the top layer of the "stakeholders" in society—the category of public was simultaneously open and restricted.[96] The restricted nature of this public emerged through controls on mobility that briefly turned Davos into a fortress of the rich and famous. During the WEF annual meeting week, the town became a high-security zone, its entry points heavily guarded to ensure the safety of the high-profile visitors. The spectacle of security also helped deter riffraff. In addition, most people cannot afford the prohibitive cost of living during the WEF.[97] Given these conditions of restricted mobility, one's very presence in this space was a testimony of one's elite status or, at the very least, of one's upward social mobility.

Yet not everyone present possessed the currency required to enter the circuits of reciprocity and exchange that constituted the social world of the elite. The effect of gate-crashing is this transgressive presence: to be present and yet remain peripheral to the circuits of reciprocity and exchange. So, what currency does one need to possess in order to inhabit this social world? The answer, unsurprising in a setting in which the prime aim is to invite capital investments, lay in the future promise of investment. The *promise* itself is the currency, the deferred possibility that investments will materialize at some future point. Those who can extend promises are first and foremost the captains of industry; they are the capitalists who either possess or can easily procure the necessary means to invest and whose promises are likely to carry weight. Thus, at the top of the pecking order are the influential CEOs of Fortune 500 companies, billionaires, hedge-fund managers, and risk analysts who can divert flows of capital toward preferred destinations. If nation branders seek to attract their attention, it is because their words or actions help create buzz in the markets and for the events that can potentially talk investment destinations up or down.[98] In short, the pursuit of promise is what remains central to the business of branding, and those who can enhance the promise can enter the social web of exchange.

I had nothing much to offer so that I could enter this circuit of exchange. My presence as a researcher was unusual in a setting in which nearly everyone was connected to the business world in one way or another. Other academics were present, but they were mainly from business schools and had been invited as experts to help enhance the brand profile of the nation. My non-business-school credentials were a sure oddity that could not readily be put in a familiar slot in this setting. But as I eventually realized, it was precisely this ambiguity, the *uncertain promise* of my presence, that allowed me to briefly inhabit the peripheries of this social world. The work of ambiguity, I figured out in retrospect, was crucial in a context in which nothing concrete was being bought or sold.[99] In fact, what appeared illusory at first was often the outcome of a deliberate strategy.

The illusory currency of promise—an entanglement between the economic and the noneconomic and between gift and commodity—makes business sense given that economic goals are pursued more effectively through noneconomic means. That *deferment* of economic goals is sometimes more profitable is ingrained in the idea of networking, which is at the heart of business transactions. The golden rule of networking is counterintuitive. What actually brings desired results is to *not* seek advancement of specific goals. Instead, business executives are advised that the best practice is to build "a robust set of connections over time" that are nontransactional in nature.[100] The hope is that nonutilitarian connections will eventually yield profits and concrete business deals in the future. Somewhat ironically, those offered the chance to partake in nontransactional social encounters were precisely those from whom future transactions were anticipated. Put differently, the currency of promise operates in a permanently deferred mode, a transaction-forever-in-the-making. This retrospective insight into the actual operation of the nation-branding world allowed me to understand my own position in the field, a field that appears to be smooth on the surface but is turbulent beneath.

If ambiguity opens doors to this elite world, it also creates a potential field of contention. During my first visit to Davos in 2012, I encountered the underlying tensions that framed personal encounters at the India Adda. The India Adda was a performance of Indian culture of hospitality and openness at which potential investors were received as guests rather than as investors. The guests also preferred to talk of how much they loved India and Indian culture rather than about the actual business of investments. At full play was the logic of the deferment of economic goals and the staging of nontransactional affective encounters. Yet the social interaction was disciplined, and those deemed to be veering off script or occupying space ahead of the prized guests (the investors) were ticked off. On the very first day of my visit in 2012, I was sitting with a group of young visitors engaged in an amiable conversation laced with occasional giggles. Ironically for an event that invited discussion, the group was told to stop the conversation, for it diverted attention from the business of investments. Thus, on several occasions, individuals deemed superfluous to the operation were quietly told to leave or, at the very least, told to not occupy the main seating area (see chapter 5, "The Magical Market"). Once someone was unambiguously categorized as unworthy of attention, they were simply ignored, and the tap of hospitality produced only a faint trickle. The officials most likely believed in all sincerity that firm discipline was necessary to produce desired results.

The nature of these personal encounters, however, remained inherently flexible and sometimes even unpredictable. In 2015, for instance, I found myself featured in the official Brand India booklet issued after the Davos event. The booklet was sent by post together with a framed photograph of me engaged in animated conversation at the India Adda. I was both surprised and pleased. After all, my presence at these high-profile events had always been a bit precarious. I never fully understood how, but over the years, I had moved from the periphery of Brand India into the main frame of its image.

The publicity events, regardless of the attention they generate, were always the proverbial tip of the iceberg, the brief moments when Brand India came to be theatrically performed for global investors. The life of Brand India itself began in less spectacular circumstances—in the routine bureaucratic work of government agencies, the creative drawing boards of advertising firms, the advocacy programs of corporate lobbies, and the public-service initiatives of private media organizations. It was everyday encounters with Brand India that generated a treasure trove of information—from policy papers and orders issued by official agencies, publicity brochures, and thematic booklets to coffee-table books, business tool kits (easy information for businesses), audiovisual promotional material on CDs and USB flash drives, logo designs, and drafts of advertisements, including those that failed to make the cut. In addition, I systematically collected material published on official websites that disappeared without leaving much trace.[101] Likewise, the online campaigns launched by private corporations have not survived in any meaningful way.[102] Thus, this unique archive could be assembled only through an ethnographic inquiry that entailed collecting bits and pieces of information as it was circulated in the present.

The book unfolds not in a chronological order but in a thematic one; each chapter is a step in the making of the brand new nation. The introduction presents the logic and form of the brand new nation, and the subsequent chapters are a journey into the investment-fueled nationalist politics that brought this form alive. It is not a teleological reading of the twenty-first-century nation-state. Instead, the chapters offer insights into the hopes and anxieties, contradictions and failures, and speculations and unanticipated outcomes that have refashioned the nation as a branded investment destination. In addition to the introduction, the book is composed of six further chapters arranged in three thematic parts.

The first part deals with the affective and bureaucratic designs of the dreamworlds of New India. Chapter 2, "Economy of Hope," looks at the moment that the economy opened up and the accompanying affective-material entanglements, which produce what I call the economy of hope in the postcolony. Here I lay out the making of Brand India as a bureaucratic operation that sells hope in and optimism about India's economic potential to global investors. The logic of Brand India is harnessed to a collective dream of realizing the nation's great destiny through economic success—its rejuvenation via capital infusion. I trace the long history of newness and the many incarnations of New India, of which the twenty-first-century investment-destination model is the most recent iteration. Chapter 3, "Remixing History" turns to the political-aesthetic project of remixing history to produce a distinct *ancient modern* identity: a seductive polychromous package of global hypertechnology and ancient civilizational culture. The spectacular imagery of India produced in the Incredible India megacampaign is at the heart of this inquiry. Produced under the sign of Incredible India at the beginning of the third millennium, an entire iconography of beautiful, digitally enhanced images came into being, a desirable photo album of how New India wanted to be seen in the world. Yet what at first seems like a low-stakes project of image *enhancement* through digital processes reveals something more fundamental at work: the production of an authentic identity inherently located in a Hindu civilizational culture, a contentious process that requires constant purging of all that is deemed foreign. Here we witness the emergence of a dominant cultural identity that is primarily Hindu, one at odds, if not in constant tension, with India's multicultural secular history.

The second part engages with the aesthetics of novelty, the idea that a new time had arrived and that India was moving ahead in fast-forward mode. Chapter 4, "Icons of Good Times," addresses one of the most iconic and perhaps most contentious image-making projects, called India Shining. It represents a distinct moment in India's post-reform history when economic reforms were publicly scrutinized and the promise of progress and prosperity deemed empty, a mere mirage. Although this campaign was declared a massive political catastrophe given the electoral failure suffered by the ruling Bharatiya Janata Party government, I argue otherwise. I offer a counterintuitive reading of the India Shining project as a moment when economic reforms received mass publicity. India Shining produced eye-catching imagery of a modern secular nation that was enterprising and inclusive and that everyone could be part of provided they signed on to the project of economic reforms. The campaign imagery unveiled the enchanting icons of prosperity that heralded good times long before Narendra Modi made "Acche din" a winning election slogan. Chapter 5, "The Magical Market," unfolds in Davos at the annual meeting of the WEF. Here we see how India's exotic tradition—*adda*, an assembly of people or a place of gathering—is performed to showcase a modern, investor-friendly India, albeit an India rooted in tradition. The adda is mobilized not only to display a specific Indian *mode of networking* in the corporate world but also to trace the roots of corporate modernity to Indian traditions rather than to Western corporate culture. The stars of this performance are the Indian "captains of industry," the capitalists, who appear in a surprising role—as nationalist resisters to Western hegemony in the financial world. Although officials sometimes try to control this performance of democratic talk, the adda nevertheless comes alive as a democratic space, albeit one exclusive to the elite. This is where state-capital relations can be seen at work—entwined with one another but always ready to upend the balance of power. The primacy of the capital in postreform New India is apparent, as is the capital's penchant for strong leadership, although the political situation of strong leaders was laced with unpredictability, as we will find.

The final part of the book is about anxieties. The story of New India is as much about hope and optimism as about the anxiety of "not making it," of being turned back from the door of a prosperous future. Given that the destiny of the nation is now tied to the speculative economic boom and bust, the fear of losing out in the economic-growth game always lurks beneath euphoria. Chapter 6, "The Second Liberation," traces the collective anxiety that led to the making of a new political subject in Indian politics: *Aam aadmi*, the common man. This was also a moment of impatience with the government, not just the government in power at that time but government as such. The domain of government was categorized as a cesspool of inefficiency, corruption, and unmeritorious people who did not deserve to be in the august offices of the state. The government was identified as an obstruction in the path of progress, even more so given the identification of the government sector with caste-based reservation policy. This chapter brings together several strands—of anticorruption politics, the caste question, and the role of media—critical in staging the second liberation of the republic. The highly mediatized popular mobilization of the *Aam aadmi* sought to liberate the nation from corruption and, in doing so, unleash the entrepreneurial spirit constrained by a corrupt government. This was also the moment that the political landscape was rearranged into a rightward coalition that consisted of a liberal economy and illiberal cultural politics. The final chapter, "Uncommon Futures," returns to the liberal/illiberal contradictions apparent in the brand new nation. Instead of seeing illiberalism as a mere aberration in the script of liberalism, I draw attention to the *bonds of investment*— "bond" meaning affective ties as well as financial instruments—that lock cultural nationalism and capitalist growth in a state of mutual indebtedness. The liberal framework of unrestrained free markets inheres the potential to unleash what is now being called authoritarian populism—the strengthening of populist cultural nationalism led by strong majoritarian leaders in the shadow of free markets.

Part I

DREAMWORLDS

CHAPTER 2

ECONOMY OF HOPE

IN 2007, the *Economist*—a promarket journal widely read in global investment–foreign policy circles—published a special report called "India on Fire: India's Economy." The journal's readers were told that "the
[Indian] economy is sizzling and foreign businessmen and investors are
swarming to Bangalore and Mumbai to grab a piece of the action. India's year-on-year growth rate could well hit double figures at some
point in 2007, and the country may even grow faster than China for
at least one quarter."[1] It was a glowing assessment of the state of India's economy, and the underlying excitement was palpable even if it
was laced with prudence.[2] Yet for regular readers of the journal, this
report may have been unusual in tone and content, a sudden departure from its earlier position on postcolonial India. After all, not too
long before, India had been dismissed from the blueprint of promising futures. Barely a decade earlier, in August 1997, the *Economist* had
etched an almost dystopic, hopeless account of India's blank future.
In an essay called "Happy Anniversary?" it mournfully and mockingly
suggested,

> On August 15th 1947, India became the first British colony to win indepen-
> dence. . . . In speeches to enthusiastic crowds around the country, they [the
> leaders] pledged to end poverty and help India regain its pre-colonial glory

as a great economic power. Today, the euphoria is gone. The champagne bottles will pop on the 50th anniversary of independence, but the bubbly will taste a trifle flat. At best, India has been a qualified political success and a barely qualified economic failure. Indian leaders believed in 1947 that colonial exploitation had kept the country poor, and that when the British went, so would poverty. In fact 320 million Indians remain below the poverty line today, almost as many as India's entire population as in 1947. A mistaken socialist experiment has cost India dear."

To the readers of the *Economist* this must have been a familiar picture of India, one that had been offered countless times before. It contained the well-known trope of India's "mistaken socialist experiment" to explain its condition as a barely qualified "economic failure" staring regretfully at its past. Yet this bleak picture gave readers hardly a hint of the economic upswing that was to come. At this point, they could not have imagined the possibility that the Indian economy would soon be described as "sizzling" and investors "swarming" to India "to grab a piece of action" unfolding there or that this India would be renamed the "New India," a hypervisible branded commodity classified as an attractive investment destination in the world of financial analysts and investors. Indian markets at this point were not only brimming with optimism and hope but also now seen as a source of hope for global capital still reeling from the financial crisis. In short, *something* had changed in the span of a single decade to dramatically alter global perceptions of India.

What was this something that had so spectacularly reconfigured the perceptions of India from an abject "economic failure" to a "sizzling" economy of hope? In whose interest had the postcolony been reimagined and classified as an "investment destination" along a graded scale of market attractiveness? What kind of newness was the sign of "New India"—an old name for an old project of modernity—called on to perform in the early twenty-first century? And if the India of the 1990s economic reforms was the "new" India, then what happened to the other new Indians who had arrived long before? Broadly speaking, what might this genealogy of the new and shifts therein, tell us about the making and remaking of the postcolony in the world of free markets?

I begin by locating this *economy of hope* within the event of the opening up of the postcolony in the late twentieth century. This is the world-historical event in which we witness the unbridled expansion of free markets into ever-new territories, especially in the old third world, which had not yet fully embraced capitalism.[3] What distinguishes this wave of expansion of free markets is how nationalist aspirations are seduced by, and seduce in return, the dreamworlds of capitalism in order to join the high table of global power and recognition. At the heart of this renewal of the nation, then, is the logic of capitalist transformation that reimagines the nation as an attractive investment destination. The event of investment by foreign and domestic capital is taken as a welcome *disruption*, an expression much loved in business circles, that functions both as a renewal of the economy and as an affirmation of the nation's worth and promising futures. The current idea of New India as a site of hope, then, is intricately tied to the unabashed makeover of the nation-form into a commodity-form that captures and encloses an entire national territory to be transformed into a site of unlimited commodification and exchange and to actualize the capitalist dream of unending growth.

The production of *hope* unfolds along with the production of new imaginaries and episteme. It requires the nation to be grasped and imagined in commodity-form before it can eventually be enclosed and put at the disposal of investors. The current production of knowledge, however, constitutes a significant departure from earlier moments of the *discovery* of the world in the early modern era, when distant territories were explored and mapped in search of valuable commodities. The present moment signifies the *rediscovery* of that already familiar world, but this time what is unknown is not its physical shape and features—both visible and legible in minute details, in high-resolution digital format on the internet—but the *potentiality* and *availability* of territories that can generate commercial value in the global economy. To be sure, the production of a new body of knowledge of the nation-as-commodity is not a one-way street. It constitutes at once the modes of knowing the other as well as making oneself known to the world. If financial analysts and investment banks produce specialized knowledge of the market potential of postcolonial nations, then the postcolonial nations themselves make their market worthiness and availability known through spectacular global publicity campaigns. The perception of emergence of the postcolony as an emerging market, then, is precisely shaped between the acts of showing and seeing the potential, of making and becoming visible as a precious commodity in the world once again.

In what follows, I address this transformative moment by tracing an older genealogy of the capitalization of territories in which exploration of the world has often been entwined with the quest to possess resources that can be controlled and brought to market. I lay out two interlinked developments in the mid-to-late twentieth century—the self-publicity of the nation as an attractive investment destination that invites global capital, and the simultaneous reexploration of the third world as the new frontier of capitalist expansion.

"SAIL FOR OUR BEAUTIFUL SHORES"

In early 2004, the Indian Ministry of Finance commissioned an advertisement to invite investors worldwide to consider investment opportunities in "India Shining"—an allusion to a resource-rich India that had regained its golden shine after a long spell of colonial darkness. The invitation was a cryptically worded advertisement meant for major international financial broadsheets (fig. 2.1). And even more curiously, it featured an image suggestive of America instead of India. The image frame contained a lithographic impression of Christopher Columbus's arrival on the American continent[4] and bold text that read, "The last time we held so much promise, Columbus discovered America." The text in small print beneath explained that "when Columbus set sail to find the rich spices of our land, destiny had other plans. Instead of finding us, he discovered America. Years later, modern day explorers have got our Incredible land back on their maps." In the upper left-hand corner, the official seal of the government of India was visible along with a partly inaccurate quote attributed to Mark Twain. It read

FIGURE 2.1. *"Sail for Our Beautiful Shores" advertisement from the India Shining global campaign. 2003. Courtesy of Prathap Suthan.*

as follows: "India is the cradle of the human race, the birthplace of human speech, the mother of history, the grandmother of legend, and the great grandmother of tradition. Our most valuable and most instructive materials in the history of man are treasured up in India only." The advertisement was obviously designed to draw and hold the attention of a highly influential and powerful consumer segment—global investors—to India's potential as an attractive investment destination in the world. What had greatly enhanced its impact was precisely the bold presence of the sign of America instead of India.

Let's take a step back here and recall the story of Columbus's "discovery of America" in 1492—a critical event in the history of the modern world. Everyone knows that Columbus sailed westward across the Atlantic and stumbled upon America, but few know that what inspired him to launch this expedition was his search for legendary India and its rich bounty. India had long existed in Europeans' imagination as the land of abundance. Consider the most influential account of ancient India, *Indica*, written by Megasthenes (ca. 350–290 BCE), the Greek historian and ambassador at the court of Chandragupta Maurya.[5] Megasthenes described India as a fertile land blessed with double rainfall that enabled "two crops in the course of the year," a natural advantage that ensured that "famine had never visited India, and that there has never been a general scarcity in the supply of nourishing food."[6] He found the soil itself to be the source of abundance that "bears on its surface all kinds of fruits which are known to cultivation, it has also underground numerous veins of all sorts of metals, for it contains much gold and silver, and copper and iron in no small quantity, and even tin and other metals, which are employed in making articles of use and ornament, as well as the implements and accoutrements of war."[7] The ancient Mediterranean accounts of India thus dwelled on the abundance of its fruits and crops; the variety and enormity of its animals, especially the elephants who were trained as war machines; and the artistic skills and stature of its inhabitants, "as might be expected of men who inhale a pure air and drink the very finest water."[8] This narrative of India as a land of abundance reappeared in the ancient world in the works of several influential historians and geographers. For example, in the first century AD, Pliny's *Natural History* described India as a country in which there are "two summers and two harvests yearly." This account was followed by the works of Caius Solinus (third century) and Martianus Capella (early fifth century), who popularized this notion.[9] That India offered innumerable sites of "commercial value" was reinforced in the writings of the thirteenth-century Venetian traveler Marco Polo, who journeyed extensively in Asia and across the Indian Ocean.[10] This tantalizing idea of a wealthy, fertile India was to have a long life in the European imagination, even up through the fifteenth-century Age of Exploration. In fact, Columbus set out precisely to possess "the great spoils expected of the Indies" based on the corpus of knowledge that had long circulated in Europe.[11] But what the European geographers had not always fully agreed on was the actual location of legendary India or how to reach it. India seemed to be of an indeterminate location within the belt of tropics, and this is why on his first voyage Columbus carried a passport that introduced him as "a royal envoy" (a title given to him in the royal charter) on his way "to the parts of India (*ad partes Indie*)."[12] India's geographical elasticity meant that it was a shape-shifting entity, and this ambivalence is precisely what allowed Columbus to insist that the newly discovered lands were a part of "the Indies," the old object of European fascination. The new land expanse was named *Indias Occidentales*, or West Indies, and thought to be legendary India until 1498–1499 when the news of Vasco da Gama's arrival on the Malabar Coast reached European courts.

The work Columbus is called on to perform in the India Shining image should be evident by now: to reify India as a desirable commodity in the world. First, the story of Columbus's search for India reconfirmed to a new audience its status as a valuable commodity through the *longue dureé* of history. The promise of India appeared as the ultimate prize that explorers, adventurers, and investors seemed to have sought out forever. It was the commodity par excellence that the world was drawn to, and it could be accessed by new transoceanic and transcontinental lines of mobility that had opened up in the early modern era. The most compelling affirmation of India's global desirability was the accidental disclosure to the Europeans of an entire new continent even as the original object of desire remained elusive. Put differently, the American continent was positioned as mere *excess*, or "fake India," produced in the race to find India in early modern times. Second, by reprojecting America as fake India at a moment when the United States was the wealthiest nation in the world, the value of "original" India was greatly enhanced. Readers were practically invited to imagine what-if: What if Columbus had not stopped halfway in his journey to the West Indies? What if he had actually completed the journey as he intended? If half a journey could enrich you, then imagine the riches that awaited you at the original destination. In short, America was a mere prop resurrected from the past that was used to enhance the attractiveness of New India as an investment destination; thus the commodity value of India was reestablished.

What we witness here is the reification of India's commodity value, albeit with a sharp twist. This time it wasn't just investors who were seeking India; India was seeking investors too. It was actively inviting investors to "sail for our beautiful shores" in the footsteps of Columbus. The ghost of Columbus returns in this image frame, although not necessarily of his own volition. At the turn of the third millennium, it is no longer just Columbus who desires India. India summons him to remind a new generation of investors to do what he could not in his lifetime—to sail further south to the fabled land of India. This massive global publicity campaign was launched to make sure that investors and explorers would indeed find their destination. Columbus had lost his way because he didn't know the exact latitudinal location of India. His successors, however, were not only being tipped off about the exact location of India but also being given a navigational guide to make it to India's shores. We can surmise that the American connection has strategic value in bolstering India's claim as the original destination for global investments in the world. Consider the presence of the celebrated American author Mark Twain in the same frame as the India Shining advertisement. The quote ascribed to him elevates India from the realm of the ordinary to something far greater, a unique entity that cannot easily be put into the routine cycle of trade and exchange. This special status is precisely what makes it worthy of possession, an object of human desire through the ages. Yet those familiar with Mark Twain's work would know that the first sentence in this quote is taken from his famous travelogue *Following the Equator: A Journey around the World*, in which he recounts his journey through the British colonies in the late nineteenth century.[13] The second part, however, appears to be an unverified internet quote on the popular theme of "What the world says about India" that enjoys wide circulation.[14] What is at stake here is not necessarily the accuracy of the quote but the attempt to recreate a palpable sense of timeless wonderment about India. If Columbus stands for the fifteenth-century fascination for India, then Twain is called on to rehearse the same in the late nineteenth century via his accounts of travel through the British Empire. These two moments are obviously not the same. What was a mere desire in the fifteenth century had become a reality four centuries later. In the late nineteenth century India was the prized possession of the British Empire, the jewel in the crown of its vast colonial territories. India was no longer just a lucrative market for commodity trade, or "an immense accumulation of commodities," as Marx had described capitalist societies in the late nineteenth century—India itself had become a valuable commodity in the imperial market.[15]

Twain's oft-quoted remark "This is indeed India!" pertains to this double moment of awestruck encounter. He writes almost breathlessly, "This is indeed India! The land of dreams and romance, of fabulous wealth and fabulous poverty, of splendor and rage, of palaces and hovels, of famine and pestilence."[16] A range of contrasts and contradictions is what he reports, because India as an imperial commodity was indeed primarily an enclosure made available for resource extraction. India as an *imperial possession* was in its full commodity-form, put at the disposal of investors in a way that Columbus could have only dreamed of. The history of Indian colonialism is a familiar one that began about a hundred years after the travels of Columbus and da Gama. In 1600, a newly formed company of 218 British merchants was granted trade monopoly to the east of the Cape of Good Hope via a royal charter. The corporation known as the British East India Company was a state-backed monopoly that not only succeeded in establishing highly profitable trade but eventually gained full control over large tracts of territory and its population.[17] The colonial enclave was the precious commodity made available to the corporation and its stockholders. The colony could be rearranged in manifold ways to yield maximum profits by diverting farmland to grow precious agrocommodities, converting forests into surplus farmland, and extracting natural resources that could be shipped to world markets via modern infrastructures of railways and telegraph networks. The colonized population offered cheap labor and tax revenues that made the colonial enterprise profitable. In short, India's commodity value was at a historic high at this point. It was this tantalizing vision of desire that was conjured in the India Shining advertisement. The difference was that this time it was India actively asking the investors to turn around and take a look at the opportunities it offered.

MAKING BRAND INDIA

The invitation to "sail for our beautiful shores" was not a solitary gesture. It was part of a sustained state-led strategic policy to position Brand India as an attractive investment destination in the world. The experts of Indian economic reforms have mostly overlooked the question of brand image or how an extensive brand-building exercise was undertaken to boost India's reputation as an investment and export destination. The foundations of the Brand India project were laid in 1996 when the finance minister P. Chidambaram allocated Rs 50 crore to the newly established India Brand Equity Fund (IBEF). He argued that the "promotion of exports must remain high on our agenda" and appealed to "industry and trade" to contribute an equal amount to the fund.[18] The fund was created under the aegis of the Ministry of Commerce with the objective to promote Made in India brands in markets around the world. The central government wanted Export Promotion Councils (EPCs) to work together with IBEF's brand-promotion apparatus "to project India as a reliable supplier of quality goods and services" at competitive prices in overseas markets.[19] To this end, the IBEF began offering soft loans for brand promotion in 1999 to export firms trading in key commodities such as tea, basmati rice, coffee, and textiles. The role of IBEF at this point was unclear, unlike the EPCs that were already dedicated to the task of export promotion. The exporters suggested the IBEF create a logo that could be attached to the export product as a mark of quality. The loan mechanism itself could be a form of quality assurance, so that only companies with ISO 9000 certificates or long-term prospects would receive support from IBEF.[20] IBEF did offer a few loans to market Indian brands in overseas markets, but it never became the strategic corporate brand that mediated Indian exports in the world, as exporters had hoped for.[21] Instead the agency was about to be reinvented altogether with a new name and objectives by the Vajpayee government. In 2003, IBEF was relaunched as India Brand Equity Foundation, a public-private partnership with the Confederation of Indian Industries (CII), to "celebrate India as a destination of ideas and opportunities" for investment and tourism in the world. The rationale behind this shift was to think at a "macro level" in order to "meet the greater challenges in the international markets" as India moved "from one threshold of globalization to another."[22] The primary objective of the reformed IBEF was "to build positive economic perceptions of India globally" as a business brand.[23] In short, the task was no longer just to promote Indian commodities. It entailed transforming India itself into a branded commodity via a nation-brand strategy.

The official strategy "to drive a holistic approach to building a strong global brand for India" becomes visible in the 2005–2006 budget reports of the Department of Commerce as well as in IBEF annual reports of the same time.[24] Here we witness the state apparatus put to work to build a business brand for India. IBEF is consolidated as the central government agency entrusted with the task of crafting Brand India as an investment destination.[25] For IBEF, the first challenge was to create an overarching identity for Brand India that would capture what the agency called the "paradigm shift in public perception" in how "India continues to grab world attention. As the world's perception of India is changing, so is India's perception of itself."[26] This shift in perception was captured in the new Brand India identity, conceived as the "fastest growing free market democracy" in the world. As would be readily evident, the tagline both refers to the high economic growth rates India was experiencing and draws sharp contrasts with an illiberal authoritarian China. Recall how China and India had come together in a hyphenated relationship in the influential discourse of the twenty-first century, dubbing this period the "century of Asia" or the "Emerging Market Century." China-India was increasingly seen at this point as the motor of global economic growth, the emerging leaders in the fast-expanding world of free markets. The core message was devised precisely to give Brand India the extra edge, the sheen of democracy that China lacked. It wasn't just a question of establishing a contrast with China but also of establishing the Indian difference at the heart of the brand identity. Brand India was now also an influential mediator of Indian difference in the world. A publicity brochure asserted that Brand India "portrays the distinctive qualities of all things Indian and has the dynamism to build an enduring reputation in the competitive global arena."[27] The drivers of Brand India were "talent, markets, growth, and opportunity," according to IBEF, the building blocks of a branded nation standing "on the threshold of years of un-precedented growth."[28] At this stage, India's economic growth rate was pegged at 8.4 percent annually and was projected to soon grow to dou-ble figures. The high growth-rate numbers were the magic code, the stamp of approval that framed each initiative to brand the nation.

Once the brand identity had been created, the next challenge was "to capture the imagination of the world by creating mindspace for 'To-morrow's India' via a new strategic path to 'Influence the Influencers' that would "turn the tide of investment in India's direction."[29] In lay terms, this meant that the challenge was to circulate Brand India to the target audience, which included global and domestic investors, policy makers, and global media organizations that would amplify "good news and success stories from India" around the world.[30] To this end, IBEF was to prepare a brand communication tool kit that contained "an In-dia brochure, presentation, film and other communication packaged in a multi-purpose folder, along with an information kiosk and several posters" to position Brand India at strategic events worldwide. This was supplemented by IBEFs Brand Ambassador Network, which recruited influential individuals as ambassadors of Brand India to help build larger networks of Friends of India around the world. The networking program included reaching out to "hubs of opinion generation" such as the Harvard Business School, MIT Sloan School of Management, Wharton, Berkeley, and others. The idea was to network with a variety of international agencies, especially US media organizations, "to allow better penetration of Brand India in the US media."[31] The influential journalists, business leaders, financial analysts, and potential investors were even invited to visit India under the Experience India Programme to witness the great transformation the nation was undergoing. The of-ficial scaffolding on which to elevate Brand India—the umbrella nation brand—and disclose it to the world was now fully erect.

Brand India made its spectacular global debut at the 2006 meet-ing of the World Economic Forum (WEF) in Davos. This is where the

FIGURE 2.2. *The India Shining global campaign ad launched in international business papers. 2003. Courtesy of Prathap Suthan.*

world's billionaires, influential business leaders, heads of states, and social and media organizations assemble once a year. Brand India was unveiled in this august assembly in a memorable high-impact campaign called "India Everywhere" that gained wide traction in Davos and beyond (see chapter 5, "The Magical Market"). The success of the Davos campaign meant that spectacular global events became the chief mode of circulation of Brand India. The trend picked up immediately with the global rollout soon after of the India Everywhere campaign from Davos to several locations across the world, including Germany, Japan, the United Kingdom, Singapore, the United States, Belgium, Switzerland, Canada, China, and Russia. Brand India became a fixture at several important global events such as Hannover Messe, the world's leading annual trade show for industrial technology. In 2006, India was for the first time invited to be the official partner country of Hannover Messe—a special status that showcased it among global manufacturers and traders of industrial goods.[32] The spotlight on India only amplified the following year when the sixtieth anniversary of independence was publicized worldwide. The India@60 events took place in major cities across the world, the most notable of which was the New York celebration that "celebrated the arrival of India on the global platform."[33] The 2010 World Exposition in Shanghai featured Brand India complete with an array of bedazzling cultural experiences.

Ajay Khanna, the CEO of IBEF, pitched the global unveiling of Brand India as bringing "out the 'realness' of the India story. Investors, journalists, policymakers and opinion leaders are flocking to India, excitedly discovering the new India. Hotels are packed, with rooms getting increasingly difficult to come by. Soaring demand for tickets on domestic as well as international flights has spurred growth in the aviation industry and investments in airport infrastructure. All these augur well for India."[34] The 2006 WEF meeting was indeed the peak moment of euphoria in the India story, a befitting celebratory prequel to the sixtieth anniversary of independence the following year. India was now the subject of intense speculation around the world, a promising story of a postcolonial nation about to make a stunning economic recovery.[35] Or at least this was the widespread discourse that Khanna was pointing to. That this experience was a bit surreal, something he had not experienced before, is evident in how he prefaces his remarks with a question: "Clearly, something has changed. Perceptions or reality or is it both?" This question is not really a question but an answer presented with an interrogative mark. What this preemptive question allows us to see is how the condition of euphoria and disbelief inhabited the elite world of Brand India all at once. The fast-unfolding present had almost a dreamlike quality that the elite had longed for—to see the world and to be seen in that world. That moment had arrived, propelled in part by another development taking place elsewhere in the world. Here I turn to the *rediscovery* of India by Euro-American investment bankers exploring the world for emerging markets—the yet untapped frontiers of economic growth.

STATES OF EMERGENCE

The history of the emerging markets is often linked to the idea of BRICs, which gained popular currency more than a decade ago. Proposed in 2001 by a Goldman Sachs banker as the growth map of the future, the catchy acronym comprising four of the world's most populous and resource-rich nations—Brazil, Russia, India, and China—came to dominate the global language of investment and policy making.[36] Yet the idea of emerging markets precedes BRICs by more than two decades. In fact, as early as 1950s, the idea of foreign investment as a development strategy had already begun taking roots. In 1956, the International Finance Corporation (IFC), a World Bank subsidiary, was formed "to stimulate private investment" as a means of "ending extreme poverty and boosting shared prosperity" with a starting capital of US$100 million. The belief that "private sector is essential to development" underpinned IFC activities in the third world, where it either offered loans to or invested directly in Asian, African, and Latin American corporations.[37] In the 1970s, IFC opened its advisory services, Capital Markets, which offered both financing and advice to strengthen local financial institutions, including banks and stock markets. The formation of the Housing Development Finance Corporation (HDFC) bank in India in 1977 is an example of this intervention, as IFC became the founding shareholder in the housing finance project. Other success stories cited by IFC in its mission to "increase the private sector's growth and its contribution to development" include Davivienda in Colombia, investments in LG Korea, formation of the first securities market in Indonesia, and finance projects for Kenya Commercial Bank.[38]

In 1981, the role of private capital in third-world economies was further consolidated in a new IFC initiative. Named the Third World Equity Fund, it invited investors to take a look at developing countries given the "possibility of making real money" in these territories.[39] This moment is remembered as a key shift that unfolded in a dramatic manner. Antoine van Agtmael, the investment banker credited with initiating this project, recalls the initial lack of enthusiasm among the investors who had assembled at the headquarters of Salomon Brothers in New York City. He was entrusted with the task of making a pitch to the potential investors by convincing them with data that showed that developing nations enjoyed higher economic growth rates and promising companies that had been ignored thus far. The assembly included about thirty bankers from major investment institutions such as JP Morgan, TIAA-CREF, and Salomon Brothers. Although they found the idea interesting, the name Third World Equity Fund was a turnoff, as his pitch failed to have the desired impact. Agtmael writes,

> We had the goods. We had the data. We had the countries. We had the companies. What we did not have, however, was an elevator pitch that liberated these developing economies from the stigma of being labeled as "Third World" basket cases, an image rife with negative associations of flimsy polyester, cheap toys, rampant corruption, Soviet style tractors, and flooded rice paddies.[40]

The name "third world" came with heavy baggage that could not be easily offloaded.[41] If it invoked the moment of decolonization in several nations across Asia, Africa, and Latin America, it was also a reminder of the global development-aid regime, of the newly independent although supposedly underdeveloped nations forever lagging behind their developed Northern counterparts. And if the Non-Aligned Movement and Bandung Conference celebrated third-world solidarity in their newfound freedom, the discourse of corruption and immature democracies hinted at the unpreparedness of these nations for full autonomy. Given these considerations, Agtmael found "a term that sounded more positive and invigorating: *Emerging Markets.* 'Third World' suggested stagnation, 'Emerging Markets' suggested progress, uplift and dynamism."[42] The new name was designed, he later recalled, "to give it a more uplifting feeling to what one had originally called the Third World Fund."[43]

What we witness in this name-change act is a desire to make a *clean break* in history intended to keep the third world and emerging markets in separate enclosures. The new name is deployed as an instant mood booster that can potentially uplift a part of the world that has long been imagined as sliding down on the political-economic ladder. The prefix *emerging* works to brighten the mood, to enhance the positive outlook while creating clear distance from all the negatives attached to the idea of the third world. This transition from the third world to emerging markets received another helping hand when the Cold War ended and the free markets became a firm foreign policy agenda pursued aggressively by the Clinton administration in the 1990s. A documentary film called *The Commanding Heights* shows how the new agenda was termed "a triumph," as "more countries than ever adopted market economies." The then prime minister of Malaysia, Mahathir Bin Mohamad, wearily described the moment as follows: "Once communism was defeated, then capitalism could expand and show its true self. . . . There is nothing to restrain capital, and capital is demanding that it should be able to go anywhere and do whatever it likes." Interestingly, this section in the film, entitled "Emerging Market Hunters," emphasized not only the elements of rediscovery of the already familiar world but also the thrill of the chase and capture of new nations turned markets.[44] And indeed the goal of "captur[ing] that growth, and of course mak[ing] money for investors" was what drove investment fund managers to the third world.[45] Yet the difference between the third world and its new incarnation as emerging markets is far-reaching. If the third world was forever waiting to catch up with the developed world, the newly classified emerging markets, buoyed by the enthusiasm of potential investors, seemed to be accelerating their entry into the future. The wide gap between these perceptions might lead one to believe that it was two different parts of the world, or two different worlds as such, being spoken of. Yet it was the same region, just projected to be on parallel tracks that seldom seem to overlap. But these supposed parallel tracks do, in fact, run into each other, or more accurately, one track merges into the other.

This dramatic shift is particularly captured in the aid-for-trade policy measures that began taking shape about a decade later under the aegis of the World Trade Organization. In 2001, a new consensus had already begun gaining ground in what is popularly called Doha Rounds, which identified the role of international trade in "the promotion of economic development and the alleviation of poverty."[46] In 2005, this consensus that "many poor countries lack the basic infrastructure to take advantage of the market access opportunities" led to further policy initiatives, including diverting development aid into creating trade infrastructures, granting loans, and providing technical assistance. The traditional donors were asked to "scale up their aid for trade" commitment in order to "build capacity and infrastructure they need to benefit from trade opening."[47] In the next decade, this shift was visible in the aid policies outlined by Western donors. For example, the Danish Development Aid Agency (DANIDA) adopted the aid-for-trade principles and identified "trade as a driver of development" in its poverty reduction programs.[48] An estimated US$264.5 billion was disbursed worldwide between 2006 and 2013, and nearly 38 percent of traditional aid was diverted toward trade facilitation.[49] This shift mirrors the wider trend within the international donor community, which moved development aid to build and launch advocacy initiatives and monitor investments in free-trade infrastructure.

What we witness here, then, is the gradual diversion of the old development aid politics toward the agenda of opening up developing economies to market forces. This trend gained traction at the same time that the potential of BRIC economies was identified. The World Trade Organization agenda of bringing "coherence in global economic policy making" that encompasses developing nations to help them "fully exploit their potential" gained broader acceptance.[50] Donors began viewing developing nations in terms of their unexploited potential, and the language of partnership, responsibility and accountability increasingly entered this changing donor-recipient relationship. The development aid agenda has since continued to recede in order to help shape the further opening up of third-world economies. As we will see, it is in this world of open markets that we witness how the old dichotomies of first/third, core/periphery, and developed/developing are readily subsumed and rearranged in commodity form.

INDEX OF ATTRACTIVENESS

What makes a nation turned market attractive in the eyes of investors? And how do investors explore and imagine this commodified world in the twenty-first century? If spectacular expeditions undertaken by adventurous explorers were the hallmark of an earlier era, contemporary exploration is a routine practice facilitated by financial experts and a fast-growing body of popular and specialist literature on markets and investments. The twenty-first-century investor-explorer, we are told, doesn't "need a passport, only a desire to discover more about the economic opportunities in the world today."[51] This mode of discovery—or more accurately, rediscovery—entails taking "a long, hard look at the world. You may not have done this at any great length since the sixth grade, but time spent studying a world map can never be wasted, and can be critical to your success as a global investor." This advice to rediscover the world, whose physical contours ought to be familiar even to a sixth grader, is offered by Mark Mobius, the executive director of the group and, in the 1980s, one of the early investors in the emerging markets. The "long, hard look" he prescribes is an invitation to see what might have been long overlooked, namely, the full economic potential of the third world. As he puts it,

> The first thing you'll probably notice is the relatively small size of the developed markets compared to the vast swaths of land covering the emerging countries. Emerging economies cover 77% of the world's land mass, have more than 80% of the world's population, hold more than 65% of the world's foreign exchange reserves, and account for about 50% of the world's gross domestic product (GDP). In 2010, about 5.7 billion people resided in emerging countries; that's about five times the 1.2 billion population of the developed markets. China and India alone account for more than 2.5 billion people; that's almost four times the approximately 700 million in the United States and European Union.[52]

This fresh gaze on the world and its cartographic reimagination in the age of open markets is significant in at least two related ways. First, the very language of classification and naming of the world regions in terms of "developed" and "emerging" both invokes and overcomes the

earlier taxonomies shaped in the moment of mid-twentieth-century decolonization. Second, the regions outside the developed world are now
seen in terms of potential and promise and even an attractive source of
economic optimism. These two features appear in tandem to grade and
rank world regions in commodity-form. The principle of this world order unfolding along the readily apparent axis of economy and politics
is captured succinctly in Mark Mobius's popular guidebook, *The Little
Book of Emerging Markets*, in which he directly asks (and then answers),
"Why invest in emerging markets? Because that's where the growth
is."[53] That economic growth is crucial in the pursuit of national interests has now become a matter of common sense, and that explains the
never-ending search for new market territories that can be opened up
to investors. Using this logic of economic growth potential, then, the
world in its commodity-form is graded and ordered in four categories:
(1) developed markets, (2) emerging markets, (3) frontier markets, and
(4) preemerging markets. This classification is not restricted to expert
policy papers, scholarly interest, or major corporate investors but is now
circulated widely, prescribed in popular literature, and consumed by
an ever-growing number of small investors. Consider the vastly popular guidebook for those keen on building individual investment portfo-
lios, *Emerging Markets for Dummies*, which defines the order as follows:
"Emerging markets are those countries that have growing economies
and a growing middle class. Some of these countries were once poor,
and some still have high rates of poverty. Many are undergoing pro-
found social and political change for the better. Another class of country, *frontier markets*, includes those nations that are very small, are at
an early stage of economic development, or have tiny stock markets.
These markets present opportunities for patient investors with an appetite for risk. The poorest of the world's nations are considered to be
pre-emerging: these markets have few opportunities for investors now,
but they could become really interesting in the years to come so they're
worth watching."[54]

What is left unsaid in this description is that each of these market categories eventually aspires to become developed, or mature, just
like Euro-American markets. As should be obvious, the world in its

commodity-form is imagined and ordered along a scale of temporality that mimics the earlier discourse of development. If developed, developing, and underdeveloped were the stages of modernity that defined the mid-twentieth-century decolonized world, the categories of developed, emerging, frontier, and preemerging mimic those, albeit in the twenty-century-framework of markets. This promise of modernity, of "catching up" with the developed world is reiterated in the language of markets too. The difference is that the markets need not sit in the "waiting room of history"[55] forever, they can fast-forward their arrival on the global stage by "opening up" to global investors.[56] In other words, the shift to markets is presented as a matter of choice, of greater autonomy to accelerate the process of joining the modern world.

The temporal order of world regions in the commodity-form differs from the previous development discourse on yet another significant count. Here, to lag behind is not necessarily a disadvantage but, on the contrary, precisely what makes the nation attractive to investors. Consider the proposition of the "appetite for risk" that Ann C. Logue refers to in connection with frontier and preemerging markets. The popular dictum of capital investment—the higher the risk, the higher the profit—is a hint well understood in investment circles. These regions are positioned on the higher scale of risk and are deemed to be yet untapped, waiting to be opened up at a later date. To put it differently, the lower the scale of development, the higher the risk, and consequently, the higher the potential that remains to be exploited. The world, then, is arranged along speculative stages of market and a range of unending possibilities in the present and future for lucrative investments. The investment experts describe these stages of market as unique "states of emergence" in which the world continues to "evolve" into profitable markets that can shape fortunes across the globe.[57] This imagination of the world is reflected in the new form of investor-friendly cartography that maps the world according to different states of emergence. Consider the heat map of the world produced by Morgan Stanley Capital Investments (MSCI).[58] The publicity brochure begins with a suggestive question: "Can you feel the heat?" that then leads customers to an interactive world map. Loaded with sexual connotations, the notion of heat refers to how ripe and ready a nation-market is for investments and what profits it might yield at a given moment. The map promises to "capture the world" via interactive tools that can help plot its current market position as well as trace its development over the past decade. The green and red dots illustrate at a glance how hot or cool a market is—green stands for profit and red for stagnation. A vast number of green dots scattered across Asia, Africa, and the Americas signals booming economic opportunities, whereas the red clusters in Europe show the decade-long effects of economic stagnation. The heat factor is indeed monitored and measured continuously in markets considered attractive overall.

At the heart of attractiveness is the old question of profitability—or what is perceived not only as potentially rich but also accessible to investors. The broad markers of potentiality on a world scale are thus already familiar—nations with large territories, a large population, a skilled and cheap labor force, and a vast middle-class consumer base are deemed to be the most lucrative by investors. For example, the idea of BRICS (Brazil, Russia, India, China, and South Africa) effectively packages some of the largest territories and populations across continents together as a coherent market proposition.[59] It also signals the post–Cold War transformations that saw postsocialist and postcolonial nations gearing up to large-scale promarket reforms. The BRICS have thus come to occupy an enviable status within the larger notion of emerging markets—they signal both potential rich returns and entry into that abundant market territory. Yet the attractiveness of markets is not a given; it is characterized precisely by speculative fluctuations. It requires a constant performance of iteration that can confirm—or unconfirm, for that matter—the status of attractiveness. The market territories, therefore, are monitored, measured, and graded on a scale of attractiveness. If high ratings on the attractiveness scale serve to boost the fortunes of a given market territory, lower ratings serve as critical moments of course correction, producing political pressure to introduce more reforms to liberalize markets ever further. A number of tools and market indexes have emerged in the past decade, each of which promises investors an accurate measure of market territories around the world. Whereas the MSCI heat map monitors markets on a daily basis, others appraise on a biannual or annual basis. The release of these appraisal reports often turns into national events, sewn seamlessly into national publicity campaigns and into electoral battles.

Consider the single-country attractiveness survey conducted by Ernst and Young (EY). Entitled "Ready, Set, Grow," the survey is "designed to help businesses make investment decisions and governments remove barriers to future growth."[60] The report promises to present both "reality" and "perception," that is, the actual inflow and impact of direct foreign investment as well as future scope. The twofold methodology thus draws on financial data as well as feedback from international business leaders and policy makers. In fact, the perception of international decision-makers is crucial and forms a kind of *endorsement* of a given market. The 2015 EY survey endorsed India as the most attractive investment destination in the world. The verdict was that "while the speed of economic reforms may vary, the direction is firmly set toward higher growth."[61] It was both an endorsement and a gentle encouragement to bring the long-awaited second line of economic reforms up to speed.[62] In short, the perception of attractiveness is something that needs to be constantly boosted. And this is where we witness the production and consumption of quantifiable knowledge predicated on measurement of the nation along a number of economic indicators.

THE MAGIC NUMBER

If there is a showstopper in this routine spectacle of market attractiveness, it indeed comes in the unlikely form of cold numbers: GDP growth rates and global business rankings. These numbers receive wide attention not only among specialists—financial analysts, investors, policy makers, and economists—but also the public at large, albeit in different ways. What is of critical importance is the fact that these numbers don't shape up or work in isolation. They remain locked in a speculative web of interconnections in which each possesses the potential to boost or hurt the other. Consider how the upward climb on the scale of economic growth or the ease of doing business can boost the speculative value of nation such as India that pitches itself as an investment destination in the world. The downward slide can likewise undo the gains or, worse still, plunge the economy into negative growth. A high GDP rate can draw new investments to the nation, and in return, the fresh investments can reaffirm the faith of markets in the nation's economic potential. The numbers, then, are central to the making or unmaking of global perceptions of the market worthiness of the nation. Put differently, the quantification of market is crucial in whetting the appetite of investors who like to imagine their future returns before allocating capital to new projects. The market statistics, unsurprisingly, are often unveiled in a highly publicized ritualistic manner and become spectacular public events in themselves that keep the nation preoccupied on an everyday basis. The numbers and ranks, then, occupy (and shape) a large space in contemporary politics as markers of current economic value as well as signposts of future potential in the arena we call the economy.[63] To unravel this complex maze of economic indicators, I begin with the GDP—the most famous form of quantitative value in this story.

Gross Domestic Product (GDP), put simply, is the sum total of the monetary value of all goods and services produced within a year in a given national territory. It is a high-impact quantified indicator of a nation's prosperity known as "economic growth" that is popularly held up as a measure of societal well-being. The presence of GDP in public life is so outsized and its political power so enormous that it is difficult to believe it did not exist until the 1930s. The long history of the making of GDP discloses how nations came to be imagined and produced as spaces of capitalist growth; citizens as consumers and manufacturers of commercial goods and services; and social well-being as aggregate economic wealth. How did this shift come about? The standard accounts of the invention of GDP begin in 1934 when the Harvard economist Simon Kuznets together with the US government and the official-sounding but private National Bureau of Economic Research (NBER) began counting America's national income and thereby defined the economic-growth metrics. In this story, the macroeconomic indicators emerged from the twentieth-century economic and social ruination that followed the Great Depression and the two world wars, and they became useful planning tools for the experts charged with overseeing the course of the national economy.[64] Yet the arrival of GDP on center stage in liberal-capitalist societies is not the beginning of the rise of economic indicators but the culmination of pre-twentieth-century developments including the making of land enclosures, the enslavement of human bodies, and the consolidation of financial capital. Eli Cook has convincingly traced this long history of economic indicators, which fully came to the fore in the early-twentieth-century crisis of American capitalism.[65] At this moment, private capital desired to be seen as a force of good just as the fear of labor unrest and the collective labor movement was gaining ground. The idea was to counter the "untruths" about the "the great business interests" via "some intelligent, well conceived, broad, non-political effort to educate public opinion" and make it appreciative of wealthy corporations as producers of affluence.[66] The eventual outcome of this effort to produce "non-political" facts was the making of Gross National Product (GNP) and then GDP, which were designed to aggregate all the legal financial transactions within a given national territory. This is when accounting practices to measure wealth moved from the realm of business to the realm of national policy and culture. The shift meant that the statistical formula used to measure the performance of a business was now applied to the nation-state. It was a critical step toward imagining the entire national enclosure as a capitalized investment capable of generating economic growth. The invention of GDP eventually transcended US borders to become a global story—"from narrow tool to global rule"—of measurement and ranking of the wealth of nations around the world.[67] In the mid-1940s, following the Bretton Woods deliberations, the GDP was adopted by international agencies such as the International Monetary Fund in order to rebuild a postwar world. The nations were now expected to compute the national economic data, including national income, and share it with the world community.[68]

The centrality of GDP in the affairs of the nation is a phenomenon that gained currency particularly once the economy opened up to foreign investments. Once the nations began to be constantly measured and ranked on a global scale, their economic worth was taken as a sign of their standing in the world. In postreform India, then, GDP numbers became familiar actors who appear regularly in the political theater of national economy. They are unveiled on a quarterly basis, leading up to the grand finale in the final quarter when the annual rate of growth is released. These numbers are often contested, their highs and lows taken as signs of government's success or failure. The government that presides over soaring GDP rates is deemed successful, and the one that oversees a downward slide stands to lose its legitimacy. Authority is constructed within the political domain around the speculative (and actual) rise and fall of GDP.[69] Consider these news headlines, which keep the nation hooked, including stories of *growth boom*: "Big Boost for Narendra Modi, GDP Growth Powers to 6.3% in Q2, 5 Quarter Slide Reversed";[70] "GDP Live: Growth Boost Has Happened Due to Rise in Manufacturing, Says FM";[71] and "IMFs 7.4% GDP Forecast Is a Gift to PM, but Why Are Foreigners More Optimistic about Growth than CSO?"[72] Stories of *anxiety* are included too: "ADB Downgrades India's GDP Growth Outlook to 7% for 2017–8";[73] "In Aftermath of Demonetization, India's GDP Growth Sees Sharp Fall to 5.7% in Q1";[74] and "As GDP Growth Slows, India's Demographic Dividend Could Turn into a Disaster."[75] And there are also the inevitable *comparisons* between the current and the former government: "PM Narendra Modi Tears into Critics; Says GDP Slid to 5.7% or Below 8% under UPA";[76] "Jaitley Praises GDP Rebound, Chidambaram Says Pause in Declining Trend";[77] and "GDP Flop-Show: Manmohan Singh Has the Last Laugh in War of Words with Narendra Modi over Note Ban."[78] It is important to note that the thing we call "the economy" or "GDP" is not a theme exclusive to newspapers in the niche of business and finance. It lies at the heart of the political debate about the present and future of the nation.

The affective obsession with GDP numbers is indeed entwined with the story of the postcolonial Indian economy: a story of stagnation, slight recovery, and then a sharp upward turn. Consider the low decadal growth between 1950 and the 1970s, which averaged 3.5 percent with marginal annual variations, a condition that has been variously labeled the Hindu rate of growth, socialist rate of growth, or, simply,

License Raj stagnation.[79] This period is often seen as a missed opportunity, especially in comparison to the fast-growing East Asian economies. This was followed by post-1980s economic recovery and then the
1990s reforms that are said to have leashed an upward explosion of economic growth.[80] The GDP numbers that buoyed India and projected
its accelerated growth story worldwide first appeared in 1999–2000
(8 percent) on the eve of the third millennium and then between 2006
and 2008 (9.48, 9.57, and 9.32 percent) to coincide with the sixtieth anniversary of India's independence.[81] At this point, India's self-percep-
tion and its perception in the world changed dramatically—together
with China, it was now the world's growth engine, but as the "world's
fastest growing free market democracy" it was also a liberal-democratic
alternative to authoritarian China. India's newfound global stature was
connected to its high GDP growth rates, a correlation that was understood by policy makers, investors, and the prosperous middle class
alike.[82] GDP was no longer just a factual statement of national output,
it was also a magical instrument that, if kept in optimal order, could
bring the dreamworlds of capital to a nation desirous of re-creating its
lost glory.

What kind of output counted as GDP, and how should it even be
computed? It should be obvious that the question of quantitative data
and methodology has been an essential point of policy deliberations in
the making of GDP. The work of this metric tool has long been subject
to critique given how it equated economic activity with societal well-
being. This move to privilege market transactions as a sign of human
progress has come with a cautionary note right from the beginning,
including from Kuznets, who is credited with devising the formula.[83]
The critique built up in the subsequent decades. A memorable articulation of this critique was offered by Robert Kennedy, who described
GNP as a measurement of everything "except that which makes life
worthwhile," such the health, education, and safety of citizens. In recent years, a particularly forceful challenge to the metrics of progress
emerged, with calls for modification of GDP calculations. The economists Joseph Stiglitz, Amartya Sen, and Jean-Paul Fitoussi described
GDP as the "mismeasuring of our lives," as market production is an

insufficient indicator of quality of life, sustainable development, and a healthy environment.[84] The GDP metrics, after all, did not capture the risks of high economic growth and industrial production to the well-being of citizens and the environment. They recommended instead that GDP calculations measure well-being rather than just market production by focusing on material consumption together with dimensions of health, education, work conditions, environment, and political governance.[85] This proposed modification to GDP calculations has not yet made inroads into the actual measurements, although concerns about human development and sustainability have now gained wider currency.[86] In India, the methodology has often been a matter of contestation. Most recently, in 2015, the Central Statistical Organisation announced a change in methodology that included changing the base year to 2011–2012 to reflect current prices and Gross Value Added (GVA), which brought indirect tax income earned by the government into purview as well. It led to what the *Wall Street Journal* described as a "dramatic revision [that] could shake up the way the current trajectory of India's economy is perceived both at home and abroad," because India's growth rate was now closer to that of China. It quoted a London-based economist, who remarked, "It kind of changes everything, at least at face value." And despite doubts about the actual state of the economy, this change in face value, or perception, in itself garnered global attention. Although the new methodology was in line with global practices of how GDP is calculated, its timing became a source of political contention. The Indian GDP had improved substantially due to this change, and in 2017, India regained the status of the fastest-growing economy in the world, with a growth rate of 7.2 percent.[87] Nevertheless, doubts persisted about the actual state of economy and numbers that told two divergent stories.[88] What adds weight to the claim of economic growth is a potential reification from a different set of numbers generated by another agency. As we will find out, these numbers work in tandem to (mostly) reinforce the legitimacy of what is called the "growth agenda" in free-market economies.

The Indian GDP is often juxtaposed with a number of global indexes and rankings, such as the World Bank's ease of doing business index, the World Economic Forum's *Global Competitiveness Report*, Moody's sovereign credit rating, and its rival Standard & Poor's credit ratings, to name the most prominent ones. These rankings are keenly watched events, much beyond the community of investors, that keep the nation transfixed each time they are made public. The rankings serve as a kind of external verification—global audit systems—of the claims made by national governments. Broadly speaking, the rankings are quantified expressions of how business friendly the nations are, and if not, to what extent have they have undertaken (or promised to undertake) economic reforms to become business friendly. While the rankings are pitched as detached and objective knowledge production of nation-states, in practice they are deeply entwined in the rough-and-tumble of national politics. Consider the World Bank's ease of doing business ranking, which probably has the widest political impact in the Global South. The *Doing Business* report issued by the bank since 2004 offers keen insights into the work of cold numbers in producing knowledge that enhances the commodity value of nation-states. The key aspect of its methodology is that it measures the "distance to frontier"—the gap between ideal market practices and the nation's actual economic performance. The ranking ranges from 1 to 190 nations, which are given scores based on the aggregate distance to frontier on topics such as starting a business, getting construction permits, getting electricity, getting credit, paying taxes, registering property, enforcing contracts, protecting minority investors, resolving insolvency, and cross-border trade.[89] The nations are measured entirely from the point of view of businesses mainly as territorial enclaves that can generate the highest output and profits. This methodology provokes a competitive race among the economies to close the gap as quickly as possible. The reward for implementing the idealized best practices is to be moved up in the ranking order—a verified quantity that becomes a cause for celebration (or public goading to bring more reforms, in case of a failure to move up). Onno Ruhl, the former World Bank country director for India, describes the rankings as a support mechanism for economic reforms. He said that they "strengthen the hands of the reformers, the politicians who work in favor of reforms."[90] The rankings work as external audit systems with inbuilt incentives—globally publicized moments of glory—for reform-minded politicians to do more, to keep on rolling reforms to reach the top. A nation's place in the ranking order, then, becomes a sign of its market worth—both actual and potential—that can be harnessed by investors and policy makers alike. Let's take a close look at the 2018 report, which was particularly eventful, as India was ranked in one hundredth place for the first time ever.

In 2018, India's upward climb on the scale confirmed and even boosted the government's claims that it was transforming the nation into the fastest-growing economy in the world. The event was widely splashed by official publicity machines like Brand India and Make in India as "India: Ranks 100 in World Bank's Doing Business Report 2018 Up by 30 Places." It was likewise covered in the media in such euphoric terms as "India Makes Highest-Ever Jump to Rank 100 Out of 190 countries";[91] "India Breaks into Top 100 for First Time";[92] "India Leaps 30 Places to 100th Rank in World Bank's 'Ease of Doing Business' Index";[93] and "World Bank Endorses Modi Government's Reform Credentials."[94] The improved ranking was labeled as the "historic jump" when India "hit a century" and was even addressed by the minister of finance, Arun Jaitley, as an occasion to set the next ambitious target for his government: to take India into the top 50 of the index.[95] He remarked that "the Prime Minister has given us [a] goal that we must try and come within [the] first 50. So, at a time when you were at 142, to come within [the] first 50 is somewhat challenging."[96] The official Indian information agency, the Press Information Bureau, credited India's improved ranking to "the mantra of 'Reform, Perform, Transform' given by the Prime Minister [Modi] wherein a strong leadership has provided the political will to carry out comprehensive and complex reforms, supported by a bureaucracy committed to perform. . . . India is the only country in South Asia and BRICS economies to feature among most improved economies of the Doing Business report this year."[97] The press release underscored the fact that the elevation of India on the global business scale had not happened by chance; instead it was a result of sustained efforts undertaken by the government in power. In fact, the rankings were taken so seriously as to set the official machinery of the Department of Industrial Policy and Promotion (DIPP) in motion making advance preparations for achieving the target "to be in the top 50" nations in the 2019 rankings. This time India was targeting ninety reform measures across sectors of finance, urban development, and corporate affairs to achieve higher rankings. The entire exercise was a continuous reconfiguration of the self—an exercise of looking down at oneself from the high end of the global ranking and making anticipatory changes in the hope of making it up there. It also required being creative in finding loopholes to better the score. An unnamed senior government official, for example, suggested easy-to-do steps to bring down the number of procedures needed to acquire digital signatures, saying, "The World Bank does not count obtaining a national ID as a separate process. We can easily reduce time by 10 days, which will improve our rank globally."[98] The official had clearly cracked the World Bank's methodology to make a shortcut to the desired target.

The larger story we witness here is not about bureaucratic maneuvering as such but about how perceptions of spectacular economic progress are manufactured and reified via global rankings. For what's it worth, the incentive to short-circuit the process in order "to get there" is the promise of windfall publicity that may follow. The event of the unveiling of rankings offers a global stage on which nations can perform as reform friendly and draw attention to themselves. The prospect of breaking into the top 100 or top 50 is a made-for-publicity moment with enormous potential for generating attention. It's a script that is rehearsed annually for the double-ended *spectacular value* it creates for the nation that is ranked as well as for the agency that creates the rankings. If the spectacular value can help change perceptions of the nation as a reform-minded open-for-business economic unit, then it also helps make the institutions that rank nations relevant players in the world of free markets. In this instance, the World Bank becomes an important voice, the key arbiter of what *frontiers* of free trade should look like. In offering ranks to nations deemed business friendly, the World Bank gains prestige as the authority that sets the global benchmark standards. What is ultimately at stake is the idea of free markets, which receives a fresh dose of publicity via the theater of global rankings. Once national prestige is linked to the rank the nation occupies in a given index, it potentially becomes a national project almost akin to a popularity contest. In its popular form, the national rank on a given global scale is no longer restricted to the world of bureaucrats, politicians, and lobby organizations. It is brought to the public sphere, an important precondition in shifting public opinion toward capitalist growth. By now, performance-based rankings predicated on the "desire to outrank others" have filtered down and have even been incorporated as a mode of governance within the national enclosure.[99] The rankings are no longer mere quantitative abstractions; they have become a matter of common sense that shapes the imaginaries of a brand new nation.

SHAPES OF THE NEW

I finally turn to that unnamed *something* that changed how the sign of India came to be perceived as an emerging power called New India in the early twenty-first century. We might ask what kind of work the prefix *New* is summoned to perform in conjunction with *India*. To be sure, the prefix *New* is not an objective status but an ontological possibility or even an expression of the desire to rediscover or reform what is there. It is a purely subjective category, a rhetorical packaging that seeks to isolate, to break off from all that was before even as it regenerates the archaic. The idea of newness always appears in temporary flashes, for the moment of its recognition is also the moment of its effacement, and therefore it is in need of endless repetition to keep it from lapsing. Put differently, for all its claims of being unfamiliar, of having never existed before, the idea of newness is a vastly familiar project of "eternal recurrence" that coheres what is forever with yet-once-again.[100] Each invocation of newness is an invitation to look at the object with fresh eyes—"Come and look; here is something you haven't seen before"—a call to reorient one's way of looking at the world. For newness to come into being, both the object and how others look it at are required to be different. In its eternally recurring form, then, newness itself becomes a spectacular value that

continues to feed the engines of capitalist growth.[101] In what follows, I
trace the long genealogy of newness in New India and its many shifts,
within folds of which we can witness vast sweeps of historical transformations. As we will find, it wasn't just that India was changing; the
way the world looked at India had also undergone a fundamental shift.
It was once seen as a hopeless postcolony and was now seen as an exciting emerging market.

I will give a brief history of New India here before we turn fully to
the contemporary moment. Although the idea of New India is popularly associated with the 1990s economic reforms, it makes an early appearance already in the mid-nineteenth century, albeit in a different
form. The description of India as *new* first began emerging at a critical moment of transition—the end of the East India Company's rule
over India and the formal absorption of India into the British Empire.
The expression *New India* was a popular one invoked in the debates
and reportage that followed the brutal repression of the 1857–1858 rebellion and the eventual dissolution of the East India Company. The
"New India bill" was a common reference to the official Bill for the
Better Government of India, which proposed transfer of the territories
in possession or under the government of the East India Company to
the British Crown. The newness alluded to the decision that "the entire
control of Indian affairs is to be taken away from the East India Company and put in the hands of the Queen."[102] This new turn was more
than a mere transfer of power. It stood for an accelerated territorial expansion of capitalism that would bring disparate geographies and networks of financial interdependence under the arch of British imperial
economy. Dressed up in the garb of liberal modernity, the transition
from mercantile to territorial colonialism opened up for large-scale reconfiguration the political-economic structures that incorporated India fully into what Giovanni Arrighi has called the "imperial foundations of Britain's free trade regime of rule and accumulation on a world
scale."[103] This is when we witness the unfettered transformation of the
"geographical space of colonial India into a commodified 'second order'
space embedded within rather than merely tied to the broader imperial economy through external relations."[104] Territorial acquisition and

control were seen as the keys to capitalist expansion where land was a prime factor of production as well as a field of capital investment. Between 1858 and 1869, colonial India became the destination for about 55 percent of all British capital investment in the empire and more than 21 percent of all British investment outside the United Kingdom.[105] A bulk of this unprecedented flow of capital investments was in infrastructures of transportation (railways) that helped create efficient connections between inland territories and port cities, thereby opening up the entire colony to trade and military movement.[106] This renewal of India as a capitalized space indeed bears an uncanny resemblance to the contemporary reign of unbridled free markets that has spread in the past decades. The difference is that it is no longer a single hegemonic economy that either drives or controls the processes of capitalist growth.

The late nineteenth century also saw the building up of national awakening and frequent discussions of "the India question," in which the transitory sign of New India came to stand in as a possible resolution, transformation, or even recovery of the colonized nation.[107] What bound these rather different accounts of newness of India was the common theme of *transition* that appeared simultaneously as a challenge and as a desired outcome. The most prominent idea of New India arose at the moment of decolonization in the mid-twentieth century when India transformed from an imperial possession to an independent democratic republic. This transition is captured in Jawaharlal Nehru's speech to the Constituent Assembly of India when he announced the birth of the new sovereign nation: "At the stroke of [the] midnight hour, when the world sleeps, India will awake to life and freedom. A moment comes, which comes but rarely in history, when we step out from the old to the new, when an age ends, and when the soul of a nation, long suppressed, finds utterance." The newness here was the awakening of the national soul that colonialism had long suppressed, an awakening harnessed to the spirit of modern democracy that came to be seen as a defining feature of postcolonial India.[108] The story of New India from early on was an upbeat story of the triumph of democracy in the third world. The democratic framework would soon become a visible marker of separation that set the old colony apart from its new decolonized incarnation. Consider this reintroduction of India to the western world soon after its first general election in 1951–1952.

> Some Western visitors to India, for instance, still see only the Rudyard Kipling–Katherine Mayo land of tiger hunting maharajas, sacred cows and cobras, against an endless backdrop of tradition-bound, poverty stricken humanity. But for the visitor who looks below the surface, there is a new and immensely exciting India—a five-year-old democracy of 360,000,000 people working earnestly and with considerable success to solve their country's staggering problems. The outcome of this great Indian effort will profoundly affect the world in which we live. . . . The future of Asia, and eventually the world balance of power, may rest on the competition between democratic India on the one hand and Communist China on the other."[109]

In its garb of democratic modernity, New India was not just a dramatic subversion of the exotic colonial imagery popularized by Kipling and Mayo but also an ideological and material bulwark against the rising threat of a communist China and Soviet Union in the postwar world. The enchantment with India's democratic ethos was more than mere appreciation; it offered strategic counterbalance in Asia during the Cold War. That the success of New India's experimentation with liberal democracy was key to the shape of the rapidly decolonizing world was widely recognized. In India, the heady moment of freedom was also a moment of responsibility—the newness of the nation was seen in broader international terms as the end of an epoch, an inevitable step toward decolonization across Asia. In 1949, an unnamed India official laid out the blueprint of New India as a moral power in the decolonized world.

> It is time for a wider recognition in the west that we have come to an end of an historical epoch. The eclipse of India in the eighteenth century was not an isolated phenomenon; it was part of the world movement by which the science and technology of Europe captured Asia and turned it, under different forms, into an appanage of the west. India's re-emergence is likewise related to the revival of the entire continent. It is not a racial movement: it is not

animated by any hostile intent. It does not further the aggrandizement of any nation. Its purpose is wholly pacific and constructive—to broaden freedom and raise the standard of living. It is in consonance with all that is liberal, humane and disinterested in the western tradition. Its ultimate result must necessarily be to transform the politico-economic map of the world, and establish a new relationship between east and west.[110]

What we witness here is the idea of decolonization expressed not just in the usual sense of a "transfer of power" from the colonial to the postcolonial state but as a wide-reaching reflection on what freedom in its full moral and material senses could look like. To be decolonized was to broaden freedom in a liberal and humane way without hostility, aggrandizement, or racial motives; to raise the standard of living; and to establish a more equitable political-economic power dynamic between the erstwhile empire and the colonies. If the emphasis on the pacific mode of engagement recalled Gandhian ideals of nonviolence, it also augured what would be the cornerstone of postcolonial India's foreign policy crafted by Nehru: nonalignment and Panchsheel. The pursuit of freedom was also the pursuit of material development in the making of a new nation. At the heart of this renewal, then, was the project of modernity envisioned in five-year plans and concretized in giant industrial plants and big dams erected across the national territory. A particularly rich set of insights into this idea of newness is offered in an official report called *Face of New India*, published in 1960. The report was billed as a kaleidoscopic album of New India taking shape at the dawn of freedom.

> This album presents portrait studies of New India. It shows an India which is speeding towards modernity, not an India where time had had a stop. The new, however, does not disown the old. It retains the best of the past, but refuses to inherit poverty, injustice and stagnation. The new India aspires to be a welfare state of the socialist pattern. Unlike other albums on India, this is not content to show chiseled idols and sculptured temples. Instead it shows the temples of the new age, as Prime Minister Nehru has called them: places where man works for the good of man, the projects large and small, where water is captured and power is generated. . . . More particularly, the album

strives to present the achievements of our [five-year] Plans. . . . It is in mighty
projects like Bhakra, Damodar Valley and Hirakud, in giant industrial plants
like Chittaranjan, Bhilai, Rourkela, Durgapur and Sindri, in hundreds and
thousands of rural uplift schemes, and in the smile on the face of the Harijan
lad that the India of today is to be seen.

This short extract captures the broad contours of what has been
called the developmental state, the state as the prime force of progress
in which planned development was harnessed to the engines of capitalist accumulation.[111] This official kaleidoscope of New India carried
the distinct stamp of a Nehruvian utopia of development featuring big
dams and heavy industries that he memorably termed the "temples of
modern India"—an expression that cohered affirmation of secularism
with that of planned economy. The invocation of the "Harijan lad" in
this vision of New India suggested the inherent belief in the capacity
and will of the state to be a social equalizer. The idea of newness in the
postcolony hinged on the socioeconomic development of a newly liberated people now responsible for their own progress and prosperity.
Yet this very model of New India came to be regarded in the subsequent decades as a *failure*, a roadblock, or even a missed opportunity to
better the socioeconomic conditions of its people. In contrast to South
Korea, Japan, Southeast Asia, and, more recently, China, India's slow
economic growth sticks out within the landscape of Asian economic
miracles. This sense of perceived failure to fulfill the promise of independence via economic self-reliance became the foundation on which
the 1990s economic reforms were staged.

The moment of economic reforms was also the moment of *renewal*
of the nation, of finally effacing its colonial past, and of dressing up
anew in the image of great powers. If India was making a wager on its
future, the wager was on the magic of capitalism to accelerate the journey to the epochal threshold of modernity. The twenty-first century
would be the age not just of capitalist transformations but also of resur-
rection of ancient culture and branded nationalism. As we will see, the
economic reforms would realize anticipated as well as unanticipated futures: history and future would unfold all at once.

CHAPTER 3

REMIXING HISTORY

Hop aboard for this ride of your life. India 2.0 is hurtling down the information superhighway, carrying its mind-boggling baggage of ever-accelerating GDP, extreme geography, kaleidoscopic culture, deep-rooted spirituality and photogenic chaos into a fascinating future. Watch history being remixed right in front of your eyes. Incredible! But true.

—India 2.0, ITB Berlin, 2007

THE INVITATION to watch "history being remixed" was displayed at the India pavilion at ITB Berlin at the spectacular global launch in 2007 of Incredible India—postreform India's largest and most visible national public city campaign—which sought to transform India's image from a third-world nation to a global player. Imagined as a fast-paced, colorfully decked-out auto rickshaw, India 2.0, the visitors were told, boasts of a "digital entertainment system with a selection of Bollywood hits; satellite TV for cricket and stock market updates; smog/fog lights for all weather urban/rural capability; incense stick holder for mobile meditation; eco friendly engine powered by compressed natural gas."[1] In an instance of clever wordplay, a number of keywords associated with India—the familiar *Bollywood, cricket, spirituality, culture,* and *incense sticks* and the new seductions of *GDP, stock market, information superhighway,* and *satellites*—are humorously strung together for a greater recall value to create India 2.0 with unique features (see figure 3.1). Each of these high-technology features is represented in the form of graphic icons that technofriendly publics across cultures are familiar with. The choice of the usually slow-paced auto rickshaw as the vehicle to represent New India is noteworthy—it depicts the desire to reimagine what is our own as the vernacular forerunner of global futures. India 2.0, then, appears as a seductive polychromous package of

FIGURE 3.1. *The India 2.0 installation at ITB Berlin. 2007. Courtesy of V. Sunil.*

hypertechnology and great civilizational culture with wide-ranging aspects difficult for anyone to grasp at a glance. Yet this is precisely what the designers of India 2.0 seemed to be aiming at—to condense and make legible the vast complexities and contradictions of India across temporalities to the outside world. The global publics could now witness a live performance of an ancient civilizational culture morphing itself into a state-of-the-art high-speed vehicle prefiguring the twenty-first-century futures.

The aesthetics and politics of *remixing history* is at the heart of India's image makeover into a commodity brand for global consumers. The use of the term *remix* is telling about the nature of the image-making project. What makes it significant is the prefix *re-* (to indicate repetition or even backward motion) added to the verb *mix* (to blend different elements together), which changes its meaning. To remix, put simply, is to blend different elements together *again and again* to create something different. Brought in from the world of popular music, the technique of remixing entails a series of actions: to cut up the original, isolate elements, repeat, rearrange, and add contemporary effects in order to create an altogether different version of what already existed. The function of remixing usually is to dress up older compositions in the aesthetics of the contemporary in order to introduce them to a new generation or audience. The remix is never an altered copy but an original composition in its own right that rearranges the sensory experiences of the audience. In short, the remixed version retains traces of the original even while erasing those—ultimately morphing into its own being, a thing in itself.

So what does it mean to remix history? What kind of political-aesthetic project is at stake in this ongoing rearrangement? Which elements of the past are preserved or erased in this remixing? And what new form do the remaining traces of the past take? A key presumption underlying this project is the prior existence of an *original* composition of history, a master copy that can be recovered from the past and remixed into the present. And here lies the ontological fault line that runs deep through the image-makeover exercise: the question of an original, authentic past is deeply contentious and never fully settled but is, at the same time, a key ingredient in the making of the nation's brand identity. The moment of remixing history, then, paradoxically entails simultaneous distillation of India's authentic past and its rearrangement in the aesthetics of the contemporary global. The imaginaries of an authentic past somewhat implausibly become visible precisely when they are being morphed into a global commodity-brand legible to its consumers around the world. Once brought into the realm of market, the cultural politics of originality emerges through the logic of the brand—what is authentic culture generates brand value, and what generates brand value is deemed authentic culture. The emergence of a globally legible Hindu civilizational cultural identity, one that sees itself as the motor engine of India's capitalist transformation, can be located in this moment of remixing history.

The image makeover of India into a global commodity-brand is often explained in tactical terms, as a purely utilitarian exercise to attract positive attention from the "right" kind of people—global investors, policy makers, and wealthy tourists—to generate economic growth in India. Yet the larger effects of these image-making processes extend beyond what is anticipated or even understood by the image makers. Far from being a mere mechanism of producing India's brand identity, the image-makeover project is a step toward the drawing board. It opens up a creative space in which India can be reimagined and redesigned, this time as an ancient Hindu civilization turned economic powerhouse. The effect of brand imagery, then, extends beyond investments; it makes visible a new blueprint of the modern nation, one that people can aspire to and policy makers can bring to reality. In this sense, the potential of remixing history is more than a clever sales pitch or the immediate utilitarian goal of selling India in the global economy—it brings to the surface the desirable image of the nation and the attendant rearrangements in the social landscape.

At the core of this ongoing rearrangement is the paradoxical cultural politics of originality and the inalienable essence of a *timeless* India—at once ancient and modern, old civilization and young nation—which occupies a contested domain in contemporary Indian politics.[2] The Incredible India campaign built on these inner contradictions, with a visible pride in antiquity and modern ambitions for India to be seen and desired as a global player. Or put differently, the claim of the pure difference of India, the ancient modern, lies precisely in its imaginary as a timeless being, its capacity to dress up in ever-new garbs of modernity without losing itself. The formula seems simple enough, even alluring. Yet it is fraught with a variety of contestations and inconsistencies that underpin the images of India's old civilizational culture dressed in the global aesthetics of advertising. If the romanticized pre-Islamic Hindu civilizational culture forms the core of the postexotic archive, the other is the familiar exotica—natural landscape, wildlife, and cultural forms and practices—through which India has long been perceived in foreign eyes. The paradox of Incredible India images is this: if the exotic draws attention to the enigma of India, it also risks overshadowing postreform India's desire to be seen as the high-technology, investor-friendly land of limitless opportunity in the world. Connected with this is the logic of external representation that inevitably rearranges the insides too. The beautiful images are not a matter merely of representation but of making public what is deemed desirable. The making of publicity images invariably reveals the shifting ideas and accounts of the nation itself.

I trace here the tensions and conflicts in the image-makeover project at two levels: (1) the actual visual framing of a *postexotic* nation in the Incredible India campaign that seeks to re-embed the exotic features within the global political economy and (2) the ontological tensions that underpin this new self. The postexotic self, as I show, is not produced by effacing the exotic past but by condensing, accelerating, and fast-forwarding it into a timeless, infinite global present. And in doing so, it reveals the blueprint of the ongoing visual rearrangement of the nation's civilizational past in the making of New India.

IN SEARCH OF THE SMART IMAGE

The origins of the Incredible India campaign are located in the sense of deep crisis that came about when the nascent India growth story was said to have experienced its first serious setback in 2002. It was a critical moment that was often re-created passionately for me during my conversations with government officials, commentators, and journalists attempting to narrate India's upward mobility toward the high table of global politics. The account was roughly along the following lines. A decade into the economic reforms, the magic of the India story was unraveling after losing the momentum of the boom years. Whereas policy makers in 2002 had modestly pegged that year's growth prospects at 5.4 percent, the actual growth, at 4.3 percent, was turning out to be the lowest since reforms were initiated.[3] The constantly sliding figures were edging worryingly closer to the much feared Hindu rate of growth—signifying the economic stagnation of the prereform decades—causing alarm in policy circles and among the middle classes.[4] As this sense of panic seeped into the public discourse, the crisis became "a time for reflection" among policy makers, calling for a serious rethinking of India's failure to reach its full potential.[5] How might India recover and realize its rightful place in the global scheme of things? This question became the basis of a variety of intense debates within the government apparatus that sought to bring India's potential into the realm of possibility. At this stage, the Ministry of Tourism commissioned a market survey that revealed India's lack of a discernible identity, or rather, a "strong and clear image that could enhance [its] desirability."[6] Although India's rich history, culture, and economic growth potential were well recognized internationally, its actual performance was found to be suffering from a deficit of "positioning, common branding or a clear, precise message."[7] In other words, India had an image deficit that was causing the exchange value of its assets to not be fully realized in the global markets. It was not that India did not have a prior image; the problem was found to be just the opposite. It had too many images, or as I was repeatedly told, India had a crowd of images mostly consisting of clichés and stereotypes: spirituality, wildlife, ancient civilization, maharajas, and magic, in addition to chaos and poverty. What it did not have was a *smart image* with a contemporary global aura—clean, minimal design enlivening India's authenticity and appeal among global publics—through which India could reconnect with the world. It was this perceived deficit that became the basis of the search for a unified smart image that would make visible "the contemporary feel of a young nation" rather than reinforce "the clichéd visuals, such as saffron-clad sadhus in the Himalayas and rope tricks performed amidst crowds."[8] These cultural stereotypes that equate India with ancient mysticism, material deprivation, and dystopic visions are particularly loathed by the Indian elite for aligning the sign of India with the nonrational world of superstition and, consequently, backwardness. This disquiet with representations of India that are deemed clichéd or stereotypical has a long history. A quick bird's-eye view is in order.

India has long been chronicled by travelers, traders, missionaries, pilgrims, settlers, and colonists. From the earliest travel records written BCE to the early twenty-first century, the geography, climate, culture, and society in the subcontinent has been described in varying forms and detail.[9] A consistent theme that has emerged is wildlife, nature, and spirituality. If the early accounts were descriptions of a new utopic land and its people, the early modern chronicles were of what the travelers found to be exotic, magical, grotesque, and even outlandish. Consider, for instance, how the ancient Chinese pilgrims tended to focus on similarities between the two lands and found India to be a "mystical land inhabited by 'civilized' and sophisticated people" such as their own. For European travelers, in contrast, the mysticism was a sign less of civilization and more of the primitive other, of deception, unreason, and ignorance. Nineteenth-century Europe was particularly replete with images, for example, of jugglers, magicians, rope tricksters, and a panoramic vision of the exotic oriental lifestyle, imperial pageantry, and luxury commodities. The oriental images of India were indeed more than just negative clichés, as Eastern wisdom was often romanticized as a corrective to Western materialism. Yet even in the celebration of its ancient wisdom, the East was posited in opposition to Western rationality and scientific temper. In the early nineteenth century, for example, the travel accounts of Ibn Battuta were translated into English, which led to the tale of the levitating *faqir* (ascetic) in the court of Emperor Shahjahan gaining popular circulation. This incredible story iterated the magical otherworldly life in India. By the mid-nineteenth century, the story of the girl-in-the-basket magic trick, of the magician who could conjure bad weather, or of the snake charmers who hypnotized snakes into absolute obedience were part of the standard repertoire of the India story in Europe. If these accounts imparted exoticism to the newly colonized land, they also unhinged its people from the European march to modernity. Central to this act of exotic image making was the transforming role of Europe as the prime mediator of technomodernity to rest of the world. In the postcolony, this archive of exotic imaginary of India created a different dilemma. The exotic imagery was a resource, readily recognized and associated with India in the wider world even if loathed at home. And recognition is what makes it valuable for the purpose of advertising to begin with. The question was this: How should economic value be extracted from the very cultural exoticism that one otherwise wished to erase? How should the concerns of the designers and policy makers be articulated? How could one imbue *smartness* to the postexotic nation as it made its debut on the world stage?

I encountered the word *smart* frequently during my fieldwork among the advertising professionals. It was an oft-used catchphrase, and at first its almost reflexive use made it seem meaningless at some level. It appeared in all possible combinations—smart vibes, smart frame, smart image, smart look, smart feel, smart logo, smart design, or just being smart—conjured to describe the quality of a given image campaign. The word *smart* invokes a range of meanings—sharp, intelligent, quick, witty, and neat—to paint a picture of impressiveness. Among the advertising professionals, it is seemingly used to indicate a presentable self that exudes "quick-wit, tongue-in-cheek humor, confidence, and intellect"—personal qualities that can be proudly displayed without a shade of embarrassment to the outside world.[10] The work of the Incredible India images, I was often told, was to imbue and convey the attributes of smartness to the nation—to effectively transform the old exotic into the new postexotic. The smart images appeared to be the labor of seductive signs—alluring forms that establish and reiterate the potential of the nation even as they disclose the sense of crisis within which they were conceived and fabricated. Through these signs, contours of the postreform nation were made visible that simultaneously sought recognition from and defied the global publics and also helped transform thus-generated attention from the outside world into surplus value. The work of the smart image, it was emphasized, was not only to imagine the nation anew but also to redirect the foreign gaze so as to "correct" the long-held perceptions that mar the nation's image. The smart image was clearly as entwined with the circulation and accumulation of global capital as it was with the visualization of new histories that sought to construct "coherent and intelligible picture of modernity."[11] This is not to suggest that the goal of creating visual coherence is necessarily realized but to underline how a unified image is perceived as the essential frame within which the postreform nation's legitimacy is established at home and around the world.

In the nation-branding parlance, the making of a smart visual identity is pitched as a policy measure toward a "better stewardship of the national identity," a profitable formula that promises to turn nations into market destinations as well as to make them the "global brand owners of the future."[12] Put differently, the project of remixing history to produce smart images positions the state as the central authority that claims an exclusive right to visualize, to be able to look, or to see—first, at the people, resources, and landscapes within its territory in order to enumerate, classify, and order the inside, and second, at the world outside as a legitimate representative of the nation's interest as well as its honor, culture, and history. As will become evident, the ability and privilege to look, then, is easily transformed into the power to design the look or appearance of the nation to be displayed in a global spectacle. The making of Incredible India is located on this interface of state policy, bureaucratic negotiations, and the aesthetic sensibilities of advertising professionals shaped against the weight of history and neoliberal economic dreams.

THE WONDER THAT *IS* INDIA

The brief that V. Sunil, a Delhi-based advertising professional, received from the government of India in 2002 was quite straightforward.[13] He had been asked to initiate a global branding exercise "to create a distinctive identity for the country."[14] It was hardly a coincidence that Sunil had been offered as strategic and important a task as branding India. In the advertising circles in Delhi, he had already made his name as one of the most creative minds of his generation.[15] Sunil took up the project readily, as he recalled, because all signs suggested that the creative project would not run aground in the maze of bureaucratic machinery. In fact, the bureaucratic hurdles had already been cleared. In a vision statement, the Ministry of Tourism had earlier that year outlined its aim to position India as "a global brand, with worldwide brand recognition and strong brand equity, especially in the [tourism] trade and among the target audience" as well as "a premier holiday destination for high yielding tourists."[16]

The stage was further set when the Planning Commission substantially increased its annual budget for tourism and heritage that year and earmarked nearly one-fifth of that budget for "brand building of India."[17] The bureaucratic apparatus, as it turned out, was for once not only operating efficiently but taking the lead in what was said to be a "moment for action" in the nation's interest.[18] The need of the moment was, as the official brief translated into the language of advertising said, to create "a smart image that would present India smartly in front of the world."[19] In the official narrative, the origin of the campaign is presented not as a routine instance of creative outsourcing by a government department to an advertising agency but as a joint effort in which the bureaucracy opens space for "thinking big, focusing on professional promotion and marketing, and creating an environment of working with the best creative minds" to shape a brand identity for India.[20] The need for thinking big could not be exaggerated in this case, as the assembled group found it

> extremely difficult and complex to establish a clear, precise identity for a multiproduct destination like India. India is a land of contrasts, a combination of tradition and modernity, a land that is at once mystical and mysterious. India is bigger than twenty-three countries of Europe put together and every single state of India has its own unique attractions.[21]

Could a single word or expression capture the rich cultural heritage, civilization, and economic potentiality of India? The only word that the creative team found to be close enough was *incredible*, said to be appropriate for a country that is "at times overwhelming, but always incredible."[22] The word *incredible* literally suggests the qualities of being "so extraordinary as to seem impossible; beyond belief; improbable" and, in a more informal sense, "amazing; marvelous."[23] Yet it was not the improbability of India that was being communicated here but rather its awe-inspiring and seductive landscape, natural beauty, millennia old civilization, and rich modern culture that was being turned into its global signature. The use of *incredible* was meant precisely to invoke the alluring mix of magic and modernity in everyday life that draws the world to India.[24]

Yet *incredible*, I was told, was not the original choice of policy makers. It was an outcome of matter-of-fact market calculations, aesthetics of smart design, and tightrope bureaucratic maneuvering.[25] The original idea proposed by the minister of tourism, Jagmohan, was to call the campaign "The Wonder That *Is* India" (emphasis added), because that felt more representative of how India is known in the world.[26] The tagline was evidently a play on A. L. Basham's famous work from 1954,

The Wonder That Was India: A Survey of the Culture of the Indian Sub-Continent Before the Coming of the Muslims. The title already indicates the temporalization of Indian history along the event of the arrival of Islam in the subcontinent, dividing it into before and after, with specific and separate histories. This widely read work has long been used as teaching material on ancient India, but it is also invoked by the Hindu nationalists as scholarly evidence of India's authentic, magical, and celebratory past that flourished until the arrival of Muslims. In this widespread discourse, the onset of the Islamic era is seen as a temporal transgression and ultimately the loss of the high Vedic culture. The minister's suggestion was to revive this long-lost essence of India that was familiar in the outside world through orientalist scholarship and somehow transport it from the past to present. The only alteration in the text, therefore, was to change the tense—from *was* to *is*—and fast-forward the past into the present. This change of tense offered important insight into how the Indian nation is seen, at once as a unique entity performed eternally in timelessness and one that temporally lags behind in the global race toward progress and development. The ideological persuasions at work were apparent, as the minister's directive invoked the familiar Hindu nationalist discourse in which India's authentic past remains essentially Hindu and that which effectively defines its difference and exclusiveness in the world. Yet the project was cast in what can only be called strange irony: the discovery and representation of authentic India, the nonforeign, was to be mediated via foreign knowledge of India. The foreign knowledge in this instance became a source of reification, and even legitimization, of what was deemed the original, untouched spirit of India.

What is palpable in this turn to orientalist scholarship for inspiration is a clear indifference to the project of imperialism, the very subjugation of India with which this particular form of knowledge was entangled. As Bernard Cohn memorably put it, "The conquest of India was a conquest of knowledge," that is, the knowledge and power to collect, order, and represent facts about India created the most valuable form of epistemologies with which to control vast colonial territories.[27]

Thus, what the minister saw as the authentic, uncloaked vision of India was in fact a vision manufactured by a foreign imperial power that had subjugated India. The proposal, however, was withdrawn quickly not because of any ideological turnabout but because of market surveys that showed that "the wonder that is India" would be a nonstarter, whereas "Incredible India in its creative form would be catchy, appealing, contemporary and would make an impact."[28]

Once the final bureaucratic difficulty had been overcome, the creative challenge was to obtain a semiotic translation of the idea of incredibility into a readily legible sign. The sign found to be the most accurate representation of the idea of Incredible India was the exclamation mark (!). In many ways, the sheer form of the sign was aesthetically pleasing as well as ambiguous, thus it could be interpreted in more ways than one in order to weave the India story in imaginative forms. Sunil told me that the idea first took shape when he began examining the map of India closely to look for visual clues to create a graphic essence of Incredible India. The cartographic form appeared as a long, beautifully curvaceous loop (India) that narrowed toward the bottom and was held in place by a lush round spot (Sri Lanka). The contours of India, in its more abstract form, appeared to resemble an exclamation mark. In order to sell the idea, he presented a top shot of the globe so others could visualize that the moment "when God created India, he placed a dot below to make an exclamation mark."[29] The allusion clearly was to the mythical event of *manthan*, the great churning that produced the universe and therein created Earth for humankind to live on. India was produced in this churning and shaped as an exclamation mark by the gods. The sense of awe and marvel was thus presented as a natural, innate feature of India that was etched on its very body and basic sense of being. The very physical shape of India, because of its abstract likeness to the exclamation mark, was now read as proof of its enchanting being. This was the making of a new creation myth of postreform India—which was entwined with the older creation narrative of manthan—in which Sri Lanka was reinvented as an essential ornamental accessory. The government officials readily bought the idea, as they were keen on presenting the magical difference of an ancient civilization within a contemporary frame. The exclamation mark was thus deployed to

> convey the mind-boggling depth and intensity of the Indian experience. Every aspect of India—be it its ever-accelerating GDP, extreme geography, kaleidoscopic culture, deep-rooted spirituality or even photogenic chaos—is summed up by the simple yet profound exclamation mark.[30]

Even as the exclamation mark subsumed and unified a wide range of facts, figures, sights, sounds, and images of India into an intense India "experience," it displayed its versatility and seductive appeal by invoking a variety of associations. Some visualized it as a pin with its head turned downward, holding the idea of India together. For others, it seemed symbolic of India with its iconic representation of *bindi* on the forehead in reverse. In a variety of modes, it seemed to work as the effective unifying visual symbol that the nation branders had been looking for. The original brand architecture was built around a single word, *!ndia*, that would *package* all official representations of India. The prefix *incredible* was incorporated as a compromise formula on the ministry's insistence but with the intention to eventually drop it. The three evolutionary stages of the logo were designed as follows:

> Incredible !ndia
>
> !ndia
>
> !

The idea was to ultimately simplify the logo to "!" so that the exclamation mark would turn into a signifier of India's magic and growth potential without the need for explanatory words. The logo was imagined visually along the lines of iconic brands such as Nike's Just Do It campaign, which enclosed every image with a swoosh sign in order to graphically express energy and sport without a word.[31] The ultimate success of a brand logo, I was often told, is its ability to invoke emotions and create a vocabulary of its own.[32] The essential ingredient in the recipe of a powerful brand is its ability "to express itself not just in terms of a product benefit, but in terms of a greater socio-economic truth." One might ask what innate truth Incredible India constitutes. The answer was its ability to artfully narrate the changes set in motion by the neoliberal reforms and represent

> a much bigger social phenomenon—an optimistic and extroverted new India, eager to make its presence felt in the global community. . . . It is this subtext that transforms "Incredible India" from a mere branding exercise into a pop culture milestone, denoting a turning point in the evolution of one of mankind's greatest civilizations.

The exclamation mark in Incredible India, in short, was the symbol of a confident, prosperous, smart, and even humorous India in the twenty-first century. It is telling that the symbol chosen to describe India does not actually trace its origin to the archives of Indian culture and history. The exclamation mark, originally known as "the note of admiration," was derived in the fifteenth century when print culture was becoming popular in Europe.[33] It was said to have been an artistic derivation of the Latin expression for the exclamation of joy that since has become an oft-used character in, and even a prominent sign of, the age of instant communication. It was precisely its widespread usage and near universal recognition in the teleconnected world of instant messaging, broadcasting, and sharing of ideas and images that made the exclamation mark an ideal sign of the postreform incarnation that India aspired to. Or as Sunil put it, the exclamation mark could most effectively convey "the smart new vibe, the feeling of new India" to the world.[34] Rather than choose an "authentic" sign such as Sanskrit words or letters written in Devnagari script, as many had advised him to do, he had taken the opposite route of appropriating a sign that had prior meaning for the intended global audience. The familiar sign was now framed as a smartly designed graphic device through which one could look at India just as India was looking back at the world.[35] The first step, thus, in the project of remixing history had been fulfilled. The next step was to visualize and rearrange the nation itself through the newly designed graphic device.

ART OF REMIXING

The inaugural campaign of Incredible India contained an eye-catching image of a young woman pictured in *vrikshasna,* or the tree position in yoga meditation, against a distant blue silhouette of the Himalaya mountain (fig. 3.2). She can be seen standing upright on her right leg, her left leg bent and placed on the right inner thigh in a half-lotus position. Her arms are stretched upward and her palms joined together in prayer form. Besides her serene posture, what immediately catches one's attention is her chic clothing made of a shiny stretch Lycra material that would be at home in any urban fitness studio. She was described to me as a global yogini—someone who could belong anywhere in the contemporary world yet retain her authentic Indianness. The other remarkable feature of the picture is a large shallow bowl filled with water and prayer flowers that lies at her feet. Her body stretched skyward and a bowl of flowers at her feet together create an arresting visual of an organic exclamation mark that creatively replaces the *I* in India within the Incredible India signature.[36]

This image was one of the first ones I was shown on a computer screen as an example of the kind of look the Incredible India campaign sought to create.[37] It was the desired confluence of tradition and modernity in the precisely correct proportions to publicize the contemporary version—India 2.0—of an ancient civilization such as India. The ancient art of yoga—literally meaning "drawing of connections between the human body and the Eternal Being in order to attain liberation of the spirit"— is performed here not by a *yogini* in her robes of renunciation but by a sculpted female body dressed in trendy sports attire that speaks to the contemporary urban ideals of fitness, beauty, and spiritual consumption. In this visual shift from renunciation to consumption, we witness the transformative work of the exclamation mark. On one hand, the mark superimposes itself on the natural landscape to imbue it with a contemporary quality. On the other hand, it subsumes the body to an extent that the body itself becomes a magical sign signaling the subtle rearrangement of the nation. This schema of subsuming, imposing, and interweaving the sign with material bodies to create a contemporary effect is something that we will witness repeatedly. The

FIGURE 3.2. *"The Tree Pose"—the yoga tradition featured in the Incredible India campaign. Courtesy of V. Sunil.*

encounter with the image was particularly significant because of the way it was framed for me—as smartly packaged reality. In this framework, two core ideas at the heart of the branding process—reality and smart packaging—were thus disclosed. Let us begin with the notion of reality in the process of remixing.

The framing of images as reality is predicated on the possibility of interchange, overlap, and even continuity, between the visions encountered in the image and reality—so that to view the images of Incredible India becomes a bodily experience of the landscape complete with its sights, scents, and sounds. Conversely, to physically experience the landscape is to encounter the avalanche of images created in the past decade. Images, in such a frame, do not intend to function as representations; they seek to replace reality itself. In fact, the strategy underpinning the project of image fixing aimed to

> veer away from the traditional advertising approach. As opposed to staging unrealistic scenarios, the core motivation was to reflect the people, landscape and emotions of India with a sincere honesty and simplicity (.) as visiting

travelers would find them when they arrived. We endeavored to portray the very same, completely real emotions they would feel when they experienced India for themselves. All the moments shown in the film, in that sense, are real and readily accessible to those who seek them."[38]

How are we to understand this specific notion of reality said to be underpinning the smart images? If we move beyond the registers of truth and falsehood, the Incredible India images begin to make sense once we position them as *sites of enhancement*, at which flawless visions of coherence are unveiled, illuminated, and amplified to the extent that all other realities are foreshadowed. The notion of enhancement suggests both embellishment as well as manipulation, not necessarily to deceive but to convey the object of publicity in the best possible light.[39] In doing so, enhancement produces an exaggerated reality that seeks to subsume and replace all other realities constituting the imaginary. Thinking of the image here as a site of enhancement and remixing in which the transformative work of seductive signs can be witnessed helps open the entanglements and tensions—between reality and image and between fantasy and materiality—that underpin this new visuality. Reality in this sense appears as a limited concept with a limited function to position the nation in its flawless and coherent form.

If reality is at one end of the framework, then at the other is the idea of smart packaging that would help highlight the deep cultural richness and economic potential of the postreform nation. The idea of smart packaging seemed to convey more an expression of a deeply rooted belief that every product can be made valuable and salable if optimally illuminated. If packaged the right way, the brand personality of the product can be enhanced and efficiently projected to the consumers. Thus, the remixed images were unified by three common characteristics. First is the creative use of the exclamation mark, which employs bodies, corporeal marks, and natural features to weave the new creation myth of India. Second is the use of the minimalist approach that traces neat lines and silhouettes to help create an unchaotic look. And third is the near absence of people and crowds in the visual framing of a country known as the second most populous nation in the world. The look of the nation framed for the viewers is that of an un-crowded, unchaotic, neat landscape in which the traveler is distracted by nothing but sheer beauty and amazing natural scenery.

The strategy used to create the smart packaging was to subject ste-reotypes to a threefold process of remixing. The first step was to treat the selected image with digital scrubbing, not in order to fantasize about a new dream landscape but to illuminate what was already there. The neat, clean, well-scrubbed India was created through digital ma-nipulations afforded by the latest technology. Thus, the images were no longer of

> sad old India. Dusty. We cleaned all that dust. This is the biggest thing we
> have done in the campaign. We just cleansed it, just scrubbed it. It's the same
> India we sold. It's not an artificial India. It's the same backwaters, unfiltered,
> but it is very cleanly designed, cleanly projected."[40]

What we witness here is how digital technology is put to use to *fix* the image, in all its senses, by removing blemishes and spots, zoom-ing in and out to highlight or blur specific parts, enhancing colors, ad-justing sharpness, cropping, splicing, and in some cases even rotating the pictured subject upside down to create an incredible effect. The ex-tra information contained in the deep copy of the image is reorganized and even erased if found to be in excess, to set the focus sharply on all that is beautiful and worthy of looking at. The image thus created is devoid of matter that is deemed superfluous and threatens to detract the viewer's attention from the object on display.

The question of excess and superfluity in the production of effec-tive image making is not merely one of a technical nature that disrupts the creation of clean, well-focused pictures. It also serves as a meta-phorical device for the nation's deep-rooted anxieties about the excess that clogs the outside gaze and risks unfixing the image itself. Human excess—the poor, the surplus labor, the vagabonds crowding the city sidewalks, the undisciplined classes, or what Marx called the lumpen proletariat—superfluous to the neoliberal economy is seen as an aberra-tion in the smart look the image makers desire to portray. The presence of excessive material waste—filth, unrecycled garbage dumps, littered streets, and toxic fumes of pollution—in urban centers similarly threatens to disrupt the clean image. The reality manufactured in the digitally scrubbed images, therefore, commands attention for explicitly drawing the desires of the reformed nation.

Once the raw images were dusted and scrubbed, the second step was to draw out the new personality of the nation from the ruins of the stereotypes. The idea was to match the smart new looks with the smart new personality of the nation—one that is clean, confident, and funny.[41] The last characteristic—of being humorous—was underlined for me as the most important ingredient in the making of a smart nation. To be able to poke fun at oneself is to betray the confidence in one's strengths, I was told. In an iconic poster, we witness the image of a lone tiger on the lookout for his prey in Ranthambore National Park (fig. 3.3). The picture is accompanied by words suggesting that "not all Indians are polite, hospitable and vegetarians." The image and text together address the long-held discourses of pre-modern India, with its primitive associations with nature and wildlife. The presence of the tiger highlights the rich wildlife and natural scenery, but it also countermands the portrayal of Indians as meek, submissive, and obedient. The old description of India as the land of tigers and elephants is turned on its head to create a different narrative of India and Indians. The very cliché of primitive, wild India is used to portray Indians as confident and humorous people, thereby turning a weakness into a strength. Clearly the aim here was not just to produce clever, witty advertising copy but to use humor as "symptomatic of a much bigger social phenomenon—an optimistic and extroverted new India, eager to make its presence felt in the global community."

These images, then, become the personification of New India, or rather, the icons of a nation that "is a far cry from the meek, tentative and 'offshore' destination of the last decade." The iconic images themselves have acquired attributes of personhood—clever, funny, smart, vital, seductive, desiring—to become totemic signs of a nation in search of its place in the global scheme of things. The smart image makeover is almost a visual restoration of pride, especially for the urban youth who imagine themselves part of a global community far more than did

FIGURE 3.3. *"Not all Indians are polite, hospitable, and vegetarian"—Incredible India advertising. Courtesy of V. Sunil.*

previous generations.[42] The popularity of the images—within and out-side—lies precisely in the projection of exaggerated realities that the nation was said to have failed to display in the outside world.

The third step toward smart packaging was to weave the old into a new narrative of exchange value and consumption. Of particular note in this frame are two eye-catching images of the Taj Mahal, one of the prime tourist attractions of India and a World Heritage site deemed to be of universal importance.[43] The iconic monument built (1631–1648) in white marble is also one of the finest examples of Indo-Islamic ar-chitecture of the Mughal era. The story of the Taj Mahal as the sym-bol of love and the story of its place in the power struggles of succes-sion in the Mughal dynasty are well known, but Incredible India places it in a somewhat different frame. For one, the two images of the Taj Mahal are the only examples of Muslim architecture and presence in the catalogue of Incredible India. To a large extent, the photographic core of Incredible India is built around its distant Vedic past and the

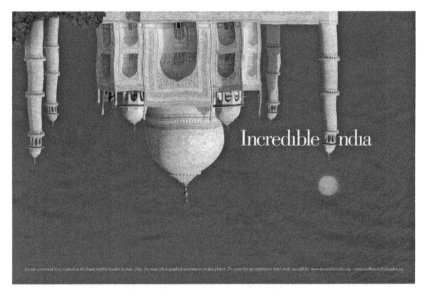

FIGURE 3.4. *Taj Mahal—Incredible India advertising. Courtesy of V. Sunil.*

contemporary present that circumvents its Muslim history. The first image depicts the inverse reflection of the white marble contours of the Taj Mahal in a pool of blue water (fig. 3.4). Here the white moon is placed as the dot on top of the minar to form the *i* in India. The Taj Mahal is now graphically framed in the familiar iconography of Incredible India to create a new/old enchanting landscape. The second image is a black-and-white postcard picture of the Taj Mahal with accompanying text that reads, "And to think these days, men get away with giving flowers and chocolates to their wives." If the image reminds the viewer of the old-world charm of the Taj Mahal and its eternal love story—as the subtext in very small print at the bottom reminds us—shorn of its full history, it also contemporizes it as a form of gift giving between lovers. The Taj Mahal, in this frame, is reinvented as a truly opulent gesture of contemporary consumption in the same genre as chocolates and flowers only much grander, almost inimitable for most people and thus possibly something to aspire to in times of prosperity. In its commodified form, the Taj Mahal overcomes its own medieval Muslim past and its original function—as a mausoleum, the final resting place of Mumtaz, in whose memory her husband, Emperor Shahjahan, commissioned it—to reappear as the ultimate object of modern desire.

Its very function is altered in the new scheme. The Taj Mahal now signals new age aspiration and consumption in this frame, and consumption itself appears to be a timeless preoccupation and an enduring feature of India. The Taj Mahal becomes the point of this double mediation. If the iconic monument is re-presented in the language of consumption to the outside world, it imbues India with the vernacular idea of consumption derived from its own timeless past. This seductive and globally legible language of consumption also shows in what form India's Muslim past can be revealed in the contemporary global. The appearance of the Muslim past in global publicity is contingent on its ability to overcome itself and then facilitate the project of economic reforms.

INDIA 2.0—THE ANCIENT MODERN

At first glance, the technoscientific language of innovation, disruption, macroeconomic shifts, and accelerated global movements might seem worlds apart from the highly contentious cultural politics of India. Yet what I want to propose is counterintuitive. It is this: the language of fast-paced, ever-evolving infotechnology at its core mimics the language of timelessness and cultural resilience used to describe India as an ancient Hindu civilizational culture that assumes new forms but never loses its original essence. It is hardly a coincidence that India, imagined as timeless, is visualized as a dazzling vehicle on the information superhighway fast-tracking the orbit of world powers. Although it is dressed up in the global aesthetics of infotech this time, the idea of an eternal, enduring, and flexible nation is a familiar one. It has been articulated in different contexts and forms and with vastly different sets of reasons. In India 2.0, unveiled in the early twenty-first century, we witness how seemingly detached temporal and epistemological spheres become deeply entangled in many unexpected ways. The making of a new technofriendly version of the Indian nation reveals inherent tensions and contradictions as it straddles between the imperatives of acceleration into the future and the authenticity of a timeless past. What also becomes apparent is how Hinduism emerges as the cultural main-frame within which twenty-first-century India begins taking shape.

Let's begin with the idea of the "version" deployed to picture the Indian nation—India 2.0—in its new and improved global form. The term *version* denotes a difference or an element of novelty inserted in the original matter, which is presumed to be stable and somewhat fixed. To create a version, then, is to overcome this tension between the change that *difference* signifies and the *core* that provides a presumably stable metaframe. And this can only be achieved if the original matter can take in the external difference even as it seeks to maintain its original edifice. In this context, the sign of India 2.0 is not just a clever reference to the IT industry; it discloses the presumption of a stable core matter that can be improved and altered periodically to fit in with contemporary times. Here we witness entanglements that on the surface seem far removed but are similar in surprising ways. If this technofriendly description of India, in its mimicry of the language of fast-paced computer programming, affirms the enormous influence of Silicon Valley in the narrative of New India, it also entwines the older discourse of (Hindu) civilizational culture that pitches India as an eternal being capable of reincarnating itself. The notion of reincarnation, widely shared among different Indic traditions, views the material body as separate from the soul (*atman*). Whereas the body is taken to be destructible, the soul is beyond decay.[44] The soul may be reborn, albeit in a new body—different matter but always the same. The soul, the inner core, is what is stable in an ever-shifting material world of consumption and desire that demands new physical forms to fit into the current moment. Thus, the version/reincarnation can be varied, renewed, or even given a fresh appearance, but its core is taken to be fundamentally unalterable. It is this potential of *remixing history* that opens endless possibilities for creating newer versions of an ancient civilizational culture. Or put differently, the grammar of novelty in New India is predicated on this potential remix, the ability to pack change and permanence into a singular moment. Although the idea of a remixed version 2.0 was honed within the aesthetics of the twenty-first-century global advertising industry, it draws on an older genealogy of knowledge of the Indian nation. One of the enduring ideas that began shaping up in the eighteenth century was of the *timelessness* that was said to have enveloped India. This was advanced as an explanation both for its ancient mysticism and for its material shortcomings, as we will see. Through subsequent centuries, this notion of India cast in eternity prevailed, albeit in many different discursive forms. I will now trace the genealogy of this epistemic edifice on which India has long been imagined.

I begin with the body of knowledge of India deemed to be "first disclosed to European observation" just as the grip of the British Empire began tightening across the subcontinent.[45] Pay attention to the use of the word *disclosed*, which hints at the act of unveiling, baring the buried secrets that could be brought to light only through the European gaze. The claim of being the first to witness this disclosure unwittingly erases everything that was before, a bit like laying the claim of imperial ownership of territories "discovered" by European explorers across the world. The nature of this epistemological enterprise becomes clear already at this point—the excavation of India's past and its future are now harnessed to the project of imperial expansion. The implementation of an imperial world order required that the colonized territories be imagined as feeble and fragmented and incapable of autonomy and self-governance. As Ronald Inden reminds us, central to this hegemonic account was an imaginary of India as the "Other" of Europe—in which "the essence of Western thought is practical reason, that of India a dreamy imagination"—and an imaginary of a "naturally" fractious India in need of control by a benevolent supreme authority (1990, 3). Throughout the eighteenth and nineteenth centuries, the intellectual labor to create this hegemonic worldview was provided by the orientalist scholars engaged in accumulating and classifying knowledge of India.[46] A consistent theme in the "India question"—oft-used shorthand for the challenges of governing a vast populous colony—that occupied the scholars, then, was that of the "immeasurable antiquity of Indian tradition" as a problem for reforms. Vincent Smith, a prominent historian and commentator on Indian political conditions warned that the ancient scriptures are neither obsolete nor dead. They still express the in-most thoughts of the voiceless myriads of to-day as truly as they record the sentiments of their ancestors in the distant past. No passing wind of doc-trine can shake the rock of Indian tradition. The shadows flee away, the wall remains. The fly on the rim buzzes for a moment, the wheel of life rolls on. Truly "it is neither safe nor easy to meddle with traditional ideas in India."[47]

This invocation of antique Indian traditions summed up both the fascination and frustration of scholars and administrators, and it even-tually shaped the frame of governance of India. It also provided argu-ments for the necessity of colonial rule of a people bound by tradition and so out of sync with the currents of modernity sweeping Europe. Let us take a closer look.

The first feature of this imaginary—of tradition as the bedrock of Indian social-political life—is the emphasis on the fixed-in-time, im-movable nature of Indian polity. India, in the imperial synoptic, ap-pears strangely resistant to change, almost stubborn in its refusal to keep pace with time. This notion of India also served as a rationale for imperial expansion: the empire would finally wake India up from its deep slumber. That colonial intervention was framed as the harbinger of liberal modernity; the power of reason; new knowledge of science, technology, and medicine; and the alluring innovations of the Indus-trial Revolution is well-known.[48] In this worldview, India, once har-nessed to the empire, would finally be in step with modern times, and maybe someday even aspire to catch up with the world that was rapidly moving ahead.[49] *Second*, the essence of Indian tradition or, more accu-rately, the task of isolating the essence itself, became a fetish for Indol-ogists who likened the social body to the physical world of atoms, mol-ecules, and the essential properties of solid masses.[50] This search for the true essence of India meant that the distant past became the focus of knowledge accumulation and production, carefully separated from the traces of Muslim presence on the subcontinent. Consider the title of Smith's work *Early History of India, from 600 BC to the Mohemmadan Conquest, Including the Invasion of Alexander the Great.* For Smith, the arrival of Muslims on the subcontinent served as a natural cutoff point, opening up the possibility of isolating the classical tradition and its imputed decline to create a neat periodization of the past. Perhaps part of the explanation for why Smith might have sidestepped the question of the Muslim presence is the fact that the British had to upstage the Mughal imperial power to gain control of India. Another probable factor is the nineteenth-century fascination of the Indologists with interconnections between Indian and European Aryan pasts. They believed the clues to this shared origin lay in the *Vedic* scriptures that could be decoded via philological translations.[51] The classical tradition of India, as should be evident, was by now associated with the high culture of early Brahmanism, and Indian tradition itself alternated with Hinduism. Third, if the account of a timeless, undisturbed antique India was posed as a stumbling block toward modernity, it was also interpreted simultaneously as its enduring strength that preserved ancient Hindu tradition even when faced with foreign interventions. The oft-used metaphor was that of a sponge that absorbed the external world—this was said to be the essence of India that defied "the Western love of definition" through its enigmatic being.

> Hinduism has been likened to a vast sponge, which absorbs all that enters it without ceasing to be itself. The simile is not quite exact, because Hinduism has shown a remarkable power of assimilating as well as absorbing; the water becomes part of the sponge. Like a sponge it has no clear outline on its borders and no apparent core at its center. An approach to Hinduism provides a first lesson in the "otherness" of Hindu ideas from those of Europe.[52]

Ronald Inden reads this metaphorical description of Hinduism—and, therefore, India—as a sign of portended weakness, of lacking "world-ordering rationality," a lack that baffles and even threatens Western rationality.[53]

I propose a different reading of this metaphor that the present moment makes possible. It is this: In a world of commodification in which cultural identity is valuable in building national-brand identity, the claim of an uninterrupted flow of the preserved original essence is a vital resource. The capacity to absorb, then, need not necessarily be a sign of deficiency. It is translated as a sign of power and stability in a global context when the world seems to be constantly reshuffling. The logic of ancient India cast in eternity is thus turned on its head. *The capacity to absorb and yet retain its core, far from being a sign of India's inability to join the march of progress with the rest of the world, becomes a powerful and even durable sign of vitality.* Gyan Prakash has perceptively noted that ancient India has long been the ground of contest, commenting that "if some of the early Orientalists had seen Europe's origin in the India of the texts, the nationalists saw the origin of the modern nation in that same ancient India."[54] The enduring appeal of the ancient in the making of the modern—the ancient modern—becomes apparent if we return to the question we began with, of versions. The techno-modern metaphor *version* suggests a quality of absorption, of frequent change that barely alters the inner substance. Stripped to their very cores, the twenty-first-century metaphor of *version* and the nineteenth-century *sponge* perform the same task of imagining India as a timeless entity. The difference is in the accelerated global language of digital infrastructure used to reincarnate older ideas to speak to twenty-first-century sensibilities. What I am proposing is that the old nineteenth-century discourse of timelessness has developed deep roots in the past two centuries and continues to shape the imaginaries of India, albeit in a new technofriendly language well understood by a younger generation enchanted with software utopias.[55]

To be sure, the idea that the essence of India lies in its forceful *capacity to endure* through time without losing its inner core is a familiar feature in postcolonial historiography. As Partha Chatterjee has shown, the nationalist imagination of a modern nation-state derived from the claim that ancient India's universal spirit was in tune with, if not ahead of, the universal spirit of modernity. Consider the accounts of anticolonial nationalism in which the edifice of the "domain of sovereignty" was built on the division between the material (outer) and the spiritual (inner) spheres. The material outside consists "of the economy and of statecraft, of science and technology where the West had proved its superiority and the East had succumbed," and the spiritual inside is "an 'inner' domain bearing the 'essential' marks of cultural identity . . . and its sovereign territory" beyond the powers of colonial interventions. The inner domain was also the domain of strong resistance in which "a 'modern' national culture that is nevertheless not Western" was fashioned by the nationalist elite.[56] It is in this hermetically sealed indigenous inside, then, that the pure difference of modern nationalist culture untouched and unchanged by colonial and capitalist practices is seemingly preserved. The point here is not just about the analytical problems in perceiving the domains of social life—the material and spiritual, the national and the colonial, the inside and the outside—as separate compartments. The contestations of the inner/outer dichotomy and the need to focus instead on entanglements in the coproduction of anticolonial nationalism have already been addressed at length.[57] What is important here is not whether a pure inner domain exists but the *speculative possibility* of an inner domain that allows a sense of being in full control even in a state of subjugation. It is in this imagined protective shell, then, that the cultural essence endures and resists externally wrought change.

The possibility of a timeless inner core makes an appearance in the account of its shift to postcolonial modernity too. This time it is seductively repackaged as the "idea of India," whose protagonists, we are told, are "at once products of ancient habits and modern ambitions, who have found in democracy a form of action that promises them control over their destinies."[58] These ideas broadly echo those of Jawaharlal Nehru, deemed the architect of modern India, who saw modern India as a new form of the ancient, a source of inspiration in the moment of chaos and strife that Partition had turned into. While moving a resolution on the adoption of the national flag and the symbolism of Ashoka Chakra in the Constituent Assembly in July 1947, Nehru connected the ancient and modern India as follows:

"[Ashoka's] wheel is a symbol of India's ancient culture, it is a symbol of the many things that India had stood for through the ages. . . . It is well that at this moment of strife, conflict and intolerance, our minds should go back towards what India stood for in the ancient days and what it has stood for, I hope and believe, essentially throughout the ages in spite of mistakes and errors and degradation from time to time. For, if India had not stood for something very great, I do not think that India could have survived and carried on its cultural traditions in a more or less continuous manner through these vast ages. It carried on its cultural tradition, not unchanging, not rigid, but always keeping its *essence*, always adapting itself to new developments, to new influences. This has been the tradition of India, always to put out fresh blooms and flowers, always receptive to the good things that it receives, sometimes receptive to bad things also, but always true to her ancient culture" (my italics).[59]

For Nehru, the inclusion of Ashoka's wheel at the center of the Indian flag was a reification of India's immemorial essence in a modern context, an enduring symbol of India's timelessness. Its symbolic appearance on the flag of a modern democratic republic merely affirmed India's ancient spirit, which continues to take ever-new forms in harmony with the contemporary world. The idea of India, then, is simultaneously ancient and modern, and in its new form it is intimately entangled with the political principle of democracy and the values of inclusiveness, tolerance, development, and pluralism. This popular narrative of India's shift to modern democratic structures plays on a familiar fracture that separates the inner core (shielding indigenous identities) from the public arena (contact with the outside world), a seemingly split screen of parallel politics that almost never transgresses allocated territory. What makes this split work is the assumption that India's social order has always been "extraordinarily resistant to political molding" by the state power.[60] This deeply rooted resilience is attributed to the distinct form of community—*jati* and *varna* order—in which the dominating social group, the Brahmins, created a self-disciplining social order by renouncing political power so that "India could be defeated easily, but the society itself remained unconquered and unchanged."[61] The split social space—of private and public arena—allowed contact and containment of the alien without fully exposing the self.

What is noteworthy here is how this vision of "unusual fixity and cultural consistency"[62] of the society overlooks and erases the forms of popular resistance to the dominant social order, the slow churning set in motion by the Bhakti and Sufi traditions in the precolonial period.

The Brahminic temporal authority to regulate social structures, knowledge, and rituals was challenged from below, a challenge that hardly left the social landscape in medieval India unchanged.[63] Yet the idea of a static, unchanging inner core has found more than a firm foothold in the imaginaries of an ancient-modern India. The inner/outer split enables the notion of a stable, pure essence to coexist with dynamics of accelerated modernity. The idea of India, in many ways, is a romanticized rehearsal of the old claim of assimilation, a celebration of its sponge-like capacity to expand and absorb alterations without losing its difference. The notion that India is an eternal entity traveling through time—open, absorptive, and tolerant of all that is encountered—has gained widespread currency. Consider how the idea of secularism itself is now increasingly joined to the large-heartedness of Hinduism, and the toleration of Hindus is given as the reason for the success of the secular ethos in India.[64] Toleration appears as another expression for absorption of the outside, an attribute at once a cause for acclaim and now a grievance in Hindu majoritarian politics.

THE FOREIGN REMAINS

I return to the inherently political question of the outside, or foreignness, or more a kind of hierarchy of the foreign that can or cannot be absorbed in the imaginaries of New India. The Incredible India imagery, I have shown, brings to surface the tensions about the rearrangements taking place in the social landscape in postreform India. In this view, India in its twenty-first-century digital reincarnation remains unchanged even as it is constantly modified. It is precisely within the story of the great transformation that we witness the opposite: the claims of eternal stability that India 2.0 as Incredible India ultimately presents to its consumers. The global aesthetics of India 2.0 are located within these seeming contradictions of change and continuity—the idea of versions providing the necessary frame. Consider the repetitive themes visible in the Incredible India imagery—natural landscape, wildlife, Hindu festivals, rituals, and exotica—that recall the old colonial imagery. These themes are loathed even as they are reproduced, and their capacity to create the smart image is never beyond doubt. The point is not whether they work effectively toward their intended goal but rather how they reveal the imagined blueprint of India and the centrality of these themes therein.

Connected to this is the related question of authenticity that discloses another contradiction. Recall the India 2.0 installation we began with. It's a green-and-yellow auto rickshaw dressed up in the pink roof made of sheer luxury fabric and matching pink silk cushions positioned to display the dramatic transformations unfolding in postreform India. The choice of auto rickshaw as a symbol of the new Incredible India is telling. Auto rickshaws are a ubiquitous part of Indian urban life as a slow-paced but affordable means of transport. The very name suggests that the vehicle is an improvisation of the cycle rickshaws that are popular for short-distance travel. Yet auto rickshaws not only are *not* unique to India, given their popularity across Asia and Africa, but were introduced in India as recently as the 1950s by the Indian licensee of Piaggio, an Italian automobile manufacturer. We witness the notion of authenticity here not as an a priori true master copy but in its formation as it is produced by drawing the foreign inside and absorbing it into the vernacular texture. This quality of absorbing, assimilating the foreign, and bringing the outside inside is what is sometimes said to cast India in timelessness. The word *incredible* seeks precisely to convey that magical, marvelous quality. The very choice of this English word would appear to be the work of these contradictions too. I was told during my fieldwork that no word exists in the Hindi language that can fully describe the potential and richness of India. While India has been translated for the global publics in the shape of Incredible India, it has also been translated back for the vernacular publics as *Atulya Bharat*, which literally means "incomparable" or "unique" India. It is telling that the multitude of vernacular languages is found to be lacking words to appropriately describe the postexotic self. Similarly, the graphic identity for New India in the logo form—!—is also extracted from the global archive of the printing press. It has been effortlessly absorbed into the graphic logo of India.

In contrast, what has not been easily absorbed is India's Muslim past in Incredible India. The catalogue of images that constitutes Incredible

India is a pointer in this direction. The sole exception to this rule is the presence of the Taj Mahal—now pitched as the ultimate sign of consumption and pleasure. The monument is presented in global publicity as a priceless and unattainable commodity that consumers can only dream and aspire to. If the near absence of the Muslim past reflects the contemporary politics of Hindutva in the blueprint of India 2.0, the presence of the commodified Taj Mahal signals the postexotic futures ahead. The future is this: the absorption of the foreign in the folds of timelessness is now not merely a problem of cultural translation but equally a question of its capacity to generate commodity value in a fully capitalized nation. What can be remixed and yet allowed to retain its distinct visibility is what generates capital, a precarious balance forever in a state of temporariness.

Part II

NEW TIME

CHAPTER 4

ICONS OF GOOD TIMES

IN THE DIGITAL UNIVERSE, the remains of the once-iconic India Shining campaign are hard to find. Of the approximately 4.5 million images tagged with the search term "India Shining," barely a handful lead to the original images released in 2003–2004 to mark the success of India's economic reforms. Most of these images accompany news reports that had documented, depending on one's vantage point, one of India's most successful or unsuccessful advertising campaigns of all time. Most of the search results contain an assortment of images ranging from artistic subversion of the original theme to plain factual news reportage of India's economic growth and stories of success in various fields. The digital shards—broken links to erased websites—reveal that any presence of the original images has been carefully removed. Neither the website of the advertising agency that created it nor that of the political party popularly associated with the campaign has retained any links with the images. The official portal of India Shining (www.indiashining.com), which once proudly displayed images of the newfound prosperity and well-being of Indians no longer exists.[1] It is telling that the vacant domain name itself has been available for sale for some years now without being able to attract a buyer.

This deliberate erasure of one of the most publicized and probably most acrimonious megapublicity spectacles by the very forces that created it remains mired in controversy. Of the many image campaigns launched in the past two decades, India Shining gained a distinct singularity for being disowned and even actively wiped out by its makers. In short, it is most remembered for being a spectacular failure. The specific question I address here concerns the disintegration of the spectacle[2] and what the effacement of the publicity campaign might mean. Put differently, what did the popular notion of the failure of India Shining actually signify and what did it not?

When the Bharatiya Janata Party (BJP) abandoned the India Shining campaign, few were surprised given the public discourse that firmly connected India Shining to the party's stunning defeat in the 2004 general elections. In fact, the BJP leadership itself cited the campaign as the prime reason for its electoral defeat.[3] The campaign had seemingly failed to connect to the true aspirations of the people and realities on the ground. Its critics labeled it a "feel-good factory" that made "fool good" false claims about the state of the nation to the public.[4] The images were likened to the fallen icons, the ones that concealed reality and turned out to be hollow when hammered and scrutinized by the desiring publics.[5]

Yet if India Shining stands out in the history of publicity campaigns for this ultimate betrayal and abandonment, it also stands out for precisely *not* fading out of the collective vision of the population despite all attempts to erase it. India Shining not only is now deeply etched in public memory as an old promise and its subversion but also is a popular catchphrase invoked in all shades of irony and desire to describe the state of the nation. Thus, for Rama Bijapurkar, India Shining is a popular symbol of the good life that the aspirational middle class remains forever in search of.[6] Similarly, Christiane Brosius takes it as a marker of new sites, spaces, and events in which the Indian Dream becomes fully visible.[7] Whereas for the economist Jayati Ghosh, India Shining was a gloss over on-the-ground realities that were "at the best a mixed economic picture, and at worst, a story of stagnation, decline, neglect, and even deterioration for a substantial part of India's population."[8] This dichotomy between representation and reality constitutive of India Shining visuals is what Shaila Bhatti and Christopher Pinney call a struggle between the shiny surface and the dark interiority of the Indian nation.[9] Whereas the various themes of clash and contrast have framed the India Shining debate thus far, the nature of disenchantment itself that growing inequality and deprivation have produced in the postreform years has been less explored.

In this chapter, I make two interlinked and somewhat against-the-grain claims. First, the visible disenchantment with the India Shining campaign in the popular domain was never about disenchantment with the neoliberal project of economic reforms as such. The discontent accrued from the failure of individuals to fully profit from the good times seemingly ushered in by the reforms. Second, the India Shining images helped popularize the reforms on an unprecedented mass scale that until then had largely been limited to elite policy debates and governmental reform packages. Even as the India Shining controversy brought out the tensions at the heart of the economic reforms, it helped firmly establish the reforms as the prime strategy of social mobility and prosperity in India. It is in this controversy too that we witness the lack of alternatives to the capitalist visions of prosperity. The stubborn, acrimonious absence/presence of the India Shining images and their very indelibility in the popular domain indicate the upheavals and rearrangements beneath the surface that have taken place in the reformed nation.

In order to bring these ongoing reconfigurations to the surface, I depart from the popular perception of India Shining images as desecrated signs of failure and instead approach them as the icons of good times or the hypericons[10] of neoliberal reforms that successfully conjured a desirable yet unattainable vision of the long-promised good times.[11] The discontent accumulated not because the vision was found to be wanting or even flawed but because it turned out to be far beyond reach of all those who desired it. In the theater of reforms, India Shining images appeared as characters in their own right on the historical stage and were endowed with a magical, almost mythical status by both their supporters and their critics. In contrast to other state-sponsored publicity campaigns—for instance, the 2002 Incredible India campaign—that are routinely dismissed as propaganda, the India Shining images were taken too seriously, almost as idols that had lied to and offended and thereby failed their worshippers. Yet even the most ardent iconoclasts and harshest critics did not smash and eliminate the hypericon of neoliberal prosperity; all they did was show how distant and unattainable it was for its ordinary followers.

In this chapter, I retrace the history of the India Shining campaign to locate it as the first major publicity effort that effectively publicized the promise of economic reforms, even in its spectacular failure. In this trajectory of the reforms process, we also witness how new forms of being and belonging in the upwardly mobile New India arose. Central to this shift is the emergence of the autonomous figure of the investor-citizen, whose belonging to the nation is authenticated primarily through a capacity to invest and grow with the nation. The language of political demand-making itself undergoes a change from the demand for rights and public goods from the state to the calculation and articulation of one's profits and losses as a result of being part of the nation. Even the opposition's campaign, *Aam aadmi ko kya mila*, or What did the common man gain?, spoke and authenticated this new language of investment and returns. In short, what we witness is the beginning of a large-scale internal rearrangement—of discourse as well as practice—within the nation that sharply aligned public opinion with the reforms agenda.

TRICKLE-DOWN EUPHORIA

The 2003–2004 financial year was in many ways unprecedented in India's economic history. It was the first time ever, after the reforms initiated in 1991, that India had achieved an average growth rate of 8.2 percent, which previously the policy makers could only dream of. Hidden within this average were figures that created a full sense of euphoria—the last quarter of 2003 had even shown the fabled double-digit growth of 10.4 percent, which was way more than double the depressing 4.3 percent of the previous 2002–2003 financial year.[12] The macroeconomic indicators from manufacturing, industry, agriculture, and services all showed a rise beyond expectations.[13] Soon this good news would be followed by the ultimate sign of India's growing economic strength—the unprecedented leap in foreign exchange reserves that had taken the economy to the magical threshold of $100 billion.[14] The old, oft-repeated rhetoric of "unleashing the India opportunity" appeared to be close to realization.[15]

If there was a dark edge to this upswing in India's fortunes, it was that Indians appeared to be out of step with the changing state of India. The sense of euphoria experienced in policy circles and government offices had not trickled down to the Indian public. The people still consumed and expended their income in largely the same way they had done a decade earlier. Although India's economy, after initial hiccups, was finally on its way toward much-longed-for growth acceleration—or as C. K. Prahalad put it, the "train had left the station"—these were still early days in the formation of consumer culture.[16] According to the 2001 Indian census, the use of amenities and ownership of assets was as follows: 31.6 percent of households possessed a television, 17.5 percent used cooking gas, 9.1 percent had a telephone connection, and only 2.5 percent owned a car, jeep, or van.[17] Even more telling was the fact that 34.5 percent of the population did not possess any assets, such as a television, radio, scooter, bicycle, or car, and 35.5 percent did not have access to banking services. The first mall in India had opened in 1999 and had yet, a decade later, to become a ubiquitous feature of the urban landscape.[18] The consumption of luxury items and branded retail goods was still in its infancy. And Indians still put their money in forms of fixed-term bank deposits and gold rather than circulating it in risk-prone markets. The challenge, it seemed, was how to encourage individual consumption and investment in order to stimulate the domestic market.

In early 2003, the Ministry of Finance, led by Yashwant Sinha, handed over the task of framing a strategy to move the domestic market to Financial Dynamics, a London-based British financial consultancy firm.[19] The firm conducted a market survey and returned to the ministry with the finding that "your country men and women don't believe, or don't know that the country is doing well, and that it [the state of economy] is conducive to more financial growth and will actually help you multiply your wealth."[20] The report recommended that the government launch a mass communication campaign with a simple and coherent message that the country is doing well, and "this is the right time for you to take advantage of that" and do well yourself too.[21] The first campaign that sought to fulfill this objective was called India's Time Has Come and appeared in several print publications in mid-2003. But the image of a happy farmer with a mobile phone in his hand accompanied by photos of the prime minister and the finance minister—the usual government propaganda in an unappealing style, as it was described to me—was unsuccessful in generating public attention. The campaign was short-lived and quickly abandoned. It had failed to grab attention and move the markets.

The project was revived shortly after a cabinet reshuffle when Jaswant Singh took over as the finance minister. This time the contract was awarded to a Delhi-based ad agency that approached the project with an altogether different logic. Prathap Suthan, the new campaign director, believed the failure of the previous campaign lay in its inability to appeal to the target group, who, according to the official brief, consisted of successful urban Indians, often English-speaking, who had a high disposable income and spare money but remained tightfisted, preferring instead to put their savings in nonfinancial assets.[22] The challenge, as Prathap saw it, lay in convincing this group to shift their idle money to the markets. The campaign that emerged from these deliberations was called India Shining, said to be a metaphor for the country doing well, which was immediately approved by the government officials. The other suggestions, such as India Rising and India Alive, were discarded, as Prathap found those "too soft" and argued moreover that "India had already risen."[23] India in this discourse was no longer a work in progress, and this fact was in need of communication to fellow citizens. The strategy was to embark on a two-phase campaign that would be unveiled in the domestic markets and followed by an international campaign. At this early stage, the makers of India Shining had little inkling of the kind of response the campaign would generate. It would not only become the biggest and most iconic mass publicity campaign ever undertaken by the Indian state inside the nation but also the most divisive and acrimonious the nation had ever seen.

The campaign was inaugurated in early October, but in less than a fortnight it was suspended until December 1, 2003, as India had just gone into election mode, with the Legislative Assembly elections scheduled in seven states.[24] Even in this short period, the campaign had managed to make an impression. Prathap Suthan recalled the moment he knew the campaign had entered the popular lexicon for good. On October 16, during the India–New Zealand cricket test match in Ahmedabad, Virendra Sehwag hit a boundary in a tough match. The cheerful moment was captured by television cameras telecasting the event live as they zoomed in on an "India Shining" placard that a spectator was holding up. This visual was accompanied by an Australian commentator's impromptu remark, "Indeed, India is shining," as the crowd cheered India's stride to victory. It seemed India Shining had touched a popular chord, or "connected with the people," as its makers had hoped. And if any other proof was required, the Sensex touched the five thousand mark for the first time in the days that followed. The markets were responding jubilantly to the message, Prathap felt, for "India Shining at that time was just the medicine, just the feeling the country wanted to have, that made Indians proud that the country has actually woken up, is doing well. It gave you an umbrella feeling for successful India. So, the moment the ad hit the country, it went like wildfire. It was instant. It was a true feeling, you see. It was hyperbole in its own way, but it was a feeling that encapsulated the pent-up pride of India." It seemed that the mood of optimism had found a new name—India Shining—that would be used from then on to signify any achievement of India.

Prathap recounted this narrative of India Shining's initial success when we finally met in a South Delhi café in late 2013 following several phone and email conversations. This was more than a decade after the India Shining campaign had first made its appearance and then been categorized in the public discourse as a failure of historic proportions. To hear the campaign being talked about in terms of success almost seemed a bit misplaced. But for Prathap this part of the story appeared to be of particular importance. He narrated this in as much detail as he could recall in order to "put it on record," as he put it. In a way, this was not surprising given that he had to bear the burden of India Shining's political failure all alone—shunned and distanced by the political party that had appropriated it and then disowned it. In the world of advertising professionals, he himself had become a story, with his name firmly attached to a publicity campaign that no one wanted to be associated with after the electoral debacle. I had expected him to distance himself from the images, but to my surprise he spoke about them passionately. Clearly he believed in the images he had created just as he believed in the promise of the economic reforms they had come to embody in the public discourse. To recall the initial celebratory acclaim that had accompanied the images was for him to activate a double recovery—of the promise of the India Shining images from the waste bin of history and of his professional name, which he felt had been unfairly dragged into the controversy. He pointed out that in 2003, India Shining was seen as a lucky totem, especially for the political party that had sanctioned its creation, as the BJP scored an unexpected victory in the three states of Madhya Pradesh, Rajasthan, and Chhattisgarh.[25] Its critique and subversion remained almost unanticipated at that stage.

The relaunch of India Shining in December 2003 took place in this optimistic mode, and by early January the campaign was ranked among the top four brands on the national scale. A survey of the first fortnight of January alone showed that India Shining was the second most recognizable national brand, ranked just after the Ministry of Health's Pulse Polio campaign, which was launched to advocate immunization among children. The campaign was described as "blazing across the print media" rather than merely shining, with 392 insertions in more than 450 newspapers. Of these, about 40 percent were back-page ads, and 20 percent were full-page ads. Almost 90 percent of the volume was color prints.[26]

The actual impact of the campaign went far beyond advertising, because India Shining had by then become a popular theme of national discussion. The thin trickle of skepticism that had begun surfacing in December was gaining traction. India Shining had already spawned a series of contrasting themes—India Whining, India Stinking, India

Burning, and India Declining—that played on the original and sought to draw attention to an alternative reality. The optimistic tone of the campaign, termed "feel good" in adspeak, was translated into "fool good" in the popular domain. The underlying message was obvious— the publicity campaign was an act of concealment that sought to divert attention from the poverty and deprivation visible to all but the state. Yet it was precisely within this contentious and acerbic setting that more fundamental changes had been set in motion. The very language and politics of citizenship were undergoing a massive shift, a shift that barely made its presence felt at the moment of its appearance.

INVESTOR-CITIZEN IN THE NEW TIMES

I begin with the launch advertisement of India Shining issued in early October, which occupied a prominent, full-page space in several national newspapers. Devoid of any photo images and under the official seal and sign of the Government of India, it was a lyrically composed poetic account of changing times in India (fig. 4.1). It was both a bearer of good news and an open invitation to join the enterprise that India now was. The opening lines thus began:

> Our country is prospering.
> Our lives are changing.
> Our tomorrow is promising.
> You've never had
> a better time to shine together.

Embedded in this grammatical structure is an uplifting portrait of the arrival of *neuzeit*, the new time,[27] which Indians had long dreamed of but never truly expected to be realized. The ad was telling the readers that we had not just reached the epochal threshold but had already effortlessly crossed it, so effortlessly that the shift had not even been noticed. The tense used was the present and present continuous, to invoke the sense of being in the middle of events yet unfolding, of belonging to history rather than being outside of it. The other notable feature is the use of *our*, the first-person plural pronoun, also called

FIGURE 4.1. *India Shining inaugural advertisement. 2003. Courtesy of Prathap Suthan.*

the possessive pronoun, which is invoked to indicate ownership of a given object. In this case, it is the ownership of the country, of one's life as well as of the collective future. The first three adverbs—*prospering, changing, promising*—lay out the previously uncharted map of the new times, ultimately revealing the "shining" present. In this rhetoric, the reader is drawn into the project at this point not just as a mere reader but also as a coauthor, as a participant in the project of transformation. Yet there remains a rhetorical conflict in the text—the *our* in the beginning is interchanged with *you* as the narrative progresses. The function of this shift is not completely clear, but in these blurred reader/author lines, it is almost as if one has taken to talking to oneself.

Across India, you can feel a new radiance.
The economy is looking up. Industry is upbeat.
We are on the threshold of further progress.
Prices are stable. Home loans are plentiful.
Interest rates are low.

Roads are being added. Highways are being modernized.
Markets are busy. Telecom is expanding.
Job opportunities are improving.
Rains are good, and the harvest richer.

The bouncing macroeconomic indicators that had sprung into policy documents and spreadsheets just a few months before had now found a poetic narrative and a place in the popular domain. Here we get a glimpse of the journey across the epochal threshold that readers/authors found had taken place while the public gaze was still distracted. The cold statistics—ranging from industrial manufacturing, agricultural production, financial capital, and infrastructure expansion, including highways and telecom, to inflation control and job growth—had now found a collective essence and purpose. The story of an economic upswing was no longer a collection of mere numbers; it had been manufactured as a fable in progress. All the text meant to do was to capture the attention and redirect the public gaze toward the erstwhile hidden economic miracle:

In fact, all the factors for greater growth have come together.
Ready to encourage individual enterprise.
Ready to support corporate initiative.
The environment is fertile for you to invest, build and create.

The epoch-changing transformation of India into a corporatized nation that had been set in motion more than a decade earlier had gained ground. The blueprint of India laid out here revealed the new logic at the heart of the liberalized nation—the magic formula of economic growth that was now invoked as a mantra more than ever before. The success of the neoliberal state was measured primarily by its ability to facilitate capital flows smoothly without obstructions, or the proverbial red tape, in order to aid growth.[28] Growth itself was taken as a sign of prosperity and of the well-being of the nation.[29] Thus, by extension, the natural inhabitants of this nation were those who demonstrated and lived the entrepreneurial spirit. The state identified its role in this new time quite clearly: it was no longer just the owner of capital but also an efficient facilitator of capital committed to removing barriers to success. The making of the corporatized state and its capacity to become an able manager of capital[30] are what began unfolding here:

> So go ahead, make use of this opportunity, and gain from these excellent
>> times.
> Spread this proud enthusiasm, and make India stronger and shine even
>> brighter.

The poem ends in the form of an invitation, or, more accurately, a proposal to collaborate. India itself is pitched first and foremost as a profitable investment proposition for its citizens. Readers/authors are reminded of their journey into the new epoch and then gently nudged to take advantage of the opportunities, to gain from the excellent times. The bargain is twofold. The citizen is asked to "invest, build and create" in order to profit from the new possibilities opening up, and the state expects that the entrepreneurial acts of the citizens will amplify "proud enthusiasm" and make India "stronger and shine even brighter." Clearly, the state-citizen relationship also undergoes a transformation here. The earlier compact between the state and citizen was broadly based on rights and responsibilities, of citizens receiving security, rights, and public goods in exchange for accepting the sovereignty of the state. The compact we witness here is different—it is based on the logic of economic growth, in which citizens help grow the nation by diverting their individual capital to the domestic markets. As a consequence, individuals profit from the growing economy and multiply their personal capital. What becomes apparent at this juncture is the figure of the investor-citizen, the ideal-type neoliberal subject who not only fits in the new economy but is a product of the decade-old societal transformations.

The figure of the investor-citizen sets itself apart from the citizens of a previous era involved in similar projects of nation building. The spirit of nation building in the postindependence era called for self-less service, and at times even sacrifice, for the greater common good.[31] One might even say that the parameters of development were different given the focus on large-scale infrastructure—big dams, public-sector industries, and building projects—and on acquiring self-reliance, especially in food production.

The India Shining campaign unveils a different kind of nation building altogether. For one, it does not call for sacrifice or selfless service but frames service itself in terms of individual profits and gains from national economic growth. Citizens are enticed to invest in the nation based on the possibility of gaining what in financial circles is called return on investment. Unlike the marginalized people in the "political society"[32] who actively contest and negotiate with the government for public goods, the largely middle-class investor-citizens lay claim to their citizenship rights and entitlements through investment and consumption. To invest or expend capital is now to serve the nation itself. The very notion of self-sacrifice here is replaced by its opposite: consumption and self-interest.

Another notable aspect of investor-citizenship is the implicit requirement that one possess something in order to expend and enter the new compact. This was emphasized to me again and again in my conversations: the India Shining campaign was never meant for the have-nots who did not have anything to invest or spend to begin with. This categorization—without explicitly setting out to do so—had by default created an opposing category of surplus citizens who did not fit the needs of the corporate nation. How could they contribute to or invest in the nation, given they could not even look after themselves? And how could they ever be part of the new compact between the state and the investor-citizen? These questions, it seems, were never part of the considerations and discourse from which India Shining emerged but instead became the source of frictions and chinks.

In the meantime, eight follow-up portraits of India Shining in everyday life followed the inaugural advertisement. Each of these portraits featured a face of New India that had become the human expression of economic policies pursued by the Indian state over the previous decade. New India appeared here as a catalog of images—cheerful, smiling faces, often with arms stretched upward to gesture enthusiasm, happiness, and enterprise—that visually aligned with the spirit of mass optimism that India Shining sought to convey. The telling feature of this catalog is the new classification of the ideal-type citizen in New India. The portraits are no longer representative of different regions, cultural diversity, or civilizational richness, as previous forms of representation in postcolonial India usually were, but of enterprising, skillful people who are defined by their value in the new economy.

The point here is not about mere representation, for it is that too, but about the images signaling how India and its ideal citizens should appear to be in the postreform era. Each of the eight portraits addressed a target group that policy makers wished to reach—young mothers, students, prosperous villagers, technofriendly small-town dwellers, big-city corporate executives, single career women, retired grandparents, and tourism entrepreneurs. The categorization, in some ways, recalls the microtrends approach in political advertising popularized by Mark Penn, the well-known American pollster, in the mid-1990s. The idea behind microtargeting consumers or voters was to categorize groups around a combination of demographic, psychographic, and attitudinal traits that helped ascertain consumption or polling preferences.[33] In the world of advertising, microtargeting is considered to be the most productive option that helps create "customized winning messages, proof points and offers accurately predicating their impact, and delivering them directly to individuals."[34] One microgroup that entered America's political advertising lexicon in an almost mythical way was the "soccer moms"—the suburban mothers who placed their kids' interests before their own—that were said to have altered the 1996 elections in favor of Bill Clinton. Regardless of doubts expressed about the myth of the soccer mom in the American media,[35] its strong shades could be seen in the first India Shining follow-up ad.

The first follow-up image was of an attractive mother, probably in her early thirties, clad in a bright yellow sari and playing the game of cricket with her young son (fig. 4.2). If soccer is the quintessential participatory sport for youth in America, then cricket is its all-consuming

FIGURE 4.2. *Happy mother and son in India Shining ad. 2003. Courtesy of Prathap Suthan.*

counterpart in India. The mother-son duo is seen cheerfully engaged in a celebratory posture. The "cricket mom" is seen holding the cricket bat in an upward swing, and she appears to be happy even though she has been stumped (struck out). The boy is joyous, with his arms stretched outward and one knee slightly bent. The image is accompanied by the following text:

> Expenses are settling.
> Budgets are balancing.
> Mothers are smiling.
> You've never had a better time to shine brighter.

The small print at the bottom offered a longer explanation:

> Mothers have never been happier. Prices are stable, quality has risen, choices are plenty, financing schemes are easy, and your budgets aren't getting upset. Besides interest rates on home loans have come down, and there's never been a better time to buy your own house. With India ready to progress even further, your tomorrow looks wonderful.

Unlike the American soccer mom, whose commitment to her children is what supposedly defines her, the Indian cricket mom featured in India Shining is burdened with weightier issues. Here the figure of the mother is imagined as a key decision maker in the household who is concerned with not only the choice, quality, and price of daily goods but also interest rates on loans to secure home ownership for the family.

This direct form of address to mothers recalls the growing realization among marketing experts that women are often the key decision makers when it comes to household purchases. A global survey conducted by the American consultancy firm Nielsen showed that "when it came to spending decisions, women were in control," and even more so in emerging markets such as Nigeria and India.[36] Another influential study claims that "women now drive the world economy" and that globally "they control about $20 trillion in annual consumer spending."[37] Their influence extends to purchasing not only groceries for everyday consumption but also 91 percent of homes, 92 percent of vacations, 60 percent of automobiles, and 51 percent of consumer electronics.[38] In the world of advertising, the ability of women to invest and consume not only as individuals but also as members of family units has clearly gained them particular prominence.

India Shining was in many ways a forerunner to the global trends in advertising, as it set out to target women investors and consumers. Here the scope of the maternal nurturing role was expanded and the domestic sphere recrafted in ways that Hannah Arendt[39] may not have completely anticipated in making public/private distinctions—ensuring the well-being of the family here also meant taking responsibility for the family's financial well-being and ensuring a roof over the family's head.[40] And this also meant opening up the narrowly defined domestic sphere to include full participation in the economy. Thus, the advertisement highlighted the key features of the government's economic policy aimed at the group of cricket moms. These incentives—or sops, as the critics would later call them—included stable prices, easy housing and consumer loans, phone on demand, cooking gas on demand, and friendlier tax processes.

This imagination of women as asset-bearing individuals at the center of the neoliberal economy rather than at the margins was evident in a second ad that focused on single career women (fig. 4.3). Here three smiling young women pose for the camera, dressed up in the professional attire of formal sari, salwar kameez, and Western-style pantsuit. The presence of a desktop computer and shelves in the background suggest an office-like setting. The accompanying text reads:

> Opportunities are growing.
> Options are increasing.
> Times are thrilling.
> You've never had a better time to shine together.

The text below the ad explains, "Women in India have new opportunities and more career options. Steering the education and health sectors, they also manage small-scale industries and global offices. Design software and clothing lines. Drive banking and investment ideas. Fly planes and helicopters. In fact, there's nothing they cannot achieve today." The women in this image are not identified in terms of the usual

FIGURE 4.3. *"Women in India now have new opportunities and more career options." India Shining Campaign. 2004. Courtesy of Prathap Suthan.*

familial web of relations—*beti, bahu, maa* (daughter, daughter-in-law, mother)—but rather as women framed within a different web of keywords: *opportunity, career, education, industries, software, investment,* and *achievements.* The absence of any obvious symbols of matrimony—*sindoor,* ritual pieces of jewelry—is probably meant to signify that these are single women oriented toward their careers.

The policy measures aimed at this group also reveal the ways that this microgroup is positioned. These include "guiding local self-government under Panchayati Raj, empowerment through self-help groups, lower income tax liability, scholarships for women scientists and 3% lower rate of tax for female houseowners." The last bit is significant, as the policy incentivizes female home ownership by lowering taxes slightly, just as it seeks to promote women scientists with financial support. This kind of government support stands in contrast to the usual women-centric schemes, such as *Mukhyamantri Kanyadaan Yojana* (the Chief Minister's Financial Aid Scheme for Girl Marriage), in which the state intervenes to organize mass wedding ceremonies for girls from poor families and offer financial aid to that end.[41] The women in India Shining visuals are pitched quite differently—they are middle-class, professional, empowered women who pay their taxes and are probably already on the property ladder even without being married. In these visuals, what we witness is the incorporation of female investor-citizens into the new economy.

The collective euphoria generated by the India Shining ads was largely intact at this stage. A big boost to the government's claims about the state of the economy came in the form of the Reserve Bank of India's 2003 year-end statement of foreign exchange reserves. India had for the first time in its history reached the long-desired US$100 billion mark.[42] The significance of this sum and the attendant celebrations can be understood only in the context of the economic crisis India faced in 1990 and 1991 and its fallout. The cash-strapped Indian government at this point was left with a mere US$5.8 billion in foreign exchange, which further shrunk to US$1.1 billion, or a mere two weeks' worth of imports, by the summer of 1991.[43] India was said to be in the midst of its "most serious crisis."[44] The crisis also became post-colonial India's moment of humiliation, as it had to pledge its gold reserves as collateral to gain international loans from its former colonizer. In the summer of 1991, about forty-seven tons of gold was airlifted to the Bank of England and twenty tons to the Union Bank of Switzerland to raise US$600 million. This crisis also became a turning point in India's economic history, as it agreed to open up its economy and undertake structural adjustment programs as part of a further IMF-led bailout. That the 1991 crisis is deeply etched in the national psyche was evident in 2009 when India made it a point to purchase two hundred tons of gold reserves put on sale by the IMF.[45] Almost every news report recounted the shame of 1991 and noted the reversal of India's fortunes. And in 2003–2004, India Shining set out to capture precisely that collective need to erase national shame and replace it with the "feeling of pride that the country is doing well."[46]

On January 1, 2004, the India Shining campaign issued the following message to fellow Indians:

> Happy New Year.
> You are now stronger and prouder with $100 billion shining.
> Our foreign exchange reserves have raced past the $100 billion mark.
> We have never been more robust, healthier and radiant.
> It's a moment that makes every Indian stand proud and tall.
> From the days of dreaming self-reliance, we have traveled a long way.
> It's a figure that inspires the world to applaud our resolve.

The New Year's greeting touched a raw nerve, for it addressed a topic that had long simmered below the surface but had never been openly addressed. In popular discourse, the economic reforms had been presented as a matter of choice, a carefully considered policy decision, while the actual events that had forced India to open up its markets had been glossed over. The India Shining message directly invoked the memory of that hidden national shame to put the new optimism in context. The publicity campaign was as much a celebration of the glorious present as an attempt to exorcise this humiliating past.

AESTHETICS OF THE EXTRAORDINARY

Once the first phase of the India Shining campaign had successfully established the miraculous rise of "the macros" (economic indicators) in the public mind, the challenge was "how to transfer the spirit of euphoria on to the individual" at a microlevel.[47] The answer to this challenge was the next phase of the campaign, called I Am India Shining, that I was told sought to move the "wonders of India" on to the individuals. The idea was to pitch the individual as "the personal embodiment, the reflection of India Shining" in the metanarrative of New India.[48] A noteworthy aspect of this campaign was that each advertisement was released in conjunction with policy announcements by the government that offered concessions and incentives to select groups. A prominent ad in the new series featured the success story of a weaver turned entrepreneur seen operating a weaving mill (fig. 4.4):

By taking charge of my future,
I join hands with India's prosperity.
By starting a small scale unit,
I inspire more people to be entrepreneurs.
By beginning a new venture,
I give jobs to my fellow citizens.
By starting my own little industry,
I improve the business of my suppliers.
By adding to my local economy,
I add to the wealth of the nation.
By being a partner in India's progress,
I make my India shine.
I am India Shining.

This "ode to entrepreneurship" follows the typical neoliberal narrative of an autonomous, enterprising citizen who proves his worth "by taking charge of [his] own future." Following the recipe of liberation means transforming oneself into an entrepreneur, the celebrated job giver who provides employment to fellow citizens and in doing so adds to the local economy and wealth of the nation. In many ways, the

FIGURE 4.4. *"I Make My India Shine," India Shining follow-up campaign. 2004. Courtesy of Prathap Suthan.*

narrative of taking charge is an old one that has defined citizenship in postcolonial India for a long time. In fact, this celebrating of entrepreneurial citizens as opposed to loathing of those forced to depend on the state has always been deeply ingrained in the official procedures and policies of the Indian state. The hierarchical distinction between self-reliant and state-dependent citizens was already evident in the very formative moment of the Indian nation-state when Partition refugees had to be resettled in the late 1940s.[49] Thus, the neoliberal script of entrepreneurship and wealth generation has never been an imposition from the outside alone. It is tied together with previous discourses of self-reliance that have always characterized the most valuable form of citizenship. The figure of the investor-citizen is merely the latest form in this lineage of belonging to the nation.

What is noteworthy in this India Shining image is the appearance of the entrepreneur himself. The visual and the text suggest that the central figure is a Muslim weaver who has probably scaled up his traditional vocation into a small industry. His entrepreneurial skill evidently opened up a fresh space from which a new relationship to the nation could be claimed. Given that Muslim groups often tend to be on the economic margins in India, this representation of an entrepreneur is significant.[50] In this instance, the claim to belonging is predicated on the ability to enter the neoliberal economy as a job giver, a wealth generator who enriches both self and the nation. The ability to generate wealth for oneself here almost becomes a form of national service, a coveted form of investment in the nation-building project that any enterprising individual can attempt.[51]

This advertisement appeared in conjunction with policy announcements aimed at medium-sized enterprises. The government had set up a small-and-medium-industry fund of Rs 10,000 crores that offered easy loans and concessions to develop businesses. The policy was part of a larger package of economic measures aimed at the middle class or those who aspired to join the middle class. On January 8, 2004, the finance minister announced the package that commentators saw as the BJP's early foray into the forthcoming general elections. A noteworthy feature of these measures was that unlike the usual prepoll benefits offered by governments—for example, concessions on items of mass consumption such as kerosene oil, sugar, food grains, or train tickets—this time an entirely new category of goods and services was being offered. These included reductions in customs and excise duties on consumer items such as mobile phones; computers; DVDs; automobiles, especially sport-utility vehicles; and airline tickets.[52] These commodities clearly did not belong to the category of basic necessities but instead to that of luxury items that signaled the prosperity the reforms had brought in.

The images helped conjure the ideal life of affluence and plenty lived by all those who had taken the opportunities the reforms presented. The visuals were also an invitation to all those deemed left behind to make use of fresh possibilities to invest, consume, and help grow one's personal wealth and the national economy. And in keeping with this idea, a variety of loans, Dada-Dadi retirement bonds aimed at elderly citizens, and several tax/excise concessions on consumer items were introduced.[53] A particular gesture aimed at the corporate sector was the reduction of restrictions on capital convertibility and mobility that allowed Indian citizens to transfer up to US$25,000 out of the country annually. The peak rate of customs duties was lowered from 25 percent to 20 percent, and some duties amounting to 4 percent were abolished altogether. These concessions were estimated to cause a revenue loss of about Rs 10,000 crores to the government, although they were done in the hope of aiding economic growth.[54]

The BJP government's policy announcements were met with severe critiques on two counts. First, the government had introduced significant changes in the structures of taxes, duties, and capital mobility without presenting them for parliamentary debates and procedures. Second, the concessions and benefits were solely targeted at the nation's elite—the upwardly mobile, affluent middle classes. The economic package had conspicuously left out poor citizens who were in need of public support. But what made this presence of the affluent and absence of the poor in the images noteworthy was the insistence that the images represented ordinary life in India. And the proof of this claim, I was told, lay in the assemblage of the photographs themselves, in which real people were featured.

> No, these were not models, these were real people. The teacher in the ad is a teacher, the farmer is a farmer, and the schoolchildren are real schoolchildren. The ads were shot in and around Delhi. The second campaign, "I Am India Shining," was shot all around the country. We went to the streets to take these images. We saw a bunch of schoolgirls, and asked them if we could take their pictures, real life pictures.[55]

The girls mentioned here were featured in an ad focused on education and student loans. The image shows three young women on bicycles, probably on their way to college. The titles of their notebooks in the cycle baskets allow us a glimpse into the education they are receiving: "Technology Today and Tomorrow" and "Digital Logic and Computer Design." The accompanying text in the ad reads:

By choosing to study further,
I widen my knowledge.
By taking a loan for my education,
I share the burden with my parents.
By taking care of their savings,
I help them live a richer life.
By specializing in bio-genetics,
I gain wisdom for our rice fields.
By learning how to enhance our harvests,
I strengthen the backbone of my nation.
By being a partner in the nation's progress,
I make my India shine.
I am India Shining.

Whether the subjects in this photo assemblage are real people or professional models is irrelevant. What is important is their position as representative models, as the ideal-types who are able to convey the desired impression. At the heart of this image is the claim of being ordinary, of bringing unexceptional scenes from everyday life into the frame of national publicity. The photographer had seemingly captured a commonplace scene on the street that could plausibly be witnessed by anyone. Yet the image is far from the ordinary representation it seeks to be. In fact, it breaks far too many barriers to be categorized as a routine, unexceptional feature of Indian life. For one thing, the young women represent a face of modern Indian womanhood as innovators and entrepreneurs in the fields of science and technology. In a nation in which a lopsided male-to-female sex ratio, a marked preference for sons, gender-based violence, and low human-development indicators define the lives of female citizens, this frame of representation is noteworthy.

In sheer numbers, India actually ranks high among BRIC nations, with a 65 percent female representation in science and engineering higher-education enrollments, a figure buoyed by high numbers in the more traditionally female caregiving roles of nursing and other medical fields. Yet, in contrast, the female presence in the science and engineering workforce is merely 12.7 percent, which places India at the bottom.[56] The disparity in these figures is not clearly explained but suggests that women do fall off the professional ladder or perhaps switch to the more conventional female occupations, such as teaching, rather than stick with, say, research innovation, as gender stereotypes in science and technology continue to prevail.[57]

Whereas in some ways the image of young women engaged in science and technology education represents these statistics because it shows the women as students, the image also exceeds the figures by positioning the young women as future professionals. The students here are expected to contribute to the economy not only by "specializing in bio-genetics" and "gaining wisdom for our rice fields" but by "enhanc(ing) our harvests" and thereby "strengthen(ing) the backbone of [the] nation." The young women also appear to be challenging norms by taking loans and "shar(ing) the burden with [their] parents" instead of being the financial and social burden that a daughter presents in the patriarchal context.

A part of the architecture of this extraordinary masked as ordinary was its temporal performance as the present. In the eyes of its makers, India Shining was not a vision of the future. It was, as Prathap put it, "a vision of the present, of currently where you are—a very prosperous environment. It was a mirror where you could see yourself. You are right here. Why are you not taking advantage of the growing prosperity around you?"[58] This conception of the ordinary presented a built-in antagonism. To be ordinary is to be unexceptional and mundane, a condition that is shared by many. The claim to represent the ordinary, then, was an attempt to speak for everyone even when the speech itself was addressed to a particular class of people: the highly educated, prosperous, professional, upwardly mobile elite. So the euphoric invitation to the haves, a category that Prathap invoked frequently, was also revealed to the have-nots who did not possess the surplus necessary to invest and grow with the nation.

During my conversations with Prathap, there was only one moment when he did not have an immediate, thoughtful, witty response to my queries. The question I had asked him was about his much-favored analogy: India Shining as a mirror to the present. What if you were not able to see yourself in the mirror the state had set up, I asked. And wasn't the desire to see only yourself, apart from others, in the frame of prosperity indicative of a kind of selfishness? After a long pause, he replied, "Listen, in India I am not bothered about you because my survival comes first. . . . We come from a land of famine, a lot of hardship, huge population, fewer resources and all that. So India Shining in a way was pandering to that spirit in you, your survival instinct." In other words, the focus here was not on the collective but on individual interest. Or as Prathap reiterated, "If you do well, your nation will benefit too, so look after your own interest first."[59]

The spirit of India Shining, then, embodied a new subjectivity constitutive of self-centered individuals who had seceded from the collective. This possibility appealed to the newly prosperous middle class and legitimized that appeal in the public discourse.[60] But this spirit of self first that India Shining successfully invoked is precisely what created acrimony, given the widespread feeling of exclusion from the celebration that India Shining represented. It is within these factions and antagonisms that we need to rethink the notion of failure with which India Shining is popularly associated. What appeared to be failure in the aftermath of the 2004 electoral defeat was, in fact, a decisive turn toward a broad consensus in favor of economic reforms. The icons of good times never really disappeared; they returned in full force in the new form of *acche din*, or "good times," in the 2014 general elections.

THE INDELIBLE ICON

I will begin unpacking the controversial moment of failure here by addressing the countercampaign launched by the Congress Party in 2004 to oppose India Shining. Provocatively called *Aam aadmi ko kya mila*, or What did the common man gain?, the emotive campaign channeled the feeling of being left behind, of being excluded from the forward march of a nation on the move. As would be clear from the slogan itself, the campaign set out to voice the discontent brewing over increasing wealth disparity, socioeconomic gaps, and the triumph of the privileged.

The campaign was noteworthy on several counts. First, in contrast to the India Shining visuals assembled in vivid, striking colors, the

Aam aadmi visuals were in shades of black and white, creating a stark, austere appearance. If the colorful India Shining ads sought to depict modernity via an accelerated present firmly tied to the future,[61] Aam aadmi ads stirred up the uncomfortable past from which the present was unable to disconnect. Absent in these visuals were objects such as computers, industrial machinery, mobile phones, and other devices, which India Shining deployed as a means to convey progress and technofutures. Second, the hope, happiness, and satisfaction visible in India Shining was replaced in Aam aadmi by a sense of dejection and hopelessness. The subjects in these photographs rarely look into the camera; their eyes remain downcast; and expressions of angst and uncertainty are conspicuous. Third, the catchy slogan itself was posed in the interrogative form, which questioned the promises and claims of prosperity made by the ruling government. If one of the advertisements reminded the public about the failure of the government to provide the five-crore jobs it had earlier promised, another raised the issues of higher education and diminishing possibilities for the young generation. The interrogative form unsettled the poetic narrative of economic reforms that India Shining had publicized. It successfully questioned what the common man had gained, or rather failed to gain, from the growing prosperity that the rising macroindicators signaled.

The last feature of the Aam aadmi campaign is probably the most telling, however, and the one that has been mostly overlooked—the ways in which the campaign reproduced the language and logic of the India Shining campaign even while seeming to oppose it. Consider the language of loss and gain to the individual, a hallmark of India Shining, which was internalized in the Aam aadmi campaign. The discourse of public good and welfare for all was replaced by that of profit for one's self. Similarly, the campaign never questioned the logic of the economic reforms themselves, which privileged economic growth over equitable distribution within the population. To be sure, the Congress Party, the chief architect of the 1991 economic reforms that paved the way for the emergence of the kind of prosperity and consumption featured in the India Shining campaign, could hardly be expected to do that. The only battle it could engage in with the BJP was about bringing more reforms and managing capital more efficiently. In a surprise electoral upset, the Congress Party was able to successfully spin the rhetoric of India Shining to make it seem like a political liability. When the Congress-led United Progressive Alliance (UPA) formed a government in 2004, the blame for the BJP's electoral loss was attributed to India Shining images that were said to have presented a false impression of prosperity and well-being to the people.

We might ask if the electoral defeat of the BJP signaled the demise of the iconic India Shining campaign. At first this would appear to be the case, as the BJP distanced itself from the images that had been popularly identified as the cause of its defeat. The website was erased without leaving any trace, and any leftover digital links that might connect the political party to India Shining had also been carefully removed. This act of erasure could indeed be read as a symbolic death, or more accurately, the consignment of India Shining into the waste bin of history. Yet on closer examination it becomes obvious that the notion of the failure of India Shining is a conflation: it misreads electoral failure as the failure of the idea of capitalist growth itself. To pick the two apart, one needs to trace the decade between the closure of the India Shining campaign in 2004 and the beginning of Narendra Modi's *Acche din* campaign in the 2014 general elections. What becomes palpable is the way the idea of capitalist growth presented as the India growth story took firm root in the Indian sociopolitical landscape.

That the logic of growth was now the inner logic of political mobilization was revealed in the very opposition to the India Shining campaign. The Congress Party's *Aam aadmi ko kya mila* campaign, as I have shown, mirrored the language of profit and self-interest over that of the collective, which had become the hallmark of India Shining images. The political claim of the Congress Party was based on its credentials as the original party of reforms and its experience as the successful manager of capital in the first decade of reforms. What the Congress Party now promised was more reforms and consequently greater growth, which the NDA government had been unable to deliver. During the two terms (2004–2014) of the Congress-led UPA government, this promise to bring more growth—albeit people friendly, or "reforms with a human face"—became the prime policy prescription. The difference was that the old question of growth was now tied in this period to the question of distribution of growth. In short, the Congress Party offered the same model that it had originally introduced in the 1990s but with a difference—it articulated the need for greater distribution of gains from reforms to the common man.

To be sure, the political consensus around the question of economic growth in various gradations goes beyond the Congress-BJP contestations. The political parties across the spectrum, including regional parties, have been keen on establishing their probusiness and progrowth credentials following the example of Modi's Vibrant Gujarat initiative and Chandrababu Naidu's transformation of Hyderabad into a hub of cybertechnology. Even the state of West Bengal, ruled by the Communist Party of India (Marxist), sought to rebrand itself as the hub of special economic zones, although that strategy ultimately led to the downfall of the state government following conflict with farmers over land acquisition. In 2006, Kamal Nath, then minister of commerce and industry, had accurately remarked, "Irrespective of the occasional grumbling about liberalization, Indians want more reform. This paradigm shift in public perception is the greatest guarantee that the reforms process is irreversible."[62] In other words, the spirit of prosperity embodied in the India Shining images not only remained intact but became more influential in the intervening decade.

The most forceful manifestation of the indelibility of the India Shining images is the success of Modi's 2014 electoral campaign. The campaign built on and eventually usurped public anger and frustration in the form of the India Against Corruption movement, which ultimately led to the formation of the Aam Aadmi Party. The public disenchantment over unfulfilled promises and wasted opportunities was articulated around the agenda of anticorruption, because corruption had been identified as the prime cause of India's failure to grow. In this politically volatile mood, the uplifting promise of *acche din* was offered by the Modi campaign. This notion was both vague and exhilarating; it was deliberately kept undefined to allow its consumers to create their personalized dreamworlds of good times. The one concrete and uncontested thing in the idea of good times was the expected mode of arrival, via successful economic reforms.

During the campaign, Modi had successfully positioned himself as the agent of good times.[63] This turnaround is crucial especially because the BJP—pushed by the *Swadeshi Jagran Manch* (Forum for the Awakening of Swadeshi),[64] an offshoot of *Rashtriya Swayamsevak Sangh* (RSS), or National Volunteer Organization, to promote self-reliance rather than opening up to foreign investments—was ambivalent about the neoliberal economic project. Groups such as Swadeshhi Jagran Manch shared the Left's opposition to the market economy even if the former's argumentation was based on indigeneity and self-reliance. The ideological opposition of the Left was not much of a surprise; more significant was how the *swadeshi* argument became the locus for countering the liberalization program in its first decade. An equally important development in the second decade of liberalization was how, in a complete volte-face, RSS made economic reforms a part of its political agenda. This turnaround in the economic policy of RSS, the parent organization of the BJP, sought to align the party with the global trend of right-wing neoliberal discourse on the one hand and to counter the strong proreform credentials of the Congress Party on the other. The fact that the Congress Party had facilitated the opening up of the Indian economy in 1991 meant that it was considered the natural party of reforms in the popular sphere. If this policy rearrangement helped the RSS/BJP to counter the political appeal of the Congress Party among the reform-minded middle class, it also augured a more or less consensual space in which the opposition to the reforms assumed a token form. This shift was enabled by first creating an internal consensus within the RSS that is still occasionally seen as the roadblock to full reforms. The logic that underpinned this change was the prospect of appealing to a broader electoral constituency of the reform-minded public that did not necessarily adhere to the agenda of cultural conservatism. The current *sarsanghchalak*, or chief of RSS, Mohan Bhagwat, is said to have altered the status quo when he unambiguously stated to a group of industrialists, soon after Modi was selected as the BJP's prime ministerial candidate, that the RSS was "not opposed to liberalization, privatization and FDI. . . .

Times change and views should change with the times as well"[65] This much-publicized change in stance addressed two concerns at once. First, it allayed middle-class anxiety about price inflation, diminishing employment opportunities, and general economic gloom. And second, it helped divert attention from public scrutiny over the 2002 Gujarat violence, from which Modi has never been fully able to distance himself.[66] As growth and development became the core ingredients of the carefully manufactured Brand Modi, it became easier for foreign governments and agencies that had thus far held back from Modi to move beyond the 2002 violence. That the BJP under Modi transformed itself into a more dependable facilitator of capital, thereby wresting the reforms agenda from the Congress Party, is a significant development in the history of India's economic reforms. Consider the ironic twist that could hardly have been imagined in 1990s—the Congress Party, the original party of economic reforms, is now deemed to be less committed to its own economic agenda in relation to the BJP. This change in perception is often blamed on the Congress Party policy of reforms with a human face that allowed concessions such as the Food Security Bill and right to work schemes to provide subsidized food and one hundred days of work, respectively, to the poorest citizens. In this shifting map of liberalization, the BJP has now assumed the mantle of the most reform-minded party.

The day Modi won the electoral battle, he sent out a single tweet—*"Acche din aa gaye,"* or "The good times have arrived"—that became the most retweeted in India's social media history. Clearly, the message that good times are intertwined with capitalist growth had been etched powerfully in the public consciousness to an extent that it became a matter of common sense even though the BJP had carefully erased any association with the India Shining images. Although less spectacular than the original India Shining icons, the idea of good times had even more effectively repackaged the tantalizing prospects of the future that capitalist growth held. In short, the icons of good times had found a new, enduring life-form harnessed firmly to the ever-enchanting dreamworlds of capitalism.

The overarching question I have pursued in this chapter is what the controversial failure of the spectacular India Shining publicity campaign constitutes in the *longue durée* of India's postreform history. If the productive value of the spectacle is in capturing attention and creating enchanting dreamworlds[67] where the idea of the good times to which human beings forever aspire is firmly harnessed to the magic of capitalist growth, then what does the deliberate erasure of the entire website as well as campaign images from the internet and the complete disassociation of the political party that commissioned the campaign mean?

Guy Debord's conception of spectacle offers an opening for discussion. For Debord,[68] spectacle signifies the transformation of all "that was once directly lived" into representation, and life under capitalism itself is "an immense accumulation of spectacles" in which appearances mask reality even while projecting a unified worldview of the dominant powers. The making of the spectacle presupposes a split, an alienation of humanity from its very essence that—as Feurbach pointed out—leaves behind an empty shell, an incomplete version of itself.[69] If the spectacle veils reality, then what does its obliteration or disintegration signify—the disclosure of a more organic, enchanting social world unmediated by images and commodities? If the hope was that the spectacle in disintegration would reveal the organic reality that had been masked by mere appearances seeking to mimic reality, then that hope remained unrealized. Instead of recovering a lived reality unmediated by appearances, we find ourselves questioning Debord's idea that such an organic, unmediated social world exists to begin with.

To be sure, the campaign was deemed to be a success for several months, following which it was incorporated into the BJP's electoral campaign and even translated across the nation into L. K. Advani's *Bharat Uday Yatra* (literally, India Rising/Shining Journey). The talk of failure was more a retrospective commentary, an afterthought that came to define India Shining after the BJP's stunning electoral defeat. The beautiful dreamworld of India Shining was blamed not only for causing the BJP's electoral failure but also for being a failed project per se and for circulating false images of prosperity. The publicity itself was an act of concealment in that it masked the state of deprivation in the nation, as its critics argued.

The perception of failure evolved within the double work of the spectacle—its productive value in bringing to the fore the potential of a good life and simultaneously revealing to people their distance from that life and the difficulty they face in realizing it. Here we witness how—unlike Debord's spectators, who presumably can be duped into taking the spectacle at face value—the spectator-consumers of India Shining demonstrated more awareness of the vast gap that separated them from the good times depicted in the images. Despite this recognition, the dream and prospects of a good life remained vibrant. What emerged unscathed from the ashes of India Shining is the notion of good times, most recently in the form of *acche din*, which BJP rode to a landslide victory a decade later in the 2014 general elections.

Even during the height of the India Shining controversy, the critics[70] never offered an alternative dreamworld in which the masses could imagine a different path to a good life. The simmering resentment at being excluded was instead redirected by the proreform challenger, the Congress Party, toward paving the way for a further opening up of the Indian economy.

Thus, the investor-citizen, the extraordinary Aam aadmi, who privileges personal gain as a form of nation building, has become a lasting legacy of India Shining. This figure has defined the kind of self-centered, middle-class politics that has gained strength in the Indian polity. It is not a coincidence that the 2011 anticorruption movement was mobilized on a shared mistrust of the political class that had allowed crony capitalism, bled the nation's wealth through corruption, scared away foreign investors, and thus slowed down the pace of economic reforms.

It is telling that the exclusion depicted in the Aam aadmi campaign never transformed into resentment and anger that challenged the structures of inequality. It was more like a knock on the door of prosperous India to be let in than a call for radical political change. In this edifice of opposition, the gradual shift to a dreamworld facilitated by capitalism became apparent. It is in the very spectacle of disintegration[71] of India Shining—its memorable failure—that we witness the withering away of the old order, even as its logic steadily takes root in the Indian social landscape.

CHAPTER 5

THE MAGICAL MARKET

IF YOU VISIT the World Economic Forum (WEF) annual meeting in Davos—the famous "magic mountain" in the Swiss Alps—you will most likely be beckoned to "Join India, Lead the World" at the India Adda lounge. This proposal, composed in many lyrical ways since 2011, has been displayed prominently on giant posters on Promenade, the main arterial street in Davos, and around the WEF convention center. The message is often creatively displayed in mobile form—as eye-catching advertisements displayed on local buses crisscrossing the town. The graphics on buses are arranged so that the "India Adda" inscription appears on doors and windows. The passengers about to board the bus are greeted by an India Adda invitation, as though they are rehearsing their potential entry into India. The signs of India are widely scattered—from buses, billboards on walls, bus shelters, and parking lots to colorful pamphlets distributed in public places—all within the visual reach of most visitors. If you are unsure about the nature of this invitation, then look for clues embedded in the publicity script. Here the nation is reinscribed in the affective language of promise and potentiality. Consider the publicity taglines: "India: Ancient Civilization, Young Nation: Build Your Future with Us" (2011), "India: 500 million under 25 Years of Age: Ambitious, Talented, Focused" (2012), "India:

Aspirational Nation of Potential and Promise: Land of Limitless Opportunity" (2013), "India: World's Largest Middle Class Consumer Market by 2030" (2014), and "From Satellites to Submarines: Whatever You Want to Make, Make in India" (2015). India, a pioneer in the field of nation publicity, can be visited on the premises of Café Schneider, where the colorful India Adda lounge exhibits the nation's enticing promise and potential in the global markets.

To an outsider, the nature of exchange performed in this global marketplace may not be readily apparent. After all, the India Adda does not exhibit any specific material either manufactured and designed in or even extracted from Indian territorial enclosure. The usual assemblage of artifacts—objects, art installations, curios, and commodities—that visitors to exhibitions or shopping malls expect to set their gaze on are absent. The lounge, in fact, is sparsely furnished in the global aesthetics of comfortable and functional offices or even airport lounges frequented by busy travelers. The "thing" offered for exchange here is the nation itself repackaged as an attractive investment destination in the global markets. The global elite are invited to explore the nation-as-commodity—Brand India—dressed up seductively as an abundant and yet untapped container of vast natural resources, a technofriendly labor force, middle-class consumption, and scientific innovation.

Adda appears here as the exotic tradition within which this showcase of investor-friendly India is designed to take place. It is mobilized not only as a mark of India's modern corporate culture but also as an Indian *mode of networking* that draws on indigenous traditions rather than imitating the corporate culture of the West. Adda, simply put, is a mode of assembling people in public or private spaces. The very practice and meaning of *adda* has undergone many genealogical shifts in the past centuries. If the nineteenth-century adda was seen as a negative practice, a waste of one's precious time in endless conversations, the twentieth-century adda was a marker of rich cultural values, good literary taste, and the art of conversation among the emerging middle class. In the twenty-first century, the practice of adda has morphed once again, this time into the logic of capital as a sign of India's market-oriented culture.

FIGURE 5.1. *India Brand Equity Foundation (IBEF) bus advertising India. Davos, 2012. Taken by author.*

I take the India Adda at Davos as an enchanting theatrical space in which Brand India's unique commercial culture is illuminated for a global audience. The adda, in its new nationalized form, stands for India's inherent liberal essence, translated and improvised into an array of desirable attributes legible to the global consumers of Brand India. I propose that the day-to-day operation of the redesigned adda allows us to witness two key transformations. First, the adda reveals how cultural difference is mobilized not only to confirm India as a mature commercial player, an old hand at the game of markets, but also to establish its inherent civilizational superiority to Western modes of commerce. The hypervisible adda iterates Brand India's potentiality and availability to investors in a highly competitive global market. It serves both as a performative frame through which India is pitched as a commodity and as a mode of translating the essence of India to a wider global audience. Second, this performance of commercial culture also discloses the shifting relations between the state and the capital in postreform India. Here we witness the emergence of the capital as a key actor—as the prime agent of resistance against Western dominance that can be effectively unshackled only via India's full shift to capitalism. It positions itself as the main promoter of India—reimagined as an investment destination—the force charged with bringing back India's glory as it continues to enrich the nation "not because of the government, but despite the government," to quote a widely popular phrase. Yet the state is reluctant to let go of its dominance, and instead it appropriates capitalist tools to augment its power and influence. The reconfigurations in the adda reflect these ongoing shifts within Brand India, which is entangled in the boom and bust of the global political economy. But we are getting ahead of ourselves here.

First, some background. The word *adda* is commonly used in several Indian languages to denote a place of gathering, dwelling, assembly, or platform. It appears in everyday life to signify a wide range of routine functions, spaces, and objects—from bus stations, wooden frames, and work platforms to a gregarious assembly of friends—intimately connected with modes of work and rest.[1] Adda also signifies a more specific form of sociability that was honed in twentieth-century Bengal. This form of adda, simply put, is the practice of friends getting together for long, informal, open-ended conversations. In his essay on adda in Calcutta, Dipesh Chakrabarty traces the history of this social practice, which came to be seen as the quintessential feature of urban life of Bengal—a vital signal of life and one's very sense of metaphysical being.[2] The routine performance of adda as a literary and political enterprise became a much-desired marker of rich cultural value among the emerging middle class in the early twentieth century. The notion of adda before that, or for that matter in other regions of India, had not always been a celebrated cultural trait. In northern India, the word *adda* is associated with a range of mundane functions if not outright negative personal qualities. The etymological tensions are evident in this nineteenth-century Hindi/Urdu dictionary entry that described *adda* as "the shed or place in which *kahars*, palanquin bearers, carters assemble or abide; stand; station, assembly room; lounge or meeting place of idlers or pleasure seekers; a square frame for embroidery; perch of a bird cage; heel of a shoe; one of the (usually) two divisions of land watered by a well."[3]

Although some of these meanings carry a trace of rural life in a time when the primacy of manual labor had not yet been displaced by modern technologies of production and transport, the description of "idlers" or "pleasure seekers" offers insight into a prevalent work ethic laden with moral disapproval of those appearing to shirk labor. The semantic associations of adda with laziness, rowdiness, and moral vices remain intact in many North Indian languages in which the practice was never fully reconfigured into a middle-class vocation. The recovery of adda in twentieth-century Bengal as a respectable social form was made possible only through its association with the public spaces of production of modern reading publics—a cultivated idleness as an alternative to industrial productivity. It is this lively version of adda as a social practice that the visitors to Davos were invited to participate in. We might ask what kind of enterprise is signaled in this convivial invitation to talk about India in global publicity? And what work is assigned to the form of *adda* once the prefix *India* is added to it in a setting such as Davos? This inquiry becomes all the more relevant given that adda has been perceived to be dying for some decades now and that its imminent expiration has been the subject of mourning and nostalgia, especially among Bengali intellectuals. For Chakrabarty, nostalgia for the perceived loss of adda is not a sign of error but an unarticulated sign of anxiety caused by the desire to retain a sense of one's self in the ever-changing currents of capitalist modernization.[4] If nostalgia for adda indeed is a sign of modernist angst, then how are we to read its recovery from the very edge of nostalgia and its colorful revival in a location such as Davos? The recovery of adda, as we will find, precisely entails its reification as a natural form of sociability in Indian public life and its amplification as an attention-grabbing practice in the fast-paced circuits of global capital.

ADDA, DAVOS

I was drawn to the adda at Davos during my fieldwork in Delhi. Since 2009, I had been following the work of nation-branding experts tasked with generating global publicity for Brand India. In 2011, the pace and enthusiasm of the experts seemed to have quickened. India Adda at Davos, I was told, was the new initiative that would finally showcase the magical effect of the fabled India story on a global scale. The popular refrain was, "If you truly want to see India's arrival on the world stage, you should go to the WEF annual meeting in Davos." This was clearly an exciting and very busy moment, and it was soon to become a high point on the annual calendar of Delhi-based advertising agencies. The India Adda, I learned, was designed to entrench India's position as an attractive investment destination following its global debut in 2006 in the form of the India Everywhere campaign launched in Davos. The story of India's spectacular debut at Davos has itself become somewhat of a legend in branding circles by now. Ajay Khanna, then CEO of India Brand Equity Foundation (IBEF)—a public-private partnership between the Ministry of Commerce and the Confederation of Indian Industries (CII, the agency charged with promoting Brand India among global investors)—recounted this story when I met him in Delhi.[5] According to him, India Everywhere was coscripted by Nandan Nilekani, the CEO of Infosys, the corporation that had come to symbolize New India's entrepreneurial ambitions as well as his own. Ajay recalled the moment when they choreographed India's appearance as the "new economic superstar" in the world.

> "Nandan and I were in Davos in 2005 and felt that there was too much focus on China. India wasn't visible. When we came back from Davos, we met at the Taj Palace coffee shop in early February to make a strategy—how can we promote India? It is not easy to brand a country of India's size and diversity to position it so that the world's perceptions improve. Nandan then wrote on a paper napkin 'world's fastest growing free market democracy' to list India's unique advantages. It all made sense. Indeed India was experiencing high growth rates, had a vibrant democracy, but the world wasn't aware of it. We had to let the world know that India was open for business."[6]

India Everywhere was the campaign designed to change the world's perceptions. The *New York Times* reported on the campaign as follows: "There were few places one could go, on this first day of the World Economic Forum's annual meeting here, without seeing, hearing, drinking, or tasting something India. . . . The total cost of the campaign and travel expenses [is] $5 million. Never before, officials of the forum said, has a country mounted such an elaborate charm offensive at Davos."[7]

The unprecedented branding exercise reported as "the most ambitious, artful, and extravagant in the country's history" began at the Zurich airport, where giant billboards announcing the "world's fastest growing free market democracy" greeted the WEF delegates.[8] And when they reached their hotel rooms in Davos, the delegates found complimentary gifts waiting for them, including Pashmina shawls, a "gift from the Himalayas to keep you warm in the Alps"; a tiny Apple iPod with Indian music; and an India promotional CD.[9] The accompanying card invited delegates to "experience India" in all its shades—its "vibrant democracy, robust economy, competitive industry, [and] rich culture."[10] This "charm offensive" was carried out by the 150-member Indian delegation, which included government officials "all intelligent and articulate, and all selling their country," 41 captains of Indian industry, and 3 cabinet ministers.[11] In 2006, India had become the talk of the town, the front-runner in the economic race with China, and the place to be for global investors. As *India Today* further reported, "For the first time Indians, from being the guests at Davos, had become the hosts."[12] India was now at home in Davos, and in the world, as an attractive emerging market on an upward swing. Indian policy makers and CEOs were featured prominently on WEF debate panels and in exclusive breakfast sessions hosted by leading investment consortiums. The title of *Newsweek*'s article about the event read, "New India: Asia's Other Powerhouse Steps Out," and the magazine featured the glamorous New York–based Indian model Padma Lakshmi on its cover. This was the moment of India's long-anticipated arrival on the global stage. The adda at Davos was conceived to consolidate this euphoric moment, to keep the momentum going in India's favor in many creative ways.

As I prepared for my visit to Davos, it seemed a familiar world at first. After all, the name *Davos* is scattered in the media in a variety of contexts. If the Davos-Klosters landscape is a popular fixture in gossip magazines as the preferred haunt of the world's wealthy elite, it has gained even more visibility in its negative form, "anti-Davos," which has spawned several anticapitalist social movements in the Global South.[13] The sign of Davos has long stood for the unhindered march of capitalism in social theory.[14] It is invoked to signal not only enormous income

and wealth disparity but also the outsized influence of wealth and privilege on government policy around the world.[15] The WEF meeting annually reinforces the innate association of the world's billionaires with
Davos, their favorite habitat. This is hardly surprising given that the
WEF is an exclusive, by-invitation-only private club whose members
are the corporations with an average turnover of over $5 billion.[16] The
annual membership fee ranges between $60,000 to $600,000, allowing different kinds of perks and levels of access.[17] The basic ticket itself
costs about $19,000 over and above the membership fee.[18] The visitors
to WEF Davos, then, can expect to mingle with the world's wealthy fi-
nanciers—the top leaders of corporations and institutions who are offered access to the invited heads of state and influential celebrities. The
WEF, established by Klaus Schwab, an enterprising management professor, has evolved over the past four decades from a forum for Swiss
businesses to "the international organization for public-private cooper-
ation" that is "committed to improving the state of the world."[19] It sees
itself as the agent of world progress "by bringing together people from
all walks of life who have the drive and the influence to make positive change."[20] Yet this stated altruism is not what steers the actual operation of the WEF annual meeting. Its main attraction remains its
global status as the high-profile "festival of networking" celebrated by
the world's rich and influential people.[21]

Davos, seemingly familiar and close because of incessant media ex-
posure, was remote and nearly inaccessible when I began figuring out
my travel plans. The basic tip I received from my acquaintances in Delhi
was to fly to Zurich and then take a bus or train to Davos Platz Station. It seemed simple enough until I arrived at the Zurich airport for
the first time in January 2012. The public route to Davos was shielded
in elaborate security arrangements, given the assembly of some of the
world's most influential and important people in one place. Unable to
figure out how to make my way to Davos, I reluctantly approached the
WEF help desk. A young woman at the desk asked me the purpose of
my visit to WEF Davos. I told her that I was an academic working on
the history of economic reforms in India and that I wanted to see the
India Adda pavilion in Davos. I wasn't sure whether she fully grasped

the details I offered, but she helpfully offered me a seat on the WEF bus about to leave for Davos Platz. At first, I wondered whether the fact that I spoke fluent English and had remembered to bring items that visibly mark class—for example, an iPhone and a handcrafted leather bag with an understated monogram—had played a part in gaining me a seat on the bus. It was only later that I realized how this short interaction at the help desk had revealed an important feature of how social dynamics at WEF Davos unfold. The basic perception everyone seems to work from is that Davos is an assembly of important people. And turned on its head, this dictum means that anyone who assembles at WEF Davos is likely to be important. This sliver of uncertainty shapes how strangers interact with each other. The *uncertain potential*, which can't be readily dismissed, almost guarantees politeness and best behavior, because "you never know if the stranger sitting next to you is a CEO of a Fortune 500 company, high ranking bureaucrat, or famous author" in the hope of making valuable networks. This uncertainty, most likely, got me a seat on the WEF bus meant for its delegates. I was probably taken to be a potentially important person from India.

Like me, my copassengers on the WEF bus were not the famed billionaires we read about. The billionaires, as I later learned, take a short helicopter ride of about thirty minutes to Davos. The free bus service was provided by the WEF mainly for media professionals, social entrepreneurs, young global leaders, and academics.[22] During the journey of about two hours, I got acquainted with an Indian entrepreneur who sold lightbulb kits powered by solar energy to poor households, a vice chancellor of a major European university, an enthusiastic graduate of an Ivy League college who wanted to change the world—this young person was called a "global leader" by the WEF—as well as media correspondents who were regular visitors to Davos. The WEF bus smoothly passed all the security checkpoints installed to monitor traffic entering Davos. The driver dropped us at the WEF reception center, where invited participants could receive the all-important badges, their key to an exclusive world. We parted ways here. India Adda, my destination, thankfully was not located inside the high-security convention center that was accessible only to those wearing official badges. India

Adda was located on the bustling main street of Davos—open to the public, just as the invitation had suggested.

WASTE TO VALUE

The path uphill from the WEF Convention Center toward the Promenade is dotted with landmarks such as the exclusive Hotel Belvedere, the Kirchner Museum, upmarket boutiques, and busy cafés. On this lively street, Café Schneider is ensconced to the left overlooking the mountain peaks. India Adda assembles annually in a specially marked area of Café Schneider, a nearly century-old cafe that ostentatiously describes itself as "die grand dame" of Davos coffeehouses, the old haunt of global celebrities and visitors in search of an authentic European coffeehouse experience.[23] Visitors to the India Adda can enter directly from the main street through a glass door decorated with giveaway signs of India—*phool booti* (flower) motifs in earthy deep-red hues framing the silhouettes of elephants dressed in ceremonial gear. A wooden sign at the entrance displays a graphic image of people holding hands in an ever-widening infinite circular loop. The inscription beneath the signboard reads "Adda—Join in the conversations on India, Widen your circle."

That the idea of adda is meant to invoke an open, harmonious, and level playing field is evident at the entrance itself. The graphic image of human figures at the door joined together in a circle of friendship in a seemingly infinite loop signals unlimited possibilities and potentialities. This sense of openness was reinforced when I stepped inside the adda. Only later would I discover that the adda was actually split into two zones—*andar* (inside) and *bahar* (outside). The inside was the private space in which the minister of commerce or high-ranking bureaucrats from the Ministry of Commerce would meet potential investors. The outside was the public space in which the act of seeing and showing India would be rehearsed. I was in this public space where all visitors were invited to experience India. The pièce de résistance in this spacious sitting area is a wall plastered with colorful imagery of New India on the ascent. The cheerful images, I was told by one of the organizers, were of ordinary Indians who have tasted the fruits of liberalization. To the left was an image of a young woman in what seemed like a university setting holding a smart tablet, *Aakash* ($35 only), developed and manufactured indigenously in India.[24] And to the right was the image of a cheerful farmer atop a tractor in a mustard field, his arms suggestively stretched heavenward as if in the embrace of progress. The inscription beside him indicated that he was the beneficiary of an indigenously developed drip-irrigation kit for farmers ($160 only) that weaned him off his dependence on unreliable seasonal rains. In between these two images appeared a stylistically arranged bold sign announcing "India Adda" followed by this inscription:

> The "adda" is the quintessential Indian hangout intricately woven into the country's social fabric. This is where bonds are built, games are played and dreams are dreamt and shared.

At first, the inscription seemed to work as a translation of the idea of adda for a global audience. Yet a closer look revealed an ongoing shift in the very meaning and function of adda—rather than being a *wasteful* practice, it is pitched as a *valuable* form of sociability that can be harnessed to market needs. Recall that adda has not always been a desirable form of social interaction. Prior to its nineteenth-century recovery as a literary endeavor, the adda was associated with noisy, disruptive behavior of young men in the urban neighborhoods of Calcutta. The young men who gathered on *rowak*, the raised platforms built around houses, to hold their boisterous adda often caused discontent in the neighborhood, as middle-class residents viewed these gatherings as a threat to their respectability.[25] The perceived negative consequences of adda did not end at neighborhood conflicts but also extended to supposed idleness and useless talk among the young men. Dipesh Chakrabarty has shown how critical attitudes to adda were built not only on the capitalist colonial theme of the lazy native but also on preexisting notions of what work and idleness constituted. Although the association of adda with these negative traits was somewhat disrupted on its rediscovery as a desirable cultural value linked with

literary production in Calcutta and as conversation as an aesthetic end
in itself, it never completely overcame moralistic overtones in parts of
north India, where adda is still seen as a waste of precious time.

In Davos, the adda is fully recovered from negative associations.
Instead, it is pitched as "a cool way to project that we [Indians] are
people who do business in a friendly, peaceful and non-threatening
way," which was an obvious allusion to its rival and neighbor, China.[26]
Aparna Dutta Sharma, the CEO of IBEF, told me in a somewhat busi-
nesslike manner that "adda offers a unique Indian experience of networking, making new friends, and creating new ideas." The practice
of adda was thus rearranged in a different species of global practice—
of corporate networking, albeit with an Indian difference—considered
fundamental and indispensable to business transactions. This unique
Indian experience of networking is what the practice of adda was now
mobilized toward. Consider this promotional invitation:

> The Indian Adda at the World Economic Forum takes this concept of idea
> exchange and conversations to a different level. The Indian Adda is more than
> a physical space, it is a concept of sharing and communications—an ambience
> that encourages the free and frank exchange of views. It is meant for sharing.
> For networking. Or just for soaking in the atmosphere and enjoying Indian
> hospitality. Hope to see you there.[27]

Central to this shift is the art of conversation, which is now assigned a dramatically different function to perform. Instead of being
a sign of idleness or a waste of precious time, it has been transformed
into a productive mode of labor as innovative ideation or even corporate-style brainstorming. To engage in conversations at the India Adda
now is to engage in the profitable task of generating value for the nation. In fact, the very capitalist notions of efficiency, production, and
"time is money" are turned on their heads. The adda invites the captains of industry and top policy makers, highly esteemed individuals
who barely have a minute to spare, to take *time out* and let go. In a 24-7
world constantly on the move (Wark), the most precious gift one can
offer is the time to relax, to take a rare pause that promises to replen-
ish one's energy. Adda represents this global space of rejuvenation, and

India is the large-hearted sponsor of such luxury. India, as the host of adda, positions itself as the chief patron of important exchanges in the global arena.

In this global translation, the adda was always carefully framed as more than a utilitarian tool for corporate networking. It was an authentic sign of Indianness, of its unique commercial culture. That the adda was a matter of the heart, an exclusive marker of Indian difference, and that India itself was a large-hearted nation were sentiments that were frequently articulated during my visit. For this claim to be effective, adda had to be reconceptualized as a metaphysical identity widely shared by Indians. Aparna Dutta Sharma cited the indelible "romance" of adda as the existential core of being Indian and, therefore, the perfect cultural frame to display India abroad.

> The idea of adda is exactly the way it is, every nook and corner of India has an adda. Typically you see in a city like Bombay people pull out benches and sit down. It is like a *nukkad* [street corner] thing. Every *nukkad* will be dotted with benches and chairs. Invariably for all you may say, whether you are urbane or not urbane, an Indian is an Indian at heart. There are some things that are very close to you, things that are common—like spontaneity in India. India is innately about adda, chairs, and conversations. Adda provides an ambience and makes people comfortable.[28]

In this reconceptualization, adda was taken very broadly to indicate any gathering in a public space—from a street corner or park to an open space in an urban neighborhood—that might potentially result in social interaction. Its main characteristic is said to be spontaneity, a natural impulse that brings people together without premeditation or design, an indication of the deep-seated inner desire to connect with others. Although comparisons with similar forms of socialization in the West—for example, salons and coffeehouse gatherings—are not explicitly made, it is quite clear that a relational Indian difference seeks to be created through the rhetorical deployment of emotions and spontaneity that places adda in the metaphysical domain and invests it with a greater emotive depth and substance. This notion of adda seems to invoke the idea of an ancient art of conversation in which even the unlettered are accomplished masters. The visions of chairs and benches being drawn to fill up street corners and of an unceasing public conversation conjure a sense of civic orderliness and passionate civility as naturally occurring features of India. Adda was thus positioned as a quintessential feature of India that is not only inextricably enmeshed in the social structure but also deeply inculcated with the very sense of being Indian. It is tantalizingly held as a kind of key that opens up intricacies of the social order and modes of being in everyday life in India. The key lay in the articulation of adda as a *hangout*, an easy and globally accessible term that instantly strikes a chord. It is defined as an open, playful space in which unrestricted imagination, ideas, and innovations take shape. This aspect of adda as an enabler of visionary ideas is crucial, as it helps establish innovation and imagination as natural parts of a playful Indian lifestyle. Implicit in this description is the nature of adda as an uncomplicated, democratic space in which people gather and partake in conversations. This emphasis on openness, freedom, and a democratic ethos is entangled in the evolving narrative of New India as the "world's fastest growing free market democracy." To this end, the adda offered a theatrical performance of democracy, and that too in a setting that is not the chaotic, dusty, noisy, and crowded space of India's actual democracy. Consider this official description:

> Amongst the hubbub of conversations sparked by minds meeting across continents, relationships were renewed, fresh bonds were built, and the awareness spread that India means business. . . . And everyone who visited the India Adda went away with India's message firmly etched in their minds. And in their hearts.[29]

Note how the success of the adda is linked not only to its capacity to enhance India's commercial value but also to its capacity to build affective connections. The invocation of "hearts" here raises the stakes. It seems as though the adda is expected to activate a deeper sentimental commitment among foreign investors rather than a purely rational economic engagement prone to cycles of boom and bust. Brand India not only seeks global capital flows but also wants to be loved by its consumers.

This frequent weaving of affective language—of hearts, friendships, relationships, and hospitality—in the quest for foreign investments sometimes seems innocuous, inconsequential, or even misplaced. Yet it hints at a deliberate ambivalence, camouflage, or perhaps plain discomfort in the project of *selling* India to foreign investors. The reluctance to present adda as a purely instrumental space and yet being unable to fully integrate its noninstrumental implications is apparent. This probably stems from the ambiguities and splits inherent in the Indian difference that the adda is meant to signify in which soaring Indian culture seems to be constructed in opposition to Western materialism. In the ideal version of Indian hospitality—*atithi devo bhave*, the guest is akin to God—the presence of a guest is considered the true test of the host's generosity and may even involve a degree of sacrifice, as the needs of the guest must assume priority.[30] The very notion of *atithi* is derived from the negation of the Sanskrit word *tithi*, which literally means "time/date or some form of certainty." This means that *atithi* by definition is someone whose arrival and departure is not predetermined and whose very presence may test the limits of the host's benevolence. Thus, true hospitality is deemed to be that which does not enter the cycle of exchange and reciprocity and is offered without creating a sense of obligation.[31] This idealized version of Indian hospitality, incidentally, underpins the internal marketing campaign within India— *atithi devo bhave*, launched by the Ministry of Tourism—that seeks to retrain the Indian opinion and reception of foreign tourists.[32] The performance of hospitality in India Adda is fraught with these inherent contradictions. The very objective of India Adda, to market India to a global audience, means that hospitality is offered in the distinct hope of getting profitable returns in the form of investments.[33] The conflict in this project is inevitable—how does one perform the idealized version of Indian large-heartedness while pitching India as a commodity in the global marketplace?

ORDER OF THE IMAGE

Tucked amid the colorful imagery of New India was a bare wall with a flat-screen TV. This visual surface displayed in real time the actual

events being performed in the adda as well as video recordings of selected moments that had already unfolded. These included photographs, interview videos, and endorsements of New India and its market potential offered by celebrity guests who had visited India Adda.
The display was nonstop. It signaled the obsession with manufacturing
and circulating moments deemed photo worthy and valuable to Brand
India. As I watched simultaneously the events unfolding around me
and the on-screen version of those events, it was soon evident that the
TV screen wasn't merely replaying what was happening in the adda.
In fact, the adda was being constantly rearranged so as to create the
proper image worth displaying. The constantly flickering visual surface revealed how the logic of image production arranged the actual
events in the adda. The performance of adda was subject to *social editing*
exercised to blur, hide, enhance, or boost individuals and events. This
control mechanism was geared to manufacture perfect moments that
could enter the image frame. This meant that spontaneity and openness, publicized as a sign of Indian essence, had to be scripted in advance. This a priori dissonance invites us to think along the lines of
what William Mazzarella calls "performative dispensations" enacted
by an ambiguous sovereign power that is both patron and police, or at
once "the umbrella under which the performance may take place and
the weapon that crushes those who challenge its integrity."[34] But what
enables policing as well as ways to escape it is the peculiar condition
within which the performative space of adda operates in Davos. India Adda at once facilitates face-to-face interaction and mass-mediated
publicity of that interaction. This meant that the patron could police
the actual physical space but not always the space of mass publicity.
The censorial role of the patron was thus layered in these manifold ambiguities and gaps. The tensions and conflicts in disciplining what was
publicized as an inherently liberated, and liberating, form of sociability then were inevitable.

The first time I visited the India Adda, a courteous young woman
received me at the door. She was warm and pleasant in the manner of
someone trained to welcome strangers and make them feel at home.
Despite her easy demeanor, her ambivalence about where to place me

FIGURE 5.2. *The images of VIP visitors were displayed on a large screen at the center of the lounge. Here, David Cameron visits India Adda. 2012. Taken by author.*

in the hierarchy of guests was apparent. I didn't seem to fit in any of the usual categories of visitors to whom India's hospitality was extended. I was neither a recognizable global celebrity nor a billionaire investor who would add glory to the adda. The likelihood that I was an Indian government official or media correspondent or, better still, a social entrepreneur of some worth was swiftly dismissed when she handed me her business card. The ritual demanded that I return the courtesy by offering my business card, and via this exchange of cards I identified myself as a university academic writing about the history of postreform India. This position was evidently not without merit, I could tell, but the fact that I was not from a business school, which would have made me the preferred type of guest, meant that no clear value could be affixed to my presence. This rapid assessment enabled me to partake in the rituals of hospitality in the adda. India was the host of this convivial gathering, where guests were nourished via a range of corporate sponsorships. The super-deluxe ITC hotel chain served piping hot Indian delicacies from its famous Bukhara restaurant; the Tea and Coffee Boards of India presented exclusive selections of tea, coffee, and spicy chocolates; and a gift set of Indian wines by Sula Wines was reserved for very special guests. The courteous young woman ensured the guests were well looked after in a style befitting a generous and playful host. Yet the unofficial hierarchy of guests was readily visible in the way guests were encouraged to enter or stay out of the image frame.

Foreign investors were the most treasured guests at the adda. This was hardly a surprise given that the adda had been set up primarily to draw the attention of this very group. What was more intriguing was the double role of the figure of the investor—foreign and domestic— at the adda. The investors here were not merely actual brokers of financial deals; they were valuable objects of display whose presence at the adda was exhibited and circulated widely in global publicity materials. To invoke Walter Benjamin here, the bodily presence of the foreign investor at the adda signaled more than just the possibility of financial transactions—it accrued exhibition value to India's status as an investment destination that in turn anticipated the generation of even more financial investments. The investor-guests at the adda, then, were not mere spectators partaking in the rituals of Indian hospitality but key actors performing a crucial role as desirable guests in the script. The theatre of adda can be imagined as what Rancière calls a "theatre without spectators" in which the distinction between the audience and spectators collapsed.[35] The investor-guest was drawn in the adda script as a prime actor probably without ever fully realizing this transition.

The script *Join the Conversation on India* performed at the adda was well rehearsed. It involved a team of Indian communication experts— a journalist and a social media whiz kid besides the staff of IBEF— charged with re-creating the spirit of adda in Davos. Armed with a video camera and a microphone, a team member would approach important figures in the corporate world to generate conversations on India. The CEOs of major global companies were the most sought-after commodity in this enterprise. Consider the following scene that unfolded on the second day of adda.

A distinguished-looking American man walked in the adda. The hostess greeted him warmly and invited him in. His business card was passed on to the journalist in a side office, who jumped to her feet in visible excitement—the CEO of Tupperware, Rick Goings, was here! She moved quickly with her video camera while instructing the photographer to click pictures of this adda encounter. Goings was offered masala chai and helpfully informed about the Indian practice of adda in which people spontaneously mingle and talk. The conversation proceeded from the ubiquity of Tupperware parties in India to the journalist's mother's love for Tupperware to the crux of the matter: Brand India.

> Journalist: When I say Brand India, what does it stand for you?
> Rick: It doesn't speak to a country, it speaks to a people. I have eyes and faces come up to me when I think Brand India. I think credibility, I think intelligence, I think heart. So it's a wonderful combination of head and heart. It's part of the [Indian] culture.

This brief interview was recorded on camera against the colorful background of India Adda wallpaper. It was almost instantly streamed on the TV screen and the India Adda blog and publicized on Facebook, YouTube, and Twitter with the hashtag #Indiaadda. What was most crucial in this encounter was not what Goings said, which was mainly niceties, but his actual presence in the adda. Goings, the CEO of a global company with a turnover of more than $2 billion in annual sales, was framed together with India while sipping masala chai in the adda.[36] This moment was replayed many times over in the global circuits of publicity. His presence itself was an *endorsement*, a reiteration of the investor's belief in India's market potential. The cozy setting imbued a sense of friendly intimacy between a world-wise investor and a nation seeking to be a global investment destination.

If the irony of generating spontaneous talks via structured interview was noticed by anyone, it was surely never mentioned. The interview form remained the main mode of purposefully initiating and guiding conversations toward Brand India. While some guests, such as Goings, deemed worthy of interview-conversations had found their way to the adda by themselves, others were especially sought out to be part of the performance. A junior adda team member was often seen to be on the lookout, just outside the main door on the Promenade, for famous people who could be invited into the adda. She was especially pleased for having invited both David Cameron and Boris Johnson to the adda "for a cup of Indian tea," she told me, when they happened to be in the vicinity to launch their 2012 Britain Is Great publicity campaign. The presence of Cameron and Johnson had brought a touch of celebrity to the adda that day. The picture-perfect moment had been assembled successfully to generate a catalogue of images to boost India's global credentials.

The spectacular catalogue of images wasn't manufactured only by assembling influential guests at the adda. It also entailed keeping the "extra" guests—surplus to the enterprise of Brand India—strategically on the edges of the image frame. In the surplus category were all those who were not implicated in the investment apparatus in some way—investors, policy makers, government officials, media publicists, brokers, and financial experts. I will call them extras; their presence is crucial to the background but can never be flaunted. Like extras in the cinematic frame, they are actors who are required for the scene to come to life yet whose voices are scripted to remain mute. In this case, the performance of adda required the presence of surplus actors who would occupy sofas and chairs, engage in small talk, sample Indian delicacies, and drink masala chai. Or as one of the organizers told me, "We need the crowd to make the adda lively." But this role entailed neither recorded interviews nor an invitation to endorse or talk about India.

During my visit to the adda, I encountered an Austrian yoga instructor passing through Davos, an Indian adventurer cycling from India across Europe, friends of a well-known European TED talks speaker, a freelance journalist of Indian origin based in Europe, the wife of an Indian newspaper editor, an Indian nanny minding young children of a distinguished business consultant, minor officials accompanying

Indian business leaders, and a group of young Swiss artists from a nearby museum who visited the adda to eat free Indian food during their break, among many others. Given my status as a nonplayer in the investment game, I too belonged to this group of extras. What distinguished the extras at the India Adda from their cinematic counterparts was their lack of awareness of the role they were expected to play. Most took the idea of adda in the spirit it was publicized—an unrestrained space in which playful conversations, ideas, and bonds were shaped. But this became a point of tension and sometimes a cause for confrontation. One of the frequent lamentations voiced by the adda staff was that "there were too many Indians" who came to the adda just to eat Indian food and indulge in noisy merrymaking. "They behave as if they are still in India," was the common complaint. In contrast, the "foreigners" in the group of extras, especially those of European descent, were not subjected to the same kind of critique. Their bodily presence still bore some value as they represented the "world's love for India," a staff member told me. The Indian guests, though, had to be constantly disciplined so that the India Adda would not turn into a convivial hub of merriment. When I was talking to a visiting banker, we were told to lower our voices when we giggled during a conversation. Under watchful eyes, we took to near whispers to continue our chat. But sometimes these tensions resulted in a dramatic emotional outburst, for example, when a staff member of the CII delegation tried to evict the freelance journalist from the adda premises. The charge leveled at her was that "she was hogging too much space." The gossip being shared in hushed tones was about the journalist trying to be in every frame of the picture, getting too close to celebrity guests, and probably disrupting important business conversations. The freelance journalist indeed had been visible in the adda as she sought comments and views on India from the potential investors. She was talking about India just as the invitation had asked of the guests. And this is precisely what the CII official had found annoying; the task of talking was reserved for the prized guests, and the journalist had broken this invisible rule. The simmering tensions ended in a spectacle that was most likely never recorded on camera. After being constantly monitored and snubbed, the journalist stunned everyone. She angrily refused to be restrained by the CII functionary trying to bar her from talking with other guests. This moment of loud confrontation drew everyone's attention, including that of the minister of commerce, who was also present. He intervened to let the journalist talk to those she wanted to, if only to reiterate the idea of adda as an open democratic space. Yet this spectacle had brought to the surface the underlying antagonisms in this enterprise. Although spontaneity was publicized as the hallmark of conviviality at the adda, the project collapsed precisely when unmediated conversations began flowing. The unrestrained moment when strangers begin talking to each other was the idealized form of a unique Indian sociability. But it was this very moment of noisy chatter and plain fun that had to be constantly disciplined.

The irony and contradiction in this enterprise are all too obvious—a practice of spontaneous interaction publicized as the hallmark of Indian sociability is disclosed to be a tightly edited operation. To be sure, adda has not always been a "pure practice of democracy" or of gender and class inclusion, as Dipesh Chakrabarty has shown.[37] He traces the shifts within the genealogy of adda—from the nineteenth-century gatherings or *majlis* in *baithakkhana* of important men who acted as patrons-cum-editors-censors of the conversations that took place under their roofs to the twentieth-century adda in a public place that assembled without the hospitality of a patron. What separates these two early forms, he suggests, is the "emergence of a democratic sensibility" that was made possible precisely in the absence of patron.[38]

The twenty-first-century adda at Davos marks a sharp turn in this genealogy. First, we witness the return of the patron at the India Adda in the form of the corporatized Indian state as the main sponsor. What is noteworthy is that the outward *secession* of the censorial role of the patron-sponsor is crucial to establishing India Adda as a celebration of democratic sensibility. The public performance of spontaneity and limitless hospitality demands that the patron-sponsor exercise editorial control, albeit in a concealed mode. Second, the public performance of adda circulates beyond the actual premises in digital form, replayed infinitely via videos, photographs, press releases, and blog updates on the

FIGURE 5.3. *In 2015, the India Adda was renamed the Make in India Lounge. The lounge was decorated with colorful images of the new logo: the roaring lion. Davos, 2015. Taken by author.*

internet. This means that even if the patron-sponsor's attempts to impose order and discipline in the adda end in dramatic failure, the very mode of digital publicity allows editorial control over what images circulate in the public domain. It is as though the adda is imagined a priori as raw footage from which to select moments that can be transformed into seductive images. The objective is not just to illuminate, blur, or delete elements in order to create the perfect visual narrative of the India growth story but to funnel the images right back in order to produce the India Adda as it happens. In short, the desire to create the perfect image—of India's market attractiveness—is what seemingly created order in the open-spirited Indian hangout.

RESISTANCE INCORPORATED

An exception to this symbolic order of openness was the figure of the entrepreneur, the most prized guest, who was beyond the censorial reach of the patron. What was particularly noteworthy was how entre-preneurs had appropriated the old language of anticolonial resistance to position themselves on the forefronts of postcolonial resurgence. As we will see, the expansion of Indian capital in the West was presented as a proverbial beating-them-at-their-own-game situation, a final nail in the coffin in the history of European colonialism. In this narrative, by extending their business interests into Europe, the Indian capital was "liberating" the nation just as the anticolonial freedom fighters had once done. In short, the figure of the entrepreneur here represented not only economic power, the "prime engine of economic revival," but also the moral argument of the resurgence of the postcolony. This ex-ceptional status of entrepreneurs also accrued because CII at that time was the copatron of the adda due to its partnership with the Minis-try of Commerce in this initiative. In technical terms, the entrepre-neur was as much a host as a guest and was as responsible as the state in creating the perfect image of a market-oriented nation. The fracture in this unified body of the patron—the state-capital partnership—was revealed when the government was scrutinized in full public view and found wanting in its ability to facilitate capital smoothly. The possibil-ity for dissent, then, did exist, albeit as "repressive tolerance"—in the words of Herbert Marcuse—that allowed toleration and space when exercised by the powerful faction within the fractured self. To be able to speak freely and without fear was to signal the extent of one's power and influence. Or, to put it differently, the expression of dissent and criticism—the true spirit of adda—was a privilege exercised only by the most powerful actors, in this case, the entrepreneurs. And as we will see, the collapse of the order also revealed the ever-shifting locus of power in the state and capital dynamics in postreform India.

I turn now to a televised conversation, the 2012 India debate, that took place under the banner of *Davos Direct* on the India Adda prem-ises. ETNOW, a Mumbai-based television channel owned by the Times Group, offered direct telecasts from Davos to its viewers in In-dia on the theme of the Indian economy. The debate was hosted by Shaili Chopra (SC), a feisty business journalist, and the participants were celebrity CEOs representing India Inc., including Adi Godrej

FIGURE 5.4. *The captains of Indian industry convene to discuss the state of India's economy. India Adda, 2012. Taken by author.*

(AG), the suave chairman of the consumer goods conglomerate Godrej Group; Hemant Luthra (HL), president of the Mahindra Group; Shivinder Singh (SS), then vice chairman of Fortis Healthcare; Vikas Oberoi (VO), director of Oberoi Realty; and Sanjeev Bajaj (SJ), managing director of Bajaj Financial Services.[39] In 2012, Adi Godrej was also the chairman of the CII. These were the most valuable voices, the corporate celebrities who featured regularly in Indian and foreign media. These voices were uncensored and unedited.

The theme of this mediatized talk was familiar: the future of the India growth story. What was remarkable was the backdrop against which the conversation was unfolding—the crisis of capitalism, which was a crucial point of debate that year in Davos. The official theme of the 2012 WEF annual meeting was "The Great Transformation: Shaping New Models," a cunning appropriation of Karl Polanyi's critique of market society.[40] The gathering was overshadowed by a sense of gloom amid negligible signs of financial recovery in the United States, the fall of the euro, and the ensuing anticapitalist protests across Europe and

America. The Occupy movement had even made its way to Davos that year with their call for "remodeling capitalism."[41] At this point, Indian policy analysts were getting worried about the state of the economy, about the specter of turning the "world's largest free market democracy" into the "fastest falling financial market in Asia" given slowing growth rates.[42] The media attention India was receiving at this juncture was about massive corruption schemes—the Commonwealth Games scam, the 2G spectrum case, and the coal mining scandal—that had mobilized popular anticorruption protests in several cities.[43] The earlier narrative of the inherent robustness of the Indian economy in the face of the global economic crisis had begun to wane as the magical growth rates of the preceding years gave way to critical warnings from international financial bodies.[44] In this gloomy scenario, India Adda had assembled in Davos to showcase India's magical growth story. The stakes were high. The need to establish India's image as an economic miracle had never seemed more urgent. What follows is an extract from the India debate that reveals the highly contentious nature of the state-capital relations in postreform India. Shaili Chopra sets the tone of the conversation.

> SC: There is plenty to be done. Things are turning around, but two years from now we are going to have the general elections in India. Clearly, you all are factoring that in. What are your expectations in terms of the reform story? And more importantly, will India Inc. have the choice to select the government?
>
> VO: Politicians should be very clear that their report cards are going to be seen in the next two years. So they better buck up.
>
> SC: You mean they are empty so far?
>
> VO: I don't know that, and I would rather not comment. Let the term get over, and then we will decide who fails and who passes, but I would clearly see them bucking up, because they really need to do that. And you know they are the drivers. We probably will put the fuel in, but at end of the day, they are the policy makers. We can influence them to make policies around growth, job creation, and so on, but at end of the day they have to take action.

I guess they really need to know what people are looking at and what people want. And they should perform.

SC: Sanjeev, you have seen what happened to Maharashtra. Another example of a great story that could have been much better, but gave everything to the neighboring Gujarat. This is part of the government story. I mean, two years from now we have general elections. What are industrialists like you going to say, that your local government also let their huge opportunity go?

SB: See, people are clearly voting more and more for performance over casteism, over religion or just status quo. And for every Maharashtra, you have Gujarat, you have many other states, like Bihar, etc. Rather than seeing each one of us as businessmen or industrialists, I think each one of us as a citizen casts our vote and believes that we can make a difference. We will hopefully see that we are left with those [politicians] that are accountable, [are] transparent, and lead by action.

. . . .

HL: I have a contrarian view on this. I think we need to take a look at how the whole electoral system in India works. I don't think we can afford the luxury of the government we have now for us to recover and catch up with rest of the world. We will need a presidential form of government [like] what Italy has been able to do just now. A real powerful bureaucrat, [Mario] Monti, said we have to throw out the last prime minister and get our act together.

. . . .

HL: I have already said that there is a golden moment you can strike now. The risk appetite has come back. The second thing I will tell the [Indian] prime minister is that you ask your political masters to either, you know what, take action or let me go.

SC (*Giggling*): The phrase "political master" gives us a lot to think about. Vikas, you talked about "despite the government"—what is the one picture of India "despite the government" that we will continue to sell at WEF?

VO: Everything that [has happened] until today is despite the government. And that probably is a clear story. I will tell the prime minister that you know we need a leader, a single leader who can drive the country to a particular focus, and I think he is the man. You rightly said that he has the talent, he's got the knowledge, and you know people love him. So I guess he should really put it through.

SS: My comment to the prime minister would be—India has the opportunity; let's seize it.

SB: Okay, I am going to be critical here. Six years is a long enough time. Not seen enough action. We need somebody different to act.

This conversation was unusual in more ways than one. Take the topic itself—the evaluation of the current government's performance as an effective agent of capital. Although this is a familiar discussion witnessed regularly in TV studios and opinion columns, it was the location that made it worthy of attention. The panel had not only voiced open discontent with the government's performance, which they perceived to be dismal, but did so a few meters away from the minister of commerce, Anand Sharma, seated inside his private office in the adda. A sense of awkwardness was palpable as this conversation proceeded along clearly demarcated positions of *they* and *we*; *they* were the politicians leading the government, and *we* was a more ambiguous, albeit high, moral identity adopted by the captains of industry. The capital had positioned itself as the prime engine of economic growth whose forward march was constantly thwarted by the political class. This move is unsurprising given the recently established discourse of Indian entrepreneurs as combatants who bring glory to the nation by acquiring companies in foreign lands. Consider, for example, the acquisitions of British brands such as Land Rover, Corus, Jaguar, and Tetley Tea by the Tata group, which were described as "a-ha moments" for Indians;[45] the takeover of the French steel and mining corporation Arcelor by the Mittal group;[46] or the relaunch by an Indian entrepreneur of the historic British East India Company as a luxury food store in its old headquarters in London.[47] These corporate victories of India Inc. have even found popular expression, for example, in a poem titled "Two India's," recited by the Bollywood superstar Amitabh Bachchan, who narrates the emergence of New India as "an India that no longer boycotts foreign-made goods, but buys out the companies that make them instead."[48] Of these triumphs, it is the purchase of the British East India Company that has made the most impact, because "the company that ruled India for more than 200 years is now ruled by an Indian, Sanjiv Mehta." The conquest of foreign companies by Indian entrepreneurs has now been added as a "new page" in the postcolonial history of India.[49] The project of entrepreneurship has acquired a fresh twist; it is now spoken of in the language of anticolonial resistance. To speak of the success of the capital on foreign shores is to speak of the success of a resurgent postcolonial nation. Thus, in this view, the national interest is now firmly aligned with the interest of the capitalist class, and narrow self-interest is itself folded within the larger framework of speaking back to the empire or, rather, of buying up the old empire. By failing to facilitate the capital, then, the government had seemingly failed the nation too. This is the "despite the government" narrative Vikram Oberoi was hinting at, a hint fully understood by the proponents of liberalization. In liberal circles, the idea that "India grows at night" is deeply entrenched; that is, economic growth happens almost by stealth when the state is fast asleep.[50] The state, said to be trapped in proverbial red tape, is seen as incapable of acting decisively, an unlikely saboteur hindering India's upward economic swing. The old question of national interest and its most effective mode of management was at the center of this tug-of-war that unfolded between the state and the capital in the adda.

What made this critique particularly stinging was the language of mock subordination used by the powerful faction to position itself as vulnerable. (That is, "They are the drivers. We probably will put the fuel in.") Recall here that this discussion in Davos was taking place just a few months after the 2011 popular anticorruption movement in Delhi. Described as an antiestablishment mobilization, the movement reflected popular disenchantment with the figure of the politician, who was seen as morally bankrupt and inefficient.[51] The sphere of politics was itself located as the prime obstacle in the path of economic growth.[52] The ordinary man, *Aam aadmi*, emerged in this discourse as the main agent of change pitted against corrupt politicians. It is this language of antipolitics that we see reflected in the capitalist critique of the government. The power dynamics are turned upside down here, as India's billionaires, especially in a highly influential setting such as Davos, express their dissatisfaction as mere "citizens," as Sanjeev Bajaj said, in possession of just one vote like everyone else. Yet it is precisely this display of vulnerability that allows the capital to distance itself from the sphere of politics, throw its lot in with the people, and demand a full reconstruction of the political system. Hemant Luthra's invocation of a "presidential form of government" was a call to replace the democratic parliamentary system seen as a "luxury" the nation could ill afford as it sought to "catch up with rest of the world." India could show it meant business by handing the reigns to a "real powerful bureaucrat" such as Mario Monti, the prime minister of Italy (from 2011 to 2013) whose "government of technocrats" had vowed to "rescue Italy from financial ruin."[53] The collective distaste for democratic rituals was articulated as the need for a "single leader" who could drive the country in a specific direction even while striking a conciliatory note toward then prime minister Manmohan Singh. The oblique reference to the "political masters" was an invocation of the satirical depiction of the prime minister as a mere front figure, remote controlled by Sonia Gandhi, the Italian-born president of the Congress Party. That the patience was running thin was clear, and as Sanjeev Bajaj said, they had "not seen enough action. We need somebody different to act." The captains of the industry had spoken in near unanimity; the stage was set for a strong leader to emerge.

THE RETURN OF THE VISIBLE HAND

In January 2012, the key corporate players would have barely guessed how this conversation was in some ways a harbinger of the future. At that point, the coalition government led by Manmohan Singh was firmly in power, the anticorruption movement had just about created a new political constituency seeking moral cleansing of the nation, the Aam Aadmi Party was yet to be formed, and Narendra Modi's formal confirmation as the BJP's prime ministerial candidate, which dislodged the old favorite, L. K. Advani, was still more than a year and a half away.[54] Yet what was readily apparent was the deep longing for a strong government led by a single leader who would centralize political-economic governance with a firm hand. In this teleological reading, the ascent of Narendra Modi two years later in the 2014 general elections seemed to be long anticipated. Many observers called the 2014 polls India's first "presidential style elections" dominated by the personality cult of a single leader.[55] The mediatized Brand Modi combined the old agenda of muscular Hindu nationalism with that of economic growth that put the economic agenda at the center of the political domain. If the Congress Party, the original party of economic reforms, veiled its economic liberalization policy as "reforms with a human face," Brand Modi publicized capitalism as the ultimate path to prosperity and himself as the efficient manager of capital. The electoral promise of *acche din*, or "good times," captured this vision of the future, this time harnessed even more firmly to the ever-enchanting dreamworlds of capitalism.[56] The wish for a strong leader articulated by the capital in the India Adda debate would indeed be fulfilled. But what could not have been foreseen at this moment is how the strong state led by a single powerful leader would co-opt the capital in the name of national interest and in doing so speed up its own ongoing transformation into a corporatized state power.

To be sure, the Indian state, even in its neoliberal corporatized form, has long remained reluctant to let go of its power to shape the socioeconomic landscape. Far from receding, the state has emerged as a dominant player within the realm of free markets.[57] It remains firmly in control of the "commanding heights" of the economy even while aggressively courting private foreign and domestic capital.[58] Yet it is not the old-style state capitalism that we witness here. What we see here, I propose, is a new strong state buoyed by populist nationalism that guides, cajoles, and even enforces its economic vision with a heavy hand. This dynamic gained a fresh impetus with the change of government in 2014 and the arrival of the much-longed-for strong leader. The myth of the invisible hand that guides the market economy has now been replaced by the very visible hand of the state power that lays out the blueprint of the free market. This difference is crucial in making sense of the state-capital relations in postreform India, as I discuss in the following section.

In the neoliberal playbook, the successful state is the one that limits its own role in opening the economic field to private actors. The axiom of "minimum government, maximum governance" seeks to reduce the government to the mere supporting role of aiding and facilitating the capital. Yet small government is not a precondition for markets to flourish. The state itself can be an all-powerful free-market actor that makes use of capitalist tools in a new phenomenon unfolding across the world.[59] The current description of the state-capital dynamic in neoliberal economies as a hybrid public-private model, even capitalism 2.0 or capitalism 3.0, does not fully capture the complex modes of state governance.[60] To make sense of the new role of the state, I suggest, it is useful to think of the state as the *mai-baap sarkar,* the "benevolent patriarch," or the sublime power that guides the restless capital meaningfully toward desired goals, albeit with a heavy hand.[61] If the sublime state derives authority and legitimacy by elevating itself above the petty squabbles of turbulent everyday politics as a knowledgeable keeper of secrets, it reaffirms that authority by displaying its willingness to use absolute power without hesitation. It is this duality that underpins many of the recent government policies introduced the past couple of years in India. Consider, for example, an array of campaigns and initiatives, such as Cashless India, which promotes a "faceless, paperless, cashless" society;[62] Digital India, which seeks to "transform India into a digitally empowered society and knowledge economy";[63] Skill India, which promotes professional skill-development programs together with corporate partners;[64] and Udaan, which is a job-training program in private companies specially aimed at the unemployed youth in the Jammu and Kashmir regions.[65] The government initiatives point toward impending opportunities for economic growth, including the building of key infrastructures and services. The state appears at once as a vision-ary guide and as an enabler of concrete opportunities for entrepreneurs.

The invitation to invest in government initiatives to build infra-structure and services is a way of endearing oneself to the state author-ity while earning assured profits. A telling example of this phenome-non is what is now popularly known as the event of demonetization. In November 2016, the Indian government announced the withdrawal of rupees 500 and 1,000 currency notes, ostensibly to curb black money, or untaxed wealth that was said to finance illegal activities such as terror-ism and drug trade. The sudden withdrawal of 86 percent of the total cash in circulation led to long queues and chaotic scenarios, and even deaths at banks and ATMs across the nation. This massive "disrup-tion," an oft-used term in policy circles, did not result in open backlash against the government. Instead it widely publicized the message that the government was trying to do "something" to eradicate counterfeit currency and check untaxed wealth. Some compared the act of stand-ing in bank queues with that of soldiers standing at the borders. To participate in this ritual of demonetization was to fulfill your patriotic duty to the nation. It even reinforced Narendra Modi's reputation as a muscular politician who wasn't afraid of making unpopular decisions in the larger national interest. Although the lack of cash in the mar-ket had tragic consequences, especially for the poor outside the formal banking system, it was also a major opportunity for companies offering digital payment solutions. Paytm, an Indian e-wallet start-up, was a loss-making venture before demonetization became its biggest benefi-ciary. Within a few days of the currency withdrawal, Paytm registered seven million transactions worth 120 crores per day,[66] a 700 percent in-crease in overall traffic on its platform, and 1000 percent growth in the value of money added to its user accounts.[67] The government has since launched its own BHIM mobile application, named after Dr. Bhim Rao Ambedkar, that enables a range of mobile banking services. A number of major corporate players—for example, Reliance-Ambani's Jio Money, Airtel Money, and HDFC Zapp—have also entered the digital banking sector in order to help realize the government's vision of a cashless economy. The private corporations have been quick to take the hint and invested in digital infrastructure development to help realize the prime minister's "pledge to make India a cashless society."[68] The service to the nation can now be performed while earning handsome profits for the shareholders. In short, capital is firmly harnessed to the nationalist cause. And in these manifold state-capital entanglements, we clearly see the collapse of the old myth that the domain of economy is distinct from the domain of politics.

I return here to the question of recovery posed at the beginning of this chapter. What might the recovery and revival of the cultural practice of adda mean within the fast-paced circuits of capitalist modernization? Recall here that the visible nostalgia for adda, perceived to be a dying art, has long been articulated as a desire to make oneself at home, to somehow "get a grip on the modern world," said to be transforming at an accelerated speed.[69] The adda, in this landscape of anxiety, represented an intimate world, an essential fulcrum around which a sense of identity and belonging could be realized. Yet, as we witnessed in Davos, the cultural practice of adda not only has not vanished but has instead been spectacularly revived in an altogether new form. The very essence of intimate belonging that adda signified has now been recovered and brought fully under the arch of capitalism. This twist in the history of adda could hardly have been anticipated by those fearful of losing their cultural essence in the currents of globalization. The difference that adda represents has not only survived globalized capitalism but also strengthened and been strengthened by those forces.[70]

The India Adda, in its new colorful, commodified form redesigned for global consumers, signals the shift toward a market economy. The very revival of adda shows how any aspect of human life that can be assigned a market value can be recovered; the waste matter can be deemed valuable if it becomes market worthy. In this instance, the theatrical performance of adda in Davos generates market value for Brand India by showcasing Indian culture as naturally predisposed to human collaboration and innovation crucial to businesses. By invoking its ancient civilizational heritage, India reiterates its position as an old hand at the game of trade and cross-cultural connections. The practice of adda, a sign of openness, hospitality, and warmth, marks the Indian difference that separates India from Western cultures that are seen as inherently materialistic. It also appears as a window through which to encounter the dramatic changes in the social-political landscape.

The first disclosure the India Adda offers concerns the power play, negotiations, and even compromises that constitute the free market. It reveals the ways in which state power and capital cohabit and even shape the contours of the fully opened-up Indian market enclave. We witness here how the state, at once sublime and profane, increasingly seeks to appropriate the capitalist tools and corporate look as it assumes the role of patron even as capital positions itself to be in active pursuit of the larger national interest. The first sign of these possible tensions was already visible in 2012 during the Davos debate when the call to dismantle the democratic government was articulated by some business leaders. What was unclear then was that the 2012 debate—characterized by freewheeling, open, critical speech—would be the last of its kind to be telecast from the India Adda premises. The reasons were never made clear, but India Adda was no longer host to such unedited televised debates. Instead in 2013, the IBEF introduced Café Conversations, which featured video interviews with important guests about the brand perceptions of India.[71]

When I returned to the India Adda in January 2015, another dramatic change had taken place. India Adda had been renamed the Make in India Lounge. In his first address to the nation from the ramparts of the historic Red Fort in August 2014, Narendra Modi launched a new campaign called Make in India that aimed to make India the manufacturing hub for the world. The initiative was "designed to facilitate investment. Foster innovation. Enhance skill development. Protect intellectual property. And build best-in-class manufacturing infrastructure. There has never been a better time to make in India." Those familiar with the 2004 India Shining campaign would have immediately noticed how Make in India subtly invoked the lyrical language of India Shining. Whereas India Shining let the Indians know, somewhat too soon, that "you've never had a better time to shine brighter," the Make in India initiative asserted to the world that "there has never been a better time to make in India." That euphoric moment of 2004, charged with peddling empty dreams, had eventually unraveled the BJP government. That same project was now being restarted, this time with more fuel to turn India into a factory of the world. The India Adda in Davos was a strategic instrument to this end, and it was now fully enfolded within the state-led Make in India initiative complete with a new name—Make in India Lounge—and imagery. The new name was meant not only to mark the arrival of the Modi government but also to help erase the legacy of the previous government. Yet the actual operation remained unaltered. The performance of Indian hospitality for potential investors continued as before. The new name, however, never gained currency among regular Davos visitors. For most, it remained the familiar India Adda.

This theater of commerce discloses the anxiety that underpins the making of a brand new nation. At the heart of this anxiety is the question of national interest and its most effective form and agency of promotion and management. It also reveals the collective fears of squandering the promise, of drifting away from a future deemed to rightfully belong to India. For now, the corporatized state had seized control of the national enclosure, and its natural and cultural resources, in its march to the future. Its spectacular exhibition uninterrupted in Davos, Brand India was at home in the world.

Part III
ANXIETY

CHAPTER 6

THE SECOND LIBERATION

ON MARCH 3, 2009, the front page of India's largest English-language newspaper, the *Times of India*, carried a sensational feature. With a background covered in sepia tones and fading, official-looking stamps and signatures, the full-page advertisement carried a lyrical oath titled "I Swear" for its readers (fig. 6.1). The oath exhorted the readers to swear to cast a vote "against [their] own helplessness. Against [their] own laziness. Against two words called Chalta hai. . . . Because only by voting against all that is destroying [their] today, will [they] give [their] children something to vote for tomorrow." This oath—informally dubbed an anti-vote oath by its creator—was accompanied by a series of news reports, features, and editorials on the themes of change and of simmering anger against government and politics as such. The coverage prominently included inspirational profiles of the *Aam aadmi*, "common man," who had brought about change through individual action without having waited for the government to intervene. Given the enormous response the campaign received on its website, it was clear that this campaign, called Lead India, had captured the mood of the nation eager for change. In the days leading up to the 2009 general elections, the campaign kept asking its readers to vote against politicians and government that had held India back from reaching its potential. The campaign was framed as an Aam aadmi's battle to take

FIGURE 6.1. *The opening ad of the Oath campaign. Lead India. 2009. Courtesy of the* Times of India.

back the nation from corrupt powerful politicians under whose watch India's progress had come to a halt. The tone and pitch of the campaign had the feel of an impending revolution, as if the postcolonial nation was seeking its liberation once again.

The intriguing part of the campaign was not just its revolutionary appearance and language but that a private media corporation like the Times Group was investing massively and boldly in what are broadly labeled as selfless public-interest causes. The Times Group was seemingly an unlikely patron given its hard-nosed profit-driven business model and open support for free-market reforms. Its procapitalist position was laid out clearly on its editorial pages day after day. In the Indian media, the Times Group has long had a dominating presence, boasting of the world's biggest-selling English-language newspaper, the *Times of India*; the most popular English-language news website; and the Times Now television channel. The newspaper, the group's core product, was rein-vented in the early 1990s along with the liberalization of markets to ap-peal to a new aspirational class. Over the years, the *Times of India*'s con-tent has come to be primarily known for its colorful supplements filled with images of beautiful people and their enviable lifestyle. The edito-rial space in the paper has shrunk, allowing ever more space for adver-tisement revenue. Its quest for more revenue has even led it to innovate a new genre called advertorials in which companies can place advertise-ments framed as editorials. Yet this very precious advertisement space was allocated gratis to a political campaign—fully sponsored and dra-matically choreographed by the newspaper itself—in order to give voice to the Aam aadmi. That the Times Group had taken on revolution-ary garb to wage a battle for the Aam aadmi was made starkly vis-ible far and wide in every possible way. It wasn't just the newspaper and its digital media platforms that were promoting the common man's battle; even the Times office building was dressed up in a style befit-ting the sponsor of a revolution. A large, colorful billboard featuring the old globally recognized symbol of revolution—the fist—adorned the Times flagship building in Delhi. The visitors to India's busy Fleet Street could bear witness from early 2009 onward to this unlikely spec-tacle: the Times building now homed the spirit as well as the operating machinery of the nation's imminent second liberation.

This strange spectacle of a private corporation choreographing the theater of national liberation raises a number of questions. What does this particular notion of liberation, or taking matters into our own hands, mean in post-reform India? Whom precisely does the Aam aadmi seek to liberate the nation from? When, and in whose inter-est, did private capital become the prime sponsor of public interest, and what might constitute this specific form of public interest? Entangled in this puzzle is the figure of the Aam aadmi, whose appearance as the prime *agent of change* is central to the unfolding script of the second lib-eration of the nation. Who is the Aam aadmi? What kind of political agency and representation is harnessed into this conceptual category?

These questions are critical given that the figure of the Aam aadmi appears in this script almost in lieu of the category of "the people"—the popular sovereign—that has long been central to democratic politics. This shift asks us to consider how the human collective, its vitality and creative force, is being reimagined in a society that is rapidly undergoing capitalist transformations. The human collective has appeared in modern mass politics in many garbs—crowds, mobs, the multitude, or the people—each associated with many potentialities and misgivings. Whereas crowds have been associated with raw potentialities of mass democratization, albeit passive and lifeless, the mob signifies unruliness and disorder, urban anonymity, and even violent destruction. In contrast, the multitude takes the collective to be the site of freedom, of progressive politics, of the vital force of democratic spirit and action.[1] If crowds and multitudes stand for the raw material from which to cast democratic politics, it is the imaginary of "the people" that has allowed the actual realization of that democratic potential, of legitimizing mass politics. Yet this imaginary has been displaced in postreform politics, even if momentarily, by the figure of the common man. The collective is no longer a faceless people but is embodied in the singular figure of the Aam aadmi, dressed up in the language of liberal freedoms and a different kind of unfettered political energy.

In this chapter, I unpack the fragment of history in which the Aam aadmi emerged as the primary agent of change in Indian politics. The political subjectivity of the Aam aadmi, I propose, took shape in the specific historical experience of inhabiting a new time (variously expressed as New India, India Shining, *acche din*, or good times), an epochal change produced in the shift to capitalism. This experience of a new time, I further suggest, unfolds in a double-edged temporal contradiction—of acceleration in the pace of history and its deceleration at the same time. In the *longue durée* of history, the rhythm of the temporal sense of our times has always been in terms of acceleration, of things in motion, of endless transition, and of being torn apart between the experience of the past and the expectations of the future. But the perception of transition we witness here is not just the euphoria of moving ahead at a quickened pace on the path of progress. It is intimately tied to the fear of slowing down, of being stuck in reverse gear, and even of sliding back into the waiting room of history, the old India one had seemingly escaped from.

This anxiety of being put in reverse gear, of never crossing the threshold to New India, is what frames the antigovernmental discourse central to the Aam aadmi's battle. Here, the temporal signs of new and old India are harnessed to the dreamworlds of capitalism: the new stands for the promise of markets, of a variety of freedoms on the path to progress, while the old stands for barriers—government, bureaucratic red tape, and corruption—on that path. In other words, the domain of politics and government is the sphere of moral and material decline in which the spirit of enterprise is said to be held back in incarceration.

What energizes the antigovernment discourse, I further propose, is not just the logic of free markets but the identification of the sphere of government with a specific logic of caste politics. To approach popular mobilization of antigovernment sentiments solely from the perspective of liberalized markets would be to miss a crucial change in the very constitution of the sphere of government in postcolonial India. More than six decades of caste-based reservations in government institutions—that is, affirmative action—have made the government more diverse, as they allowed entry of groups historically outside the power/knowledge circuits into the structures of power. But precisely this caste diversity has meant that the sphere of government was seen as depleted of merit once quotas for the most deprived caste groups became a tool of recruitment.[2] In contrast, the domain of market, the private sector ungoverned by affirmative action quotas, was deemed the domain of undiluted merit. It is in the caste-free and therefore merit-based market that innovation and enterprise, the keys to the future, are thought to reside. And this faith in market/merit persists despite the fact that even after two decades of economic reforms the market mechanism has not fulfilled its promise to trickle-down wealth to the poorest citizens.[3] The incessant calls for minimum government are rooted in this double-edged anxiety of quota versus merit and government versus market, and it is in this anxious state that the political subjectivity of the Aam aadmi is shaped too.

In what follows, I trace the genealogy of the figure of the Aam aadmi through the 1950s and its political debut as an action figure in the second decade of economic reforms. The Aam aadmi first appeared as a cartoon figure in the pages of the *Times of India* as a reluctant, wry observer of Indian politics, the excesses of politicians, and the helplessness of the people. Drawn by R. K. Laxman, the Aam aadmi soon became a familiar rallying point for national conversations on the dismal state of politics. About half a century later, the Aam aadmi made a new appearance in Indian politics as a political actor, the prime figure in the popular politics that spoke in the name of ordinary people. To be sure, what I offer is not an account as such of the Aam Aadmi Party (AAP) that emerged out of these processes. Instead I foreground the figure of the Aam aadmi in Indian politics that almost every political party, including the AAP, has sought to appropriate in various ways. In 2004, for example, the winning political campaign of the Congress Party— *Aam Aadmi ko kya mila* (What did the common man gain?)—featured the common man's woes to challenge the narrative of the prosperous India (that is, India Shining) celebrated by the ruling party, Bharatiya Janata Party (BJP). The most recent incarnation of the Aam aadmi was the political makeover of Narendra Modi—a powerful three-time chief minister of Gujarat before he became India's prime minister in 2014—as the humble *chaiwala*, the tea seller, that enabled him to position himself as one of the people embattled with the Congress Party elite. The key phenomenon I follow is this: the emergence of the Aam aadmi as a pure, unblemished political subject that transcends as well as shapes politics in India. I begin, then, with the moment of its spectacular appearance as a political figure in postreform politics.

"A PUBLICATION THAT CARES FOR THE SOCIETY"

Like millions of Indians in early 2009, I was captivated by the intriguing call to "Lead India" issued by the Times Group. Each day, the *Times of India* carried an entire full page to create public awareness on themes such as corruption, criminal politicians, lack of merit in recruitment, reservation policies, and communalism. The page was split into two parts—one part carried an image and the other an editorial piece that dwelled on the image and offered facts and figures as well as views of ordinary people. The show-business celebrities and public personalities well known in social work and academic circles were sometimes invited to endorse the theme. The almost daily reiteration of the campaign created a fever pitch: a kind of emergency about the state of the nation, about the internal threat to its being posed by its inefficient, corrupt, and outright criminal politicians. The *Times of India* had located itself as the lone voice carrying the revolutionary flame as the nation was being delayed, if not stopped altogether, on the path to prosperity. Keen to make sense of the Times Group's reasons for investing in and articulating public interest, I called the editorial office in Delhi to speak to the editor responsible for the campaign. To my surprise, the receptionist transferred my telephone call to the brand marketing office. Taking this to be a mistake made at the switchboard, I apologized when the call was answered and asked to be redirected to the editorial office. The voice at the other end politely assured me that it wasn't a mistake. I had indeed reached the home of the Lead India campaign, which was conceived and executed by the Times Group brand team and not the editorial section, as I had first imagined. I learned that the voice at the other end was one of the brand managers who coordinated the campaign between the advertising professionals in Mumbai and the editors in Delhi to create a seamless narrative of a nation brought to the brink of crisis. Impressed by my curiosity and interest in the campaign idea, he invited me to the brand marketing office to talk about the *Times of India*'s "service to the nation," as he put it.

I arrived at the Times building the next day and made my way through the usually crowded reception area to the more orderly marketing department, lined with identical small cubicles and remarkably tidy wooden desks. A slightly built man, polite and eager to talk, received me at the door. He was Nitin, a management professional in his late twenties, who had spoken to me when I had called the previous day.[4] He immediately suggested that we go out for a cup of tea at a popular tea stall in the back lanes of Bahadur Shah Zafar Marg. As we walked out of the Times building, he told me that the quality of tea was better at the roadside stall famously patronized by journalists. But the real reason for walking away from the Times office, he added a little later, was his discomfort in talking about the newspaper's brand strategies and the operation of the Lead India campaign. So why was the Times Group devoting so much valuable advertising space, funds, and labor to make the voice of the Aam aadmi heard? And why was the brand management team steering this campaign, I asked? Nitin looked slightly amused that the reason wasn't readily obvious to me. He stated with practiced professional ease: the Lead India campaign was a strategic brand-building exercise "to shift popular perception of *Times of India* from a page 3 newspaper to a publication that cares for the society."[5] It seemed this line had been rehearsed many times before, perhaps in corporate-strategy brainstorming sessions or just alone, if only to search for some greater purpose in the exercise.

The phrase "a publication that cares for the society" could easily be dismissed as a glib, meaningless, albeit emotive, formulation that brand-marketing professionals routinely indulge in. Yet the choice of words and their intended effect disclosed the moral lineages of public service that the campaign drew on and the manifold contradictions therein. To care for something is not only to disclose empathy but also to take responsibility, to take charge of the situation. Thus, the structuring assumption of this statement instantly brought overlapping groups—readers and citizens—together into a single orbit and allocated a degree of responsibility to the newspaper. In doing so, the interests of the newspaper and the nation were packaged in a common frame. This particular conjunction of readers and citizens, however, is not fully transparent when the latter are increasingly seen as consumers and investors in the nation turned market.

I turn now to the older connections between the press and the public interest and the contemporary twists therein. The idea of a socially responsible newspaper, a publication that speaks for the people, is not particularly new. The world of print has almost always been entwined with some form of advocacy of various causes and their intended publics. Consider how the formation of the so-called vernacular press in nineteenth-century colonial India came to be imbricated with the nascent struggle for autonomy and, eventually, liberation from imperial domination. One of the influential Bengali-language newspapers, *Amrita Bazaar Patrika*, for example, was started in 1868 as a response to the "helplessness of the peasants . . . under the high handed ways of the European indigo planters."[6] Similarly, the foundation of the Urdu-language monthly periodical *Dil Gudaz*, among others, came to be connected with the spirit of public activism, volunteerism, and the making of an *Islami pablik* in the post-1857 period.[7] The idea that the "life of nations and the life of the mind" were inextricably connected had become a foundational concern of Urdu-language publications that aimed to counter Western intellectual domination in the early twentieth century.[8] Print culture had vastly expanded the public sphere in colonial India—the older oral networks of communication, "the Indian ecumene"[9] with a variety of actors and informal mechanisms now joined by newspapers, periodicals, pamphlets, and books.[10] The difference between the oral and the print media was that the former was more difficult to control for governments forever seeking to quell any signs of threat to its authority. The print media, in contrast, was more easily monitored. Already in the late nineteenth century, the colonial government introduced the Vernacular Press Act of 1878 for "better control of publications in Oriental languages" to quell any disaffection arising from "seditious writing" in the vernacular press.[11] The Indian Press Act of 1910, similarly, sought to curb any words, signs, or visual representation of "disaffection, . . . incitement, . . . or seduction" of "soldiers or sailors from their allegiance or duty, to bring into hatred or contempt for the British Government, any Native Prince."[12] Yet it is precisely in this imperial context of control and censorship that the ideal of a free press as a "sacred duty" to give voice to public opinion "with the object of serving the country" began taking shape.[13] Although the notion of press as a profit-making enterprise was but a distant thought in the early twentieth century, some journals had been launched as business ventures. This meant that the question of commercial gain versus public good—a very contemporary debate—had already become a moral dilemma in Indian journalism. A glimpse of this debate is visible in a 1929 essay written by Ramanand Chatterjee, the editor of the Calcutta-based *Modern Review* and *Pravasi*, on the subject of ethics in Indian media.

> I do not mean to suggest that no journal conducted for pecuniary gain can do good to the country, though in starting and running newspapers the sole or chief object should not be money. It is true, newspapers cannot be conducted without money; but sufficient money can be earned for running a journal without sacrificing moral principles and public good. The average young Indian journalist who works for money takes to the profession with a high object. His achievement can, however, only be commensurate with his character, attainments, capacity and industry. . . . We must not sacrifice our convictions for any advantage whatsoever.[14]

The position taken by Chatterjee was quite clear: money was merely the means to keep newspapers and journals running; it was not the end in itself. Although advertising as a source of revenue had become a familiar feature of the publishing industry by the late nineteenth century, newspapers had not yet become profit-driven enterprises. If there was any moral dilemma between the imperatives of public good and private profits, then that debate had clearly been settled at this point in favor of public good. The pursuit of ever more advertising revenues or of newspapers as profit-making operations was still half a century in the future. In short, the role of the press as a public watchdog perched on a wall between advertising and news was an established premise in the world of journalism.

This picture began altering dramatically in the early 1990s as India embraced market reforms. The most significant change was that the desire to make a profit no longer had to be a secret—it could now be pursued openly and unabashedly. The media landscape was expanding rapidly at the turn of the second millennium, with new city editions and new publications across India. Many publications even engaged in the so-called acrimonious newspaper wars at that point.[15] The competition to enter new markets and sustain the existing ones meant a shift in how newspapers were produced and sold. A critical change was the reconfiguration of the established divisions between news and editorial content and advertising space. In the conventional newspaper model, news and editorial content were kept apart in one watertight compartment and advertising was kept in another. But in a bid to garner more revenues from advertising, this separation was less strictly enforced.[16] For instance, the front page now no longer exclusively belonged to the editorial section; it could also be fully sold to advertisers by the marketing department.[17] Another example is a hybrid feature called advertorials—advertisements dressed up as news features—that further encroached on editorial space.[18] The very practice of buying and selling advertisements had changed—a media company could provide advertising to another company in exchange for stock. In this field, the *Times of India* set the trend in 2003 when it launched an innovative initiative called Medianet to manage corporate ad sales. In a tongue-in-cheek promotion for Medianet, the *Times* pitched itself to prospective advertisers as the "industry leader . . . constantly cloned by competitors." At the heart of this innovation was a simple yet profitable idea: advertising as a form of information. Consider this passage, which I quote at length:

> The purpose of a newspaper is to act as an information provider. That has remained unchanged over time. But the definition of information has changed. For the reader, information is no longer restricted to the conventional parameters of news about the nation-state, party politics and the government. Today, the reader not only expects reportage and comments on issues of nation and state, but also on a range of information in the realm of lifestyle, fashion and entertainment. . . . Advertising is recognized as a legitimate source of information about products and services, delivered in an engaging and enticing manner. Likewise, advertorials about products or services are seen as another form of information. . . . Those who are apoplectic about the perceived invasion of "message" into the domain of "content" may want to consider that the two have long since ceased to be strangers, and are sharing an increasingly symbiotic relationship. Marshall McLuhan famously declared that the medium was the message. In all humility, we'd like to say that Medianet is the messenger—heralding a brave new world of innovation.[19]

By placing news and advertising in a single domain, the proverbial wall between the two, the very foundation of journalism, had been

erased almost effortlessly. What is particularly noteworthy is the invocation of Marshall McLuhan, one of the most influential thinkers of
the twentieth century, sometimes designated as the "prophet of the information age," to give intellectual authority to this move.[20] McLuhan
was prescient—in fact, ahead of his time—in his reading of new media
and the ways in which technologies transfigure the human sensorium.
He approached *medium* as an extension of the human body, mind, and
senses, and *message* as the change of scale, speed, or pattern introduced
by any new technology in human affairs. Seen from this vantage point,
it is not entirely clear what the "invasion of 'message'" in the Medianet
promotion pitch stood for. But given the nature of enterprise Medianet
represented, it can be safely inferred that the message versus content
dichotomy was a way to reframe the old advertising versus news debate.
McLuhan, here, is not given full credit, but in the 1960s, he had already presented the idea that newspapers were "mosaic forms," a patch-
work of the older "book form" and "pictorials" that appeared as news
and advertisements in the broadsheet. The entanglements between
news and advertising were inevitable for him, as "the classified ads (and
stock market quotations) are the bedrock of the press. Should an alternative source of easy access to such diverse daily information be found,
the press will fold."[21] To think otherwise, he asserted, was simply an
expression of one's "unawareness of the nature of the press."[22] This is
the view—that the press exists because of and for advertisements—
that the *Times* Medianet promotion seems to be rehearsing, in an effort
to preempt any moral arguments about the decline of the press. Any
moral responsibility is displaced to the ever-astute reader, said to be
hungry for information and actively seeking it from multiple sources.
The newspaper, in contrast, is projected as merely serving the interests
of the reader by providing a range of information in a single platform.
Conventional journalism is dismissed as being out of sync with readers,
who are apparently being shortchanged—it is fashion and lifestyle they
want, not news about politics, Parliament, and the government. The
old news versus advertising hierarchy was effectively erased, the unnec-
essary vestige of a bygone era. Or so it appeared at first.

The *Times of India*, in its post-1991 reincarnation as a mosaic of information, continued to gain substantial new market territories across India. During 2003 and 2004, it became the world's largest English-language newspaper, with 7.4 million readers and a print circulation of more than 2.4 million, thus surpassing broadsheets such as *USA Today*.[23] The newspaper described its success as "a victory for India" on a global scale and put it down to the importance "of shedding traditional journalistic biases in favor of a reader-centric approach to news reporting."[24] In other words, the blurred news/advertising model was bearing fruit—the readership was soaring just when print newspapers were folding up in many parts of the world.[25] Vineet Jain, the managing director of the Times Group, explained the phenomenon succinctly: "We are not in the newspaper business, we are in the advertising business. . . . If ninety per cent of your revenues come from advertising, you're in the advertising business." Although this approach initially caused shock and dismay because advertising was "masquerading . . . as news"[26] and because ethical values and integrity were being compromised, it was soon adopted by other media corporations. The greater reliance on advertisement as a source of revenue meant that the sale price of the newspaper became almost irrelevant. By 1992, the unit price of the *Times of India* had been reduced to an invitation price of rupees 1.50, just half of what other newspapers cost, an unexpected move that helped vastly expand its readership by undercutting the competitors.[27] The expansion of readership is what made the newspaper attractive to the advertisers. In short, it affirmed what McLuhan had predicted several decades before: advertising was the bedrock of the press.

This iteration, however, poses a puzzle about the nature of the press that even McLuhan was never fully able to resolve, which is that the newspaper, even in the age of advertising, continued to be linked to its original functions: "to correct rumors and oral reports," to speak truth to power, and to be a public watchdog.[28] In *Understanding Media*, McLuhan recounts an occasion when one of his friends tried teaching forms of media to secondary-school students. He reports with disbelief, "The students could not for a moment accept the suggestion that the press or any other public means of communication could be used with base intent. They felt that this would be akin to polluting the air or the water supply, and they didn't feel that their friends and relatives employed in these media would sink to such corruption." He put this down to a "failure of perception" in understanding how media operate, the inability of the literate classes to come to terms with the ground reality of the economy of information.[29] But what he dismissed as the failure of perception was, in fact, a pointer to more vexing questions about the anticipated role of press in society. We might ask: If advertising was what the readers actually wanted, then why was the news section never fully erased from the newspaper? What kind of value did news represent, so much so that advertisements had to be dressed as news reports—advertorials—to appear credible to readers? These questions lie at the heart of the unsettling dynamics of the news/advertising mosaic. McLuhan seems to have missed the crucial point that even in the age of advertising the task of the newspaper as a credible source of information never really vanished. Even "free" newspapers—distributed at no cost to consumers—that depend on advertising revenue have kept the news format at the center of their operations.[30] It seems that advertising masquerading as news has added impact value that advertising on its own cannot muster. McLuhan was right in pointing out that information was a commodity, but he did not anticipate that reputation itself is an equally valuable commodity that is crucial to the brand identity of the newspaper. The reputation of a newspaper remained entangled with its original function: to make and circulate credible news, a vital condition to draw in readers and advertisers. Long before the concerns about fake news and post-truth reinvigorated newspapers on digital platforms, ad-blocking applications had already gained currency; readers wanted more credible news and little or no advertising. It even spurred the trend to crowd-fund ad-free news platforms via public donations. In India, the blurred lines between advertisement and editorial spaces have long been a major concern. In 2010, the phenomenon of paid news—advertising masquerading as news— even became the subject of an inquiry by the Press Council of India.[31] The ethical problems in the advertising-based business model were not just moral questions that could be discarded; they unsettled the core enterprise of the press.[32] As the industry leader who had pioneered some of the advertising innovations, the *Times of India* brand seemed to be growing and corroding at the same time. And this paradox, as we will find, could be resolved only by making over the brand anew—by noisily incorporating public-interest issues into its brand identity.

Back in the crowded tea stall, Nitin addressed the newspaper's quest to "shift popular perception" vis-à-vis the fast-expanding middle class, new consumption habits, or the "mindscape of the reader," as he called it. He recalled a market survey conducted by the Times Group a few years ago that set out to create a post-1991 profile of newspaper readers. The survey showed that a new middle-class Indian was emerging that he described as the "I, me, myself variety—the youth who wants to be liberated, woman who wants equality, middle class that consumes and shows off more, and yet wants to feel a certain guilt for not participating or contributing to the society." The new middle class, the survey had further found, was disenchanted with politicians, their lack of initiative, and, particularly, the malaise of corruption. Nitin said that the Lead India type of campaigns (or Teach India volunteer scheme to teach English)[33] "make them feel that they are doing something. This way they can express their dissent and yet participate" in the society. An additional gain in the initiative to teach English was that it helped forge a new potential readership among the aspirational middle class—the low-income, non-English-speaking groups aspiring to join the "proper" middle class by inculcating their cultural practices. It is this segment of reader-citizens that was waiting to be tapped, and the Lead India campaign was clearly designed to capture this unrealized market opportunity.

What Nitin had described as the "I, me, myself variety"—a plain acknowledgement of survey results mixed with a bit of contempt—has been described elsewhere as the secession of the prosperous urban middle class from the mess and chaos of India. In the first decade of the twenty-first century, the postreform middle class, deemed the sign of the economic boom and new consumption practices, began moving into gated communities that offered order, the latest amenities, and more importantly, distance from the teeming poor. These immunized residential zones offered everything the middle class wanted, including the option to be "free from India" in everyday life.[34] The sign of India, in this context, stood for dystopic visions of a postcolonial nation that seemed reluctant to join the march to capitalist modernity. In this emerging narrative, the beneficiaries of capitalist reforms saw themselves as future-oriented subjects who were victims of a warped system that didn't allow enterprise and progress. A frequent refrain, for example, that I often heard during my fieldwork was that "businesses are successful not because of the government, but despite the government." The government was seen as the roadblock that had to be circumvented in order to succeed. Thus, pushed to the wall, the entrepreneurial middle class had chosen to withdraw itself from India and its political class and instead create its own exclusive dreamworld. The blame for segregation, in this worldview, lay squarely with the government and politicians for having failed society.

So what did it mean to be "a publication that cares for the society" when the sphere of government was being identified as the sphere of moral and material decline of society? Nitin giggled and asked me if I recalled a famous scene from the Bollywood film *Phir bhi Dil hai Hindustani* starring Juhi Chawla and Shahrukh Khan. I hadn't seen the film, so he recounted it for me. In a romantic sequence, Chawla asks Khan,

"Tum aadmi ho ya bandar?" (Are you a human being or a monkey?)
"Jo tumhe pasand ho" (Whatever you want me to be), replies Khan.

The point, he said, was to mirror the ongoing changes and aspirations in society. At this particular moment, the middle class appeared to be rudderless, disenchanted with the government. This simmering discontent had created a vacuum, a feeling of neglect, and even anger. This is the empty space the newspaper was seeking to take charge of—as a sponsor of social change, the large-hearted anchor of public interest. What was left unsaid was that in this shifting political landscape, the arena of public interest had also become a lucrative financial opportunity. The sponsorship of public interest, this particular expression of "care" is what precisely enriched its corporate brand value as a credible publication. The object of care here was the Indian nation—neglected by the government and unable to fulfill its rich potential—that needed to be rescued from itself, from its politicians. The rise of antigovernment politics, or the mobilization of the apolitical middle class, can be witnessed here in full public view.

ANTI-VOTE

On the sixtieth anniversary of its independence in 2007, the fabled India story was soaring high on the global stage. It was a heady moment. India was a rising economic powerhouse, an exemplary success story of a third-world nation transformed effortlessly into a lucrative emerging market. It had even unhinged itself from its old hyphenated relationship with Pakistan and instead become one half of the China-India engine leading the world economy. The international media was dazzled by the high economic growth that had averaged 8.1 percent the past three years. The previous year, in 2006, the *Economist* magazine had even carried a provocatively titled special in-depth report called "Can India Fly?" The report was accompanied by an image purportedly of Indian men and women in a cross-legged meditational pose. One of the men is shown working on a laptop and a remote device but, like several others, is chained to the ground, unable to soar higher than his chains allow. The visual metaphor of chained Indians is woven in the report, which is filled with facts and figures of economic growth, red-tape barriers, the global success of Indian businesses, and the vast potential of India's demographic dividend that is yet untapped. The writer then goes on to answer the puzzle enthusiastically by arguing, "Indian business has secured a niche in the world economy that can only grow in importance. The question is no longer whether India can fly, but how high—and whether the success of the business class can be spread throughout the country. . . . India has taken off. Just think how high its people could fly without all those chains."[35] This was a highly sought-after endorsement of India's fifteen-year-old economic reforms; it was effusive praise and confirmation of Brand India's global market equity. India was now impatient to be unfettered, and the India Story was even scripted to soon eclipse China on the global stage.

The image of a people chained in governmental red tape was a powerful one, and one that chimed with the unfolding public discourse in India. Recall here the 2004 India Shining controversy that had disclosed acute disaffection caused by growing economic inequality (see chapter 4). The notion that "we are doing well" was not shared across social groups, given that the high growth rates had not exactly trickled-down wealth to the lower rungs.[36] The widespread resentment simmered, but it never fully spilled over in the political theater. Two years later, though, this pent-up anger had found fresh resonance in a somewhat surprising set of circumstances. The Indian economy was booming—an event that unexpectedly became a cause for both euphoric celebration and overwhelming despair. This contradictory response accrued from the notion that India—with its vast resources, young population, and entrepreneurial potential—was in shackles. So a moment of celebration of economic success was marred instead by the speculative loss of what could have been if the nation had not been constricted by governmental policies. It is in this counterfactual imagination of what-if that we begin witnessing the mobilization of anger and resentment against the sphere of politics and government. The chief catalyst in this mobilization was the Lead India campaign sponsored by the *Times of India*. What is particularly noteworthy is that by 2009, the campaign had been conferred an unofficial name—the anti-vote campaign—by advertising professionals and media executives responsible for its creation. This unofficial moniker would fully disclose the main script that the official name—Lead India—had carefully tried to conceal: outright skepticism toward the very machinery on which the rhythms of Indian democracy were performed. The response to the rhetorical question, Can India fly? had already started taking on people versus government overtones, a trend that would be consolidated in the anti-vote campaign. I will return to this theme, but first I will provide some background.

The foundations of the anti-vote initiative were laid in a high-pitched campaign called India Poised sponsored by the *Times of India*. The campaign was launched on January 1, 2007, with a poem called "India vs. India" to mark the sixtieth year of India's freedom. The anthem, as it came to be popularly known, was made available in print, digital, and video form and was endorsed and recited by Amitabh Bachchan, the Bollywood superstar. It starts as follows:

> There are two Indias in this country. One India is straining at the leash,
> eager to spring forth and live up to all the adjectives that the world has
> been recently showering upon us.
> The other India *is* the leash.
> One India says, "Give me a chance, and I'll prove myself."
> The other India says, "Prove first, and maybe then, you'll have a chance."
> One India lives in the optimism of our hearts.
> The other India lurks in the skepticism of our minds.
> One India wants. The other India hopes.
> One India leads. The other India follows. . . .
> For over half a century, our nation has sprung, stumbled, run, fallen, rolled
> over, got up and dusted ourself, and cantered, sometimes lurched on.
> But now, in our sixtieth year as a free nation, the ride brought us to the edge
> of time's great precipice.
> And one India, a tiny little voice at the back of the head, is looking down at
> the bottom of the ravine, and hesitating. The other India is looking up at
> the sky and saying, "It's time to fly."[37]

The vivid imaginary of the nation's two bodies—deeply estranged yet intimately entangled in strife—becomes palpable here.[38] If one part of the fractured body appears impatient to move across the epochal threshold, the other seems to be standing still in time, even moving backward. The urgency of this moment is engraved in the vision of India on "the edge of time's great precipice," waiting to take off. That India, poised on the edge of the future, is unable to unleash itself because the "other India" itself is the leash. In other words, the problem lay deep inside the nation. If there was any doubt about the nature of internal barriers holding India back on the path of progress, the accompanying editorial commentary made it clear. The editorial, titled "A Passage from India," identified the problem as "the collapse of governance and the erosion of our institutions. Corruption is at a high, faith in the ability and inclination of our politicians and bureaucrats to run an efficient, honest and just administration is at a low. . . . Increasingly, there's a sense that India is ticking in spite of its babus (bureaucrats) and political leaders. . . . As a paper, we have advocated that government's role in business should be minimal."[39] The nature of the obstacle had been laid out in plain words: the domain of government was the dead end of progress. The conclusion was that the only way to realize the true potential of the nation was to overcome the government.

The most compelling part of the anthem, however, was not the message but the messenger—Amitabh Bachchan, "the most sought after and most expensive brand endorser in the country," who had volunteered to do the video for free.[40] For Agnello Dias, the creative director of JWT India, who wrote the anthem, this star endorsement was the ultimate confirmation of the mission they had embarked on. It unexpectedly transformed a mere print advertisement into a powerful, high-impact campaign series that would run in many incarnations for almost a decade. It would also be deeply entangled in the remaking of the Indian political landscape. He told me how Bachchan Senior, as he is popularly called, was approached by the *Times of India* for a celebrity interview series on India's sixtieth anniversary of freedom. The media team had taken the "India vs. India" ad as part of the brief for their interviewees. When Mr. Bachchan saw the ad, he asked, "Instead of me giving a few bites [quotes], why don't I read this out?" The ad had moved him, and he wanted to do his share for India. Arranged on very short notice, the video was shot at the Bandra Worli Sea Link and then on a partially constructed bridge meant to connect the suburbs of Mumbai to its fast-paced financial district.[41] It was "kind of symbolic of two Indias," said Dias, who was surprised at the emotional outpouring that followed the release of the video, which was also on January 1, 2007. He recalled how people were "writing back that this is India's big chance. It became quite jingoistic in a manner that was not planned for. Suddenly, prominent musicians wanted to do a song; the renowned Gulzar agreed to write for it as well. We realized that a lot of people had [been] and were getting involved." It was then that Rahul Kansal, the brand director of the *Times of India*, "sat down with all of us and decided to convert the ad into a really big initiative . . . a kind of reality search for someone who would probably circumvent the traditional murky path of politics, and maybe we catapult him to a more promising position in the political future of the country."[42] This search for alternative politics is what would eventually end up as the influential Lead India campaign, mediated in print and digital format, a lively website, and a television reality show that would help identify future leaders worthy of state office.

The newspaper, it was evident, was not only identifying the problem but also planning to help find an array of solutions "that should go a long way in accelerating the progress of an India Poised for its rightful place under the sun."[43] Pay attention to the emphasis on the longing for acceleration—the problem was not necessarily the path India was on but the slow speed at which it was moving. At this point, India was already a decade and a half into its economic reform program. It was the sense of growing impatience or, worse still, the fear of slowing down that the newspaper was tapping into. The website India Poised: Our Time Is Now (www.indiapoised.com) became the public platform where people could debate "what's holding us back?" At this point, an important shift in language took place. The newspaper no longer saw itself as a mere mediator of public opinion; it pitched itself as "your representative" who will "carry civil society's torch of change to key figures in government, Opposition and others in office." It was now an agent for a particular kind of politics that a few years later would be labeled apolitical and fully embraced by the middle classes. The reader-citizens, then, were invited to "poise yourself with the *Times* for a better India. Pick up your pen or hit the keyboard to become part of the Citizen's Common Minimum Programme." The citizen's program referred to here is the "Citizen's Charter," dubbed "your charter," that spelled out "what the people of India want" to lay the ground for a second liberation (fig. 6.2). The charters asserts:

We, the citizens of India, resolve to seize the moment and leverage the unprecedented explosion of talent, entrepreneurship and innovation to catapult
this dynamic country to the status of a developed young nation. We affirm
our intention to propel India to a global leadership position, while ensuring that no Indian is left behind in the quest for a significantly better quality
of life. We call upon policymakers to take proactive steps to further catalyse
the immense potential that is just being unleashed within India. We also demand that they immediately initiate remedial measures to solve the problems
that threaten to shackle India and prevent it from soaring. We recognize that
sweeping reforms are urgently needed so that this country can finally attain
the stature that is its rightful due.[44]

The tone and tenor of the charter immediately invokes another document that also speaks in the name of Indian people: the Constitution
of India. The Indian Constitution framed a newly unfettered nation,
or what Jawaharlal Nehru called "a nation on the move," emerging
from the shackles of colonial rule to recover its full sovereignty and
its place in the world.[45] The spirit of the postcolonial nation was constituted in this moment of freedom, buoyed by the promise of liberation. But six decades on, the same nation seemed to be yearning for
another liberation, this time from its internal yoke that keeps its entrepreneurial spirit in prolonged confinement. The mode of unleash-
ing that spirit, the charter demands, is to undertake further sweeping economic reforms. Ironically, the charter advises the government
to take action, an action that precisely constitutes "maximum governance, minimum government" and an eventual effacement of the government. The charter was made available on the India Poised website,
where reader-citizens could offer comments suggestions that would be
presented to the prime minister of India. About seventeen areas of development had been identified that required government intervention.
An editorial argued that "along the way, we hope that with your feedback we can put together a few transformational ideas and solutions for
an India whose only real obstacle to progress is itself. . . . We know that
we haven't tapped even a fraction of our potential. It will be the modest
endeavor of this paper to help realize this potential."[46]

FIGURE 6.2. *The Citizens' Charter was issued together with the inscription, "They say democracy is of the people, for the people and by the people. Here's what the people of India want." India Poised campaign. 2007. Courtesy of the* Times of India.

By making India the transformative object of its intervention, the newspaper was enacting a tried-and-tested branding formula it had perfected during the previous few years. Rahul Kansal, the brand marketing director of the *Times of India*, described it for me as the "hearts and minds" strategy when I met in him in 2009 in his Delhi office. He was visibly excited at the vast impact both India Poised and Lead India had created, far beyond what a newspaper campaign could ever have hoped for. He recalled how the newspaper had successfully started several city editions in India's major urban centers at beginning of the new millennium. The strategy was "to first appeal to the heart and then the mind" of the reader by actively taking up urban causes, such as decaying urban infrastructure, long neglected by the public authorities. He gave the example of the 2006 Kolkata Rising campaign that focused on reclaiming disused public spaces, encroached sidewalks from hawkers, bad roads, and reduced green areas in the city. A number of initiatives such as Clean Kolkata, Drive Kolkata, and Happy Streets made the problems of the urban citizen the fulcrum of the newspaper's strategy to attract new readers. As should be evident, the category of the urban citizen in this worldview largely comprised the newly prosperous middle class. The poor, the street hawkers, the slum dwellers— as much a part of an unequal urban landscape as the upwardly mobile middle class—were pitched as intruders, the excess weighing down the city infrastructures. They were also implicitly seen as subjects of political patronage, the constituents of an ostensible "vote bank" politics; therefore they were presumed to be shielded by successive governments. It is hardly a coincidence that the urban problems picked by the newspaper as signature issues were all about the faltering state of the infrastructure—the failure of the government to provide civic amenities for its subjects. The problems of urban inequality, the livelihood of the poor, and their right to the city were not part of this conversation. In this narrative, the government had abandoned the interests of the middle-class urban citizen, and the newspaper had now vowed to do something about that state of neglect. By championing the causes close to the heart of the urban middle class, the newspaper connected with potential new readers. Or at least this appeared to be the strategy. The success of the city campaigns—Chalo Dilli, Mission Mumbai, Happening Hyderabad, Kolkata Rising, and Refresh Bangalore— meant that this became the blueprint for newspaper-led activism across India. The arrival of the sixtieth anniversary of independence, then, seemed to be a ripe moment to implement the blueprint on a national scale "and make a difference through a combination of public service advertising and editorial campaigns."[47] In this city-to-nation shift, the nation was now deemed the object of political neglect, one that had to be reclaimed by the people. The nation was also the launch vehicle on which the *Times of India* hoped to reinvent itself as a public-service minded, serious newspaper for the anxious and increasingly impatient citizens of New India.

It is in this context too that the anti-vote campaign began taking shape. In 2009, the rhetorical question, Can India fly? had gained new urgency, but this time it was shorn of the optimism and hope that the sixtieth anniversary of freedom had come to symbolize. Increasingly, the focus was more on the fettered people who had seemingly not done enough to break off their chains. In this connection, the phenomenon of the low turnout of urban middle-class voters and, by extension, their nonparticipation in the decision-making process, had become a major theme of discussion. A number of studies showed the decline in the proportion of urban voters compared to their rural counterparts and showed how poor Indians displayed more commitment to electoral democracy than the wealthier citizens.[48] Christophe Jaffrelot calls this the exceptional "Indian pattern of absenteeism," or the alienation of the urban middle class coinciding with the 1990s caste politics that propelled hitherto marginalized caste groups—OBCs and Dalits—into mainstream politics. Thus, the increased participation of the poor rural, and often lower-caste, population had an unintended effect—the urban middle class now saw itself as outnumbered and therefore grew indifferent to the elections.[49] This apathy of middle-class, upper-caste voters was a challenge that the anti-vote campaign was precisely designed to address. According to Dias, the objective of the 2009 edition of Lead India was simply to get people to vote in the upcoming general elections, the kind of people who would otherwise keep away from political participation.

> A lot of people said that I don't want to vote because there is nothing to vote for. A lot of people said it makes no difference. But we turned it on its head and made a campaign about—maybe you don't want to vote for, but what if we told you there's a chance that you could vote against. And you should go to vote because you can vote out some people.[50]

In many ways, the anti-vote campaign is a neat reversal of the celebration of electoral democracy, particularly among poor rural populations. The act of casting one's vote is seen as an act of recognition when even the ordinary voter is said to become "the object of attention of the powerful."[51] But the anti-vote emerged not from this sense of playful participation, of belonging to a larger *communitas*, but from anger against the very sphere of politics. The political tool of voting was now mobilized to perform a negative task, to register disenchantment with politics that had undergone unbridled "plebianization" in the past decades.[52] That the middle class was ready to participate in anti-vote politics was becoming apparent. Consider the popularity of the 2008 Lead India reality TV show that ostensibly gave "every right-thinking Indian a chance to step out of the comfort zone and take on the task of stewarding the nation" and to "shrug off their indifference and put a shoulder to the wheel."[53] The aim of the reality show was to find bold leaders who would be worthy of the government office.[54] The critical turning point, however, was the call for solidarity march that thousands of Mumbai residents responded to following the 2008 Mumbai terror attack.[55] Agnello Dias recalled how when the call for solidarity march was given, no one expected anybody to turn up. Yet the large turnout exceeded all expectations. He said, "When we started talking to people next day, they said, 'We went to the solidarity march because we want things to change.'" The solidarity march had shown that the middle class was not completely averse to participating in public causes. On the contrary, there seemed to be a pent-up desire to contribute. One of the participants is said to have described the scene as "surreal" as he pointed to a group of affluent women, some holding Louis Vuitton handbags, and gasped, "All the aunties have showed up."[56] The two Indias—of slums and of high-rises inhabited by the wealthy—seemed to have momentarily leveled in this public show of solidarity. The *Times* magazine described the scene as follows: "Amid the press of bodies were a few scattered pockets of space and light—either candle-lit shrines left by the public in vigil or camera crews surrounded by the vocal and vociferous crowd. They called for an inchoate assortment of things: the heads of bungling politicians, the end of taxes, the bombing of Pakistan."[57] The crowd was pointing fingers not just at Pakistan for the massacre but also at its own political class for failing to address the security and

safety of its citizens.⁵⁸ The familiar theme of antigovernment was being
replayed, but this time in a highly charged setting.

Although Dias was moved by this show of solidarity in his city—
"The whole of Bombay was shut down"—it disturbed him that this
public gesture did not translate into electoral participation. He recounted how the day after the solidarity march, a local NGO had or-
ganized a voter registration drive for the 2009 general elections. The
event had failed to get any response, as hardly anyone turned up. There
was a clear distance between the solidarity march and the electoral
booth to cast one's vote. It is this distance he set out to bridge via the
anti-vote campaign.

OATH EATERS

The image-world conjured in the anti-vote campaign was at once a
world of disenchantment and awakening. It disclosed the ongoing exercise in moral stocktaking, a cathartic public examination of the state
of the nation. More specifically, it was a spectacular act of sounding out
the idols in Indian politics—the political leaders—and finding them
hollow. This hollowness was now being openly curated, a spectacular disclosure of a public secret presented as an image trail the reader-
citizens were invited to follow.

We might ask what these anti-vote images wanted. The obvious answer, evident in the campaign name itself, is that they wanted the politicians who had not performed to be voted out. But the images were
hinting at more than replacing one politician with another—they were
asking the reader-citizens to *exile* the idols that had failed them. In
the prevailing discourse of, Can India fly?, the politician as the representative of the state symbolized all that had kept India from fly-
ing high. It wasn't the abstract category of the politician that needed
to be shown the door but of a specific type of politician, often drawn
from the margins, who was found to be hollow, incompetent, and out
of sync with the fast-paced, market-friendly India. Although the figure
of the politician was never given an actual physical form in the Lead
India campaign, a parallel series of Bleed India advertisements drew a

caricatured portrait of the specific type of politician who was unwanted in the domain of politics. Through an interocular assemblage of photos, texts, icons, and traces of official documents, the common man and his simmering anger became visible in the sphere of Indian politics.[59] I draw on these scattered images, jumbled with editorial articles, statistical tables, and opinion polls: the chaotic image-world of the Aam aadmi's battle as the new site of middle-class activism. I begin with an advertisement called "Against the Best" that was featured in the month of March (fig. 6.3). The text read as follows:

> Against the best of the worst.
> Against having to choose from the least tainted.
> Against dubious reputation and unclean records.
> Against those who have criminal convictions
> but not personal ones.
> Against dark truths and white lies.
> Against legal sentences that are covered by glib ones.
> Against vote bank traders and political salesmen.
> Against all that is working against this country.
> I swear to vote against it all.

This oath was placed beneath a striking picture of a man and a young girl, most likely a father and daughter, seated in a modest home. The first noticeable feature in this image is the corporeal gesture—the father's hand is placed on his daughter's head—which might simultaneously convey meanings of *ashirwaad* (blessing), and *saughand* or *kasam* (oath in Hindu and Urdu, respectively). To touch another body while taking an oath, *chhoo ke kasam khana* (literally, to eat the oath by touching), is to consume the oath and thereby make an unbreakable *corporeal contract* between the two bodies. The contract is based on a double assumption that the one who is being touched will be sacrificed if the oath is not fulfilled and that she is too precious to the oath taker to be scarified. This double assumption is what makes the bodily touch a powerful sign—the oath taker would not put at risk what is precious to them if they were not serious about fulfilling the oath. The corporeal contract, then, is a sign of uncompromising resolve to do everything

Against the best
of the worst.
Against having to choose from the least tainted.
Against dubious reputations and unclean records.
Against those who have criminal convictions
but not personal ones.
Against dark truths and white lies.
Against legal sentences that are covered by glib ones.
Against vote bank traders and political salesmen.
Against all that is working against this country.
I swear to vote against it all.

LEAD INDIA '09
Let's make this vote count.

FIGURE 6.3. *"Against the Best," the Oath campaign. Lead India. 2009. Courtesy of the* Times of India.

possible to carry out the oath. It is an expression of utmost love and trust. There need not be a witness to this form of contract, for what makes it binding is the fear of losing what is mutually valuable to the two parties. In this picture, however, the act of eating the oath is performed on a public stage, with millions of reader-citizens bearing witness. In doing so, they do not remain untouched by the gesture. The public enactment is as much an affirmation of the father's will to protect his daughter as a mode of persuasion for others to emulate him. This visualization of Aam aadmi as the oath eater, the strong-willed facilitator of change, was a feature common to all the images released in the I Swear series. Each image featured a father who posed together with his male or female child. The figure of the mother was starkly absent, as if irrelevant to the project. The intergenerational pact to secure the future of the nation's youth was mostly a masculine enterprise. The call to join the Aam aadmi's battle, then, appeared to be an appeal to the patriarchal anxiety of having lost control over one's destiny.[60]

The picture and text stood in contrast to the dull, worn-out background. It is precisely in this faded, blank-looking space that we find crucial clues about the Aam aadmi and his enemy, the proverbial system he had set out to confront. The paper itself appears to be a bit soiled, crumpled at the sides and dotted with tea stains left by someone handling them carelessly while sipping tea. Look carefully and you begin noticing the old, discolored official stamps on the paper, and sometimes you see traces of government legislation. These are the markers of state power that make the paper look like an official document. In an Against the Best image, for example, one can read traces of the A. P. Revenue Recovery Act of 1864, a British colonial law that empowered the district collector to confiscate property upon the failure of the landholder to pay revenue.[61] In the "I Swear" oath, the trace of the official seal on the Indian passport is faintly visible. The signs and symbols of the state and the torn edges and stained appearance suggest the paper has been retrieved from an official archive. In the anti-vote image, they are called on to perform different work. Instead of projecting power and awe in the public domain, they stand in as mere representations of the system that has kept India chained to the ground. The faded sepia-tinted background serves as a contrast so that the oath printed on it in bold typeface is visible. In fact, the faded symbols and text appear together with the bold text in a way that symbolizes that the citizen's anti-vote overshadows the system quite starkly.

The sepia-tinted background and faded color scheme framing the image are no coincidence. They are used to create an aesthetic distinctive of a bygone era, or more precisely, a visual portrait of the "other" half of India that has been "left behind" in the global race. Consider the spatial arrangement carefully assembled to indicate lower-middle-class setting in the picture. The walls are dressed up in old marine-blue paint, mismatched and stained, that is often a standard feature of government-built flats for those with low income. The room is cramped, with a bed pushed to the wall on one side and a small table on the other. The space seemingly doubles as a bedroom and a living room for a small family. The folded plastic carpet kept on the bed signals multiple uses—it is probably used to transform the floor as an eating space during waking hours and/or an extra sleeping space during the night. The wooden table with an old glass cabinet on top appears to be a study surface placed next to a round aluminum container and an old table fan. The presence of a book and trophies on the table/cabinet suggest that the family has invested in the child's future even when it has little resources. This in itself is a strong signal of aspiration to join the ranks of the educated, upwardly mobile class. The other items on the cabinet top are a picture of Jesus and Maria and a plastic figure of a seemingly Christian bride and groom. These are set against a large poster of Saibaba and a Kal Niryanay *pachang* Hindu calendar popular in Maharashtra. Read together, these different items suggest the secular home of a working-class family headed by an aspirational father who has ambitions for his daughter. In short, this is a visual biography of the Aam aadmi, his debut in the national political theater, and the moment of his transformation into an action figure.

The act of transformation unfolds in the image. Pay attention to the logo—the symbol of the fist—placed along the inscription "Lead India '09: Let's make this vote count" on the lower right side. Here we witness the hand of the oath eater—the instrument of corporeal contract—reincarnated as a fist. Recall here that the fist is an old radical sign widely used by revolutionaries across the world. It's a call for rebellion, even war, against the *ancien regimen* that the people desire to overthrow. The sign of the fist is often drawn together with weapons or flags that the hand of the revolutionary holds. The fist we see in the Lead India images is a rehearsal of the aesthetics of revolution barring one crucial difference: it holds a rubber stamp to mark the election ballot paper.[62] The rubber stamp is transformed into a weapon of choice in this impending, aptly named anti-vote revolution. If in revolutions the people beheaded their leaders through violent means, the Indian voters were merely expected to exercise their right to vote to peacefully banish the corrupt politicians. The aesthetics of revolution were now liberal and democratic.

To be sure, the figure of the Aam aadmi is no stranger to the political discourse in postcolonial India. It first appeared as a popular cartoon figure in the chaotic and heady years of India's independence. A number of cartoonists across India drew the common man as representative of Indian publics, their perceptions, and their never-ending struggles in everyday life. The Indian common man is said to have occupied the kind of space inhabited by John Bull, a cartoon figure that sought to represent the average man in eighteenth-century England.[63] Of the many drawings of the common man, R. K. Laxman's depiction in the You Said It series became especially popular. Laxman's common man made his debut in 1951 mostly as a daily feature and has run ever since on the pages of the *Times of India*. The common man became a key element of the newspaper's brand identity not too long before branding came to be recognized as a key element of the newspaper business. That the Aam aadmi was a central figure in the affairs of the nation and was inextricably bound with the *Times of India* was recognized in 1988 when the government of India issued a golden stamp to commemorate 150 years (1838–1988) of the newspaper.[64] The commemoration stamp showcased the portrait of the common man together with the masthead of the *Times of India*. The mass appeal of Laxman's common man was said to be due to his ability "to represent the whole of India. This Common Man is a lower-middle-class chap and can fit anywhere in India."[65] The pan-Indian everyman seemingly stood out among the many versions of the common man drawn, for example, by well-known cartoonists Shankar, Kutty, and Bireshwar. Consider Shankar's common man, modeled on a north Indian farmer dressed up in a dhoti (wraparound) and a big turban. Kutty and Bireshwar also drew variations of the emaciated-looking barefoot farmer—with different regional touches—attired in loincloth and holding a wooden staff. The prevalence of the farmer as the preferred model for the common man in a primarily agrarian economy was not especially surprising.[66] The poor farmer was seen as the neglected hero who "fed the country. He bore the brunt of the taxation, too. The rich man had loopholes to evade tax: the poor farmer was exploited to the maximum."[67] Yet the primarily urban reading publics, even if sympathetic, could not always identify themselves with this depiction of the common man. In contrast, Laxman's common man is more difficult to pin down in either regional or occupational terms, and therefore he is a constant subject of speculation. For Kutty, "Laxman's Common Man is a sort of peon. He looks like the fellow who gets paan (betel leaves and nut), cigarette or tea from outside for the people in the office. He is neither an observer nor a participant."[68] This reading of the common man is telling in a way, given that the category of peon—derived from its Spanish American usage of landless laboring class—forms the lowest rank, an unskilled attendant, in South Asia's official hierarchy. The peon is seldom an active decision-maker but is nevertheless a permanent fixture in the official machinery. It is precisely this routine presence that allows him a long-term, unhindered vantage point to clearly see the nature of tumultuous events unfolding around him. Laxman called his common man "the little man,"[69] a symbol of "the mute millions of India, or perhaps the world, a silent spectator of marching time."[70] Indeed, Laxman never attributed any words to his common man and instead made him appear as a permanent bystander, as if he were eavesdropping on conversations. The reader was invited to see the world the way the common man was seeing it—through carefully arranged sketches of everyday life.

What made the cartoon popular was not just the figure of the common man but his powerlessness in relation to the politician *Mantri* (minister), the other main character in the story. The recurring theme in the series is of a postcolonial nation in decline precipitated by morally corrupt, self-serving, and often intellectually weak politicians. The cartoon dwells on the excessive lifestyle and reckless decisions made by the politician as a contrast to the austere and responsible life lived by the common man. He is deeply cynical of the political theater in which uncaring politicians "take the country and its people for a jolly ride," as Nitin from the brand-marketing department put it. In this narrative, the Aam aadmi, six decades after independence, had gotten tired of watching the nation fall apart. He wanted to take charge of the nation by stepping into the leadership vacuum the corrupt politicians had created. What we begin witnessing, then, is a visual shift, as the figure of the Aam aadmi undergoes a radical transformation from a disenchanted bystander in the affairs of the nation to an active participant seeking to steer the course of history. This reconfiguration in the political-aesthetic domain is predicated on the availability of an archive of familiar signs that can be requisitioned and pressed into the service of ever-new causes and occasions. The strategy recalls what Christopher Pinney calls the "recursive archive"—highly dynamic and inherently unstable—that enables the future to draw on familiar signs from the past. The Aam aadmi, in its incarnation as an action figure, invokes the familiar that has already been "half-seen in advance" to constitute a "not-so-new" political subjectivity.[71] Crucial to the moment of renewal of the familiar is its relationality to other signs in the political landscape. In this instance, the political vitality of the Aam aadmi is animated primarily in relation to the recurring reference to the corrupt politician who had morally stained the sphere of government.

GOVERNMENT OF CORRUPTION

I turn here to the sign of the politician who at first sight seems to be conspicuously absent within the frame of Lead India images. But a glance at the newspaper page, not too far from the images of Lead India, reveals another set of images, called "Bleed India '09: No Tension. Why Vote in Elections?" that focuses entirely on the figure of the politician. That Bleed India is designed to stand as dark comedy, a spoof, in opposition to Lead India is obvious. It is the distorted mirror that reveals the malady afflicting the nation: the politician. The word *bleed* is loaded with double meanings—it rhymes with the word *lead* even as it suggests the siphoning off of the nation's resources by the corrupt politician. The Lead/Bleed entanglements seem inseparable on the Bleed India website.

> Lead India? Where to? Up the garden Path? Round the Bend? And by who? Our Leaders? Lol! So while the Times of India tries to find new leaders for a new age (good luck gentlemen!), we focus instead on those who Bleed India; Masters of the Scam, Tigers of the Tightrope: Surely they deserve some acknowledgement of their genius—in staying above the law, beyond the law,

in making it and breaking it. . . . Wah! Wah! Ladies and gentlemen, . . . you have led us and yes you have bled us."[72]

The contrasting images of Lead/Bleed India amplify the familiar discourse of the corrupt politician, albeit in very different ways. If the Lead India images foreground the woes of the Aam aadmi deceived by cunning politicians, Bleed India sets the focus on the "money-eaters," the politicians and their modes of deception. If the raised revolutionary fist represents Lead India, Bleed India displays a clenched hand whose little finger is covered in blood. If the affective language of anger and resentment draws the Aam aadmis to the sphere of politics, it is the language of mockery and ridicule that frames the Bleed India campaign. And if Lead India is rendered in a lyrical poetic style, Bleed India campaign is written like a quick text message on a mobile phone. These differences are brought into play as mobilizational tools to address different audiences. Consider the use of *lol* (laugh out loud), an oft-used internet slang term popular among youth. This distinct youthful style is probably what made the campaign a popular internet phenomenon in March and April 2009. That the www.bleedindia .com website addressed the tech-savvy population was no coincidence. In 2009, political analysts were expecting about "100 million first time voters in the age [group] 18–24, and [who are] most likely connected via the Internet and mobile phones."[73] These estimates and projections had led both the BJP and Congress Party to make significant investments in online mobilization to persuade the youth population. The 2009 general election also saw an extensive use of social networking for the first time "to connect with the country's young and plugged-in generation."[74] These were still the early days of what was being called India's "cell phone revolution," which brought access to network technology across social classes.[75] The speed at which mobile networks expanded in India is indeed dramatic. In 2006, there were about 140 million mobile phone subscribers, and in 2012 that number grew to 900 million, covering a vast spectrum of the Indian population.[76] By 2016, India had more than a billion subscribers, a distinction it shares only with China.[77]

In terms of technology and style, then, the Bleed India campaign was perfectly at home with the fast-growing networked population. Quite unsurprisingly, the content of the Bleed India website mainly consisted of interactive features designed for mobile phones. These included games, netashopping (literally, politician shopping—the sale of Netaji-branded merchandise), ring tones, polls, wallpapers, screensavers, e-postcards, e-greetings, and message boards. The visitors were invited to download ring tones called Scam Tone, Booth Capturing, and *Netaji Ki Jai* (Victory to the leader) and "make every phone call a fun call with these crazy ringtones and callback tunes. Download the ringtones and scam your pals. Immortalize our leaders voices and keep them close to your heart." They could play games such as *Kissa Kursi Ka* (The Story of the Chair), in which the player needed to grab chairs quickly to win, and the Big Booty game, which required the players to "find the booty hidden by our King of Corruption with your hawk eyes and razor-sharp memory" and expose the corrupt politician. Each week they could bestow awards such as "The Fodder of the Nation Award: For Scam Masters and no. 2 deals"; the "Golden Chappal FoR services to mankind"; or the "Pink Chaddi FOR Moral Magnificence" (capitals in original). The invitation to send nominations explained the idea as follows: "Let's award our bleeders. They may have high offices but they also have low standards. So let's give these corporate scamsters, crooked cops or public servants working for private gains an award befitting their stature." The thrust of these interactive features should be evident by now—to publicly shame the corrupt, a category primarily identified as being composed of public officeholders. The strategy seemed to work, or "hit the nail on the head," as a newspaper report described. The report quoted a businessman from Goa saying that "Lead India is good, but Bleed India is better. It actually makes your blood boil and makes you want to go out there and vote!" The metaphor of boiling blood suggests the internalization of collective anger, the condition of feeling the anger in one's own body. It is a greater outcome than the campaign could have ever hoped for.[78] What we see is the strengthening of the corruption/politics theme, a trend that would be consolidated in the 2011 anticorruption movement and the subsequent making of the Aam aadmi political party in India's capital. But we are getting ahead of ourselves. Before addressing this theme, we turn to the portrait of the politician unveiled in the Bleed India campaign.

The character of the politician appears in a series of print ads and on the website. He is dressed in a white kurta pajama and a boat-shaped cap—attire that has come to be identified with the political class—and is adorned with garlands around his neck. He stands with folded hands holding a few rupee notes. He stares into the camera as he opens his mouth in an extrawide mocking grin. He is clearly having fun. The visual clues are not lost on the viewers—the politician is laughing, and the joke is on them. If there were any doubts, they were set aside in the accompanying Hinglish text.

> "Bhaiyo aur beheno (Brothers and sisters), I am Pappu Raj of Bleedindia Party requesting you, please, not to give vote in this election. Apka kaam to ho jaata hai Aap samjhe na? Thoda chai paani idhar udhar accha hai. (Your work does get done. You do understand? A bit of contribution to [my] daily expenses is good.) We are all friends only. Let it flow, no?"

That Pappu Raj was addressing the globalized middle class and those desiring to join it is clear in the use of informal Hinglish. The phenomenon of Hinglish—mixing Hindi and English words—is rooted in colonial history, but it gained popular credence in the 1990s as the preferred language of the globalized middle class.[79] It was especially put to work in the fields of advertising, TV serials, news, and films, in which unique Hinglish phrases were seen as innovative and commercially valuable. The young urban population showed a particular preference for Hinglish as it came to be seen as a sign of privilege and worldliness. The use of Hinglish demonstrated at once the knowledge of the English language and a casual disregard for it. Paradoxically, it could also be seen as an expression of low competence and could assign the speaker to the category of those who are yet to make it on the social ladder. English, the language of the educated elite, was no longer on a pedestal; it could be twisted and bent to the needs of the vernacular sphere. In this instance, Pappu's treachery is exposed, made starkly visible to the Hinglish-speaking aspiring middle class. The choice of the name Pappu Raj is instructive in itself, as it is a code widely understood in the popular sphere. Pappu is a common nickname in north India that is now associated with the qualities of being a dim-witted, unmeritorious, or good-for-nothing person. Its transformation from a proper noun to an adjective in the popular sphere can be traced to a well-known 2005 TV ad for chocolates. The ad features Pappu, a middle-aged balding man who has finally passed his class X exams, an achievement that he celebrates by distributing chocolates in the neighborhood.[80] The irony is obvious—Pappu has cleared an exam that is ordinarily meant for fifteen-year-olds. This popular association is alluded to in the Bleed India campaign; *Pappu Raj* translates to "the rule of the dimwit." In short, Pappu Raj, the archetype politician, is occupying the powerful chair that he neither deserves nor is qualified for. And as if this is not enough, he is mocking middle-class viewers from his cozy perch, shielded from the grind of everyday struggles. This multitude of visual codes is what ignites widespread outrage and therefore constitutes the main appeal of the campaign.

It should be apparent by now that the image of Pappu Raj far exceeds the meanings allocated in the frame. Perhaps that precisely is the point—to let the image work as an allusion, be suggestive, and bring the excess inside the frame while retaining the option of deniability. The image of Pappu Raj is more than a representation of a corrupt politician, the incorrigible money eater. His image coheres a number of scattered themes—merit/demerit, (lack of) intellectual prowess, and (lack of) moral integrity—in the sphere of popular politics. A close look at the appearance of Pappu Raj allows us to unpack these multiple entanglements.

The first noticeable aspect of the image is the presence of Johnny Lever, a popular Bollywood actor who was called on to play the part of Pappu. During the past three decades or so, Lever has built a considerable reputation as a comedian in supporting roles—hero's friend, henchman, and comic sidekick—in the film industry. The choice of Lever—a dark-skinned school dropout from a poor working-class home—to play the corrupt politician is rich in cultural-political symbolism.

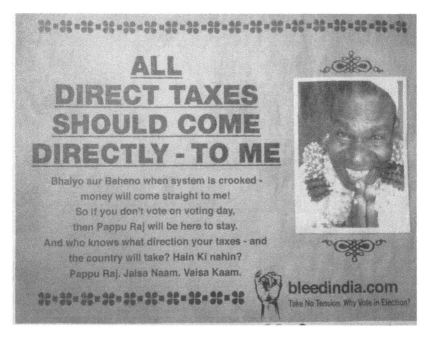

FIGURE 6.4. *The Bleed India campaign featuring corrupt politician Pappu Raj. 2009. Courtesy of the* Times of India.

Lever's Pappu stands in sharp contrast to the role given to Amitabh Bachchan in the "India vs. India" video—as the heroic voice of the nation, its conscience keeper—and the roles given to other fair-skinned Bollywood superstars. Shahrukh Khan received a prominent role in the same campaign in which he read a motivational text to the nation called "Do," which was inspired by Gandhi's 1942 Quit India speech, "Do or Die" that vowed to liberate India from colonial rule.[81] Similarly, Amir Khan was invited to join the oath eaters in the Lead India '09 campaign together with his young daughter.[82] That the Bollywood stars were on the side of the Aam aadmi, embodying his pure, anxious spirit, is readily ascertained. Lever is placed on the other side of the fence. He is dressed up as the reviled money eater, the comic-villainous character that the Bollywood stars have set out to vanquish. He is asked to represent the "other" in both overt and covert ways. Whereas Lever's low social class is never in doubt given his portrayal as a crass, uncouth character, his caste is left open to speculation. So ingrained is the discourse of upper castes, merit, and moral superiority, and vice versa, that it does not need to be rehearsed. The audience is offered visual clues and subtle markers with the expectation that they will work out the social profile of Pappu themselves.[83]

The cauldron of resentment around the discourse of caste and corruption has continued to simmer over the years.[84] A persistent theme that has emerged is that the structures of the government were clean and unstained before they came to be governed by hitherto "backward" castes. The lower-caste origins are identified as the locus of the moral stain in politics. This assumption surprisingly ignores instances of corruption among the privileged castes. In the past two decades, a number of prominent upper-caste politicians and business have been associated with a variety of corrupt practices, including accusations of the misuse of public office, disproportionate wealth, bribery, and financial fraud.[85] Yet the dominant discourse has been about the preponderance of corruption among the less-privileged caste groups, who have historically had no share in the power structures.

The historical context of this caste-corruption discussion, then, needs to be located in what is sometimes called the 1990s Mandal politics, or the politics of caste-based mobilization that gained considerable ground. In 1990, the Indian state decided to implement the *Mandal Commission Report* that required 27 percent of government institutions to promote caste groups identified as socially and economically backward. The new OBC reservation (27 percent) together with the previous reservation for Scheduled Castes (15 percent) and Scheduled Tribes (7.5 percent) meant that nearly half of all government employment was reserved for underprivileged groups. This move sparked a wave of protests and countermobilization by privileged "forward" caste groups, who found their job opportunities diminished. This rupture also opened up fresh space for social polarization and new alliances along caste lines. The 1990s saw the rise of new caste-based political leaders Mulayam Singh Yadav in Uttar Pradesh and Laloo Prasad Yadav in Bihar. The resurgence of caste politics consolidated the position of Dalit leaders such as Kanshi Ram and Mayawati who made profitable alliances with the new OBC parties. This caste mobilization resulted in the entry of new players in politics who had historically been out of power structures. The number of OBC elected representatives grew from 11 percent in 1984 to 25 percent in 1996; and during that same period, the number of upper-caste representatives fell from 47 percent to 35 percent in northern India.[86] In the same period, the most populous state in India, Uttar Pradesh, saw the emergence of the first Dalit woman chief minister when Mayawati led the Bahaujan Samaj Party (BSP) to power.[87] For the first time, deprived social groups had gained not only *access* to power but also the authority to *exercise* that power. They had acquired a share in the government machinery, not as mere recipients this time but as distributors of public goods.

This shift from being clients to major stakeholders in government operations was critical to opening paths of social mobility. But the change in the constitution of the government also led to the *flight* of the middle classes from the sphere of government. As Partha Chatterjee writes, "After 1991 . . . no self-respecting person from the middle classes wants a job in government. The private sector, they believe, rewards merit and performance. Government is the place of political patronage and corruption. In fact, government now is the same as the domain of politics, and politics breeds and protects corruption." The against corruption = against politics equation is the outcome of shrinking space for the privileged castes in government machinery and of the opening up of the Indian economy that created new job avenues for those turning their back on government.[88] Add to this the popular idea that corruption is primarily the misuse of public office that leaves corrupt practices, bribery, and kickbacks in the private corporate sector completely outside the purview.[89] In short, the sphere of government was smeared with the moral stain of corruption, whereas the private sector was the domain of pure merit and industriousness.

A prime manifestation of how government was composed of hitherto marginalized groups was the appearance of architectural landmarks such as memorial parks and museums that featured Dalit symbols. These included larger-than-life bronze statues of the Dalit pantheon, including B. R. Ambedkar, Kanshi Ram, and Mayawati; Buddhist stupas; and elephants, the election symbol of the BSP. In the

elite world of art and architecture, these material signs of Dalit assertion were dismissed either as plain "deification with no artistic or
architectural merit" or as environmental disasters—the kind of questions that are seldom raised about memorials for leaders from privileged castes.[90] As Kajri Jain has argued, the significance of the new
monuments lay in bringing visibility to a community that has historically been invisible on the social landscape.[91] To be visible is to mark
your presence, and unsurprisingly, it is this visibility of Dalit assertion that has often been a prime ground of contestation.[92] It also at-
tracted charges of blatant corruption.[93] The new leaders were subjected
to close scrutiny; for example, under suspicion were Mayawati's extravagant lifestyle, birthday bashes, the "garland of cash" offered by
her party,[94] and even her handbag, which was interpreted as a sign of
money power.[95] In Bihar, the OBC leader Laloo Prasad Yadav was accused of the fodder scam;[96] and in Jharkhand, tribal leader Madhu
Koda was accused of masterminding a coal-mining scam.[97]

The crucial point here is about the epistemic imaginary within
which the Dalit/Shudra subjects forever appear to be on a steep learning curve, lagging far behind their middle-class, upper-caste counterparts. The subtext is that even when Dalit/Shudra subjects indulge in
corrupt practices, they are not as good as their counterparts from privileged castes. They *lack* capital not only in economic terms but also in
cultural terms, given their inability to make smart transactions. This
diagnosis, however, overlooks a critical reason why caste is amplified
in instances that involve individuals from less privileged castes. The
problem lies in how privileged caste groups are enabled to see themselves as "casteless" individuals subsumed in the "general category," as
opposed to scheduled-caste/scheduled-tribes/other-backward-classes
groups that are explicitly identified by their caste. This visual asymme-
try, Satish Deshpande reminds us, means "hypervisibility for the so-
called lower castes and . . . invisibility for the so-called upper castes" in
postcolonial India.[98] In the discourse of corruption, then, caste identity
remains muted when "casteless" individuals are involved and amplified
when individuals who do not have the privilege of being casteless are
involved. This predicament of caste and castelessness in the corruption

discourse is sometimes described as the "caste differential of corruption" that determines differing consequences for corruption: caste identity decides who is named and shamed and who escapes public ignominy.[99] The problem lies in the skewed vision that makes caste starkly visible among those less privileged and invisible among the privileged groups.

The appearance of Johnny Lever dressed up in the garb of the corrupt politician, then, is not a random occurrence. His body is made to work as a hypervisible apparatus that fuses the moral stain of corruption with caste, the sign of double affliction holding back the nation in seemingly interminable confinement, its utopian futures forever out of reach. It is against this background that the Aam aadmi—the morally pure, unblemished subject—stepped out into public-square activism in search of liberation.

SUBJECT OF LIBERATION

The moment of the Aam aadmi's appearance in the public square seems at first to be what Frantz Fanon might have called collective catharsis, the climactic event that appears frequently in the histories of revolutions. To collectively experience catharsis is to purge and cleanse the collective body of impurities, of dead weight that continues to stall the march to modernity. It also means a recovery of the lost sense of self and to re-create that self in the image prior to the experience of disempowerment. But what we witness in this fleeting image is an unusual script of liberation, one that reveals the nature of the transformation reshaping postreform India. Consider the following snapshot from Delhi.

Anna Hazare, a septuagenarian activist leading the Aam aadmi's struggle against corruption, is seated on a stage surrounded by a growing crowd of supporters, activists, journalists, and photographers at Jantar Mantar, a site in the heart of New Delhi marked for protests. The simple, crisp, stainless decor—white sheets covering the platform and a white tent overhead to give shade from the relentless April heat—offers a sharp contrast to the colorful banner in the background. The large banner features the familiar cartographical imagination of

Bharat Mata (Mother India) superimposed on the map of India, holding aloft the national flag in one hand and blessing her devotees with
the other. The inscription in Hindi makes the purpose of the assembly clear: "Against Corruption, for Jan Lokpal (Ombudsman) Law—
Indefinite hunger strike." Hazare is on a fast unto death, a Gandhian
mode of protest that entails self-denial of nourishment and eventually
corporeal sacrifice in order to demand measures against corruption in
public life. This was also the moment of arrival of the Aam aadmi, the
resourceful middle class dressed up as disempowered ordinary people,
as a full political subject in the theater of street activism.

The assembly of bodies in the public realm is indeed the oldest form
of enactment of popular sovereignty, a form that predates any formal
organization of government. To assemble as a collective is to make an
appearance, to become visible and mark one's presence and acknowl-
edge the presence of others. The act of appearance is the very first ac-
tivation of bodies, an event that brings the collective into being even
before the proclamation of "We, the people" as the popular sovereign.
This is perhaps the founding act of the fabrication of we, the people as
a unified body, one that comes into being by excluding those undeserv-
ing of this claim to popular sovereignty. Hannah Arendt has reminded
us that this "space of appearance" only comes into being for a fleeting
moment before it disappears with the dispersal of bodies and cessa-
tion of activities.[100] But even this brief appearance, I suggest, leaves an
invaluable trace that reveals underlying ambitions and contradictions,
processes and agents that precede and might outlive the sovereign assembly of bodies. So what kind of popular sovereignty was being performed in this particular moment?

The 2011 protests had indeed captivated the nation's political imagination. Hazare, described as "a quintessential traditional Indian by
looks and mannerism," was hailed as the popular face of India's struggle against corruption.[101] Specifically, the protest was said to have inspired and mobilized "ultra-modern Indians, Indians for whom the
word 'social' only means having a profile on social networking sites."[102]
It gained support from many groups including business owners, sala-
ried professionals, students, Bollywood stars, cricketers, and even the

famous Mumbai *dabbawalas*—tiffin delivery workers—who stopped their work for the first time in their 120-year-old history.[103] The protests were experienced as "a carnivalesque celebration of the pure ideas of democracy—of the idea that 'we, the people' are sovereign, that politicians are the servants of the people, that laws must originate in the needs and demands of the people."[104] Inevitably, the protests were dubbed the Indian Summer, the slightly deferred counterpart of the many Arab Spring revolutions that had galvanized youth activism across West Asia. The calls to "make Jantar Mantar another Tahrir Square of India" were becoming louder, and in the popular imagination Jantar Mantar was now placed in the same genealogy as Tahrir Square in Cairo or the public square in Sidi Bouzid, Tunisia—the seismic centers of political earthquakes that sought to overthrow authoritarian regimes. The media coverage was abuzz with the discourse of a "second freedom struggle of our country, to free our motherland from its worst enemies, the corrupt" and "the second freedom struggle, the real one—against the world's rich and powerful mafia [Indian politicians]."[105] This desire to liberate the nation a second time from the internal enemy is what had brought teeming crowds into the public square.

At first glance, the milling crowds in Delhi are indeed hardly discernible from the prodemocracy activists assembling in public spaces in Cairo, Sidi Bouzid, Benghazi, Tripoli, Hom, Sanaa, or even New York (for the anticapitalist Occupy Wall Street protests). What is common is the raw force that assembled crowds across these locations represented, a force that drew on the "anarchist energy" that is always at the core of the permanent principle of revolution.[106] Yet the nature and outcome of the Indian Summer could hardly have been more different from those of the Arab Spring. Let me begin with the grammar of appearance of the Aam aadmi in the rough-and-tumble of political activism.

A noteworthy feature is the use of the singular form to describe the multitude that had appeared in Jantar Mantar. The prime agent in this story is the Aam aadmi, a singular noun invoked to make visible the individual, an agent who also claimed to represent the multitude. As the protests unfolded, Aam aadmi activists began appearing in

T-shirts, caps, and other popular merchandise that simply stated "*Mein hun aam aadmi*" (I am the common man). What we witness here is the shift from the familiar plurality of "We, the people" to the yet unfamiliar singularity of "I, the common man" in this specific space of appearance. The faceless crowd of people is replaced with an assembly of individuals asserting their personal claims as political subjects. This shift in the grammar of political representation is not a mere coincidence. It reflects the undercurrents that had long been in the making in postreform India. The 1990s turn to liberalization was in not just the material domain of economy but also the aesthetics of self, the individual expectations and aspirations that came to be reshaped in the liberal frame. The liberation here also meant liberation of the individual from the faceless collective of the people, which was now deemed to be a hallmark of the collectivist impulses of the so-called socialist era.[107] The collective, if it appeared at all in the liberal discourse, was the quicksand in which innovation, enterprise, and individual talent were sent to disappear. The recovery of the *I* from the *we*, the individual self from the collective, bears the discursive imprint of liberalism that came to define India at the turn of the third millennium. It prefigures the possibility that "the people" can be fragmented into individuals who are brought together in open pursuit of self-interest (see chapter 4, "Icons of Good Times").

A connected strand is the political ontology of antigovernmentalism that seeps through the assembly of bodies in Jantar Mantar. The disenchantment with the government among the protesters in Delhi did not accrue from the failure to perform as such but from the supposition that the very inner constitution of the government had transformed beyond recognition. This ontological crisis stemmed from the perceived collapse of the government as a pure space of merit, a space that had been corrupted over the decades through caste-based affirmative action. Unlike the protestors elsewhere, the crowd in Delhi was not explicitly rallying for social justice and equity or against economic inequality that capitalist reforms had exacerbated.[108] It is hardly a surprise, then, that the main thrust of the second liberation had shaped itself around the identification of the combination of corruption and

government as the main cause of India's deprivation and misery. The
figure of the politician, the symbol of moral deficiencies and official red
tape, was the internal enemy, the agent who sapped the unbound energy of an innovative and meritorious people and eventually hollowed
out their potential to make strides on the world stage. Politics itself was
a space of disorder in this worldview, a barrier to progress and development that could be overcome only by effacing all that stands for corruption of the pure self. The Aam aadmi, then, is the site of the fabrication of the new political subject, the one who remains uncorrupted,
the symbol of unblemished and uncompromised intellectual merit and
moral purity. It also stands for a barely hidden fascination with strict
discipline and authority, the strong patriarchal figure who promises to
restore order and prestige to the nation.[109] It is a theme that will find an
enduring presence in Indian politics, the search for strong leaders who
can deliver the nation out of the quicksand of history.

The dispersal of bodies from Jantar Mantar at the end of the Indian
Summer did not mean the end of Aam aadmi politics. It was merely
a brief hiatus, a moment of rest before the raw force was reassembled
into a political force that vowed to dismantle corruption from within
the system.[110] The anarchist energy of this anticorruption mobilization was capitalized by two political formations. One was the Aam
Aadmi Party (AAP), a political start-up, as its well-educated, technofriendly promoters like to call it; the other was the BJP, the avowedly
Hindu hypernationalist party. In late 2012, Arvind Kejriwal, a bureaucrat turned activist as well as a key figure in the anticorruption protests who had parted ways with Anna Hazare, launched the AAP.[111]
In 2013, buoyed by the success of the anticorruption movement, the
party tasted its first electoral victory in Delhi. The urban poor and mi-
grants received AAP enthusiastically, expanding its base beyond the
middle class, a development that could not have been foreseen given its
grounding in middle-class interests. In 2015, it made a near clean sweep
in the Delhi state elections even though its ambitions to be a national
party had largely been thwarted during the 2014 general elections. The
urban middle class, in contrast, opted for a double deal during those
elections that voted in AAP at the local level and BJP at the national

level. This was the ground of popular disaffection on which Narendra Modi would design his 2014 electoral victory. Dressed up as a humble *chaiwala* (tea seller), Modi would appeal to those beyond his political base as one of the people battling the corrupt elite, the one who would restore moral and material progress to India. This churning revealed the foreseen and yet unforeseen political realignments altering the social fabric. What was beyond contestation was this: the return of the privileged, emboldened by an upswing in their economic fortunes, to the political center stage to reshape the nation in their own image.

CHAPTER 7

UNCOMMON FUTURES

We have made it so easy to invest in India, manufacture in India, and work in India. We have decided to uproot licence and permit Raj. We are replacing red tape with red carpet.

—Narendra Modi, World Economic Forum, Davos

In Davos the Prime Minister is trying to project India as "open for business" and in India his chief ministers cannot prevent goons from vandalizing cinemas just because they don't like a movie. The rule of law for investment. Right?

—Journalist Tavleen Singh, Twitter, January 23, 2018

ON JANUARY 23, 2018, Prime Minister Narendra Modi addressed the world's billionaires, the celebrated captains of industry, and world leaders assembled at the annual meeting of the World Economic Forum in Davos. The address was a highly anticipated event—it was the first time in twenty years that an Indian prime minister was present in Davos. He had already been billed as a bold leader who did not hesitate to undertake tough measures to fully open up the Indian economy. The frequent reference was to two major economic interventions he had initiated—demonetization of high currency notes and the implementation of the goods-and-services tax—to transform India into a single unified market. While policy experts were still questioning the economic benefit of these reforms, his supporters held these measures up as examples of his strongman appeal and popularity among the people. Smitten with his well-crafted, market-friendly image and the promise of *acche din* (good times), a section of the Indian media had even begun describing him as the "smartest salesman India has had in a long while,"[1] the "best salesman India has ever had,"[2] or simply "salesman-in-chief" of the Indian nation.[3] This famous sales pitch is precisely what

Modi rehearsed in his Davos speech. He invited the world to come and invest in India, and he promised to replace "red tape with red carpet" to nudge and entice those who were still hesitant.[4]

His speech, however, was largely drowned out in the cacophony of foreign and Indian media. The news item that had grabbed headlines and the attention of TV anchors instead was that of violent protests raging in northern India. The supporters of a little-known Rajput Hindu group, Karni Sena, were protesting against a Bollywood film due to be released on January 25 in cinema halls across India. The film in the eye of the storm was called *Padmavat*, a musical extravaganza based on a sixteenth-century epic poem about a legendary Rajput Hindu queen who had committed *jauhar* (self-immolation) to avoid being captured by the victorious army of Alaudin Khilji.[5] The objections to the film ranged from Padmavati's stunning, albeit scandalous, midriff-baring costumes to a widely speculated dream sequence of romance between the Hindu queen and the Muslim emperor. The protestors had accused the filmmaker and the actors of "demeaning the glorious heritage of Rajput women" and threatened to behead Deepika Padukone (the actor playing Padmavati) or at the very least cut her nose for bringing disrepute to the Rajput community.[6] A frequent ritual performed by protestors was the burning of Padukone's effigies, the theatrical enactment of symbolic killing as an expression of collective outrage. In Chittorgarh, the historical town associated with Padmavati, thousands of Rajput women brandishing swords marched in a *Chetavani* rally (Warning rally) to force the state authorities to either stop the film's release or face the community's wrath. On short notice, about 1,908 Rajput women had reportedly registered to perform jauhar to protect their community's honor, under attack this time from a Bollywood filmmaker.[7]

It seemed as if the medieval past, packaged in its violent legacy, had broken through the compartments of history to paralyze the present. And in doing so, it was threatening to corrode the modern investor-friendly image and even undo the great spectacle of Brand India that the state had carefully nurtured during the previous decades. Consider the irony: Narendra Modi had courted the world's attention to market

Brand India as the most desirable destination for global capital, but what had become prominently visible instead were the less desirable "primitive" features of identity politics that lurked beneath the brand's glossy surface. The past appeared to be holding back the future of the nation. Or so lamented the political commentators.

This was indeed a strange moment in the life of the brand new nation. But it was neither anomalous nor exceptional. In fact, it brought to the surface the messy entanglements of capitalist growth and cultural politics on which the logic of the brand new nation has evolved for the past several decades. To many observers, the protestors brandishing swords seemed at first to be unwelcome guests from the past—the intruders who had not received the memo that India had moved on to matters of economic growth and progress. The stark contrast between Modi's "liberal" defense of global free trade and the "illiberal" demands of protestors appeared to be a deep rift between modernity and tradition, the rational and irrational, reason and passion, and the future and the past. What made these dichotomies somewhat inadequate, however, was the fact that the prime minister's party, the Bharatiya Janata Party, and the Karni Sena protestors belonged to the same broad ideological spectrum of Hindutva politics. So how could primordial identity politics cohabitate with a globalist vision of boundless freedoms? Had we not left identity politics, the ethnonationalism, and violent conflicts behind in the prereform decades? While this moment clearly eschewed prefabricated explanations, it brought to the fore what is described as one of the most pressing crises of our time: that of liberal politics. Yet it is here the inherent contradictions of liberalism become apparent. Identity politics had never gone away; it had merely been reshaped into an identity economy—the brand identity that packaged the nation as a distinct investment destination—and even been emboldened in the process. The old nationalist politics had been rejuvenated too, this time fueled on capital investment flows. What we witness here are the deep ties between cultural nationalism and capitalist growth, or how the old cultural politics continues to play out but is now boosted by the promise of investments.

BONDS OF INVESTMENT

At the heart of this conundrum is the neoliberal script of opening-up territories for capital investments, a script increasingly embraced by hypernationalists across the world. Recall here the promise of the brand new nation—to not only attract capital investments but in doing so also activate its destiny to be a great nation. In India's case, capital flows are what promise to activate its old civilizational glory and renew its cultural nationalism in the twenty-first-century global economy. Global capital flows are taken as a form of legitimization of the sovereign state power and a global recognition of its cultural essence. This dynamic is well understood by nationalists who craftily combine the investment destination model with the revival of their versions of the cultural past and of cultural nationalism. If the inflow of capital investments is what boosts the sovereign power of the nation-state, it also ensures that the management of the nation's "domestic affairs" remain a no-go territory for external actors. The unspoken bargain is this—the state facilitates the mobility of capital into investment-ready territories, and the capital in turn enables the rearrangement of the domestic sphere without external sanctions or censure. This is what I suggest are the *bonds of investment*—*bond* in a double sense of affective ties and financial instruments—that lock cultural nationalism and capitalist growth in a state of mutual indebtedness. It is in this liberal framework of free markets that we begin to see the foundations of what is now being called authoritarian populism—the strengthening of populist cultural nationalism led by strong majoritarian leaders in the shadow of free markets.

This script has been enacted time and time again in the twenty-first century. Its most dramatic iteration is the renewal of Hindu cultural nationalism and centralized state governance on the back of neoliberal economic reforms. Ironically, the capitalist reform project was kick-started by the secular Congress Party in the 1990s, but its political capital extracted by its opponent Bharatiya Janata Party led by the current Prime Minister Narendra Modi—the man who would make a case for more liberalisation of markets in Davos even as personal liberty to watch a film was being jeopardized in India. Far from being in opposition, the manifestation of Hindu cultural nationalism and market liberalization were indebted to one another.

The alliance between Hindu cultural nationalism and market liberalization began taking shape in the aftermath of the 2002 anti-Muslim pogrom in Gujarat during Narendra Modi's tenure as the state's chief minister.[8] What activated this alliance was the wide condemnation of the pogrom by several foreign governments and external agencies.[9] The failure to control violence had become a source of embarrassment for India and threatened to tarnish its image in the world.[10] In order to repair the reputational damage, Modi undertook two initiatives that would become foundations of his long-term strategy, a reliable path that would eventually lead to his electoral victory as India's prime minister in the 2014 general elections.[11] The first was *Gaurav Yatra*, literally "pride" or "honor journey," which directed the Gujarati Hindus, the internal political base, to counter the "sustained propaganda" against Gujarat and restore the hurt collective pride.[12] In doing so, Modi had crafted himself into an embodiment of Gujarat's *asmita* (self, ego, or pride) that made his personal crisis into a collective crisis. The extensive journey through Gujarat was a vital part of his winning 2002 electoral campaign there.[13] The second initiative was his transformation into *vikas purush* (development man), the one who promised to bring material progress and prosperity to the people.[14] The domain of economy was to become the arena where the social-political landscape would be redesigned even as it addressed an external political constituency: investors. This took the form of Vibrant Gujarat, a spectacular event that brought together Indian and foreign investors who could infuse capital in Gujarat and, in doing so, legitimize the political-cultural order.[15] This invitation to capital was not just to make a business transaction but also to verify that "vibrant, colourful Gujarat" was "completely normal" and that "there is no red tape, only red carpets and green signals and blue chip companies."[16] The Modi-led transformation of Gujarat into a pro-business, investor-ready territory was the crucial turning point.[17] It not only led to his political rehabilitation in India and abroad[18] but also laid the groundwork for a key coalition that combined "primitive" features of cultural nationalism and with the "modern" thrust of global capitalism. This coalition is what bought immunity to the violent streak of Hindu cultural nationalism and, in so doing, disclosed the inherent violence of capitalism in pursuit of profits that made the dichotomy of liberal versus illiberal almost superfluous. It also produced Brand Modi: a key feature in the life of the brand new nation.

Brand Modi is an embodiment of the entanglements between the imperatives of capitalist growth and the cultural nationalism that shapes twenty-first-century politics. The informal addition of the prefix *brand* is not only an acknowledgment of Narendra Modi's procapital credentials but also a reference to his personal brand identity as the Hindu nationalist strongman loved by the capital. The main pillars of Brand Modi are his strongman image—the one who doesn't flinch in the face of opposition—and the promise of good times that is held out as an agent of economic growth and prosperity. In its twenty-first-century edition, the good times, or *acche din*, are a popular rendition of the dreams of progress, the long-held-back aspirations of the common man that only capitalism can bring to life. By harnessing the dreams of good times to the vehicle of Hindu nationalism, Modi, a longtime RSS *pracharak* (volunteer/propagator), instrumentalized the neoliberal formula of economic growth toward the making of a Hindu nation. This transition is crucial. Recall that since its inception in 1925, the RSS was largely disinterested in matters of economy, and its offshoot, Swadeshi Jagran Manch, even became a strong critic of the economic reforms initiated by the Congress Party. But this stance was quietly overturned, first under the Vajpayee government that publicized the growth agenda via the India Shining campaign and simultaneously in BJP-ruled Gujarat at the beginning of the millennium. What allowed Hindu nationalism to create a broad coalition with the progrowth, middle-class Indians was the appropriation of the global language of neoliberalism—good governance, growth/investment, and development—that was well understood by policy makers, investors, and consumers at home and abroad. If the growth agenda enabled Brand Modi to circumvent associations with communal violence, the aggressive communal polarization in Gujarat strengthened his strongman image in the public eye.

It is no coincidence that Modi used the rhetoric of his "56-inch-large chest" repeatedly to establish himself as the desirable embodiment of masculinity, especially in comparison to the then prime minister Manmohan Singh, who is of slender physical build. Put simply, Brand Modi is manufactured and marketed[19] on a well-calibrated play of attention and diversion, of secrecy and excessive publicity that creates its own truths and "public secrets" that people know not to know.[20]

Like all brands, Brand Modi seeks to mediate certain qualities and affects that promise to change the lives of its consumers. What sets it apart is the ability to conjure attention-grabbing spectacles that keep its consumers constantly hooked. From mass publicity of the fantasy worlds of good times to bland policy measures,[21] this quality has seeped into routine functions of government.[22] His signature quality is the capacity to make swift decisions—unilateral and almost entirely conducted in secrecy but released in the public domain as a thrill-inducing series of spectacles. Nearly every major policy decision—from demonetization and the implementation of the Goods and Services Tax (GST) to the abrogation of the special status of Kashmir—followed a familiar playbook of secrecy and spectacle.[23] The dramatic surprise element is what the followers of Brand Modi admire, and each move is celebrated as "bold," a "masterstroke,"[24] or even a "blockbuster" thriller unfolding in real time.[25] These heavily marketed and mediatized performances bolster Brand Modi's strongman credentials and promote public celebration of muscular Hindu majoritarianism. They shape the boisterous public mood even as the public is distracted from more pressing issues such as employment and growing social inequality.[26] These are the building blocks of unabashed illiberal majoritarian politics taking shape in liberal democracies.[27] The majoritarian populists draw raw energy from the spectacle of power even as they flex their free-market economic muscle to redraw the nation in their own image.

This turn from liberal to illiberal politics seems an aberration at first. After all, the script of the twentieth-century liberal reforms was predicated on the universalization of liberalism—liberal democracy in alliance with liberalized markets—as the road to progress and prosperity. If the twenty-first-century push toward majoritarian strong leaders with a penchant for illiberal authoritarian populism seems to be an eruption from the past, it's because the liberal condition itself has been misread. I turn here to some of the influential ideas that shaped the twentieth-century liberal world order and how those overlooked entanglements between liberalism and what is now called authoritarian populism.

THE ENDLESS HISTORY

An article of faith among the proponents of neoliberalism was that the cumulative arc of human development "underwritten by the abundance of a modern free market economy" would ultimately lead to liberal democracy.[28] Dubbed "the end of history," this influential idea held that the "only coherent political aspiration" that remained after the defeat of "strong dictatorships, whether they be of the world's authoritarian Right, or the communist-totalitarian Left," would be liberalism.[29] The natural alliance between political and economic freedoms would lead to the triumph of liberalism, Francis Fukuyama proposed, so that the only prospect that lay ahead was "centuries of boredom at the end of history" before history would start again.[30] The future of history, at this point, seemed predictable, even lackluster, and its form liberal.

Yet in less than three decades of the "triumph of liberalism," the twentieth-century liberal world order is said to be breaking apart. Instead of "centuries of boredom," we are confronted with "authoritarian populism," "illiberal democracies," and the return of "identity politics," the signs of an impending breakdown in the liberal world order. The fear of boredom has been replaced with the fears of majoritarian populism. This rupture in liberal democracies, diagnosed as "democratic recession,"[31] has puzzled many political theorists who struggle to explain why many people across Europe are turning to populist ethnonationalism or authoritarian traditions. Or why they appear to have rejected global cosmopolitanism and freedoms including free markets, all of which are the essential building blocks of liberal politics. Some attempts to explain this conundrum have dwelt on the theme of global inequality. In this view, the ever-widening gap between the "global elite" and "the people," or the "fat plutocrats" and the "squeezed middle," is a prime factor in the rise of illiberal democracies. Economic inequality is seen as the bedrock of authoritarian populism that stokes as well as thrives on the politics of resentment. But what it doesn't explain sufficiently is why the Right has been more successful than the Left in channeling this resentment toward their political program. The clues perhaps lie in how the liberal utopias of globalization were sketched out in the late twentieth century.

Two discursive shifts are critical in the story of globalization. The first is the use of the expression *free markets* or *globalization* instead of *capitalism*. The idea of a "market" or "economic interdependence" invokes an egalitarian condition within which exchange and trade takes place of pure free will. These discursive shifts override questions of accumulation, appropriation, and exploitation of labor and resources, the conditions of unfettered neoliberal capitalism that in turn produce and exacerbate social inequality. The second is the conjoining of the ideas of multiculturalism and cosmopolitanism to free-market globalization. To be sure, multiculturalism does not require capitalism to thrive, for the mingling of cultures and people long preceded the era of unabashed and unrestrained capitalism. But by harnessing itself to multiculturalism, capitalism in the garb of globalization acquired wider acceptance. It is this association of multiculturalism with free markets that has created backlash against the former. In the meanwhile, as we have seen, capitalism is reforming itself once again, this time as a national enclosure of investments in alliance with hypernationalist cultural politics: the brand new nation.

The current focus on identity as the crux of the crisis of liberalism, however, continues to underestimate the capacity of capitalism to refashion itself in ever-new forms. Once again, Francis Fukuyama is at the forefront of this debate. He has argued that the focus on economic conditions overlooks the principle condition that drives human history—the struggle for recognition of one's identity. The demand for recognition of one's identity, which he calls the "true inner self," is in his view a "master concept that unifies much of what is going on in world politics today . . . and cannot simply be satisfied by economic means."[32] While not ruling out the effect of economic inequalities in contemporary politics, he suggests that "economic grievances become much more acute when they are attached to feelings of indignity and disrespect. Indeed much of what we understand to be economic motivation actually reflects not a straightforward desire for wealth and resources, but the fact that money is perceived to be a marker of status and buys respect."[33] Fukuyama's intention is to steer us away from what he sees as "simpleminded economic models" that presume human beings to be rational individuals and instead work toward "a better theory of the human soul" to capture the complexity of human behavior. But in doing so, he overlooks that material and spiritual worlds are not always opposed to one another. It is in these seeming contradictions that we begin to see the peculiar entanglements that cohere the imperatives of capitalist growth and identity politics that frame the contemporary world.

To begin with, the world of globalization had never evolved in contrast to national identities (despite the dominant discourse) or sought to overcome the ethnonationalism of the past. Instead, by the end of the twentieth century, ethnocultures, or national identities, were being capitalized to become commercial brand identities that generate economic value. In fact, Fukuyama's observation that the politics of resentment and demands for the recognition of identity cohere as "money is perceived to be a marker of status and buys respect" points to deep interconnections between the domain of politics and the domain of economy. This is precisely how "identity economies" have long operated and how the crux of Nationality Inc. has been fashioned for the market. The dynamic of the exchange of value has always been clear—the authentic identity (inner self) could be branded successfully, and what could be branded was authentic identity. Fukuyama's project is to find a better theory of the human soul that is not weighed down or corrupted by economic motivations. Yet his quest to find a pure space for the assertion of human dignity that is above utilitarianism is undone when he insists that economic grievances are mere proxies for feelings of indignity and disrespect. He is right in pointing out the importance of human dignity but wrong in overlooking that fulfillment of material needs is a condition for human dignity too. The pure space for human dignity can exist only if we imagine material and spiritual worlds to be completely detachable from one another. What is at stake at this point is not just the quest for human dignity but the lure of fulfilling the nationalist dreams of "arrival" in the world as a great power, of undoing the history of colonial subjugation, and even of establishing one's cultural superiority. This is the messiness within which capitalism and identity politics can occupy common ground—the brand new nation is the key to understanding these apparent contradictions.

The emerging worlds in the twenty-first century appear to be familiar, even though epistemic scaffolding has changed in dramatic ways. Consider the twentieth-century internationalist imagination of the world as a "family of nations"[34] that celebrated diversity predicated on spatial segmentations, or "culture gardens separated by boundary-maintaining values—as posited essences" that imagined the world as a series of bounded spaces.[35] Although the family of nations continues to exist, its logics and effects have undergone a major transformation. Recall here the idea of rootedness—of cultures and people anchored in national territories—which continues to persist even in this internationalist vision of the world. The irony is that the decades of globalization did not dilute this cultural-spatial arrangement. Instead, the culture gardens were reterritorialized into enclosures of capital, each an exclusive brand that capitalized its essential cultural identity and sought to draw ever more investments to the enclosure. If once the world was a family of nations, it is now a family of brand new nations that thrive on the promise of capitalist growth and hypernationalism. This proliferation of nations turned investment destinations has created a new dynamic that allows the states to lay full claim to the national territory and even expand inward by bringing more untapped territory into the fold of investment destination. The promise of investments is held out as a mode of national integration, the healing balm that accompanies any coercive political move to extend centralized governance to the peripheries.[36] And in turn, the hypernationalism fueled on investment flows continues to capture and control ever more peripheries into the fold of capitalist transformation.

The investment-fueled hypernationalism is the force that drives the brand new nation. The staging of the brand new nation is often explained as a tactical move by policy makers, a necessary policy that the state needs to pursue in order to attain economic ascendance. Yet the politics of brand making helps open a vast space for social-political experimentation, the consequences of which are not always fully anticipated. In India, a quarter century of the nation-branding project has helped sharpen a specific kind of cultural politics that lives off branding of the authentic Indian difference in the world. The push to brand the original Indian cultural essence, for example, has led to a predominance of pre-Islamic imagery combined with the globalized aesthetics of Hindu cultural identity in the nation-brand campaigns. This has also boosted the search for the uncommon—the cultural difference that is not shared with the other—that can be achieved only by continuously peeling back layers of history to reach into a mythical ancient past. The increasing focus on yoga and vegetarianism to brand India's Hindu identity is an example of this trend. The uncommon difference, the exclusive identity not shared with others is the prime ingredient on which a successful brand is built. If this exclusive identity is deemed a profitable asset that generates economic value, then generation of economic value in turn brings recognition and respect to the uncommon and even reifies it. This also means that in order to market the exclusive inner self, the brand needs to evict the other—the Muslims, the poor, the Dalits—from the image frame, to seek the uncommon in what had once been a common cultural existence. The eviction of the matter surplus to the brand is not always limited to the image frame; the brand creates its ideal world as it ought to be in the image of the dominant group. This is where we begin to make sense of majoritarian impulses and the return of ethnonationalism (that had never left in the first place) to the field of politics.

Witness, then, the populist politics that shape the brand new nation: consumed with an endless supply of good news, the nation is forever in a state of optimism and anticipation of the long-promised good times. The ones who express doubts or troubling questions are at best dismissed as pessimists[37] and at worst categorized as traitors.[38] In fact, pessimism is itself a form of treachery, for what keeps the engine of the brand new nation running is the constant production of hope. To continue to hope amid falling economic growth is not just to trust the strong leader to manage capital but also to trust in the promise of capitalist growth to trickle-down to the poorest citizens one day. The paradox of the brand new nation is that economic downturn does not necessarily lead to the weakening of the political leadership; indeed, it potentially even strengthens it. For what keeps the brand new nation afloat is the promise of good times, the permanent state of anticipation, the dreamworlds forever a work in progress. History is endless, and the brand new nation is merely the latest manifestation of manifold futures that await us.

ACKNOWLEDGMENTS

This book began as a fascination with publicity images. I became enchanted with the colorful images of the "India Story," or of "New India," that were gaining attention in the global circuits of publicity more than a decade ago. The India in this India story was an alluring proposition—a land brimming with optimism and opportunity, a resource-rich nation of enterprising people, an ancient civilizational culture that was fast morphing into an economic powerhouse. It was a familiar place and yet also unfamiliar in many ways. The India I had grown up in was dubbed a developing nation, a nation in standby mode, forever waiting to arrive as a great power in the world. In contrast, the India in the publicity images I was witnessing was no longer biding time; it had arrived on the global stage. Or so the official publicity posters and advertisements proclaimed, and this euphoric view was echoed in the world of global investors and policy makers. I began collecting bits and pieces of this unfolding India story, of spectacular artifacts from many places I have lived—from Copenhagen to Delhi and from Tehran to Tel Aviv. The image trail eventually led me to Davos and the World Economic Forum, the influential venue at which the global elite assembles annually to network and speculate on global futures. This is one of the key sites at which India made its spectacular debut as an attractive investment destination in the global economy. And this is where many entanglements between the state and the capital, between culture and commerce, and between the many modes of capitalization of the nation-state can be witnessed. What began as mere curiosity eventually turned into a study of the past and the future of nation branding and the ongoing capitalist transformation of the nation-state. The publicity images of Brand India as a destination for global capital became a unique entry point into a much larger phenomenon: the speculative opening up of the old third world, or the BRICS nations—the promise of good times and of an investment-fueled hypernationalism in the twenty-first century.

I have incurred many debts over the years while pursuing this subject. I want to extend my deepest gratitude to those who offered their critical engagement with my work at various stages: Rina Agrawala, Mukulika Banerjee, Amita Baviskar, Tarini Bedi, Lisa Bjorkman, Sharad Chari, Manuela Ciotti, Lawrence Cohen, John Comaroff, Faisal Devji, Nandini Gooptu, Thomas Blom Hansen, Keith Hart, Kajri Jain, Jukka Jouhki, David Ludden, Nayanika Mathur, Saloni Mathur, William Mazzarella, Kenneth Bo Nielsen, Kavita Philip, Chris Pinney, Arvind Rajagopal, Sumathi Ramaswamy, Mahesh Rangarajan, Anupama Rao, Srirupa Roy, Ornit Shani, Aradhana Sharma, Sarabjeet Singh, Sanjay Srivastava, Luisa Steur, Nandini Sundar, Sharika Thirangama, Peter van der Veer, and two anonymous readers for Stanford University Press. I particularly owe William Mazzarella gratitude for offering valuable comments at the formative stages of this work.

In the professional field of nation branding and public diplomacy, I want to thank those who generously gave me their time and invaluable leads: Agnello Dias, Aparna Dutt Sharma, Vistasp Hodiwala, Sudhir Horo, Amitabh Kant, Ajay Khanna, Onno Ruhl, Navtej Sarna, Amit Shahi, V. Sunil, Navdeep Suri, and Prathap Suthan. These interactions—facilitated via a variety of media, from Skype, WhatsApp, and email to old-fashioned personal meetings—have been crucial to my work. I am especially thankful to V. Sunil and Prathap Suthan for allowing me to use their image archive.

This work has benefited immensely from critical comments and discussions I received at the Department of Sociology, University of Delhi; School of International Studies, Jawaharlal Nehru University; Center for Indian Studies in Africa, Johannesburg; Center for Modern Indian Studies, Gottingen; Max Planck Institute for Ethnic and Religious Diversity; Nehru Memorial Museum and Library; Wits Institute for Social Economic Research, University of Witwatersrand; International Institute for Asian Studies, Leiden; Department of Anthropology, University College London; and South Asia seminar series at Aarhus

University; University of Chicago; Haifa University; Hebrew University, Jerusalem; Oxford University; Lund University; New York University; University of California, Berkeley; University of California, Los Angeles; School of Oriental and African Studies, London; University of Jyväskulä; Uppsala University; and Stanford University.

At my own department in the University of Copenhagen, my colleagues have provided me with a stimulating and collegial environment. I owe gratitude especially to my colleagues in the Asia group: Rune Bennike, Rune-Christopher Dragsdahl, Bani Gill, Dan Hirslund, Maansi Parpiani, Stine Simonsen Puri, Elmar Renner, Atreyee Sen, Marie Yoshida, and Emilija Zabiliute. Thanks are also due to Joan Ellingsgaard Kindberg, Therese Boje Mortensen, and Sofie Rosa Hviid Mønster for helping me prepare the notes and bibliography and transcriptions at different stages.

This work has been made possible through a generous research grant offered by Danmarks Frie Forskningsfond (Independent Research Fund). It allowed me the freedom to develop my own ideas across disciplinary boundaries. Parts of the following articles have been reworked into three chapters in the book: "Post-exotic India: On Remixed Histories and Smart Images," *Identities: Global Studies in Culture and Power* (2016) 23(3):307–326; "'I am India Shining': The Investor-Citizen and the Indelible Icon of Good Times," *Journal of Asian Studies* (2016) 75(3):621–648; "World as Commodity: Or, How the 'Third World' became an 'Emerging Market,'" *Comparative Studies of South Asia, Africa and the Middle East* (2018) 38(2):377–395.

A special word of gratitude is due to Thomas Blom Hansen, who offered unstinting support to this interdisciplinary endeavor. Marcela Cristina Maxfield at Stanford University Press steered the publication of my work from manuscript to book with unwavering encouragement and exemplary patience. Sunna Juhn and Jessica Ling offered professional editorial assistance during its final makeover into a book. I remain thankful for this support.

Finally, I want to thank my family in Delhi and Copenhagen who stepped in to help with childcare at crucial points. Without this support network, I could not have undertaken archival work and fieldwork. Anders, my husband, has been a steady source of encouragement and support through this process, which involved travels and absences. Anton and Noor, my children, have grown up with the fact that their mother's "book work" never stopped, even during vacations. Without their love and affection, my work would not have come to life. This book is dedicated to them.

NOTES

CHAPTER 1

1. Dipesh Chakrabarty, "Adda, Calcutta: Dwelling in Modernity," *Public Culture* 11, no. 1 (1999): 118.

2. This radical vision of the world, by India's first prime minister, Jawaharlal Nehru, eventually became the guiding principle of the Non-Aligned Movement (NAM) of nations, which desired to move beyond the bipolar hegemony of the United States and Soviet Union.

3. Vijay Prashad, *The Darker Nations: A People's History of the Third World* (New York: New Press, 2007), xvii.

4. This approach represented the middle path between free market and planned economy that would be used to create the modernist vision of an industrialized society. The mixed economy eventually came to be seen as a roadblock in India's path to growing its economic muscle and becoming a great power.

5. The advertisement poster featured boldly in the 2007 International Tourism Bourse in Berlin, in which India was a partner country. The sign was hung at the main entrance to the convention. See also Dilip Bobb, "India Excel at International Tourism Bourse in Berlin, 2007," *India Today*, March 26, 2007, https://www.indiatoday.in /magazine/leisure/story/20070326-india-at-international-tourism-bourse-in-berlin20 07-748967-2007-03-26#close-overlay.

6. The gendered nature of this transaction is apparent—the (masculine) outside capital fertilizes the (feminine) earth of the investment-ready nation.

7. Fernand Braudel, *Civilization & Capitalism 15th–18th Century: The Perspective of the World* (Berkeley: University of California Press, 1992), 19.

8. Jean Comaroff and John Comaroff, "Millennial Capitalism: First Thoughts on the Second Coming," *Public Culture* 12, no. 2 (2000): 291–343; and Joseph E. Stiglitz, *Globalization and Its Discontents* (New York: Norton, 2003).

9. Susan Buck Morss has shown how the twentieth century dreamworlds of mass utopias were once drawn in the socialist frame. I show how the twenty-first-century collective dreamworlds have a distinct capitalist foundation wherein the "collective" is inherently exclusionary—it relies on the irredeemable promise of the trickle-down theory to bring prosperity to all. See Susan Buck-Morss, *Dreamworlds and Catastrophe: The Passing of Mass Utopia in East and West* (Cambridge, MA: MIT Press, 2000).

10. Arjun Appadurai, *Modernity at Large: Cultural Dimensions of Globalization* (Minneapolis: University of Minnesota Press, 1996), 19, 169; Appadurai, "Deep

Democracy: Urban Governmentality and the Horizon of Politics," *Environment and Urbanization* 23, no. 2 (2001): 23–44; and Saskia Sassen, "Spatialities and Temporalities of the Global: Elements for a Theorization," *Public Culture* 12 (2000): 215–32.

11. The idea of globalization entered the scholarly and policy discourse in full force in the 1990s. This was the moment of liberal triumphalism, and it generated both critical and euphoric accounts of how liberal capitalism was reshaping the world. The world was seen as constitutive of flows, movements, and fluidscapes that ran their courses unhindered, and this phenomenon was dubbed globalization. A vast literature has been generated on this now ubiquitous idea. See, for example, Appadurai, *Modernity at Large*; Saskia Sassen, *Globalization and Its Discontents: Essays on the New Mobility of People and Money* (New York: New Press, 1999); J. India and R. Rosaldo, "Introduction: A World in Motion," in *The Anthropology of Globalization: A Reader* (Malden, MA: Blackwell, 2002), 1–34; D. Held and A. McGrew, eds., *The Global Transformation Reader: An Introduction to the Globalization Debate* (Malden, MA: Polity, 2000); Zygmunt Bauman, *Globalization: The Human Consequences* (New York: Columbia University Press, 1998); Anna Tsing, "The Global Situation," *Cultural Anthropology* 15, no. 3 (2000): 327–60; Stiglitz, *Globalization and Its Discontents*; and Jan Nederveen Pieterse, *Global Melange: Globalization and Culture* (London: Rowman and Littlefield, 2003). Also, a number of journals dedicated to the theme of globalization or bearing the prefix *global-* sustain scholarship in this field. See, for example, the journals *Globalizations* (https://www.tandfonline.com/action/journalInformation ?show=aimsScope&journalCode=rglo20) and *Global Networks* (https://onlinelibrary .wiley.com/journal/14710374).

12. See, for example, Saskia Sassen, *Territory, Authority, Rights: From Medieval to Global Assemblages* (Princeton, NJ: Princeton University Press, 2008). See also Jürgen Habermas for a critical discussion of postnational utopias in connection with the 1990s European Union debate. *The Postnational Constellation: Political Essays* (Cambridge, MA: MIT Press, 2001).

13. The imagination of the world seemed to have come full circle—it was now said to be flat, limitless, and open, its barriers swept away in the accelerated momentum of "globalization 3.0," further contracting an already shrinking world. It was not that mobility or connections were new to human history, marked as it has been since ancient times with long-distance trade, wars, travel, pilgrimages, and cultural exchange. What was new was the sense of accelerated momentum at the end of the Cold War, epitomized in the end-of-history thesis that claimed the triumph of liberalism. If the fall of the Berlin Wall and the Soviet Union expanded the domain of free markets, then cheaper air travel, ever-new media technologies, modes of consumption, and the digital world opened by the internet fueled the sense of social acceleration.

14. A case in point is the large-scale infrastructure-development projects—multilane highways, high-speed trains, ports, cargo and storage facilities, smart cities, and special economic zones—undertaken by states to connect the interior regions to coasts to enhance mobility of goods and make the territory investment ready.

15. In neoliberal economies, nation branding is also in the sphere of political contestations. The opponents often challenge the branding project, in an effort not to demolish it but to claim that the state has not done it well enough. See Andrew Graan's study of branding Macedonia, "Counterfeiting the Nation? Skopje 2014 and the Politics of Nation Branding in Macedonia," *Cultural Anthropology* 28, no. 1 (2013): 161–79.

16. See William Mazzarella, *Shoveling Smoke: Advertising and Globalization in Contemporary India* (Durham, NC: Duke University Press, 2003); Constantine V. Nakassis, "Brand, Citationality, Performativity," *American Anthropologist* 114, no. 4 (2012): 624–38; and Nakassis, "Brands and Their Surfeits," *Cultural Anthropology* 28, no. 1 (2013): 111–26.

17. A telling example is Brand India, known as the "mother brand" in the world of advertising, which is now composed of regional states turned subnational brands—Sunrise Andhra, Awesome Assam, Magnetic Maharashtra, Happening Haryana, Vibrant Gujarat, Odisha: New Opportunities, Brand Uttar Pradesh, Invest Punjab: Opportunities Unlimited, Momentum Jharkhand: The Investment Destination, Magnetic Mizoram: Get Mesmerized, Invest Karnataka, Bengal Means Business, and Organic Uttarakhand.

18. I particularly invoke works such as Karl Polayni's *The Great Transformation: The Political and Economic Origins of Our Time* (Boston: Beacon Press, 2001) that seek explanations of change in national and international institutional politics.

19. Susan Sontag, *The Art of Revolution: 96 Posters from Cuba* (London: Pall Mall Press, 1970), vii.

20. Publicity offers a provocative encounter that can potentially interrupt the status quo. On encounter as provocation, a calling forth, see William Mazzarella, *The Mana of Mass Society* (Chicago: University of Chicago Press, 2017), 6–7.

21. William Mazzarella calls this the "illusion of premediated existence," which is fundamentally constituted through mediation, an irony that requires masking in order to be effective. See "Affect: What Is It Good For?," in *Enchantments of Modernity*, ed. Saurabh Dube (London: Routledge, 2009), 210–309.

22. Until the sixteenth century, the Latin term *propaganda* meant "reproduction" in a biological sense. In the middle of that century, the Catholic church established the College of Propaganda to train missionaries to spread Catholic doctrines in newly "discovered" territories outside Europe.

23. What the archive does is to activate images that already exist in those dreams that publicity campaigns seek to address. See Mazzarella, *Mana of Mass Society*.

24. Outward appearance notwithstanding, the secular figure of the nation has always absorbed and made acceptable all that could never be rendered in the form of economy. On the modern origins of nation and nationalism, see Benedict Anderson, *Imagined Communities: Reflections on the Origin and Spread of Nationalism* (London: Verso, 2016).

25. John Hutchinson, *The Dynamics of Cultural Nationalism: The Gaelic Revival and the Creation of the Irish Nation State* (London: Allen and Unwin, 1987), 13.

26. Isaiah Berlin, *Vico and Herder: Two Studies in the History of Ideas* (New York: Viking Press, 1976), quoted in Hutchinson, *Dynamics of Cultural Nationalism*, 13.

27. Hutchinson, *Dynamics of Cultural Nationalism*, 13.

28. Johann Gottfried Herder, *Outlines of a Philosophy of the History of Man*, trans. T. Churchill (London, 1803). See especially Book VI, "Organisation of the Man," in which he lays out the history of mankind as a natural history wherein "varieties in the organisation of different races . . . are already noticed in elementary treatises on natural history" (234–91).

29. Ernest Renan, "What Is a Nation?," in *What Is a Nation? and Other Political Writings*, trans. M. F. N. Giglioli (New York: Columbia University Press, 2018), 261.

30. Anthony D. Smith, *The Nation Made Real: Art and National Identity in Western Europe, 1600–1850* (Oxford, UK: Oxford University Press, 2013).

31. Sumathi Ramaswamy, "Maps, Mother/Goddesses, and Martyrdom in Modern India," *Journal of Asian Studies* 67, no. 3 (2008): 819–53.

32. Joan B. Landes, *Visualizing the Nation: Gender, Representation, and Revolution in Eighteenth-Century France* (Ithaca, NY: Cornell University Press, 2001), 2. See also Ramaswamy, "Maps, Mother/Goddesses, and Martyrdom."

33. Anderson, *Imagined Communities*.

34. John Comaroff and Jean Comaroff, *Ethnicity, Inc.* (Chicago: University of Chicago Press, 2009), 118.

35. Comaroff and Comaroff, *Ethnicity, Inc.*, 125.

36. George Paul Meiu, Jean Comaroff, and John Comaroff, introduction to *Ethnicity, Inc. Revisited* (Bloomington: Indiana University Press, forthcoming), 21.

37. William Mazzarella addresses the problem of how value is managed and harnessed in a situation of routine exchange and how the inalienable element is absorbed in the system of alienation. See *Shoveling Smoke*.

38. Wally Olins, "Branding the Nation: The Historical Context," *Journal of Brand Management* 9, nos. 4–5 (2002): 242.

39. Michel Girard, "States, Diplomacy and Image Making: What Is New? Reflections on Current British and French Experiences" (paper presented at Image, State, and International Relations Conference, London School of Economics, June 24, 1999), quoted in Olins, "Branding the Nation," 241.

40. Olins, "Branding the Nation," 247.

41. Wally Olins, *Trading Identities: Why Countries and Companies Are Becoming More Alike* (London: Foreign Policy Centre, 1999).

42. The various lives of the corporation have existed since ancient times as non-profit ventures in the Roman Empire, in the medieval church as a corporate structure, and, later, in municipal corporations.

43. Douglas Harper, *Online Etymology Dictionary*, s.v. "corporation (n.)," accessed April 20, 2018, https://www.etymonline.com/word/corporation.

44. See Ernst H. Kantorowicz, *The King's Two Bodies: A Study in Medieval Political Theology* (Princeton, NJ: Princeton University Press, 2016).

45. An apt example of these inseparable capital-state entanglements is the most influential corporation in the world, the British East India Company, which held monopoly trade rights and eventually control of vast colonies across the world. The first charter sanctioned in 1600 by Elizabeth I asserts that "we . . . for the increase of our navigation and the advancement of lawful traffic to the benefit of our commonwealth, have . . . granted . . . unto our said loving subjects (the 218 merchants) . . . that they from henceforth be *one body corporate and politic*, in deed and in name, by the name of the Governor and Company of Merchants of London trading into the East Indies" (emphasis added). The charter documents were at once the birth of a for-profit corporation through state proclamation and the foundational unity of the state and capital in pursing commercial enterprises. G. W. Prothero, "First Charter to the East India Company, December 31, 1600," in *Select Statutes and Other Constitutional Documents: Illustrative of the Reigns of Elizabeth and James I* (Oxford, UK: Clarendon Press, 1906), 448.

46. The British East India Company, like the later Dutch, French, and Danish companies that ventured in Asia, eventually turned its monopoly trade rights into a full colonial enterprise that encompassed vast territories across the world.

47. Bayly Osterhammel, *The Transformation of the World: A Global History of the Nineteenth Century* (Princeton, NJ: Princeton University Press, 2014).

48. Walter Benjamin, *The Arcades Project*, trans. Howard Eiland and Kevin McLaughlin (Cambridge, MA: Harvard University Press, 2002), 18. The first landmark world exhibition was "The Great Exhibition of the Works of Industry of All Nations" held in 1851 in London, which epitomized the technoscientific spirit of the Industrial Revolution, the enchanting world of commodities, and precious raw material extracted from Europe's overseas colonies. Although Paris had already been host to a series of industrial expositions between 1797 and 1849, the exposition in 1851 was the first one to take place on such a vast scale, including representation from European nations as well as overseas colonies. See *The Great Exhibition: The Crystal Palace Exposition of 1851* (New York: Random House, 1995), ix–xii. The site of the exhibition called "Crystal Palace" itself was a mesmerizing extravaganza—a light and airy prefabricated modern structure made of glass, iron, and wood, a "technological world wonder" of its time that represented the British industrial prowess and imperial dominance in the world. There were a record 13,937 exhibitors, of which more than half were from Britain and its thirty-two colonies. *Great Exhibition*, 179.

49. It was here the public at large could witness the "magnificent spectacle" of "human industry" that Western civilization had made possible. The displayed commodities were classified into four main categories—raw material, machinery, manufactures, and fine arts—and thirty subdivisions that enabled visitors to be, as Jerome Adolphe Blanqui, a French political economist, wrote in a series of letters describing the 1851 exhibition, "carried away by magic from country to country, from East to West, from iron to cotton, from silk to wool, from machines to manufactures." Quoted in Lara Kriegel, *Grand Designs: Labor, Empire, and the Museum in Victorian Culture* (Durham, NC: Duke University Press, 2008), 86, 167. See also Thomas

Richards, *The Commodity Culture of Victorian England: Advertising and Spectacle 1851–1914* (Stanford, CA: Stanford University Press, 1990).

50. Edward Lloyd, *The Law of Trade Marks: With Some Account of Its History and Development in the Decisions of the Courts of Law and Equity* (London: Yates and Alexander, 1862), 1. This was surely an updated version of Locke's idea of property created through labor.

51. Harry Bodkin Poland, *Trade Marks: The Merchandise Marks Act, 1862* (London: John Crockford, 1862), 5. The first British Merchandise Marks Act, in 1862, was brought simply as a measure to protect property and as a measure against misdemeanors of fraud and commercial theft punishable with fines and even imprisonment. Subsequently, an act was passed specifically to patent inventions superseding an earlier trademarks act in 1875. On the early history of trademarks, see J. E. Crawford Munro, *The Patents, Designs, and Trade Marks Act, 1883: With the Rules and Instructions* (London: Stevens and Sons, 1884).

52. Lloyd, *Law of Trade Marks*, 8.

53. The use of "Made in Germany" as an example of foreign goods flooding the British market was no coincidence. The total value of German goods imported into the United Kingdom increased by over 30 percent in a single decade between 1883 and 1893. German exports were outcompeting other manufacturers, and Hamburg was said to have left Liverpool behind in terms of shipping returns. In the late nineteenth century, unified Germany embarked on an ambitious industrialization program that made it one of the major suppliers of industrial and consumer goods in the world market. In this era of cutthroat free-trade competitiveness, the manufacturing boom in Germany and the attendant consolidation of its political power was fast becoming a cause for concern for other European trading powers. Ernest Edwin Williams, *Made in Germany* (London: William Heinemann, 1896), 138–39.

54. Howard Payn, *The Merchandise Marks Act, 1887: With Special Reference to Importation Sections* (London: Stevens and Sons, 1888), 17.

55. As Ernest Edwin Williams explained, "When it is made in Germany, the mug must state so much, lest the unwary excursionist should bear his gift home in triumph over the discovery of a native school of pottery adjoining the Hall by the Sea." But this same "Made in Germany" stamp, he regretfully added, undercut the British manufacturers and instead "(it) operates as a free advertisement of German manufactures. The colonial buyer (to take an instance) sends orders to England for goods. He receives these orders stamped 'Made in Germany.' Obviously, he says, the English middleman has made a profit; and he may add, 'I will purchase direct from the German houses, and save the commission. . . .' Having gone to Germany for one class of goods, he is made acquainted with the virtues and prices of others, and being on the spot, he purchases things he would otherwise have bought in England. So the English loss is extended beyond the particular German made article which the Merchandise Marks Act pointed out." Williams, *Made in Germany*, 138.

56. The geographical indicators were already addressed in the Paris Convention for the Protection of Industrial Property, 1883.

57. *The Madrid Agreement Concerning the International Registration of Marks from 1891 to 1991* (Geneva: International Bureau of Intellectual Property, 1991), 5, https://www.wipo.int/edocs/pubdocs/en/marks/880/wipo_pub_880.pdf.

58. "Call for Papers, Cases and Doctoral Posters," IPBA, December 5–7, 2018, http://placebranding.org/wp-content/uploads/2018/01/IPBA-Call-for-papers-posters -and-cases-2018.pdf.

59. *Place Branding and Public Diplomacy*, https://www.springer.com/business+& +management/journal/41254/PSE?detailsPage=aboutThis; *Journal of Destination Marketing and Management*, https://www.journals.elsevier.com/journal-of-destination-ma rketing-and -management.

60. "Institute for Identity," INSTID, accessed June 30 2018, http://instid.org.

61. Joseph S. Nye is credited with proposing the idea of soft power. See Joseph Nye, "Soft Power," *Foreign Policy*, no. 80 (1990): 153–71.

62. Simon Anholt, "Foreword," special issue on nation branding, *Journal of Brand Management* 9, nos. 4–5 (2002): 234.

63. Wally Olins, *The Brand Handbook* (London: Thames and Hudson, 2008).

64. Simon Anholt, "What Is a Nation Brand?," Superbrands, 2002, http://www .superbrands.com/turkeysb/trcopy/files/Anholt_3939.pdf p186. See also Anholt, *Competitive Identity: The New Brand Management for Nations, Cities and Regions* (Basingstoke, UK: Palgrave Macmillan, 2007).

65. Anholt, "What Is a Nation Brand?"

66. Philip Kotler and David Gertner, "Country and Brand, Product and Beyond: A Place Marketing and Brand Management Perspective," *Journal of Brand Management* 9, nos. 4–5 (2002): 250. See also N. Papadopoulos and L. A. Heslop, eds., *Product and Country Images: Impact and Role in International Marketing* (Binghamton, NY: Haworth Press, 1993); T. A. Shimp, S. Saeed, and T. J. Madden, "Countries and Their Products: A Cognitive Structure Perspective," *Journal of the Academy of Marketing Science* 21, no. 4 (1993): 323–30.

67. Simon Anholt, *Places: Identity, Image and Reputation* (Basingstoke, UK: Palgrave Macmillan, 2010), 3–5. In many ways, this echoes the old discomfort with market societies thought to be morally bankrupt, in which "almost everything can be bought and sold" for financial profit. See Michael J. Sandel, *What Money Can't Buy: The Moral Limits of Markets* (London: Penguin, 2013), 5.

68. Wally Olins had presciently addressed this widespread discomfort in imagining the nation as a brand as he offered his seven-step plan to brand nations. That the idea of the "nation as brand" is found to be objectionable by so many, he conjectured, was because "most business people do not know anything about the history of the nation, . . . [and] most academics know nothing about how business works, so each side assumes that the other lives in another and entirely foreign land—and there is no overlap or relationship between them." Olins, "Branding the Nation," 247.

69. Klaus Schwab, *The Global Competitiveness Report 2017–18* (Geneva: World Economic Forum, 2017).

70. The idea of enclosing and engrossing entailed fixing value on land as a factor

of market production and leasing out plots to the highest-bidding tenants. The rent on the leased enclosure was then determined by bargaining on its future capacity to improve so as to extract maximum profits and returns on investment. This shift reconfigured the relationship between humankind and nature and between land and the tiller through the vocabulary of land productivity, innovation, investment, resource, and profit generation. It also introduced a new kind of market-oriented entrepreneurial farmer on whose enclosure the dispossessed peasants now worked as wage laborers. Here we witness how market considerations came to align seamlessly with the Enlightenment-era ideas of human agency and its capacity for reason and progress.

71. Tamar Herzog, *Frontiers of Possession: Spain and Portugal in Europe and the Americas* (Cambridge, MA: Harvard University Press, 2015), 10.

72. John Locke, in his *Two Treatises of Government*, advanced arguments of land use and improvement to make a case for the dispossession of the native inhabitants in the Americas as well as of peasants from the English farmlands, albeit with slight modifications. See Herzog, *Frontiers of Possession*, 120–21.

73. Walter Prescott Webb, *The Great Frontier* (Austin: University of Texas Press, 1951), 11–13.

74. Webb, *Great Frontier*, 12.

75. This long process of enclosing and capitalizing territories into profitable enterprises was a defining moment in the emergence of European domination in the world. The unfettered political-economic expansion of Europe in overseas territories—sometimes nostalgically explained as the "boom hypothesis"—was an era of unprecedented wealth accumulation and material prosperity in Europe. This spectacular economic boom in Europe's fortunes is said to have begun with Christopher Columbus's arrival in the Americas in the late fifteenth century and petered out in the mid-twentieth-century events of decolonization.

76. J. G. Fichte, *The Closed Commercial State*, trans. Anthony Curtis Adler (Albany: State University of New York Press, 2013). Indeed, Fichte presented his arguments for commercial closure as a measure of withdrawal from world trade and to destabilize European colonialism, or what he described as Europe's great "advantage from this common exploitation of the rest of the world" (85). His model of self-contained utopias of peace never found credence at a moment when colonialism masked as free trade was rapidly changing the world.

77. Fichte, *Closed Commercial State*, 140.

78. The idea and extent of natural borders, the kind of specific natural resources that needed to be captured and enclosed for an economy to be profitable, remained blurred and subject to contingency, however. What was brought to the surface instead regarding the notion of natural borders was the unadorned conception of the nation as a vast enclosure of natural resources, an exclusive claim to vital means of production to be obtained through coercive measures if need be. It also revealed the inherent paradox of the closed commercial state—that the very viability of the enclosure depends on potentially flexible borders that could be expanded to enclose resources according to the needs of the economy. See Fichte, *Closed Commercial State*, 169–70.

79. Fichte, *Closed Commercial State*, 108.

80. The language of development was used extensively to make arguments for infrastructure investments in the nineteenth century. For example, *The Economist* continuously pressed for more systematic investment in infrastructures of trade in imperial India, because there was no tropical raw material "for which India is not as well, or better adopted than any other country; while its dense and illustrious population would seem to offer an illimitable demand for our manufacturers." The publication also claimed that India possessed "the most extensive underdeveloped resources in the world" that could be extracted via better infrastructure. Quoted in Daniel Thorner, *Investment in Empire: British Railway and Steam Shipping Enterprise in India 1825–1849* (Philadelphia: University of Pennsylvania Press, 1950), 2.

81. Thorner, *Investment in Empire*, 2.

82. Robert Melville Grindlay, the founder of Grindlays Bank, was a major advocate for British investment in steamships as a prerequisite for invigorating trade with colonial India. Quoted in Thorner, *Investment in Empire*, 4.

83. The making of the colony into a unified arena of production was undertaken through a variety of state initiatives. See Manu Goswami, *Producing India: From Colonial Economy to National Space* (Chicago: University of Chicago Press, 2008).

84. For example, the network of irrigation canals that followed the annexation of Punjab in 1849 was meant to boost commercial agriculture to feed the demand for raw materials in European markets. See Imran Ali, *The Punjab under Imperialism 1885–1947* (Princeton, NJ: Princeton University Press, 1988).

85. A telling example of this enduring association is *Makers of Modern India*, which features twenty-one portraits of men and women, nearly all of whom are political leaders and reformers, credited with forming modern India. See Ramachandra Guha, *Makers of Modern India* (Delhi: Penguin, 2010).

86. The work of bureaucrats, policy experts and planners, and architects and artists who *did* the actual nation making was subordinate to the political visions. Srirupa Roy, for example, has drawn our attention to those who imagined and brought alive the vision of India as a modern secular nation via films, advertisements, and documentaries. See *Beyond Belief: India and the Politics of Postcolonial Nationalism* (Durham, NC: Duke University Press, 2008).

87. I invoke antipolitics in two ways—one technical-bureaucratic and the other mainly moral and based on caste and class distinctions. First is the idea of antipolitics developed by James Ferguson (1994) and Tim Mitchell (2005) as a form of modern governance and bureaucratic technicalities based on expert technocratic knowledge. And second is antipolitics as a moral stance that perceives electoral politics as an intrinsically dirty or corrupt sphere of social life, as Thomas Blom Hansen has shown in his work. Drawing on the longer genealogy of antipolitics to Gandhian politics, Hansen (1999) has argued that the distaste for electoral politics became even stronger when the 1980s political sphere increasingly came to be equated with the rise and power of dirty, plebeian, and unworthy popular politicians from outside the middle-class, upper-caste milieus. See James Ferguson, *The Anti-Politics Machine:*

Development, Depoliticization, and Bureaucratic Power in Lesotho (Minneapolis: University of Minnesota Press, 1994); Timothy Mitchell, *Rule of Experts: Egypt, Techno-Politics, Modernity* (Berkeley: University of California Press, 2005); and Thomas Blom Hansen, *The Saffron Wave: Democracy and Hindu Nationalism in Modern India* (Princeton, NJ: Princeton University Press, 1999).

88. Critical in this shift was the emergence of the economy as a specialized field with its own experts. The older meanings of *economy* as "thrift" or "expenditure/management of resources" were replaced in the twentieth century with the idea of the economy encompassing notions of governance of a political order or government as Foucault deployed. This genealogical shift in the making of the economy is traced in Mitchell, *Rule of Experts.*

89. In recent years, there has been an effort to position P. V. Narasimharao, instead of Manmohan Singh, as the visionary who engineered economic reforms. What is often lost in these revisionist accounts is the fact that reforms were not exactly popular in the early 1990s. So when Singh, a trained economist, was made the public face of reforms, it was also to capitalize on his expert authority and carry the moral burden in the public domain. On Narasimharao's political legacy, see Vinay Sitapati, *Half-Lion: How P. V. Narasimha Rao Transformed India* (Delhi: Viking, 2016).

90. The gendered distinctions are palpable here. The decision makers, the action-oriented agents, are mainly men. Barring few exceptions, the women present are relegated mostly to roles that require care and hospitality in establishing the cultural uniqueness of India. See chapter 5, "The Magical Market."

91. Despite stated noneconomic motivations, however, the field of nation branding remains intensely competitive at multiple levels. Nation-branding assignments are highly coveted by professionals. The chance to brand the nation helps raise corporate profiles of individuals and companies, so it potentially opens up an entire range of possibilities. Indian agencies have built up substantial reputations globally in the field of nation branding. For example, one prominent Indian branding agency I came across successfully offered their services to help brand not just regions in India but also nations in Asia and Latin America.

92. In the early 1990s, foreign companies had begun showing interest in Indian markets, and what was especially boosted at this point was the business of advertising and publicity. Indian advertising professionals came to occupy a critical role—of mediation between Indian consumer tastes and global commodity brands. On the history of advertising in India and its global turn during the economic reforms, see Mazzarella, *Shoveling Smoke.*

93. Interview by author, Delhi, March 2009.

94. The hopeful emigrants ranged from highly educated tech engineers for whom Silicon Valley remained the dream destination to low-skilled laborers in West Asia.

95. The WEF takes place in the convention center, which is accessible only to the invited delegates. But the town itself becomes a fortress, guarded at key entry points and open inside. This theme is fully dealt with in chapter 5, "The Magical Market."

96. WEF founder Klaus Schwab replaced the term *shareholder* with *stakeholder* to locate businesses in the larger societal frame.

97. I was able to fund my travel and stay through a generous research grant given by the Danish Council of Independent Research.

98. A prominent example of this phenomenon is how the investment profile of BRICS (Brazil, Russia, India, China, South Africa) was boosted once major banks put their weight behind these markets.

99. A frequent charge leveled at nation branding is that it is an empty project since the thing being sold is not apparent. Unlike routine advertising jobs in which the commodity is clearly marked out, the nation branders work in a more abstract space.

100. Dorie Clark, "The Right (and Wrong) Way to Network," *Harvard Business Review*, March 10, 2015, https://hbr.org/2015/03/the-right-and-wrong-way-to-network.

101. I have addressed the problem of archives in the digital age elsewhere. See Ravinder Kaur, "Writing History in a Paperless World: Archives of the Future," *History Worldshop Journal* 79, no. 1 (2015): 242–53.

102. Some material survives in The Wayback Machine web archive, https://archive.org/web/.

CHAPTER 2

1. "India on Fire: India's Economy," *Economist* 382, no. 8514 (February 3, 2007): 77.

2. The overall theme of the special report was overheating—the rate of India's economic growth was found to be too fast to be sustainable in the long run.

3. On the historical roots of capitalism in India, see Ritu Birla, *Stages of Capital: Law, Culture, and Market Governance in Late Colonial India* (Durham, NC: Duke University Press, 2009).

4. The lithograph is a popular illustration widely used to depict the arrival of Columbus. It is curated online as part of the Bettmann-Corbis collection held by Getty Images. "Columbus Discovers America, 1492," Getty Images, accessed November 21, 2018, https://www.gettyimages.dk/detail/news-photo/columbus-discovers-america-1492-lithograph-news-photo/517200614?#-picture-id517200614.

5. The manuscript itself is lost, but its fragments survive via references and reproductions in the works of historians and geographers of the ancient world such as Pliny, Ptolemy, and Strabo. The collection of fragments was compiled in the nineteenth century by the German classicist Dr. E. A. Schwanbeck and translated by J. W. McCrindle. *Ancient India: As Described by Megastenes and Arrian* (London: Trubner, 1877).

6. McCrindle, *Ancient India*, 31–32.

7. Ibid., 31.

8. Ibid.

9. Nicolas Wey Gomez, *The Tropics of Empire: Why Columbus Sailed South to the Indies* (Cambridge, MA: MIT Press, 2008), 177.

10. Gomez, *Tropics of Empire*, 166.

11. Ibid., 174.

12. Ibid., 167.

13. "This is indeed India! The land of dreams and romance, of fabulous wealth and fabulous poverty, of splendor and rage, of palaces and hovels, of famine and pestilence, of geni and giants and Aladdin lamps, of tigers and elephants, the cobra and the jungle, the country of a hundred nations and a hundred tongues, of a thousand religions and two million gods, cradle of the human race, birthplace of human speech, mother of history, grandmother of legend, great-grandmother of traditions, whose yesterdays bear date with the mouldering antiquities of the rest of the nations—the one sole country under the sun that is endowed with an imperishable interest for alien prince and alien peasant, for lettered and ignorant, wise and fool, rich and poor, bond and free, the land that all men desire to see, and having seen once, by even a glimpse, would not give at glimpse for the shows of all the rest of the globe combined." Foreign visitors to India often refer to Mark Twain's characterization of India. See, for example, Brookings Institution, "Mark Twain, Like Many, Overwhelmed by India," YouTube Video, April 29, 2014, https://www.youtube.com/watch?v=VsswWdkX98Y.

14. The internet quote has become a genre in itself that sometimes has little to do with the original words being cited. Internet quotes are more an assemblage than direct quotations. Since the source is not referred to, and the quote is given wide circulation in the digital space, many of these inspirational or celebratory, albeit unverified, quotes gain a life of their own. Under the broad category of "what the world says about India," many famous Euro-American figures, such as Mark Twain, Albert Einstein, and Herman Hesse, are routinely quoted.

15. Karl Marx, *Capital: A Critique of Political Economy*, vol. I (London, Penguin: 1990), 27.

16. Mark Twain, *Following the Equator: A Journey around the World* (Hartford, CT: American Publishing, 1898), 200.

17. A number of excellent studies on the history of the East India Company are available. See Nick Robins, *The Corporation That Changed the World* (London: Pluto, 2006); K. N. Chaudhuri, *The English East India Company: The Study of an Early Joint Stock Company 1600–1640* (London: Kelley, 1965); Chaudhuri, *The Trading World of Asia and the English East India Company 1660–1760* (Cambridge, UK: Cambridge University Press, 1978); William Dalrymple, *The Anarchy: The East India Company, Corporate Violence, and the Pillage of an Empire* (London: Bloomsbury, 2019); and Philip J. Stern, *The Company-State: Corporate Sovereignty and the Early Modern Foundations of the British Empire in India* (Oxford, UK: Oxford University Press, 2011).

18. P. Chidambaram, "Budget Speech of Shri P. Chidambaram, Minister of Finance Part A," July 27, 1996, http://www.indiabudget.gov.in/ub1996-97/BUDGET/.

19. Mohan Padmanabhan, "EPCs to Popularize India Brand Equity Fund," *Hindu Business Line*, June 17, 2000.

20. Mr. S. K. Ray, an exporter, quoted in Padmanabhan, "India Brand Equity Fund."

21. Some loans granted by IBEF were never recovered. One example is the loan worth Rs 4.5 crore offered to a little-known company called Vishuddha Rasayanee to

market Urvashi perfumes in Paris. The company has wound up in the meantime, but the recovery case continues. See IBEF, *Annual Report 2015–16*, section 4, "Accounts and Administration," accessed November 21, 2018, https://www.ibef.org/uploads/An nual-Report-2015-16.pdf.

22. "Towards Creating Brand India," *Financial Express*, February 15, 2003, http://www.financialexpress.com/archive/towards-creating-brand-india/73145/.

23. IBEF, "What Is IBEF?," India Brand Equity Foundation, 2005, www.ibef.org /aboutus.aspx.

24. Government of India, Ministry of Commerce, "Performance Budget 2005–2006," p. 7, accessed November 21, 2018, http://commerce.nic.in/publications/PB -2005-06-FINAL.pdf.

25. IBEF began as a government agency in 1996 and remained so until 2002, when it became a public-private partnership between the Ministry of Commerce and the CII. This partnership changed once again after 2015 when IBEF fully reverted to the Ministry of Commerce to be headed by an IAS officer.

26. Kamal Nath, "India: The Paradigm Shift," foreword to *Annual Report 2005–06*, by IBEF, accessed April 4, 2018, https://www.ibef.org/download/india_paradigm shift.pdf.

27. IBEF, "What Is IBEF?"

28. Ibid.

29. Nath, "Paradigm Shift."

30. Government of India, Ministry of Commerce, "Performance Budget 2005–2006," 8.

31. Ibid.

32. A short visual retrospective on the 2006 India at Hannover Messe can be found here: "India—Partner Country 2006: Photos," EEPC Hannover, accessed January 15, 2018, http://eepchannover.in/india-partner-country-2006-photos/.

33. India@60 brochure, Incredible India campaign.

34. Ajay Khanna, "The Year in Review," in *Annual Report 2005–06*, by IBEF, p. 3, accessed January 5, 2020, https://www.ibef.org/download/year_review.pdf.

35. That India itself is a celebrated object as well as a site of speculation would become the encompassing narrative over the next several years. On speculation on and in India, see Laura Bear, Ritu Birla, and Stine Simonsen Puri, "Speculation: Futures and Capitalism in India," *Comparative Studies of South Asia, Africa and the Middle East* 35, no. 3 (2015): 387–91.

36. Jim O'Neill, *The Growth Map: Economic Opportunity in the BRICs and Beyond* (New York: Penguin Group, 2011), 7.

37. IFC, *Six Decades of Innovation, Influence, Demonstration and Impact*, accessed July 14, 2016, http://www.ifc.org/wps/wcm/connect/CORP_EXT_Content/IFC_Ex ternal_Corporate_Site/About+IFC_New/IFC+History.

38. "Decade 2: Broadening our Scope," About IFC, International Finance Corporation, accessed July 14, 2016, http://www.ifc.org/wps/wcm/connect/corp_ext_content /ifc_external_corporate_site/about+ifc_new/ifc+history/1970s.

39. Antoine Van Agtmael, *The Emerging Market Century: How a New Breed of World-Class Companies Is Overtaking the World* (London: Simon and Schuster, 2007), 4.

40. Ibid., 5.

41. Jean Comaroff and John Comaroff, *Theory from the South: Or, How Euro-America Is Evolving Toward Africa* (New York: Routledge, 2012), 1–7.

42. Agtmael, *Emerging Market Century*, 5.

43. IFC, "Who Coined the Phrase 'Emerging Markets'?," YouTube Video, September 8, 2011, https://www.youtube.com/watch?v=-DdoiI2PFmo.

44. "Commanding Heights: The Battle for World Economy," PBS, accessed July 20, 2016, http://www.pbs.org/wgbh/commandingheights/lo/index.html.

45. Mark Mobius, quoted in "Commanding Heights."

46. "Doha WTO Ministerial 2001: Ministerial Declaration," World Trade Organization, adopted on November 14, 2001, https://www.wto.org/english/thewto_e/minist_e/min01_e/mindecl_e.htm#cooperation.

47. "Aid for Trade Fact Sheet," Development: Aid for Trade, World Trade Organization, accessed July 15, 2016, https://www.wto.org/english/tratop_e/devel_e/a4t_e/a4t_factsheet_e.htm.

48. "Transitional Strategy for Denmark's Multilateral Aid for Trade Activities 2014–2015," DANIDA, September 2014, 5.

49. "Aid for Trade at a Glance 2015: Reducing Trade Costs for Inclusive, Sustainable Growth," World Trade Organization, accessed July 10, 2016, https://www.wto.org/english/res_e/booksp_e/aid4trade15_e.pdf.

50. "Aid for Trade Work Programme," World Trade Organization, accessed July 14, 2016, https://www.wto.org/english/tratop_e/devel_e/a4t_e/aid4trade_e.htm.

51. Ann C. Logue, *Emerging Markets for Dummies* (Indianapolis: Wiley, 2011), 9.

52. Mark Mobius, *The Little Black Book* (Singapore: Wiley, 2012), 12.

53. Ibid., 9.

54. Logue, *Emerging Markets for Dummies*, 10.

55. Dipesh Chakrabarty, *Provincializing Europe: Postcolonial Thought and Historical Difference* (Princeton, NJ: Princeton University Press, 2000), 9.

56. Ravinder Kaur and Thomas Blom Hansen, "Aesthetics of Arrival: Spectacle Capital, Novelty in Post-Reform India," *Identities, Global Studies in Culture and Power* 23 (2016): 265.

57. Franklin Templeton, *States of Emergence: The Evolution of Emerging Markets* (New York: Franklin Templeton Investments, 2014), 2.

58. "MSCI Emerging Markets Horizon Index Methodology," MSCI, accessed July 14, 2016, https://www.msci.com/eqb/methodology/meth_docs/MSCI_Emerging_Markets_Horizon_Index_Methodology_Jul14.pdf.

59. These parameters form the basic indicators deployed to identify BRICs as the most lucrative territories. See O'Neill, *Growth Map*, 25–40.

60. Ernst & Young, *Ready, Set, Grow, Ernst Young Attractiveness Survey: India 2015* (Mumbai: EYGM Ltd., 2015), www.ey.com/Publication/vwLUAssets/ey-2015-india

-attractiveness-survey-ready-set-grow/$FILE/ey-2015-india-attractiveness-survey
-ready-set-grow.pdf.

61. Ibid., 3.

62. On the politics of economic reforms, see Ravinder Kaur, "Good Times, Brought to You by Brand Modi," *Television and New Media* 16, no. 4: 323–30.

63. Timothy Mitchell, "Fixing the Economy," *Cultural Studies* 12, no. 1 (1998): 82–101.

64. A substantial literature on the history of GDP and economic indicators as such is available. See Diana Coyle, *GDP: A Brief but Affectionate History* (Princeton, NJ: Princeton University Press, 2014); Zachary Karabell, *The Leading Indicators: A Short History of the Numbers That Rule Our World.* (New York: Simon and Schuster, 2014); Dirks Philipsen, *The Little Big Number: How GDP Came to Rule the World and What to Do about It* (Princeton, NJ: Princeton University Press, 2015); and Ehsa Masood, *The Great Invention: The Story of GDP and the Making and Unmaking of the Modern World* (New York: Pegasus Books, 2016).

65. See Eli Cook, *The Pricing of Progress: Economic Indicators and the Capitalization of American Life* (Cambridge, MA: Harvard University Press, 2017), 8–10.

66. Ibid., 255–56.

67. Ibid., 8.

68. See, for example, the articles of agreement at the formation of the IMF that required its members to regularly furnish national data, including national income. IMF, *Article of Agreement* (Washington, DC: International Monetary Foundation, 2006).

69. This is despite the fact that the boom and bust in the Indian market is not an isolated event; it is connected to global economic trends. It was long believed that the Indian economy was decoupled from the global markets, but that idea was debunked, especially after the 2008 global financial crisis. For example, the 2013 currency crisis in India, under the UPA II government, was linked to the global economic downturn set in motion following the American subprime crisis. Yet it was right out of the political playbook, and together with the anticorruption movement it paved the way for the election of BJP, led by Narendra Modi, who promised new reforms to unshackle the economy.

70. Financial Express Bureau, "Big Boost for Narendra Modi, GDP Growth Powers to 6.3 Pct in Q2, 5-Quarter Slide Reversed," *Financial Express*, December 1, 2017, http://www.financialexpress.com/economy/big-boost-for-narendra-modi-gdp-growth-powers-to-6-3-pct-in-q2-5-quarter-slide-reversed/955041/.

71. BS Web Team & Agencies, "GDP LIVE: Growth Boost Has Happened Due to Rise in Manufacturing, Says FM," *Business Standard*, November 30, 2017, http://www.business-standard.com/article/economy-policy/gdp-live-growth-boost-has-happened-due-to-rise-in-manufacturing-says-fm-117113000680_1.html.

72. Dinesh Unnikrishnan, "Narendra Modi in Davos: IMF's 7.4% GDP Forecast Is a Gift to PM, but Why Are Foreigners More Optimistic about Growth than

CSO?," *Firstpost*, January 23, 2018, http://www.firstpost.com/business/narendra-modi
-in-davos-imfs-7-4-gdp-forecast-is-a-gift-to-pm-but-why-are-foreigners-more-opti
mistic-about-growth-than-cso-4315555.html.

73. "ADB Downgrades India's GDP Growth Outlook to 7% for 2017–18," *Hindustan Times*, September 26, 2017, https://www.hindustantimes.com/business-news
/adb-lowers-india-s-gdp-growth-outlook-to-7-for-2017-18/story-nK0x1qp2Ay4LMo
UswzrrEO.html.

74. IANS, "In Aftermath of Demonetisation, India's GDP Growth Sees Sharp
Fall to 5.7% in Q1 of 2017–18," *Huffington Post*, August 31, 2017, https://www.huffing
tonpost.in/2017/08/31/indias-gdp-growth-sees-sharp-fall-to-5-7-in-q1_a_23192099/.

75. Sriram Iyer, "Beyond Numbers: A Slowing Economy Risks Turning India's Demographic Dividend into a Disaster," Quartz India, January 8, 2018, https://
qz.com/1173792/as-gdp-growth-slows-indias-demographic-dividend-could-turn-into
-disaster/.

76. BT Online, "PM Narendra Modi Tears into Critics; Says GDP Slid to 5.7%
or below 8 Times under UPA," *Business Today*, October 5, 2017, https://www.business
today.in/current/economy-politics/pm-narendra-modi-critics-economy-demonetisa
tion-gst-gdp-growth-inflation/story/261435.html.

77. Arun Jaitley (BJP) is the current finance minister and P. Chidambaram (Congress) is the former finance minister. "Jaitley Praises GDP Rebound, Chidambaram
Says Pause in Declining Trend," *India Today*, November 30, 2017, https://www.india
today.in/india/story/gdp-growth-bjp-congress-arun-jaitley-chidambaram-mamata
-banerjee-1097647-2017-11-30.

78. Manmohan Singh, together with former prime minister Narasimha Rao, is
considered the architect of India's economic reforms. He was the finance minister in
the 1990s and then prime minister from 2004 to 2014. Dinesh Unnikrishnan, "GDP
Flop-Show: Manmohan Singh Has the Last Laugh in War of Words with Narendra Modi over Note Ban," *Firstpost*, June 2, 2017, http://www.firstpost.com/india/gdp
-flop-show-manmohan-singh-has-the-last-laugh-in-war-of-words-with-narendra
-modi-over-note-ban-3508625.html.

79. The deployment of the term *Hindu* to describe the slow, barely unchanging
rate of growth has been contended as more an outcome of socialist stagnation. Various perspectives on and approaches to Indian economic growth can be found here:
Krishna Raj, "Some Observations on Economic Growth in India over the Period
1952–53 to 1982–83," *Economic and Political Weekly* 19, no. 41 (October 13, 1984); N. Nagaraj, "Growth Rate of India's GDP, 1950–51 to 1987–88: Examination of Alternative Hypotheses," *Economic and Political Weekly* 25, no. 26 (1990): 1396–1403; Pranab
Bardhan, *The Political Economy of Development in India* (Delhi: Oxford University
Press, 1984); Arvind Virmani, *Propelling India from Socialist Stagnation to Global Power*
(Delhi: Academic Books, 2006); and Sabyasachi Kar and Kunal Sen, *The Political
Economy of India's Growth Episodes* (London: Palgrave Macmillan, 2016).

80. On the question of post-1990s high economic growth and its effects, see Jean
Drèze and Amartya Sen, *An Uncertain Glory: India and Its Contradictions* (Princeton,

NJ: Princeton University Press, 2013); Jagdish Bhagwati and Arvind Panagariya, *Why Growth Matters: How Economic Growth in India Reduced Poverty and the Lessons for Other Developing Countries* (New York: Public Affairs, 2012); A. Kohli, *Poverty amid Plenty in the New India* (Cambridge, UK: Cambridge University Press, 2012); and Pranab Bardhan, *Awakening Giants, Feet of Clay: Assessing the Economic Rise of China and India* (Princeton, NJ: Princeton University Press, 2012).

81. Government of India, Ministry of Finance, "India—Macro-Economic Summary: 1999–00 to 2013–14," Central Statistical Organisation, May 30, 2014, http://planningcommission.gov.in/data/datatable/data_2312/DatabookDec2014%201.pdf.

82. On the elite fixation with GDP numbers, see Sankara Krishna, "Number Fetish: Middle-Class India's Obsession with the GDP," *Globalizations* 12, no. 6 (2015): 859–71.

83. Robert Constanza et al., "Time to Leave GDP Behind," *Nature* 505 (2014): 283–85.

84. Joseph Stiglitz, Amartya Sen, and Jean-Paul Fitoussi, *Mismeasuring Our Lives: Why GDP Doesn't Add Up* (New York: New Press, 2010).

85. These policy measures were first suggested in a report commissioned by Nicolas Sarkozy when he was the president of France. See Joseph Stiglitz, Amartya Sen, and Jean-Paul Fitoussi, *Report by the Commission on the Measurement of Economic Performance and Social Progress* (Paris, 2009), http://ec.europa.eu/eurostat/documents/118025/118123/Fitoussi+Commission+report.

86. The IMF's approach to measuring GDP can be found here: Tim Callen, "Gross Domestic Product: An Economy's All," *Finance and Development*, December 18, 2018, http://www.imf.org/external/pubs/ft/fandd/basics/gdp.htm.

87. "India Regains Title of World's Fastest-Growing Major Economy," *Financial Times*, February 28, 2018, https://www.ft.com/content/cb5a4668-1c84-11e8-956a-43db76e69936.

88. See, for example, doubts raised due to the absence of a revised back series of GDP based on new methodology: P. Chidambaram, "Change Begins with Words and Ideas," *Indian Express*, March 25, 2018, http://indianexpress.com/article/opinion/columns/india-economy-gdp-bjp-congress-plenary-session-5110381/; and see also the dissonance between the ground perception of economic progress and the numbers: TCA Srinivasa Raghavan, "The Economy beyond Numbers," *Open the Magazine*, March 23, 2018, http://www.openthemagazine.com/article/essay/the-economy-beyond-numbers.

89. See World Bank Group, *Doing Business 2018: Reforming to Create Jobs* (Washington, DC: The World Bank, 2018), methodology section, http://www.doingbusiness.org/~/media/WBG/DoingBusiness/Documents/Annual-Reports/English/DB2018-Full-Report.pdf.

90. Onno Ruhl, World Bank country director for India (2012–2016), Skype interview with author, February 15, 2018.

91. BT Online, "Ease of Doing Business Rankings: India Makes Highest-Ever Jump to Rank 100 Out of 190 Countries," *Business Today*, November 1, 2017, https://

www.businesstoday.in/current/economy-politics/ease-of-doing-business-rankings
-india-rank-world-bank-100/story/262976.html.

92. Deborate Ghose, "Ease of Doing Business Ranking: India Breaks into Top 100 for First Time; All You Need to Know," *Firstpost*, November 1, 2017, http:// www.firstpost.com/business/ease-of-doing-business-ranking-india-breaks-into-top -100-for-first-time-all-you-need-to-know-4186895.html.

93. ENS Economic Bureau, "India Leaps 30 Places to 100th Rank in World Bank's 'Ease of Doing Business Index,'" *Indian Express*, October 31, 2017, http://indian express.com/article/business/business-others/world-bank-ease-of-doing-business -india-ranks-100-out-of-190-nations-arun-jaitley-modi-gst-4915978/.

94. Asit Ranjan Mishra, "World Bank Endorses Modi Government's Reform Credentials," *Live Mint*, November 1, 2017, https://www.livemint.com/Companies /icjVbgr3PteKYupZlzwOtN/India-jumps-to-100th-spot-in-World-Banks-ease-of -doing-busi.html.

95. Live Mint, "Arun Jaitley: Taking India to Top 50 in World Bank Doing Business Index Doable," *Live Mint*, November 1, 2017, https://www.livemint.com/Pol itics/UftqeUiYVYiOojLekhCWGJ/Arun-Jaitley-says-taking-India-among-top -50-in-ease-of-doing.html.

96. PTI, "Possible for India to Be in Top 50 on Ease of Business Index: Jaitley," *The Hindu*, January 27, 2018, http://www.thehindu.com/business/possible-for-india -to-be-in-top-50-on-ease-of-business-index-jaitley/article22535396.ece.

97. Government of India, Ministry of Commerce and Industry, "India's Rank Rises to 100 in World Bank's Doing Business Report, 2018," Press Information Bureau, October 31, 2017, http://pib.nic.in/newsite/PrintRelease.aspx?relid=173116.

98. Ruchika Chitravanshi, "Ease of Doing Business: Government Targets 90 Reforms to Climb Rank in World Bank's Report," *Economic Times*, January 4, 2018, https://economictimes.indiatimes.com/news/economy/policy/ease-of-doing-business -government-targets-90-reforms-to-climb-rank-in-world-banks-report/articleshow /62359708.cms.

99. Jun Zhang, International Finance Corporation country director for India, quoted in Malini Goyal, "How Performance-Based Rankings Are Shaking Up the Rigid World of Government," *Economic Times*, January 28, 2018, https://economic times.indiatimes.com/news/economy/policy/how-performance-based-rankings -are-shaking-up-the-rigid-world-of-government/articleshow/62674879.cms. The federal states within the nation-state compete with one another to become investment hubs, and to that end, they seek (or are offered) quantification of progress. The performance-based rankings can be found on a variety of themes—from cleanest cities to best panchayats, from best police stations to railways stations monitored and ranked on live data generated through biometric attendance, e-payments, and apps— across many states of India. For example, Indore was ranked as the cleanest Indian city in the 2017 *swachh survekshan* conducted by the Ministry of Housing and Urban Affairs. See the list in Government of India, Ministry of Housing and Urban

Affairs, "Swacch Survekshan—2017: Sanitation Rankings of Cities/Towns State/UT-Wise," Press Information Bureau, May 4, 2017, http://pib.nic.in/newsite/PrintRelease.aspx?relid=161527.

100. Walter Benjamin, Lloyd Spencer, and Mark Harrington, "Central Park," *New German Critique* 34 (Winter 1985): 32–58.

101. The discursive history of novelty is connected with a variety of concepts including discovery, innovation, invention, and investment harnessed mostly but not exclusively to capitalist advances and progress. See also Michael North, *Novelty: A History of the New* (Chicago: University of Chicago Press, 2013).

102. See, for example, "The New India Bill," *New York Times*, May 19, 1858; and "The Old Company and the New India Bill," *Calcutta Review* 31 (July–December 1858): 412–42.

103. Giovanni Arrighi, *The Long Twentieth Century: Money, Power and the Origins of Our Time* (London: Verso, 2010), 55. David Ludden reminds us that the rise of global capitalism evolved from the very beginning in transcontinental spaces and networks of mobility across many imperial territories. See David Ludden, "Imperial Modernity: History and Global Inequity in Global Asia," *Third World Quarterly* 33, no. 4 (2012): 581–601.

104. Manu Goswami, *Producing India: From Colonial Economy to National Space* (Chicago: University of Chicago Press, 2008), 45.

105. Ibid., 42.

106. An excellent account of the imperial project of railway investments can be found in Daniel Thorner, *Investment in Empire: British Railway and Steam Shipping Enterprise in India 1825–1849* (Philadelphia: University of Pennsylvania Press, 1950).

107. For example, "New India" was the name of a nationalist weekly and a reformist daily newspaper published respectively by Bipin Chandra Pal and Annie Beasnt of the Theosophical Society. See also ICS member Henry Cotton's largely sympathetic account of a New India, or as he described, "India in transition is New India." This account was first published in 1885 when the Congress was just about taking shape. Henry Cotton, *New India: Or India in Transition* (London: Kegan Paul, Trench Trubner, 1904), 2.

108. Sunil Khilnani, *The Idea of India* (Delhi: Penguin, 1997).

109. Chester Bowles, "New India," *Foreign Affairs* (October 1952): 79–80.

110. An Indian Official, "India as a World Power," *Foreign Affairs* (1949): 550.

111. On developmental state, see Vivek Chhiber, *Locked in Place: State-Building and Late Industrialization in India* (Princeton, NJ: Princeton University Press, 2006).

CHAPTER 3

1. Text accompanying the India 2.0 vehicle at ITB Berlin, 2007.

2. Contemporary political mobilizations in India have often been about uncovering and restoring the Hindu essence of the ancient nation. This basically means "removing" the foreign elements, especially Muslims and traces of Islamic culture. The

destruction of Babri Mosque in Ayodhya by Hindu nationalist groups in December 1992 is an example of how the authentic is sometimes violently restored in contemporary India.

3. *Times of India*, "GDP Growth Slips to 4.3 in 2002," *Times of India*, June 30, 2003, https://timesofindia.indiatimes.com/business/india-business/GDP-growth-slips-to -4-3-in-2002-03/articleshow/52422.cms.

4. Swaninathan Aiyer, "The Neo-Hindu GDP Growth Rate," *Times of India*, March 9, 2003, https://timesofindia.indiatimes.com/home/sunday-times/all-that-mat ters/The-neo-Hindu-GDP-growth-rate/articleshow/39701549.cms. On the eclipse of the Hindu growth rate phenomenon in the 1980s Indian economy, see Dani Rodrik and Arvind Subramaniam, "From 'Hindu Growth' to Productivity Surge: The Mystery of the Indian Growth Transition" (NBER working paper 10376, National Bureau of Economic Research, Cambridge, MA, 2004), https://www.imf.org/external/pubs /ft/staffp/2004/00-00/rodrik.pdf.

5. Amitabh Kant, interview by the author, October 6, 2010.

6. Amitabh Kant, *Branding India: An Incredible Story* (Delhi: Harper Collins, 2009), 3.

7. Kant, *Branding India*, 4.

8. Ibid., 4.

9. While mere fragments of *Indica*, written by Megasthenes, the ambassador of Selecus Nicator, to the court of Chandragupta Maurya (sometime between 318–303 BCE), survive, the travel accounts of Chinese Buddhist pilgrims (written a few hundred years later) are more plentiful. See, for example, Upinder Singh, *A History of Ancient and Early Medieval India* (Hoboken, NJ: Pearson Longman, 2008); A. B. Bosworth, "The Historical Setting of Megasthenes' *Indica*," *Classical Philology* 91, no. 2 (April 1996): 113–27; Tansen Sen, "The Travel Records of Chinese Pilgrims Faxian, Xuanzang, and Yijing: Sources for Cross-Cultural Encounters between Ancient China and Ancient India," *Education about Asia* 11, no. 3 (April 2006): 24–33.

10. V. Sunil, interview by the author, March 19, 2012.

11. Nicholas Mirzoeff, *The Right to Look: A Counterhistory of Visuality* (Durham, NC: Duke University Press, 2011), 23.

12. See, for example, the invitation to the nation-branding masterclass *Indian Subcontinent: Managing and Measuring Subcontinent* (Delhi: India Brand Equity Foundation, 2009), https://www.ibef.org/download/India_IBEF_v0509.pdf.

13. In 2002, V. Sunil was the creative director at Ogilvy & Mather in Delhi. He went on to form an independent ad agency in Delhi that later merged with W+K.

14. Sunil, interview.

15. When he received this new brief, he had the distinction of being the youngest creative director of a major advertising agency in India. At twenty-seven, he was appointed the creative director of Ogilvy & Mather, a major advertising firm in Delhi.

16. Government of India, Ministry of Tourism and Culture, *National Tourism Policy 2002*, Department of Tourism, accessed February 10, 2018, http://tourism.gov .in/tourism-policy.

17. The budget outlay for 2002–2003 was especially enhanced so as to reserve Rs 34 crore for overseas marketing and Rs 6 crore for domestic marketing out of a total budget of Rs 202 crore. Government of India, Planning Commission, *Annual Plan: 2002–03*, p. 667, accessed February 18, 2018, http://planningcommission.nic.in/plans /annualplan/index.php?state=apo20_03cont.htm.

18. Kant, *Branding India*, 2.

19. V. Sunil, interview by the author, August 12, 2012.

20. Kant, *Branding India*, 7.

21. Ibid.

22. Ibid.

23. Dictionary.com, s.v. "incredible," 2012, https://www.dictionary.com/browse /incredible.

24. A contemporary example of such a narrative is the recent travelogue by William Dalrymple, *Nine Lives: In Search of the Sacred in Modern India* (London: Vintage, 2009).

25. Kant, interview.

26. Ibid.

27. The imperial knowledge of Indian society and history was altered to meet the specific needs of the administrators, the commercial interests of British traders, and the ultimate end of disciplining the colonized territory into the efficient production of machinery for raw materials (see, for example, Harjot Oberoi, *The Construction of Religious Boundaries* (Delhi: Oxford University Press, 1997); S. B. Cohn, *Colonialism and Its Forms of Knowledge: The British in India* (Princeton, NJ: Princeton University Press, 1996), 4.

28. Kant, *Branding India*, 44.

29. V. Sunil, interview by the author, October 10, 2010.

30. V. Sunil, quoted in Kant, *Branding India*.

31. Incidentally, W+K is the agency that created the Nike campaign as well.

32. Sunil, interview, March 19, 2012.

33. Lynn Truss, *Eats, Shoots, and Leaves: The Zero Tolerance Approach to Punctuation* (New York: Gotham Books, 2004), 137.

34. Sunil, interview, October 10, 2010.

35. Ibid.

36. Allusions to the figure of Mother India are obvious here. See Sumathi Ramaswamy, *The Goddess and Nation: Mapping Mother India* (Durham, NC: Duke University Press, 2010).

37. Sunil, interview, October 10, 2010.

38. Bharat Bala, the filmmaker, quoted in Kant, *Branding India*, 21.

39. Compare W. J. T. Mitchell, "Realism and the Digital Image," in *Critical Realism in Contemporary Art: Around Alan Sekula's Photography*, ed. J. Baetens and H. Van Gelder (Leuven, BE: Leuven University Press, 2007), 12–27.

40. Sunil, interview, October 10, 2010.

41. Sunil, interview, August 12, 2012.

42. Although Incredible India was aimed at the outside world, it has gained as much attention and popularity inside the country, especially among the upwardly mobile middle classes.

43. See UNESCO, "World Heritage List: India, Taj Mahal," accessed February 3, 2018, http://whc.unesco.org/en/list/252.

44. See Jeffery D. Long, *Historical Dictionary of Hinduism* (Lanham, MD: Scarecrow Press, 2011), 253–54.

45. Vincent Smith, *Early History of India, from 600 BC to the Muhemmadan Conquest, Including the Invasion of Alexander the Great* (Oxford, UK: Oxford University Press, 1924), 356.

46. The most influential voices in this enterprise belonged to William Jones, James Mill, Max Mueller, and Vincent Smith.

47. Vincent Smith, *Oxford History of India* (Oxford, UK: Oxford University Press, 1919), 22–23.

48. See, for example, David Arnold, *The New Cambridge History of India: Science, Technology and Medicine in Colonial India* (Cambridge, UK: Cambridge University Press, 2000); and Christopher A. Bayly, *The Birth of the Modern World, 1780–1914, Global Connections and Comparisons* (Malden, MA: Blackwell, 2004).

49. On the question of colonial modernity and the state of deferment, see Dipesh Chakrabarty "The Difference: Deferral of (a) Colonial Modernity: Public Debates in British Bengal," *History Workshop Journal*, no. 36 (Autumn 1993): 1–34.

50. Ronald Inden links this obsession of locating the essence of India to the nineteenth-century claims to get Indology classified as a natural science. The oft-used metaphors of *machine, system,* and *mechanics* sought to transfer the elements of the physical world to a body politic. See Ronald Inden, *Imagining India* (Oxford, UK: Blackwell, 1990), 12–21.

51. Max Müller, a German Indologist at Oxford, was one of the first scholars to undertake such comparative studies of Sanskrit and European, an inquiry that led to the creation of the field of Indo-European language and culture.

52. Percival Spear, *India, Pakistan and the West* (Oxford, UK: Oxford University Press, 1958), 57.

53. Inden reads this as an encounter between Hinduism as a female presence with absorptive powers and Western rationality as a male presence. He suggests that this threat arises as "European reason penetrates the womb of Indian unreason but always at the risk of being engulfed by it." *Imagining India*, 86.

54. Gyan Prakash, "Writing Post-Orientalist Histories of the Third World: Perspectives from Indian Historiography," *Comparative Studies in Society and History 32*, no. 2 (1990): 388.

55. India has the world's largest and youngest population. More than half of its total population is below twenty-five years of age. Internet usage covers more half a billion and is expected to reach more than 600 million by 2020.

56. Partha Chatterjee, *The Nation and Its Fragments: Colonial and Postcolonial Histories* (Princeton, NJ: Princeton University Press, 1993), 6–7.

57. Manu Goswami, *Producing India: From Colonial Economy to National Space* (Chicago: University of Chicago Press, 2008), 24–26.

58. Sunil Khilnani, *The Idea of India* (Delhi: Penguin, 1997), 13.

59. Jawaharlal Nehru, quoted in Government of India, Ministry of Information and Broadcasting, Publicity Division, "The Flag of the Indian Union," *New India* 1–2 (August 1947): 5.

60. Khilnani, *Idea of India*, 18.

61. Ibid., 20.

62. Ibid.

63. Across the subcontinent, popular figures such as Kabir, Nanak, Tulsidas, Ravidas, Basvanna, and Mira challenged orthodoxies in the medieval era.

64. This view is well established and shared within the popular narrative of both "liberal" Hinduism and "illiberal" Hindutva. See, for example, the liberal Hindu view from Shashi Tharoor, *Why I Am a Hindu* (Delhi: Aleph, 2018); Akshay Mishra, "Hindutva vs. Hinduism: Why I Am Proud to Be Pseudo-Secular," *Firstpost*, December 10, 2012, https://www.firstpost.com/politics/hindutva-vs-hinduism-why-i-am-proud-to-be-pseudo-secular-552399.html; and Sanam Sharma, "A True Hindu Is a Secular Hindu," *Huffington Post*, May 11, 2015, https://bit.ly/2sQaHxP. For the Hindutva view, see C. K. Saji Narayanan, "Why Fear a Hindu Rashtra?," *Outlook India*, May 7, 2018, https://www.outlookindia.com/magazine/story/why-fear-a-hindu-rashtra/300 085. See also Rajeswari Sundar Rajan, "The Politics of Hindu 'Tolerance,'" *Boundary 2* 38, no. 3 (2011): 67–86; and Manjari Katju, *Vishwa Hindu Parishad and Indian Politics* (Delhi: Orient Blackswan, 2003).

CHAPTER 4

1. A search for "www.indiashining.com" returns the following domain for sale, accessed March 9, 2018: https://www.afternic.com/forsale/indiashining.com?utm _source=TDFS_DASLNC&utm_medium=DASLNC&utm_campaign=TDFS _DASLNC&traffic_type=TDFS_DASLNC&traffic_id=daslnc.

2. Guy Debord, *The Society of the Spectacle*, trans. Ken Knabb (London: Rebel Press, 2005).

3. "False Shine, Core Flaws Resulted in NDA's Debacle," *Economic Times*, May 14, 2004, http://articles.economictimes.indiatimes.com/2004-05-14/news/27416319_1_re form-process-nda-core-issue; and P. V. Indiresan, "A Reality Check on India Shining," *Hindu*, May 8, 2004.

4. P. Sainath, "The Feel Good Factory," *Frontline* 21, no. 5 (2004), http://www .frontline.in/static/html/fl2105/stories/20040312007800400.htm; Reshmi Dasgupta, "Smokin' Slogan: On Poll Trail, It's the Call of the Jingle," *Economic Times*, March 27, 2004, http://articles.economictimes.indiatimes.com/2004-03-27/news/27381115_1_slo gan-garibi-hatao-aam-aadmi-ke-saath; and R. Deshpande and L. Iyer, "BJP Rides on India Shining Plank, Congress Counters the Feel-Good Line," *India Today*, March 22, 2004.

5. C. P. Chandrasekhar, "A Bubble Waiting to Burst," *Frontline* 21, no. 5 (2004), http://www.frontline.in/static/html/fl2105/stories/20040312007200900.htm.

6. Rama Bijapurkar, *We Are Like That Only: Understanding the Logic of Consumer India* (New Delhi: Penguin, 2007), 149.

7. Christiane Brosius, *India's Middle Class: New Forms of Urban Leisure, Consumption and Prosperity* (New Delhi: Routledge, 2010), 2.

8. Jayati Ghosh, "India Shining, India Declining," *MacroScan: An Alternative Economics Webcentre*, February 5, 2004, http://www.macroscan.net/index.php?&view=article&aid=459.

9. Shaila Bhatti and Christopher Pinney, "Optic-Clash: Modes of Visuality in India," in *A Companion to the Anthropology of India*, ed. Isabel Clark-Decès (Hoboken, NJ: Blackwell, 2011), ch. 12.

10. W. J. T. Mitchell, *Iconology: Image, Text, Ideology* (Chicago: University of Chicago Press, 1986).

11. Here the notion of hypericon is invoked to emphasize the recursive nature of an image that doubles as idea, conjured not only as a picture, figure, or form but also as a representation or the act of imagination itself. See Mitchell, *Iconology*.

12. "At 8.2%, India's Growth Only Next to China," *Business Standard*, July 1, 2004, http://www.business-standard.com/article/economy-policy/at-8-2-india-s-gdp-growth-next-only-to-china-104070101036_1.html.

13. Rakesh Mohan, "The Growth Record of the Indian Economy 1950–2008: A Story of Sustained Savings and Investment," Reserve Bank of India, February 14, 2008, http://www.rbi.org.in/scripts/BS_SpeechesView.aspx?Id=379.

14. Reserve Bank of India, "Foreign Exchange Reserves," December 19, 2003, http://rbidocs.rbi.org.in/rdocs/Wss/PDFs/50084.pdf.

15. Indian Express, "Think 'Young' for Better Growth: CII," March 10, 2004, http://archive.indianexpress.com/oldStory/42668/.

16. Cited in Amy Waldman, "Sizzling Economy Revitalizes India," *New York Times*, October 20, 2003, http://www.nytimes.com/2003/10/20/international/asia/20INDI.html.

17. Government of India, Ministry of Home Affairs, "Availability of Amenities and Assets," Office of the Registrar General & Census Commissioner, *Census of India*, 2001, http://censusindia.gov.in/Census_And_You/availability_of_eminities_and_assets.aspx.

18. Nandini Gooptu, "Neoliberal Subjectivity, Enterprise Culture and New Workplaces: Organised Retail and Shopping Malls in India," *Economic and Political Weekly* 44, no. 22 (2009): 45–54.

19. The firm has since merged with another and is now called FTI Consultancy.

20. Prathap Suthan, series of discussions with the author, November 2013.

21. Ibid.

22. Krishna Kant, "Households Put Two-Thirds of Their Savings in Houses, Gold," *Business Standard*, May 31, 2014, https://www.business-standard.com/article

/economy-policy/households-put-two-thirds-of-their-savings-in-houses-gold-114053
001457_1.html; and S. L. Shetty, "Saving Behaviour in India in the 1980s: Some Lessons," *Economic and Political Weekly* 25, no. 11 (1990): 555–60.

23. Suthan, discussions.

24. The Election Commission of India's model code of conduct bars the use of government machinery for electoral gains.

25. "BJP Sweeps Out Congress from 3 States," *Tribune India*, May 12, 2003, http://www.tribuneindia.com/2003/20031205/main1.htm.

26. AdEx India, "India Is Shining All Over the Print Media: An AdEx India Analysis," exchange4media, February 6, 2004, https://www.exchange4media.com /Print/India-is-Shining-all-over-the-Print-Media!-An-AdEx-India-Analysis_10844 .html.

27. Reinhardt Koselleck, *Futures Past: On the Semantics of Historical Time* (Cambridge, MA: MIT Press, 2004); and Hartmut Rosa, *Social Acceleration: A New Theory of Modernity* (New York: Columbia University Press, 2013).

28. David Harvey, *A Brief History of Neoliberalism* (New York: Oxford University Press, 2007).

29. Jagdish Bhagwati and Arvind Panagariya, *Why Growth Matters: How Economic Growth in India Reduced Poverty and Lessons for Other Developing Countries* (New York: Public Affairs, 2013).

30. John Comaroff and Jean Comaroff, *Ethnicity, Inc.* (Chicago: University of Chicago Press, 2009).

31. See Sunil Khilnani, *The Idea of India* (Delhi: Penguin, 1997); and Deepak Singh, "Locating the Dislocated in Globalized India," in *Facing Globality: Politics of Resistance, Relocation and Reinvention in India*, eds. Bhupinder Brar and Pampa Mukherjee (New Delhi: Oxford University Press, 2012), 245–67.

32. Partha Chatterjee, *Politics of the Governed: Reflections on Popular Politics in Most of the World* (New York: Columbia University Press, 2004).

33. Mark J. Penn, *Microtrends: The Small Forces behind Tomorrow's Big Challenges* (New York: Twelve, 2007).

34. Tom Agan, "Silent Marketing: Micro-Targeting," WPP, a Penn, Schoen and Berland Associates White Paper, accessed June 23, 2004, http://www.wpp.com/wpp /marketing/reportsstudies/silentmarketing/.

35. Neil MacFarquhar, "What's a Soccer Mom Anyway?," *New York Times*, October 20, 1996; and Michele Miller and Holly Buchanan, *The Soccer Mom Myth: Today's Female Consumer: Who She Really Is, Why She Really Buys* (Austin, TX: Wizard Academy Press, 2010).

36. Nielsen Company, *Women of Tomorrow: A Study of Women around the World*, June 28, 2011, http://www.nielsen.com/us/en/insights/reports/2011/a-study-of-women -around-the-world.html.

37. Michael J. Silverstein and Kate Sayre, "The Female Economy," *Harvard Business Review*, September 2009, 46.

38. Ibid., 50.

39. Hannah Arendt, *The Human Condition* (Chicago: University of Chicago Press, 1998).

40. Arendt's distinction between the private and the public rests on differences between life-sustaining activities and those that deal with making sense of the world in the political sphere. Yet the very notion of life-sustaining activities here is altered and broadened to bring the financial and economic spheres into the domestic.

41. See, for example, Shivraj Singh Chouhan, "81 Girls Married under Mukhya-mantri Kanyadan (Nikah) Yojna," April 15, 2013, http://shivrajsinghchouhan.org /newsdetail.aspx?id=137.

42. Reserve Bank of India, "Foreign Exchange Reserves," December 19, 2003, http://rbidocs.rbi.org.in/rdocs/Wss/PDFs/50084.pdf.

43. Y. V. Reddy, "India's Foreign Exchange Reserves: Policy, Status and Issues," Reserve Bank of India, 2002, accessed June 25, 2014, http://rbidocs.rbi.org.in/rdocs /Bulletin/PDFs/29869.pdf; Reserve Bank of India, *Report on Foreign Exchange Reserves 2004–5 (Covering Period up to March 2005)*, 2005, accessed June 25, 2014, http:// rbidocs.rbi.org.in/rdocs/PublicationReport/Pdfs/64264.pdf.; and Bernard Weinraub, "Economic Crisis Forcing Once Self-Reliant India to Seek Aid," *New York Times*, June 29, 1991.

44. T. N. Ninnan, quoted in Weinraub, "Economic Crisis."

45. Tamal Bandyopadhyay and Anup Roy, "RBI to Buy 200 Tonnes of IMF Gold," *Live Mint*, November 3, 2009, http://www.livemint.com/Home-Page/Btryp kIoTHQ1gorYq5JNgP/RBI-to-buy-200-tonnes-of-IMF-gold.html.

46. Suthan, discussions.

47. Ibid.

48. Ibid.

49. Ravinder Kaur, "Distinctive Citizenship: Refugees, Subjects and the Postcolonial State in India's Partition," *Cultural and Social History* 6, no. 4 (2009): 429–46.

50. Sachar Committee Report, *Social, Economic and Educational Status of Muslim Community in India* (New Delhi: Government of India, 2006), http://mhrd.gov.in /sites/upload_files/mhrd/files/sachar_comm.pdf.

51. A similar discourse of enterprise called Dalit capitalism has taken shape within the debates about Dalit emancipation and neoliberal potentialities.

52. V. Sridhar, "More Sops for the Elite," *Frontline* 21, no. 2 (2004), http://www .frontline.in/static/html/fl2103/stories/20040213001704100.htm.

53. *Dada Dadi* means "grandfather and grandmother" in Hindi.

54. Sridhar, "More Sops for the Elite."

55. Suthan, discussions.

56. Women in Global Science and Technology, "National Assessments on Gender Equality in the Knowledge Society, Country Results: India," p. 7, 2013, accessed July 14, 2014, http://wisat.org/wp-content/uploads/National_Scorecard_India.pdf.

57. On gender and science in India, see Abha Sur, *Dispersed Radiance: Caste, Gender and Modern Science in India* (New Delhi: Navayana, 2011).

58. Suthan, discussions.

59. Ibid.

60. Ravinder Kaur, "Nation's Two Bodies: Rethinking the Idea of 'New' India and Its Other," *Third World Quarterly* 33, no. 4 (May 1, 2012): 603–21; and Ravinder Kaur, "Remains of Difference: New Imaginaries of Otherness in Post-Reform India," in *Interrogating India's Modernity: Democracy, Identity and Citizenship*, ed. Surinder Jodhka (New Delhi: Oxford University Press, 2014), 221–43.

61. Rosa, *Social Acceleration*.

62. Kamal Nath, "India: The Paradigm Shift," foreword to *Annual Report 2005–06*, by IBEF, accessed April 4, 2018, https://www.ibef.org/download/india_paradigm shift.pdf.

63. Ravinder Kaur, "Good Times, Brought to You by Brand Modi," *Television and New Media* 16, no. 4 (2015): 323–30.

64. *Swadeshi Jagran Manch* (Forum for the Awakening of Swadeshi) was started in 1991 in response to the economic reforms. The invocation of *Swadeshi*, or "of one's own country," is a reference to the Indian anticolonial struggle; here it means self-sufficiency of the Indian economy.

65. Rahul Kanwal, "RSS Views Now More Aligned with Modi's? Mohan Bhagwat Says Sangh Not Opposed to FDI, Liberalisation," *India Today*, November 2, 2013, https://www.indiatoday.in/india/story/rss-mohan-bhagwat-narendra-modi-fdi-bjp-216245-2013-11-02.

66. Ornit Shani, *Communalism, Caste and Hindu Nationalism: The Violence in Gujarat* (Cambridge, UK: Cambridge University Press, 2007).

67. Susan Buck-Morss, "Aesthetics and Anaesthetics: Walter Benjamin's Artwork Essay Reconsidered," *October* 62 (Autumn 1992): 3–41; and Jonathan Crary, *Suspensions of Perception: Attention, Spectacle, and Modern Culture* (Cambridge, MA: MIT Press, 2001).

68. Debord, *Society of the Spectacle*.

69. Regis Debray, "Remarks on the Spectacle," *New Left Review* 214 (1995): 134–41.

70. See, for example, Radhika Desai, "Forward March of Hindutva Halted?," *New Left Review* 30 (2004): 49–67; Ghosh, "India Shining, India Declining"; and Achin Vanaik "Rendezvous at Mumbai," *New Left Review* 26 (2004): 53–65.

71. McKenzie Wark, *The Spectacle of Disintegration: Situationist Passages of the 20th Century* (London: Verso, 2013).

CHAPTER 5

1. Building on the word *ad* (अड), a variation of the Sanskrit root *ardh* (अर्ध), or *aadh* (आध) in Hindi, *adda* (अड्डा) denotes both division into two parts and an assemblage of different parts.

2. Dipesh Chakrabarty, "Adda, Calcutta: Dwelling in Modernity," *Public Culture* 11, no. 1 (1999): 110.

3. John T. Platts (John Thompson), *A Dictionary of Urdu, Classical Hindi, and English* (London: W. H. Allen, 1884). These semantic associations have survived through

the industrial age to appear as work platforms in factories and weaving mills and as bus stations across northern India.

4. Chakrabarty, "Adda, Calcutta," 111.

5. Ajay Khanna was the CEO of India Brand Equity Foundation from 2002 to 2006. IBEF is a public-private initiative between the Ministry of Commerce and the Confederation of Indian Industries.

6. Ajay Khanna, interview by author, March 22, 2012, India Habitat Centre, New Delhi.

7. Mark Lander, "'India Everywhere' in the Alps," *New York Times*, January 26, 2006, http://www.nytimes.com/2006/01/26/business/worldbusiness/india-everywhere -in-the-alps.html.

8. Aroon Purie, "Davos 2006: India Showcases Contemporary Face at World Economic Forum," *India Today*, February 13, 2006, http://indiatoday.intoday.in/story /davos-2006-india-showcases-contemporary-face-at-world-economic-forum/1/1919 68.html.

9. Purie, "Davos 2006."

10. India Everywhere publicity kit, 2006.

11. Fareed Zakaria, "India Rising," *Newsweek India*, March 5, 2006, http:// europe.newsweek.com/india-rising-106259?rm=eu.

12. Purie, "Davos 2006."

13. Immanuel Wallerstein, "New Revolts against the System," *New Left Review* 18 (November–December 2002), 29–39, https://newleftreview.org/II/18/immanuel -wallerstein-new-revolts-against-the-system.

14. See, for example, Immanuel Wallerstein, "Entering Global Anarchy," *New Left Review* (July–August 2003): 27–35; Immanuel Wallerstein, "Structural Crises," *New Left Review* (March–April 2010): 133–42; and Michael Hardt and Antonio Negri, *Multitude: War and Democracy in the Age of Empire* (New York: Penguin Books, 2005).

15. Peter S. Goodman, "Davos Elite Fret about Inequality over Vintage Wine and Canapés," *New York Times*, January 18, 2017, https://www.nytimes.com/2017/01/18 /business/dealbook/world-economic-forum-davos-backlash.html.

16. See WEForum, "Our Members and Partners," World Economic Forum, accessed December 15, 2011, www.weforum.org/members. This information has since been erased. The membership rates are no longer displayed on the website. This change occurred in response to the rising backlash against growing wealth inequality.

17. Oliver Cann, "Who Pays for Davos?," World Economic Forum, accessed March 20, 2017, https://www.weforum.org/agenda/2017/01/who-pays-for-davos/.

18. For a full view of the levels of membership and the costs of attending the WEF annual meeting, see Andrew Ross Sorkin, "A Hefty Price for Entry at Davos," Deal-book, *New York Times*, January 24, 2011, https://dealbook.nytimes.com/2011/01/24/a -hefty-price-for-entry-to-davos/. See also how badges create social competitiveness at Davos: Felix Salmon, "Davos's Status Levels," *Reuters*, January 19, 2012, http:// blogs.reuters.com/felix-salmon/2012/01/19/davoss-status-levels/. In 2015, the strategic

membership fee was hiked by 20 percent; see "Davos Corporations Swallow Sharp Increase in Fees," *Financial Times*, February 15, 2015, https://www.ft.com/content /c1935338-a47b-11e4-8959-00144feab7de.

19. Weforum, "About: Our Mission," World Economic Forum, accessed March 20, 2017, https://www.weforum.org/about/world-economic-forum.

20. Weforum, "Our Mission."

21. Jennifer Rankin, "Davos—A Complete Guide to the World Economic Forum," *Guardian*, January 21, 2015, https://www.theguardian.com/business/2015/jan/21 /-sp-davos-guide-world-economic-forum.

22. This segment of participants is what WEF's Klaus Schwab has long promoted as the "stakeholders" in the society mirroring the idea of "shareholders" in a corporation.

23. Already evident here is the language of commodity tradition that locates Café Schneider as *Erlebnis* rather than mere *Erfahrung*, to invoke the distinction made by Walter Benjamin. See Walter Benjamin, Lloyd Spencer, and Mark Harrington, "Central Park," *New German Critique* 34 (Winter 1985): 49; and Schneider's Davos, "Das Schneider's: Portrait," accessed November 21, 2018, http://www.schneiders-davos .ch/schneiders/portrait.html.

24. The images of Aakash were prominently displayed and circulated in Davos in 2012, creating a significant interest. Many visitors to the adda would ask to see a sample tablet, except that the tablet was unavailable. The tablet turned out to be a source of huge embarrassment for the human resources ministry, which had funded the project. Not only was the design found to be below par, but the capacity was too low for different functions to work. Moreover, the controversy around the manufacturing process has almost doomed the project of making low-cost tablets for schoolchildren in India.

25. Chakrabarty, "Adda, Calcutta," 118.

26. Chandrajit Banerjee, director-general of the Confederation of Indian Industries, quoted in Harish Damodaran, "'Cool' India Offers Inclusive Growth for All," *Hindu Business Line*, Davos, January 26, 2011.

27. IBEF, "India Davos," India Brand Equity Foundation, accessed October 2, 2018, http://www.india-davos-blogs.ibef.org/India---Innovates.

28. Aparna Dutta Sharma, interview by author, January 28, 2012, India Adda, Davos.

29. IBEF, "Brand India: At the Annual Meeting of the World Economic Meeting" (Davos, January 27–30, 2013), 4, 16.

30. Government of India, Ministry of Tourism, Atithi Devo Bhave (Guest is God) campaign, 2010. See also the Incredible India video, accessed November 21, 2018, https://www.youtube.com/watch?v=MMydmkiafTE.

31. The discussion on *dan* (or the gift) here is instructive. For a true act of giving to take place, it must not entail return, exchange, or reciprocity. Otherwise the gift enters a cycle of commodity exchange and can no longer be deemed to be a pure gift. Derrida has dwelt on this impossibility of the gift at length. Similarly, Jonathan

Parry and James Laidlaw have shown how the gift need not be reciprocal or non-alienated. See Jacques Derrida, *Given Time 1: Counterfeit Money* (Chicago: University of Chicago Press, 1992); Jonathan Parry, "The Gift, the Indian Gift and 'the Indian Gift,'" *Man, New Series* 21, no. 3 (1986): 453–73; James Laidlaw, "A Free Gift Makes No Friends," *The Journal of the Royal Anthropological Institute* 6, no. 4 (2000): 617–34.

32. This campaign was launched especially in anticipation of a major tourist influx during the Commonwealth Games in 2010. The idea was to professionalize the Indian tourist industry by training guides, drivers, hotel staff, and so on, on the ideals of Indian hospitality.

33. Pitching hospitality as a key cultural trait in tourism is indeed not unique to India. For a comparative perspective, see Andrew Shryock, "The New Jordanian Hospitality: House, Host and Guest in the Culture of Public Display," *Comparative Studies in Society and History* 46, no. 1 (2004): 35–62.

34. William Mazzarella, *Censorium: Cinema and the Open Edge of Mass Publicity* (Durham, NC: Duke University Press, 2013), 41.

35. Jacques Rancière, *The Emancipated Spectator* (London: Verso Books, 2009), 3.

36. Peter Vanham, "How Rick Goings Went from Dirt Poor to the CEO of a $2 Billion Company," CNBC, December 27, 2016, http://www.cnbc.com/2016/12/27/how-rick-goings-went-from-dirt-poor-to-the-ceo-of-tupperware.html.

37. Chakrabarty, "Adda, Calcutta," 120.

38. Ibid., 121.

39. The participants are CEOs of Godrej Group, Mahindra Systech, Fortis, Oberoi Realty, and Bajaj Financial Services, respectively. Adi Godrej was also the chairman of CII that year.

40. Karl Polanyi, *The Great Transformation: The Political and Economic Origins of Our Time* (Boston: Beacon Press, 2001).

41. Jill Treanor, "Occupy Activists Attempt to Take Over Davos Debate," *Guardian*, January 27, 2012, https://www.theguardian.com/world/2012/jan/27/occupy-movement-davos-capitalism-debate.

42. Jaswant Singh, "India's Year of Living Stagnantly," *Project Syndicate*, January 25, 2012, https://www.project-syndicate.org/commentary/india-s-year-of-living-stagnantly?barrier=accessreg.

43. Ravinder Kaur, "India Inc. and Its Moral Discontents," *Economic and Political Weekly* 47, no. 20 (May 19, 2012): 40–45.

44. The growth forecast bullishly pegged at double digits in early 2011 was revised a few months later to less than 7 percent. See, for instance, Rishi Shah, "9–10% GDP Growth Is History for Indian Economy: Richard Iley, BNP Paribas," *Economic Times*, December 16, 2011, http://articles.economictimes.indiatimes.com/2011-12-16/news/30525115_1_richard-iley-gdp-growth-growth-story; and BS Reporter, "India's GDP Growth in FY12 Just 6.8%: Report," *Business Standard*, January 19, 2012, http://www.business-standard.com/article/economy-policy/india-s-gdp-growth-in-fy12-just-6-8-report-112011900058_1.html.

45. "Tata Tea Tetley Merger: The Cup that Cheered," *India Today*, August 7, 2000, http://indiatoday.intoday.in/story/2000-Tata+Tea-Tetley+merger:+The+cup+that +cheered/1/76481.html; and "The Times of Tata," *Economic Times*, https://economic times.indiatimes.com/timesoftata.cms.

46. Shankkar Aiyar, "Inside Story: How L. N. Mittal Won the Bitter Battle to Clinch the Archelor Deal," *India Today*, July 10, 2006, http://indiatoday.intoday.in /story/how-ln-mittal-won-bitter-battle-to-clinch-arcelor-deal/1/180968.html.

47. Rachl Rickard Strausi, "East India Co Is Back, with Indian Owner," *Times Of India*, August 16, 2010, http://timesofindia.indiatimes.com/india/East-India-Co-is -back-with-Indian-owner/articleshow/6316784.cms.

48. dickyjones01, "Amitabh Bacchan—The New India," YouTube Video, January 30, 2007, https://www.youtube.com/watch?v=KNomFKB8sgk.

49. vivekkhat, "Great India: CEO of East India Company Is Now an Indian," YouTube Video, September 27, 2010, https://www.youtube.com/watch?v=tu4SHz DFGgw.

50. See Gurucharan Das, *India Grows at Night: A Liberal Case for a Strong State* (Delhi: Penguin Books, 2013).

51. See Srirupa Roy, "Being the Change: The Aam Aadmi Party and the Politics of the Extraordinary in Indian Democracy," *Economic and Political Weekly* 49, no. 15 (2014): 45–54.

52. See, for example, Partha Chatterjee, "Against Corruption = Against Politics," *Kafila Online*, August 28, 2011, https://kafila.online/2011/08/28/against-corruption -against-politics-partha-chatterjee/.

53. Michael Day, "Caving into Pressure: Why Mario Monti's Technocrats Couldn't Repair Italy after Silvio Berlusconi's Government Collapsed," *Independent*, February 22, 2013, http://www.independent.co.uk/news/world/europe/caving-in-to -pressure-why-mario-monti-s-technocrats-couldn-t-repair-italy-after-silvio-berlus coni-s-8507736.html.

54. B. Muralidhar Reddy, "It's Official: Modi Is BJP's Choice," *The Hindu*, September 13, 2013, http://www.thehindu.com/news/national/its-official-modi-is-bjps -choice/article5124375.ece.

55. See, for example, Amy Kazmin, "Modi Personality Cult Dominates India Election," *Financial Times*, April 8, 2014, https://www.ft.com/content/96b8ca94-bed0 -11e3-a1bf-00144feabdco.

56. Ravinder Kaur, "Good Times, Brought to You by Brand Modi," *Television and New Media* 16, no. 4 (2015): 323–30.

57. Ravinder Kaur, "Nation's Two Bodies: Rethinking the Idea of 'New' India and Its Other," *Third World Quarterly* 33, no. 4 (2012): 603–21.

58. Stanley Pignal, the *Economist* correspondent in Mumbai, suggests that "the Indian state is reluctant to let go of the 'commanding heights' of much of the economy, to use Lenin's term. The most glaring example is banking, wherein two-thirds of all loans are on state owned banks' books. . . . The Indian state does not allocate

capital, but it steers it, subtly but unmistakably, towards areas it thinks are worthy of investment. You are more likely to get land allocated to you, say, if you are pursuing some chief minister's pet cause." Email message to author, April 19, 2017.

59. Examples of this phenomenon include the Russian Gazprom; the Chinese state's role as a direct shareholder in more than 150 companies and as a guide of thousands more; the Saudi Basic Industries Corporation, one of the most profitable chemical companies; Dubai Ports, the third-largest port operator; and the Emirates, the Qatar state-owned airlines, growing at 20 percent per year. See Adrian Wooldridge, "The Visible Hand," *Economist*, January 21, 2012, http://www.economist.com/node /21542931.

60. See, for example, Elizabeth Chatterjee, "Reinventing State Capitalism in India: A View from the Energy Sector," *Contemporary South Asia* 25, no. 1 (2017): 85–100.

61. It is useful here to think of Thomas Blom Hansen's description of the duality of the Indian state. If the profane dimension constitutes the brutality, the rough-and-tumble of negotiation, compromise, and naked self-interest, the sublime qualities resurrect the state as an immensely powerful mythical being. Thomas Blom Hansen, "Governance and State Mythologies in Mumbai," in *State of Imagination: Ethnographic Explorations of the Postcolonial State*, ed. Thomas Blom Hansen and Stepputat (Durham, NC: Duke University Press, 2001), 226–27.

62. The Cashless India program promotes a number of digital payment solutions including banking cards, internet banking, e-wallets, United Payment Interface (UPI), an open-code single banking application, and the Bharat Interface for Money (BHIM) application developed by the National Payments Corporation of India (NPCI). For more details, see Government of India, "Cashless India," accessed April 24, 2018, http://cashlessindia.gov.in.

63. Digital India is a flagship program of the Modi government that promotes digital infrastructure. Government of India, Ministry of Electronics & Information Technology, "Home: About Digital India: Introduction," accessed April 24, 2018, http://www.digitalindia.gov.in/content/introduction.

64. The National Skill Development Corporation is a public-private initiative first proposed under the UPA government in 2008–2009. National Skill Development Corporation, "Organisation Profile," NSDC India, accessed April 24, 2018, http://www.nsdcindia.org/organisation-profile.

65. UDAAN—National Skill Development Corporation, "What Is Udaan?," accessed August 2, 2018, http://nsdcudaan.com.

66. Business India Bureau, "Thanks to Demonetization, Paytm Is Making Rs 120 Crore per Day; Achieves Target before Deadline, Crosses $5 Billion GMV," *Business Insider*, November 21, 2016, http://www.businessinsider.in/Thanks-to-demone tization-Paytm-is-making-Rs-120-crore-per-day-achieves-target-before-deadline -crosses-5-billion-GMV/articleshow/55541691.cms.

67. Arushi Chopra, "Paytm Claims Record Number of Transactions after Govt's Demonetization," *Live Mint*, November 14, 2016, http://www.livemint.com

/Companies/gWuı8E6zIzsIotfsANYsFL/Paytm-claims-record-number-of-trans
actions-after-govts-demo.html.

68. HT Correspondent, "Pledge to Make India a Cashless Society: Highlights
from PM Modi's Mann Ki Baat," *Hindustan Times*, November 27, 2016, http://www
.hindustantimes.com/india-news/live-pm-modi-speaks-on-demonetisation-cross
-border-ties-in-mann-ki-baat/story-QGFJfAYbderasrlGbov32N.html.

69. Marshall Berman, *All That Is Solid Melts into Air* (London: Verso, 2010).

70. Dipesh Chakrabarty poses this as an unresolved question: "how to be at home
in a globalized capitalism now" in relation to the idealized image of adda.

71. See, for example, IBEF, "Mr Sunil Bharti Mittal, Founder, Chairman and
Group CEO, Bharti Enterprises," YouTube Video, January 26, 2013, https://www
.youtube.com/watch?v=29tatOhC56A&list=PLıyEMadWev-EofqHA32myUgNpgvr
JVruc&index=12.

CHAPTER 6

1. William Mazzarella, "The Myth of the Multitude, or, Who's Afraid of the
Crowd," *Critical Enquiry* 36 (2010): 697.

2. On the long history of the merit versus quota debate, see Satish Deshpande,
"Caste and Castelessness," *Economic and Political Weekly* 48, no. 15 (2013).

3. Jean Drèze and Amartya Sen, *An Uncertain Glory: India and Its Contradictions*
(Princeton, NJ: Princeton University Press, 2013); Ravinder Kaur and Nandini Sundar, "Snakes and Ladders: Rethinking Social Mobility in Post-Reform India," *Contemporary South Asia* 24, no. 3 (2016): 229–41; and Alpa Shah, *Behind the Indian Boom:
Inequality and Resistance at the Heart of the Economic Growth* (Kolkata: Adivaani, 2017).

4. Name changed on request.

5. Nitin, interview by author, March 13, 2009.

6. Uma Das Gupta, "The Indian Press 1870–1880: A Small World of Journalism,"
Modern Asian Studies 11, no. 2 (1977): 223.

7. Ryan Perkins, "A New *Pablik*: Abdul Halim Sharar, Volunteerism, and the
Anjuman-e Dar-us-Salaam in Late Nineteenth Century India," *Modern Asian Studies* 49, no. 4 (2015): 1049–90.

8. Kavita Datla, "A Worldly Vernacular: Urdu at Osmania University," *Modern
Asian Studies* 43, no. 5 (2009): 1117–48.

9. Christopher A. Bayly, *Empire and Information: Intelligence Gathering and Social
Communication in India, 1780–1870* (Cambridge, UK: Cambridge University Press,
1996).

10. See Robin Jeffrey, "Communication and Capitalism in India, 1750–2010,"
South Asia: Journal of South Asian Studies 25, no. 2 (2000): 61–75. See also Arvind Rajagopal, *Politics after Television: Hindu Nationalism and the Reshaping of the Public in India* (Cambridge, UK: Cambridge University Press, 2001).

11. Das Gupta, "Indian Press 1870–1880," 213.

12. P. C. Alexander, "Liberty of the Press: Its Legal Restrictions," *The Indian Journal of Political Science* 8, no. 2 (1946): 688.

13. Ramanand Chatterjee, "Origin and Growth of Journalism among Indians," *The Annals of the American Academy of Political and Social Science* 145, no. 2 (1929): 164.

14. Ibid.

15. Randeep Ramesh, "Newspaper Empires at War in India," *Guardian*, July 27, 2005, https://www.theguardian.com/media/2005/jul/27/pressandpublishing.business.

16. "The Times Of India's Business Strategy Start the Presses," *Washington Post*, July 2, 2015, https://www.washingtonpost.com/business/the-times-of-indias-business-strategy-start-the-presses/2015/07/02/52d5e670-1c50-11e5-ab92-c75ae6ab94b5_story.html?utm_term=.ca55ae2dd495.

17. Ken Auletta, "Citizens Jain," *New Yorker*, October 8, 2012, https://www.newyorker.com/magazine/2012/10/08/citizens-jain.

18. Advertorials are said to be prevalent in English-language media as in Hindi and regional languages. Some media companies mark items clearly as "adverorials," and many do away with this altogether.

19. Times News Network, "Medianet: Innovative Content, Integrated Offering," *Times of India*, March 4, 2003, https://timesofindia.indiatimes.com/india/Medianet-Innovative-content-integrated-offering/articleshow/39286961.cms.

20. See, for example, the description on his official website, accessed November 28, 2017, https://www.marshallmcluhan.com.

21. Marshall McLuhan, *Understanding Media: The Extensions of Man* (Cambridge, MA: MIT Press, 1964), 228.

22. Ibid., 230.

23. Timesofindia.com, "We Are the Best," *Times of India*, April 2, 2004, https://timesofindia.indiatimes.com/nrs-2003/We-are-the-best/articleshow/596413.cms.

24. Times News Network, "Times Now Masthead of the World," *Times of India*, June 26, 2005, https://timesofindia.indiatimes.com/india/Times-now-Masthead-of-the-World/articleshow/1152489.cms.

25. "Why India's Newspaper Business Is Booming," *Economist*, February 22, 2016, https://www.economist.com/blogs/economist-explains/2016/02/economist-explains-13.

26. Paranjoy Guha Thakurta, "The Times, the Jains, and BCCL," *The Hoot*, November 11, 2012, http://thehoot.org/media-watch/media-business/the-times-the-jains-and-bccl-6425.

27. A note on business practices—combo model, advertiser: Shamni Pande, "Just in Times," *Business Today*, July 10, 2011, http://www.businesstoday.in/magazine/cover-story/bennett-coleman-and-co-among-100-year-old-indian-companies/story/16498.html.

28. McLuhan, *Understanding Media*, 234.

29. Ibid., 230.

30. See, for example, Roy Greenslade, "City AM Takes a Revolutionary Step by Opening Website to Advertisers," *Guardian*, June 3, 2016, https://www.theguardian

.com/media/greenslade/2016/jun/03/city-am-takes-a-revolutionary-step-by-opening
-website-to-advertisers.

31. The inquiry itself became the subject of controversy, as the report was delayed and its content said to be diluted. See "Press Council of India's Report on Paid News," Press Council of India, accessed November 27, 2017, http://presscouncil.nic.in/Old Website/CouncilReport.pdf; and P. Sainath, "Paid News Undermining Democracy: Press Council Report," *The Hindu*, April 21, 2010, http://www.thehindu.com/opinion /columns/sainath/Paid-news-undermining-democracy-Press-Council-report/article 16371596.ece.

32. For example, the concerns about "paid news" content have been much discussed. See Nayantara Narayanan, "Five Ethical Problems That Plague Indian Journalism," *Scroll.in*, March 19, 2015, https://scroll.in/article/714570/five-ethical-problems -that-plague-indian-journalism; and Akash Kapur, "In India, Sometimes News Is Just a Product Placement," *New York Times*, May 7, 2010, http://www.nytimes.com /2010/05/08/world/asia/08iht-letter.html. It is not just the English-language newspapers that made use of paid news content but also Hindi and other vernacular newspapers in which "favourable new coverage" could effectively be bought. See Mrinal Pande, "Hindi Media and an Unreal Discourse," *The Hindu*, November 18, 2009, http://www.thehindu.com/opinion/lead/Hindi-media-and-an-unreal-discourse /article16892944.ece.

33. "The Initiative," Teach India, accessed December 2, 2018, http://www.teach india.net/teach-india?pref=mumbai&nocache=true.

34. Anjali Puri, "Free from India?," *Outlook India*, August 18, 2008, https://www .outlookindia.com/magazine/story/free-from-india/238163.

35. "Can India Fly?," *Economist*, June 1, 2006, http://www.economist.com/node /7004433.

36. The schemes like MGNREGA or Right to Food are limited in scale and scope to the absolute poor, and even then just to bare necessities required to survive.

37. See the video form at Times Music, "India vs. India—TOI ft. Amitabh Bachchan HQ," YouTube Video, January 25, 2017, https://www.youtube.com/watch?v=XzJj -PL-kPs. The Hindi version is available here: Huzefa Husain, "India Poised Anthem (Hindi)," YouTube Video, January 17, 2007, https://www.youtube.com/watch?v=MEF MJgbLRaM.

38. See Ravinder Kaur, "Nation's Two Bodies: Rethinking the Idea of 'New' India and Its Other," *Third World Quarterly* 33, no. 4 (May 1, 2012): 603–21; and Kaur, "Remains of Difference: New Imaginaries of Otherness in Post-Reform India," in *Interrogating India's Modernity: Democracy, Identity and Citizenship*, ed. Surinder Jodhka (New Delhi: Oxford University Press, 2014), 221–43.

39. The title "A Passage from India" is a nod to E. M. Forster's *A Passage to India*, a story set in the British colonial era. The reverse passage from India hints at India's growing global role and its exploration of the world. Jaideep Bose, "A Passage from India," *Times of India*, January 1, 2007.

40. Vyas Shuchi, "The Time Is Now," *Economic Times*, January 10, 2007.

41. The bridge was eventually completed and opened to the public in 2010.

42. Agnello Dias, Skype interview with author, April 14, 2014.

43. Screenshot of the www.indiapoised.com website.

44. "Citizens' Charter for Change," *Times of India*, January 7, 2007. Available on Press Reader.

45. Javed Majeed, "A Nation on the Move: The Indian Constitution, Life Writing, and Cosmopolitanism," *Life Writing* 13, no. 2 (2016): 237–53.

46. Bose, "Passage from India."

47. Shuchi, "Time Is Now."

48. See, for example, Christophe Jaffrelot, "'Why Should We Vote?': The Indian Middle Class and the Functioning of the World's Largest Democracy," in *Patterns of Middle Class Consumption in India and China*, ed. Christophe Jaffrelot and Peter van der Veer (Delhi: Sage, 2008); Mukulika Banerjee, *Why India Votes?* (London: Routledge, 2008); and John Harriss, "'Politics Is a Dirty River': But Is There a 'New Politics' of Civil Society? Perspectives from Global Cities of India and Latin America" (London: LSE Research Online, 2005), http://eprints.lse.ac.uk/487/1/CCLSConferencePaper.pdf.

49. Jaffrelot, "Why Should We Vote?," 45–47. See also Jaffrelot, "The Caste Based Mosaic of Indian Politics" (India seminar, seminar no. 633, 2012), http://www.india-seminar.com/2012/633/633_christophe_jaffrelot.htm.

50. Dias, interview.

51. Mukulika Banerjee, "Vote," *South Asia: Journal of South Asian Studies* 40, no. 2 (2017): 411.

52. Jaffrelot, "Why Should We Vote?," 46.

53. Preethi Chamikutty, "Times of India's 'Lead India' Campaign a Success," *Times of India*, February 22, 2008, https://timesofindia.indiatimes.com/india/Times-of-Indias-Lead-India-campaign-a-success/articleshow/2801380.cms.

54. The show ran on STAR TV for ten weeks between December 2007 and February 2008. The winner was the forty-four-year-old R. K. Misra, an IIT graduate who had given up his corporate career to do social work. In March 2009, he joined the BJP as an active politician.

55. The 2008 terror attack left 160 dead and 310 injured. "How 26/11 Mumbai Attack Happened in 2008: From First Eyewitness to Kasab," *India Today*, November 26, 2017, http://indiatoday.intoday.in/story/how-2611-mumbai-terror-attack-happened-in-2008-from-first-eyewitness-to-kasab/1/1097464.html.

56. Dhruv Wadia, a young advertising professional, quoted in Ishaan Tharoor, "A Rally in Mumbai: Remember 26/11," *Time*, December 3, 2008.

57. Tharoor, "Rally in Mumbai."

58. See also Prabhu Chawla, "A Harvest of Terror," *India Today*, November 28, 2008, http://indiatoday.intoday.in/story/A+harvest+of+terror/1/21193.html.

59. On interocularity, see Martin Jay and Sumathi Ramaswamy, "Introduction: The Work of Vision in the Age of European Empires," in *Empires of Vision: A Reader (Objects/Histories)* (Durham, NC: Duke University Press, 2014), 25–46.

60. I use the pronoun *he* for the Aam aadmi, as depicted in the campaign imagery.

61. The act continues to be used even today, often to confiscate property in case of errant companies not paying their dues to farmers and workers. Srinivas Rajulapudi, "55-Year-Old A. P. Sugar Unit Closed," *The Hindu*, January 23, 2017, http://www.the hindu.com/todays-paper/tp-national/tp-andhrapradesh/55-year-old-A.P.-sugar-unit -closed/article17080098.ece.

62. Although India moved to electronic voting machines in the 2004 general elections, the stamp retains its symbolic value as a mark of democracy. "How the Voting Takes Place," Election Commission of India, accessed April 20, 2018, http://eci.nic .in/eci_main1/the_function.aspx#howthevoting.

63. See interview with Kutty in Ritu Gairola Khanduri, *Caricaturing Culture in India: Cartoons and History in the Modern World* (Cambridge, UK: Cambridge University Press, 2014), 193.

64. Ritu Gairola Khanduri, "Picturing India: Nation, Development and the Common Man," *Visual Anthropology* 25, no. 4 (2012): 304.

65. Kutty, quoted in Khanduri, *Caricaturing Culture*, 193.

66. Agriculture has been the mainstay of the Indian economy, especially prior to the 1990s economic reforms. See also Kavita Philips, "Telling Histories of the Future: The Imaginaries of Indian Technoscience," *Identities: Global Journal of Power and Culture* 23, no. 3 (2016): 276–93.

67. Kutty, quoted in Khanduri, *Caricaturing Culture*, 194.

68. Ibid., 192.

69. R. K. Laxman, interview by contractor, quoted in Khanduri, *Caricaturing Culture*, 194.

70. Laxman, quoted in Aditi De, "Creating the Common Man," *The Hindu*, June 12, 2004, http://www.thehindu.com/yw/2004/06/12/stories/2004061200060200 .htm.

71. Chris Pinney, *Photos of the Gods: The Printed and Political Struggle in India* (London: Reaktion Books, 2004), 207.

72. On commission from the *Times of India*, Bawa Broadcasting Corporation, a Delhi-based ad agency, created www.bleedindia.com. The site is now archived at "Archive—BLEED INDIA WEBSITE," Sky Design, accessed April 20, 2018, http:// www.skydesign.in/archive/BLEED_INDIA_WEBSITE/index.html.

73. Diptarup Chakraborti, a research analyst, quoted in Rina Chandran, "India Leaders Blog, Text to Plug In to Young Voters," Reuters, March 17, 2009, https:// www.reuters.com/article/us-india-elections-youth/india-leaders-blog-text-to-plug -in-to-young-voters-idUSTRE52G1CR20090317.

74. Chandran, "India Leaders Blog."

75. See, for example, Shashi Tharoor, "Meanwhile: India's Cellphone Revolution—Opinion—International Herald Tribune," *New York Times*, February 2, 2007, http://www.nytimes.com/2007/02/01/opinion/01iht-edtharoor.4431582.html.

76. Assa Doron and Robin Jeffrey, *The Great Indian Phone Book* (London: Hurst, 2013), 3.

77. Saritha Rai, "India Just Crossed 1 Billion Mobile Subscribers Milestone and the Excitement's Just Beginning," *Forbes*, January 6, 2016, https://www.forbes.com /sites/saritharai/2016/01/06/india-just-crossed-1-billion-mobile-subscribers-mile stone-and-the-excitements-just-beginning/#397556ff7dbo.

78. Times News Network, "Awareness Campaigns Draw Mixed Reactions from Electorate," *Times of India*, April 23, 2009, https://timesofindia.indiatimes.com/city /goa/Awareness-campaigns-draw-mixed-reactions-from-electorate/articleshow/44321 71.cms.

79. Francesca Orsini, "Dil Mange More: Cultural Contexts of Hinglish in Contemporary India," *African Studies* 74, no. 2 (August 2015); and Rita Kothari and Rupert Snell, eds., *Chutneyfying English: The Phenomenon of Hinglish* (New Delhi: Penguin, 2011).

80. The ad can be viewed here: "Cadbury Dairy Milk—Pappu pass ho gaya," YouTube Video, March 1, 2011, https://www.youtube.com/watch?v=xs-r6wJ7koc.

81. The video is available here: *Times of India*, "TOI Lead India Sharukh Khan," YouTube Video, January 23, 2013, https://www.youtube.com/watch?v=Z_JA6FhN9LI.

82. *Times of India*, "TOI Lead India Aamir Khan," YouTube Video, January 23, 2013, https://www.youtube.com/watch?v=gLw9aHLW-JE.

83. The persona of Pappu Raj, the corrupt politician, played by Johnny Lever, appears to mimic the flesh-and-blood politician Bangaru Laxman, who became a prominent symbol of the corrupt politician. In 2001, Laxman, BJP's lone Dalit president, became the main character in the story of India's first media "sting operation" that exposed corruption in politics. A team of journalists from *Tehelka* magazine posing as arms dealers had secretly recorded him accepting a bribe on a concealed camera. The cash received was merely 1 lakh rupees, a pittance compared to the astronomical sums running into lakhs of crores quoted in later claims of corruption. Bangaru claimed in his defense that he had been falsely framed by the journalists. He was nevertheless removed from the post of party president and left on his own to fight the legal charges. He was convicted in 2012 on the charges of corruption. Neither these details nor the name of Bangaru Laxman appear anywhere in the Bleed India campaign. Yet the availability of this information in the public domain and the visual clues in the image mean that viewers are able to work out the connections. Incidentally both Bangaru and Lever hail from Andhra Pradesh, and, like Bangaru, Lever belongs to a Dalit community. Johnny Lever is said to belong to a Dalit Mala family that converted to Christianity. See Jitesh Singh Chauhan, "Dalits in Indian Cinema," *Forward Press*, February 1, 2015, https://www.forwardpress.in/2015/02 /dalits-in-indian-cinema/. His biographies on Wikipedia and IMDB, however, do not offer details on his caste origins.

84. In 2013, this discourse fully spilled out in the public domain when Ashis Nandy, a celebrated social scientist, weighed in on the malady of corruption. He remarked, "How should I put it? It is almost a vulgar statement on my part. It is a fact that most of the corrupt come from the Other Backward Classes, and the Scheduled Castes, and now increasingly Scheduled Tribes. One of the states with the least

amount of corruption is the state of West Bengal, that is when the CPM was there. And I want to propose to you, draw your attention to the fact that in the last 100 years, nobody from the OBCs, the backward classes, and SC, ST have come anywhere near power in West Bengal. It is an absolutely clean state." Besides Ashis Nandy, the debate also featured Tarun Tejpal, editor of *Tehelka*; Ashutosh, managing editor at IBN7; and Urvashi Butalia, moderator. The transcript and video is available here: Urvashi Butalia, Ashis Nandy, Tarun J. Tejpal, and Ashutosh, "What Ashis Nandy Actually Said at JLF," *Outlook India*, January 30, 2013, https://www.outlook india.com/website/story/what-ashis-nandy-actually-said-at-jlf/283737/.

85. The names of upper-caste politicians charged, imprisoned, and even convicted of corruption include Jayalalitha, Dilip Singh Judeo, Robert Vadra, Sukh Ram, Suresh Kalmadi, and Ramalingam Raju. See FP Staff, "Jayalalithaa Convicted in Disproportionate Assets Case: How It All Began," *Firstpost*, February 14, 2017, http://www.firstpost.com/politics/jayalalithaa-convicted-in-disproportionate-assets -case-how-it-all-began-1992325.html; Sayantan Chakravarty, "Chhattisgarh Assembly Polls: Dilip Singh Judev Sting Operation haunts BJP," *India Today*, December 1, 2013, https://www.indiatoday.in/magazine/states/story/20031201-chhattisgarh -assembly-polls-dilip-singh-judev-sting-operation-haunts-bjp-791411-2003-12-01; Raghav Ohri, "Robert Vadra Made Gains of Rs 50 Crore from a Land Deal in Haryana in 2008: Dhingra Panel," *Economic Times*, April 28, 2017, https://economictimes .indiatimes.com/news/politics-and-nation/robert-vadra-made-gains-of-rs-50-crore -from-a-land-deal-in-haryana-in-2008-dhingra-panel/articleshow/58407295.cms; and "Satyam Scandal: Who, What and When," *The Hindu*, April 9, 2015, http://www .thehindu.com/specials/timelines/satyam-scandal-who-what-and-when/article10818 226.ece.

86. Christophe Jaffrelot, "The Politics of the OBCs," in *Repressing Disadvantages: A Symposium on Reservations and the Private Sector*, ed. Gurpreet Mahajan (Seminar no. 549, 2005).

87. Sudha Pai, "Rise of Mayawati in Hindi Heartland Is a Remarkable Phenomenon," *Indian Express*, January 22, 2016, http://indianexpress.com/article/blogs/rise -of-mayawati-in-hindi-heartland-is-a-remarkable-phenomenon/. See also Sudha Pai, *Dalit Assertion* (Delhi: Oxford University Press, 2013).

88. Partha Chatterjee, "Against Corruption = Against Politics," *Kafila Online*, August 28, 2011, https://kafila.online/2011/08/28/against-corruption-against-politics -partha-chatterjee/.

89. The ongoing debate on corruption has shown how the critique of government corruption per se requires that the state be imagined as an impartial, uncorrupt institution. On the corruption debate, see Akhil Gupta, *Red Tape: Bureaucracy, Structural Violence, and Poverty in India* (Durham, NC: Duke University Press, 2014); and Arjun Appadurai, "Our Corruption, Our Selves: Arjun Appadurai," *Kafila*, August 30, 2011, https://kafila.online/2011/08/30/our-corruption-our-selves-arjun-appa durai. Such imaginary overlooks the social character of the state and how the upper-caste elite consolidated power through corrupt practices. The upward mobilization of

"backward castes" meant that corruption was seen as a "naked signifier of power, now wielded by lower-caste leaders." Jeffrey Witsoe, "Corruption as Power: Caste and the Political Imagination of the Postcolonial State," *American Ethnologist* 38, no. 1 (2011): 73–85. The focus on state institutions in the anticorruption discourse, then, has also meant that corruption in the private sector has never been a major issue. See Ravinder Kaur, "India Inc. and Its Moral Discontents," *Economic and Political Weekly* 47, no. 20 (2012): 40–45.

90. Shruti Ravindran, "A Park for Maya Memsaab," *Indian Express*, January 9, 2011, http://indianexpress.com/article/news-archive/web/a-park-for-maya-memsaab/.

91. Kajri Jain, "The Handbag That Exploded: Mayawati's Monuments and the Aesthetics of Democracy in Post-Reform India," in *New Cultural Histories of India: Materiality and Practices*, ed. Partha Chatterjee, Tapati Guha-Thakurta, and Bodhi-sattava Kar (New Delhi: Oxford University Press, 2015).

92. See, for example, the spectacle of covering and uncovering the statues of Ma-yawati around election time. "Mayawati Statues: Race to Cover India Chief's Mon-uments," BBC News, January 10, 2012, http://www.bbc.com/news/world-asia-india-16481185. See also the vandalization of statues that occasionally takes place. Ashish Tripathi, "Mayawati's Statue 'Beheaded' in Lucknow, Police Call It Sacrilege," *Times of India*, July 26, 2012, https://timesofindia.indiatimes.com/city/lucknow/Mayawatis-statue-beheaded-in-Lucknow-police-call-it-sacrilege/articleshow/15161969.cms.

93. Anant Zanane, "Mayawathi's Elephant Statues: Could Be a 40,000 Crore Scam, Says Akhilesh Yadav," NDTV, May 15, 2012, https://www.ndtv.com/india-news/mayawatis-elephant-statues-could-be-a-40-000-crore-scam-says-akhilesh-yadav-482599.

94. C. J. Kuncheria, "Mayawathi's Garland of Cash Kicks Up Political Storm," Reuters, March 16, 2010, https://in.reuters.com/article/idINIndia-46965320100316?sp=true.

95. Sunil Sethi, "Sunil Sethi: In Mayawati's 'Green Garden,'" *Business Standard*, January 20, 2013, http://www.business-standard.com/article/opinion/sunil-sethi-in-mayawati-s-green-garden-111102900057_1.html.

96. Amarnath Tewary, "What Is the Lowdown on the Fodder Scam," *The Hindu*, January 13, 2018, http://www.thehindu.com/news/national/what-is-the-lowdown-on-the-fodder-scam/article22437730.ece.

97. The case of Madhu Koda, in fact, was one of the examples that Ashis Nandy had mentioned as an instance of being "brilliantly corrupt," because Koda was seen as unlike other backward leaders who did not know how to absorb ill-gotten money. In a subsequent interview, he suggested that his remarks were pro-Dalit because he was trying to highlight that the corruption of the unprivileged castes looks crude and un-sophisticated, and they get caught more often than the dominant castes. See Niharika Mandhana, "A Conversation With: Sociologist Ashis Nandy," *New York Times*, Jan-uary 30, 2013, https://india.blogs.nytimes.com/2013/01/30/a-conversation-with-sociol ogist-ashis-nandy/. See also Aditi Singh, "Coal Scam Case: Former Jharkand CM Madhu Koda Convicted by Special by CBI Court," *Live Mint*, December 13, 2017,

http://www.livemint.com/Politics/oIdl8xXT6qYR3pw8p4DBXM/Coal-scam
-case-Former-Jharkhand-CM-Madhu-Koda-convicted-by.html; and Kancha Ilaiah,
"Caste, Corruption and Romanticism," *The Hindu*, March 22, 2013, http://www.the
hindu.com/opinion/lead/caste-corruption-and-romanticism/article4534892.ece.

98. Deshpande, "Caste and Castelessness."

99. It is instructive to note the shape that the political careers of, for example, Bangaru Laxman and Dilip Singh Judeo took following conviction in corruption cases.
Both Laxman and Judeo were from BJP and were caught accepting a bribe on camera.
Yet the latter was rehabilitated into the party fold while the former was isolated and
left to his own means. Another difference is that, for example, Sukh Ram's conviction
in the telecom scandal did not lead to any generalized conclusions about Brahmins
and their collective moral flaws. He was seen as a corrupt individual. In contrast, the
corruption cases against Madhu Koda and Mayawati were interpreted as signs of collective flaws among the less-privileged caste groups. See also Shekhar Gupta, "Corruption and the Caste Differential," *Business Standard*, December 23, 2017.

100. Hannah Arendt, *The Human Condition* (Chicago: University of Chicago
Press, 1998), 199.

101. *Times of India*, "Who Is Anna Hazare?," *Times of India*, August 18, 2011,
https://timesofindia.indiatimes.com/india/Who-is-Anna-Hazare/articleshow/96447
94.cms.

102. Ibid.

103. PTI, "For the First Time in Their 120-Year-Old History, Mumbai's Dabbawalas to Take a Break for Anna Hazare," *Economic Times*, August 19, 2011, https://
economictimes.indiatimes.com/news/politics-and-nation/for-the-first-time-in-their
-120-year-old-history-mumbais-dabbawalas-to-take-a-break-for-anna-hazare/article
show/9649340.cms. See also *Economic Times*, "India Inc Rallies behind Anna Hazare in the Anti-Corruption Movement," *Economic Times*, April 19, 2011, https://eco
nomictimes.indiatimes.com/news/politics-and-nation/india-inc-rallies-behind
-anna-hazare-in-the-anti-corruption-movement/articleshow/7922112.cms.

104. Nivedita Menon, "We Should be There: The Left and the Anna Moment,"
Firstpost, August 20, 2011, https://www.firstpost.com/politics/we-should-be-there
-the-left-and-the-anna-moment-65356.html.

105. Times News Network, "India against Corruption: 'This Is Our 2nd Freedom Struggle,'" *Economic Times*, April 7, 2011, https://economictimes.indiatimes.com
/news/politics-and-nation/india-against-corruption-this-is-our-2nd-freedom-strug
gle/articleshow/7895496.cms.

106. Judith Butler, "We, the People: Thoughts on Freedom of Assembly," in *What
Is a People?* (New York: Columbia University Press, 2016), 51.

107. The prereform decades in postcolonial India are sometimes referred to as the
socialist era. Yet there is nothing especially socialist, in the sense of a social-welfare
model, about this period, as social welfare has never been an accessible public good.
The term *socialism* in the context of India often appeared as a marker of a time before
new modes of middle-class consumption took over.

108. Kaur and Sundar, "Snakes and Ladders."

109. The biography of Anna Hazare, an ex-soldier turned activist is instructive here. His preference for order and discipline and for instant justice for moral deficiencies and slipups has framed his political activism over the decades in his native Ralegaon Siddhi. See Mukul Sharma, "The Making of Anna Hazare," *Kafila Online*, April 4, 2011, https://kafila.online/2011/04/12/the-making-of-anna-hazare/.

110. Aradhana Sharma, "New Brooms and Old: Sweeping Up Corruption in India, One Law at a Time," *Current Anthropology* 59, no. S18 (April 2018): S72–S82.

111. The disagreement was over the question of active participation in politics. Arvind Kejriwal, Yogendra Yadav, Prashant Bhushan, and others argued that political participation is a precondition to changing the system. Anna Hazare, in contrast, forbade his followers from taking part in electoral politics.

CHAPTER 7

1. Dinesh Unnikrishnan, "World Economic Forum 2018: Narendra Modi Can't Ask for a Better Marketplace than Davos to Pitch India as a Hot Ticket Item," *Firstpost*, January 23, 2018, http://www.firstpost.com/business/prime-minister-narendra-modi-cant-ask-for-a-better-marketplace-than-davos-to-pitch-india-as-a-hot-ticket-item-4313817.html.

2. *Economic Times*, "Here's What Makes Narendra Modi the Best Salesman India Has Ever Had," *Economic Times*, May 29, 2017, https://economictimes.indiatimes.com/news/politics-and-nation/heres-what-makes-narendra-modi-the-best-salesman-india-can-ever-have/articleshow/58895081.cms.

3. Manjeet Kriplani, "Narendra Modi: India's Salesman-in-Chief," *Quartz India*, May 22, 2015, https://qz.com/410498/narendra-modi-indias-salesman-in-chief/. See also https://edition.cnn.com/2017/07/06/asia/india-modi-traveling-salesman/index.html.

4. Sidhartha, "India Is Replacing Red Tape with Red Carpet: PM Modi Tells CEOs at Davos," *Times of India*, January 23, 2018, https://timesofindia.indiatimes.com/business/international-business/india-is-replacing-red-tape-with-red-carpet-pm-modi-tells-ceos-at-davos/articleshow/62622556.cms.

5. Based on an epic poem composed by the sixteenth-century Sufi poet Malik Muhammad Jayasi, the story of Padmavati has long been surrounded in myths and contested narratives. See Ramya Sreenivasan, *The Many Lives of a Rajput Queen: Heroic Pasts in India, c. 1500–1900* (Seattle: University of Washington Press, 2007).

6. Ananya Bhattacharya, "Padmavati and Verna: India and Pakistan Shame Shame, Not Different," *India Today*, November 14, 2017, https://www.indiatoday.in/movies/standpoint/story/padmavati-verna-india-pakistan-deepika-padukone-mahira-khan-1086223-2017-11-14.

7. Indo Asian News Service, "Stop Padmaavat or We'll Jump into Fire, Warn Hundreds of Rajput Women," January 22, 2018, https://www.ndtv.com/india-news/women-draw-swords-threaten-jauhar-in-chittorgarh-to-protest-against-padmaavat-release-1802926.

8. The violence began on February 27, 2002, and lasted at least three days but had long-lasting effects, including more than one thousand dead (most of whom were Muslims) and about 150,000 driven from their homes. For the history of the pogrom, see Parvis Ghassem-Fachandi, *Pogrom in Gujarat and Anti-Muslim Violence in India* (Princeton, NJ: Princeton University Press, 2012), 1–2; Ornit Shani, *Communalism, Caste and Hindu Nationalism: The Violence in Gujarat* (Cambridge, UK: Cambridge University Press, 2007); Christophe Jaffrelot, "Communal Riots in Gujarat: The State at Risk?" (working paper no. 17, Heidelberg Papers in South Asian and Comparative Politics, July 2003), http://archiv.ub.uni-heidelberg.de/volltextserver/4127/1/hpsacp17 .pdf. A rich visual source on the pogrom is Rakesh Sharma, "Final Solution," Vimeo video, 2004, accessed July 31, 2019, https://vimeo.com/329340055.

9. A. G. Noorani, "India's Reaction to the International Concern over Gujarat," in *Gujarat: The Making of a Tragedy*, ed. Siddharth Varadarajn (Delhi: Penguin, 2003), 389–400.

10. The then prime minister Atal Bihari Vajpayee is also said to have expressed remorse, especially given the embarrassment. Vajpayee reportedly remarked, "I don't know how I can face the rest of the world after the shameful events in Gujarat" in a meeting with the victims. Quoted in Dionne Bunsha, "Gujarat's Shame," *Frontline* 19, no. 8 (April 13–26, 2002), https://frontline.thehindu.com/static/html/fl1908/19080210 .htm. Yet Vajpayee's position was deliberately ambiguous on the Gujarat question. See Siddharth Varadarajan. "Chronicle of a Tragedy Foretold," in *Gujarat: The Making of a Tragedy*, ed. Siddharth Varadarajn (Delhi: Penguin, 2003), 1–44.

11. The question of reputation weighed heavily at this juncture. Arun Shourie, the disinvestment minister, reminded Gujarat that "in order to focus on growth, a state needs to preserve its reputation." See Garima Singh and Basant Rawat, "Shourie Stings as Advani Shields Modi," *Telegraph* (Kolkata), September 28, 2003, https://www.telegraphindia.com/india/shourie-stings-as-advani-shields-modi/cid /799320.

12. Singh and Rawat, "Shourie Stings as Advani Shields Modi."

13. A few months after the February 2002 anti-Muslim pogrom, the Gujarat Assembly elections were held in the month of November. The *Gaurav yatra* became a central component of the election campaign that established Modi as a political leader with his own political base. The yatra covered about 4,200 kilometers, or 400 election rallies in 146 constituencies out of a total of 182 Assembly constituencies. See Christophe Jaffrelot, "Narendra Modi between Hindutava and Subnationalism: The Gujarat *asmita* of a Hindu Hriday Samrat," *India Review* 15, no. 2 (2016): 196–97.

14. On the work of development programs in making a Gujarati-Hindu identity, see Nikita Sud, "Constructing and Contesting a Gujarati-Hindu Ethno-Religious Identity through Development Programmes," *Oxford Development Studies* 35, no. 2 (2007): 131–48.

15. On Vibrant Gujarat, see Tommaso Bobbio, "Making Gujarat Vibrant: *Hindutva*, Development and the Rise of Subnationalism in India," *Third World Quarterly* 33, no. 4 (2012): 657–72.

16. Arun Shourie, then disinvestment minister, quoted in Singh and Rawat, "Shourie Stings."

17. This procapital image is what enabled Modi's rehabilitation in India and abroad. In 2005, Modi was denied a US visa because of human rights violations during the anti-Muslim pogrom. These sanctions were lifted once he became a serious contender in national politics. On the US visa denial, see Vijay Prashad, "No Entry for Modi," *Frontline* 22, no. 7 (March 12–25, 2005), https://frontline.thehindu.com /static/html/fl2207/stories/20050408003313100.htm; and Angana Chatterji, "How We Made US Deny Visa to Modi," *Asian Age*, March 22, 2005, reproduced in *Countercurrents* at https://www.countercurrents.org/guj-angana220305.htm.

18. Ellen Barry, "U.S. Reaches Out to Indian Opposition Leader It Once Rebuked," *New York Times*, February 10, 2014, https://www.nytimes.com/2014/02/11 /world/asia/us-reaches-out-to-indian-opposition-leader-it-once-rebuked.html.

19. The well-financed BJP invests heavily in marketing and advertising Narendra Modi at home and abroad. It also routinely uses government advertising contracts to reward or penalize newspapers. See Ian Marlow, "PM Narendra Modi Spent \$1 Billion on Ads, Foreign Trips," *Live Mint*, December 15, 2018, https://www.live mint.com/Politics/aSDTIh5323HhoHWsnk6mPL/PM-Narendra-Modi-spent -1-billion-on-ads-foreign-trips.html; Adam Withnall, "How Modi Government Uses Ad Spending to 'Reward or Punish' Indian Media," *Independent*, July 7, 2019, https:// www.independent.co.uk/news/world/asia/india-modi-government-media-ad-spend ing-newspapers-press-freedom-a8990451.html; and Alexandra Ulmer and Aftab Ahmed, "Modi's War Chest Leaves India Election Rivals in the Dust," Reuters, May 1, 2019, https://www.reuters.com/article/india-election-spending-bjp-congress /modis-war-chest-leaves-india-election-rivals-in-the-dust-idUSKCN1S7390.

20. On public secrets, see Michael Taussig, *Defacement: Public Secrecy and the Labour of the Negative* (Stanford, CA: Stanford University Press, 1999).

21. Ravinder Kaur, "Good Times, Brought to You by Brand Modi," *Television and New Media* 16, no. 4 (2015): 323–30.

22. The routine government schemes and policy initiatives are heavily marketed, complete with taglines and logos. Prominent examples include the Make in India inititiative that dresses up routine manufacturing policy measures into spectacular events.

23. The decision-making did not always include important stakeholders or consider expert advice. For example, the demonetization policy scrapped high currency notes of Rs 500 and Rs 1,000 overnight. This sudden annulment of currency caused a long-term economic slow down as well as chaos and hardship and even deaths across the country. See, for example, *India Today*, "25 Deaths in a Week: PM Modi's Demonetisation Drive Takes a Toll on Aam Aadmi," November 15, 2016, https://www .indiatoday.in/india/story/demonetisation-deaths-in-country-352059-2016-11-15.

24. See *Economic Times*, "Confederation of Indian Industry Hails Narendra Modi's Demonetisation as 'Masterstroke,'" *Economic Times*, November 14, 2016, https://eco

nomictimes.indiatimes.com/news/politics-and-nation/confederation-of-indian-in
dustry-hails-narendra-modis-demonetisation-as-masterstroke/articleshow/55406519
.cms?from=mdr. See also Indo-Asian News Service, "Film Celebrities Laud Modi's
'Masterstroke' of Demonetisation," *Business Standard*, November 9, 2016, https://
www.business-standard.com/article/news-ians/film-celebrities-laud-modi-s-master
stroke-of-demonetisation-116110900441_1.html.

25. Consider this description of the abrogation of Article 370: "It had all the mak-
ings of a blockbuster—deployment of security, suggestions of terror threats, house
arrest of political leaders from the Kashmir Valley, and snapping of key communications modes, including internet, at the stroke of midnight." Press Trust of India, "Government's Article 370 Revocation: Slow Burn Thriller that Kept Everyone
Guessing," *Economic Times*, August 5, 2019, https://economictimes.indiatimes.com
/news/politics-and-nation/governments-article-370-revocation-slow-burn-thriller
-that-kept-everyone-guessing/articleshow/70540420.cms?from=mdr.

26. The question of jobs and emplyment has been a sore spot—in July 2019, unemployment was reported to have touched a forty-five-year high at 6.1 percent amid
controversy of doctored statistics. See *Economic Times*, "Is the Job Scene in India Bad?
Depends on How You See It, Says Govt," *Economic Times*, June 1, 2019, https://eco
nomictimes.indiatimes.com/jobs/indias-unemployment-rate-hit-6-1-in-2017-18/arti
cleshow/69598640.cms?from=mdr; and "Cat Finally Out of the Bag: Unemployment
at 45-Year High, Government Defends Data," *India Today*, May 31, 2019, https://
www.indiatoday.in/business/story/india-unemployment-rate-6-1-per-cent-45-year
-high-nsso-report-1539580-2019-05-31.

27. The phenomenon of majoritarianism in India politics has recently been explored at length. See Angana P. Chatterji, Thomas Blom Hansen, Christophe Jaffrelot, eds., *Majoritarian State: How Hindu Nationalism Is Changing India* (London:
Hurst, 2019).

28. Francis Fukuyama, "The End of History?," *National Interest* (Summer 1989): 7.

29. Francis Fukuyama, *The End of History and the Last Man* (New York: Free
Press, 1992), xiii–xiv.

30. Fukuyama, "End of History?,"18.

31. Larry Diamond, "Facing Up to the Democratic Recession," *Journal of Democracy* 26, no. 1 (2015): 141–55.

32. Francis Fukuyama, *Identity: Contemporary Identity Politics and the Struggle for
Recognition* (London: Profile Books, 2018), xv.

33. Ibid., 10–11.

34. See Liisa Malkki's critical account of the twentieth-century imagination of
the family of nations. "National Geographic: The Rooting of Peoples and the Territorialization of National Identity among Scholars and Refugees," *Cultural Anthropology* 7, no. 1 (2012): 24–44.

35. Gyan Prakash engages with Johannes Fabian's idea of cultural relativity to lay
out the spatial-cultural segmentation. See "Writing Post-Orientalist Histories of the

Third World: Perspectives from Indian Historiography," *Comparative Studies in Society and History* 32, no. 2 (1990): 394; and Johannes Fabian, *Time and the Other: How Anthropology Makes Its Object* (New York: Columbia University Press, 1983).

36. Note how the abrogation of Article 370, a unilateral decision by the Indian state to remove the special status of Jammu and Kashmir, was accompanied by the promise of an investment summit as a path to progress and prosperity. Tanushree Pandey, "Article 370 Gone, Investor Summit Planned in Jammu and Kashmir to Boost Industry and Healthcare," *India Today*, August 7, 2019, https://www.india today.in/india/story/article-370-gone-investor-summit-planned-j-k-boost-industry -healthcare-1578042-2019-08-07.

37. ET Online, "$5-Trillion Economy Goal: PM Modi Calls Doubters 'Professional Pessimists,'" *Economic Times*, July 6, 2019, https://economictimes.indiatimes .com/news/politics-and-nation/5-trillion-economy-goal-pm-modi-calls-doubters -professional-pessimists/videoshow/70104393.cms.

38. "People Who Feel Unsafe in India Are Traitors, Should Be Bombed: BJP MLA," *Economic Times*, January 4, 2019, https://economictimes.indiatimes.com/news /politics-and-nation/people-who-feel-unsafe-in-india-are-traitors-should-be -bombed-bjp-mla/articleshow/67378122.cms?from=mdr.

BIBLIOGRAPHY

Adex India. "India Is Shining All Over the Print Media: An AdEx India Analysis." exchange4media, February 6, 2004. https://www.exchange4media.com/Print/India-is-Shining-all-over-the-Print-Media!-An-AdEx-India-Analysis_10844.html.

Agan, Tom. "Silent Marketing: Micro-Targeting." WPP, a Penn, Schoen and Berland Associates White Paper. Accessed June 23, 2004. http://www.wpp.com/wpp/marketing/reportsstudies/silentmarketing/.

Agtmael, Antoine Van. *The Emerging Market Century: How a New Breed of World-Class Companies Is Overtaking the World*. London: Simon and Schuster, 2007.

Aiyar, Shankkar. "Inside Story: How L. N. Mittal Won the Bitter Battle to Clinch the Archelor Deal." *India Today*, July 10, 2006. http://indiatoday.intoday.in/story/how-ln-mittal-won-bitter-battle-to-clinch-arcelor-deal/1/180968.html.

Aiyar, Swaninathan. "The Neo-Hindu GDP Growth Rate." *Times of India*, March 9, 2003, https://timesofindia.indiatimes.com/home/sunday-times/all-that-matters/The-neo-Hindu-GDP-growth-rate/articleshow/39701549.cms.

Alexander, P. C. "Liberty of the Press: Its Legal Restrictions." *The Indian Journal of Political Science* 8, no. 2 (1946): 683–88.

Ali, Imran. *The Punjab under Imperialism 1885–1947*. Princeton, NJ: Princeton University Press, 1988.

Anderson, Benedict. *Imagined Communities: Reflections on the Origin and Spread of Nationalism*. London: Verso, 2016.

Anholt, Simon. *Competitive Identity: The New Brand Management for Nations, Cities and Regions*. Basingstoke, UK: Palgrave Macmillan, 2007.

———. "Foreword." Special issue on nation branding, *Journal of Brand Management* 9, nos. 4–5 (2002): 234.

———. *Places: Identity, Images and Reputation*. Basingstoke, UK: Palgrave Macmillan, 2010.

———. "What Is a Nation Brand?" Superbrands, 2002. http://www.superbrands.com/turkeysb/trcopy/files/Anholt_3939.pdf p186.

Appadurai, Arjun. "Deep Democracy: Urban Governmentality and the Horizon of Politics." *Environment and Urbanization* 23, no. 2 (2001): 23–44.

———. *Modernity at Large: Cultural Dimensions of Globalization*. Minneapolis: University of Minnesota Press, 1996.

———. "Our Corruption, Our Selves: Arjun Appadurai." *Kafila*, August 30, 2011. https://kafila.online/2011/08/30/our-corruption-our-selves-arjun-appadurai/.

Arendt, Hannah. *The Human Condition*. Chicago: University of Chicago Press, 1998.

Arnold, David. *The New Cambridge History of India: Science, Technology and Medicine in Colonial India*. Cambridge, UK: Cambridge University Press, 2000.

Arrighi, Giovanni. *The Long Twentieth Century: Money, Power and the Origins of Our Time*. London: Verso, 2010.

Auletta, Ken. "Citizens Jain." *New Yorker*, October 8, 2012. https://www.newyorker.com/magazine/2012/10/08/citizens-jain.

Bagchi, Amiya Kumar, and Anthony P. D'Costa, eds. *Transformation and Development: The Political Economy of Transition in India and China*. New Delhi: Oxford University Press, 2012.

Bandyopadhyay, Tamal, and Anup Roy. "RBI to Buy 200 Tonnes of IMF Gold." *Live Mint*, November 3, 2009. http://www.livemint.com/Home-Page/BtrypkIoTHQ_1g0rYq5JNgP/RBI-to-buy-200-tonnes-of-IMF-gold.html.

Banerjee, Mukulika. "Vote." *South Asia: Journal of South Asian Studies* 40, no. 2 (2017): 411.

———. *Why India Votes?* London: Routledge, 2008.

Bardhan, Pranab. *Awakening Giants, Feet of Clay: Assessing the Economic Rise of China and India*. Princeton, NJ: Princeton University Press, 2010.

———. *The Political Economy of Development in India*. Delhi: Oxford University Press, 1984.

Barry, Ellen. "U.S. Reaches Out to Indian Opposition Leader It Once Rebuked." *New York Times*, February 10, 2014. https://www.nytimes.com/2014/02/11/world/asia/us-reaches-out-to-indian-opposition-leader-it-once-rebuked.html.

Bauman, Zygmunt. *Globalization: The Human Consequences*. New York: Columbia University Press, 1998.

Bayly, Christopher A. *The Birth of the Modern World, 1780–1914, Global Connections and Comparisons*. Malden, MA: Blackwell, 2004.

———. *Empire and Information: Intelligence Gathering and Social Communication in India, 1780–1870*. Cambridge, UK: Cambridge University Press, 1996.

BBC News. "Mayawati Statues: Race to Cover India Chief's Monuments." January 10, 2012. https://www.bbc.co.uk/news/world-asia-india-16481185.

Bear, Laura, Ritu Birla, and Stine Simonsen Puri. "Speculation: Futures and Capitalism in India." *Comparative Studies of South Asia, Africa and the Middle East* 35, no. 3 (2015): 387–91.

Benjamin, Walter. *The Arcades Project*. Translated by Howard Eiland and Kevin McLaughlin. Cambridge, MA: Harvard University Press, 2002.

Benjamin, Walter, Lloyd Spencer, and Mark Harrington. "Central Park." *New German Critique* 34 (Winter 1985): 32–58.

Berlin, Isaiah. *Vico and Herder: Two Studies in the History of Ideas*. New York: Viking Press, 1976.

Berman, Marshall. *All That Is Solid Melts into Air*. London: Verso, 2010.

Bhagwati, Jagdish, and Arvind Panagariya. *Why Growth Matters: How Economic Growth in India Reduced Poverty and the Lessons for Other Developing Countries*. New York: Public Affairs, 2013.

Bhattacharya, Ananya. "Padmavati and Verna: India and Pakistan Shame Shame, Not Different." *India Today*, November 14, 2017. https://www.indiatoday.in/movies /standpoint/story/padmavati-verna-india-pakistan-deepika-padukone-mahira -khan-1086223-2017-11-14.

Bhatti, Shaila, and Christopher Pinney. "Optic-Clash: Modes of Visuality in India." In *A Companion to the Anthropology of India*, edited by Isabel Clark-Decès, ch. 12. Hoboken, NJ: Blackwell, 2011.

Bijapurkar, Rama. *We Are Like That Only: Understanding the Logic of Consumer India.* New Delhi: Penguin, 2007.

Birla, Ritu. *Stages of Capital: Law, Culture, and Market Governance in Late Colonial India.* Durham, NC: Duke University Press, 2009.

Bobb, Dilip. "India Excel at International Tourism Bourse in Berlin, 2007." *India Today*, March 26, 2007. https://www.indiatoday.in/magazine/leisure/story/20070326 -india-at-international-tourism-bourse-in-berlin2007-748967-2007-03-26#close -overlay.

Bose, Jaideep. "A Passage from India." *Times of India*, January 1, 2007.

Bosworth, A. B. "The Historical Setting of Megasthenes' *Indica*." *Classical Philology* 91, no. 2 (April 1996): 113–27.

Bowles, Chester. "New India." *Foreign Affairs* (October 1952): 79–80.

Braudel, Fernand. *Civilization & Capitalism 15th–18th Century: The Perspective of the World.* Berkeley: University of California Press, 1992.

Brosius, Christiane. *India's Middle Class: New Forms of Urban Leisure, Consumption and Prosperity.* New Delhi: Routledge, 2010.

BS Reporter. "India's GDP Growth in FY12 Just 6.8%: Report." *Business Standard*, January 19, 2012. https://www.business-standard.com/article/economy-policy/in dia-s-gdp-growth-in-fy12-just-6-8-report-112011900058_1.html.

BS Web Team & Agencies, "GDP LIVE: Growth Boost Has Happened Due to Rise in Manufacturing, Says FM," *Business Standard*, November 30, 2017, http://www .business-standard.com/article/economy-policy/gdp-live-growth-boost-has-hap pened-due-to-rise-in-manufacturing-says-fm-117113000680_1.html.

BT Online. "Ease of Doing Business Rankings: India Makes Highest-Ever Jump to Rank 100 Out of 190 Countries." *Business Today*, November 1, 2017. https://www .businesstoday.in/current/economy-politics/ease-of-doing-business-rankings-in dia-rank-world-bank-100/story/262976.html.

———. "PM Narendra Modi Tears into Critics; Says GDP Slid to 5.7% or below 8 Times under UPA." *Business Today*, October 5, 2017. https://www.business today.in/current/economy-politics/pm-narendra-modi-critics-economy-demone tisation-gst-gdp-growth-inflation/story/261435.html.

Buck-Morss, Susan. "Aesthetics and Anaesthetics: Walter Benjamin's Artwork Essay Reconsidered." *October* 62 (1992): 3–41.

———. *The Dialectics of Seeing: Walter Benjamin and the Arcades Project,* Cambridge: MIT Press, 1991.

———. *Dreamworlds and Catastrophe: The Passing of Mass Utopia in East and West.* Cambridge, MA: MIT Press, 2000.

Bunsha, Dionne. "Gujarat's Shame." *Frontline* 19, no. 8 (April 13–26, 2002). https://frontline.thehindu.com/static/html/fl1908/19080210.htm.

Business India Bureau. "Thanks to Demonetization, Paytm Is Making Rs 120 Crore per Day; Achieves Target before Deadline, Crosses $5 Billion GMV." *Business Insider*, November 21, 2016. http://www.businessinsider.in/Thanks-to-demonetization-Paytm-is-making-Rs-120-crore-per-day-achieves-target-before-deadline-crosses-5-billion-GMV/articleshow/55541691.cms.

Business Standard. "At 8.2%, India's Growth Only Next to China." July 1, 2004. Accessed June 10, 2014. http://www.business-standard.com/article/economy-policy/at-8-2-india-s-gdp-growth-next-only-to-china-104070101036_1.html.

Butalia, Urvash, Ashis Nandy, Tarun J. Tejpal, and Ashutosh. "What Ashis Nandy Actually Said at JLF." *Outlook India*, January 30, 2013. https://www.outlookindia.com/website/story/what-ashis-nandy-actually-said-at-jlf/283737/.

Butler, Judith. "We the People: Thoughts on Freedom of Assembly." In *What Is a People?* New York: Columbia University Press, 2016.

Calcutta Review. "The Old Company and the New India Bill." 31 (July–December 1858): 412–42.

Callen, Tim. "Gross Domestic Product: An Economy's All." *Finance and Development*, December 18, 2018. http://www.imf.org/external/pubs/ft/fandd/basics/gdp.htm.

Cann, Oliver. "Who Pays for Davos?" World Economic Forum, accessed March 20, 2017. https://www.weforum.org/agenda/2017/01/who-pays-for-davos/.

Chakrabarty, Dipesh. "Adda, Calcutta: Dwelling in Modernity." *Public Culture* 11, no. 1 (1999): 109–45.

———. "The Difference: Deferral of (a) Colonial Modernity: Public Debates in British Bengal." *History Workshop Journal*, no. 36 (Autumn 1993): 1–34.

———. *Provincializing Europe: Postcolonial Thought and Historical Difference*. Princeton, NJ: Princeton University Press, 2000.

Chakravarty, Sayantan. "Chhattisgarh Assembly Polls: Dilip Singh Judev Sting Operation Haunts BJP." *India Today*, December 1, 2013. https://www.indiatoday.in/magazine/states/story/20031201-chhattisgarh-assembly-polls-dilip-singh-judev-sting-operation-haunts-bjp-791411-2003-12-01.

Chamikutty, Preethi. "Times of India's 'Lead India' Campaign a Success." *Times of India*, February 22, 2008. https://timesofindia.indiatimes.com/india/Times-of-Indias-Lead-India-campaign-a-success/articleshow/2801380.cms.

Chandran, Rina. "India Leaders Blog, Text to Plug In to Young Voters." Reuters, March 17, 2009. https://www.reuters.com/article/us-india-elections-youth/india-leaders-blog-text-to-plug-in-to-young-voters-idUSTRE52G1CR20090317.

Chandrasekhar, C. P. "A Bubble Waiting to Burst." *Frontline* 21, no. 5 (2004). http://www.frontline.in/static/html/fl2105/stories/20040312007200900.htm.

Chatterjee, Elizabeth. "Reinventing State Capitalism in India: A View from the Energy Sector." *Contemporary South Asia* 25, no. 1 (2017): 85–100.

Chatterjee, Partha. "Against Corruption = Against Politics." *Kafila Online*, August 28,

2011. https://kafila.online/2011/08/28/against-corruption-against-politics-partha -chatterjee/.

———. *The Nation and Its Fragments: Colonial and Postcolonial Histories.* Princeton, NJ: Princeton University Press, 1993.

———. *Politics of the Governed: Reflections on Popular Politics in Most of the World.* New York: Columbia University Press, 2004.

Chatterjee, Ramanand. "Origin and Growth of Journalism among Indians." *The Annals of the American Academy of Political and Social Science* 145, no. 2 (1929): 161–68.

Chatterji, Angana. "How We Made US Deny Visa to Modi." *Asian Age,* March 22, 2005. Reproduced in *Countercurrents* at https://www.countercurrents.org/guj-an gana220305.htm.

Chatterji, Angana, Thomas Blom Hansen, and Christophe Jaffrelot, ed. *Majoritarian State: How Hindu Nationalism is Changing India.* London. Hurst Publishers, 2019.

Chaudhuri, K. N. *The English East India Company: The Study of an Early Joint Stock Company 1600–1640.* London: Kelley, 1965.

———. *The Trading World of Asia and the English East India Company 1660–1760.* Cambridge, UK: Cambridge University Press, 1978.

Chauhan, Jitesh Singh. "Dalits in Indian Cinema." *Forward Press,* February 1, 2015. https://www.forwardpress.in/2015/02/dalits-in-indian-cinema/.

Chawla, Prabhu. "A Harvest of Terror." *India Today,* November 28, 2008. http://india today.intoday.in/story/A+harvest+of+terror/1/21193.html.

Chhiber, Vivek. *Locked in Place: State-Building and Late Industrialization in India.* Princeton, NJ: Princeton University Press, 2006.

Chidambaram, P. "Change Begins with Words and Ideas." *Indian Express,* March 25, 2018. https://indianexpress.com/article/opinion/columns/india-economy-gdp-bjp -congress- plenary-session-5110381/.

Chitravanshi, Ruchika. "Ease of Doing Business: Government Targets 90 Reforms to Climb Rank in World Bank's Report." *Economic Times,* January 4, 2018. https:// economictimes.indiatimes.com/news/economy/policy/ease-of-doing-business -government-targets-90-reforms-to-climb-rank-in-world-banks-report/article show/62359708.cms.

Chopra, Arushi. "Paytm Claims Record Number of Transactions after Govt's Demonetization." *Live Mint,* November 14, 2016. https://www.livemint.com/Com panies/gWu18E6zIzsIotfsANYsFL/Paytm-claims-record-number-of-transac tions-after-govts-demo.html.

Chouhan, Shivraj Singh. "81 Girls Married under Mukhyamantri Kanyadan (Nikah) Yojna." April 15, 2013. http://shivrajsinghchouhan.org/newsdetail.aspx?id=137.

Clark, Dorie. "The Right (and Wrong) Way to Network." *Harvard Business Review,* March 10, 2015. https://hbr.org/2015/03/the-right-and-wrong-way-to-network.

Cohn, S. B. *Colonialism and Its Forms of Knowledge: The British in India.* Princeton, NJ: Princeton University Press, 1996.

Comaroff, Jean, and John Comaroff. "Millennial Capitalism: First Thoughts on a Second Coming." *Public Culture* 12, no. 2 (2000): 291–343.

———. *Theory from the South: Or, How Euro America Is Evolving Toward Africa*. New York: Routledge, 2012.

Comaroff, John, and Jean Comaroff. *Ethnicity, Inc.* Chicago: University of Chicago Press, 2009.

Constanza, Robert, et. al. "Time to Leave GDP Behind." *Nature* 505 (2014): 283–85.

Cook, Eli. *The Pricing of Progress: Economic Indicators and the Capitalization of American Life*. Cambridge, MA: Harvard University Press, 2017.

Cotton, Henry. *New India: Or India in Transition*. London: Kegan Paul, Trench Trubner, 1904.

Coyle, Diana. *GDP: A Brief but Affectionate History*. Princeton, NJ: Princeton University Press, 2014.

Crary, Jonathan. *Suspensions of Perception: Attention, Spectacle, and Modern Culture*. Cambridge, MA: MIT Press, 2001.

Dalrymple, William. *The Anarchy: The East India Company, Corporate Violence, and the Pillage of an Empire*. London: Bloomsbury, 2019.

———. *Nine Lives: In Search of the Sacred in Modern India*. London: Vintage, 2009.

Damodaran, Harish. "'Cool' India Offers Inclusive Growth for All." *The Hindu Business Line*, Davos, January 26, 2011.

DANIDA. "Transitional Strategy for Denmark's Multilateral Aid for Trade Activities 2014–2015." September 2014.

Das, Gurucharan. *India Grows at Night: A Liberal Case for a Strong State*. Delhi: Penguin Books, 2013.

Dasgupta, Reshmi. "Smokin' Slogan: On Poll Trail, It's the Call of the Jingle." *Economic Times*, March 27, 2004. http://articles.economictimes.indiatimes.com/2004-03-27/news/27381115_1_slogan-garibi-hatao-aam-aadmi-ke-saath.

Das Gupta, Uma. "The Indian Press 1870–1880: A Small World of Journalism." *Modern Asian Studies* 11, no. 2 (1977): 213–35.

Datla, Kavita. "A Worldly Vernacular: Urdu at Osmania University." *Modern Asian Studies* 43, no. 5 (2009): 1117–48.

Day, Michael. "Caving into Pressure: Why Mario Monti's Technocrats Couldn't Repair Italy after Silvio Berlusconi's Government Collapsed." *Independent*, February 22, 2013. https://www.independent.co.uk/news/world/europe/caving-in-to-pressure-why-mario- monti-s-technocrats-couldn-t-repair-italy-after-silvio-berlusconi-s-8507736.html.

De, Aditi. "Creating the Common Man." *The Hindu*, June 12, 2004. http://www.thehindu.com/yw/2004/06/12/stories/2004061200060200.htm.

Debord, Guy. *The Society of the Spectacle*. Translated by Ken Knabb. London: Rebel Press, 2005.

Debray, Regis. "Remarks on the Spectacle." *New Left Review* 214 (1995): 134–41.

Derrida, Jacques. *Given Time 1: Counterfeit Money*. Chicago: University of Chicago Press, 1992.

Desai, Radhika. "Forward March of Hindutva Halted?" *New Left Review* 30 (2004): 49–67.

Deshpande, R., and L. Iyer. "BJP Rides on India Shining Plank, Congress Counters the Feel-Good Line." *India Today*, March 22, 2004.

Deshpande, Satish. "Caste and Castelessness." *Economic and Political Weekly* 48, no. 15 (2013).

Diamond, Larry. "Facing Up to the Democratic Recession." *Journal of Democracy* 26, no. 1 (2015): 141–55.

Doron, Assa, and Robin Jeffrey. *The Great Indian Phone Book.* London: Hurst, 2013.

Drèze, Jean, and Amartya Sen. *An Uncertain Glory: India and Its Contradictions.* Princeton, NJ: Princeton University Press, 2013.

Economic Times. "Confederation of Indian Industry Hails Narendra Modi's Demonetisation as 'Masterstroke.'" *Economic Times*, November 14, 2016. https://economic times.indiatimes.com/news/politics-and-nation/confederation-of-indian-industry -hails-narendra-modis-demonetisation-as   masterstroke/articleshow/55406519 .cms?from=mdr.

———. "False Shine, Core Flaws Resulted in NDA's Debacle." *Economic Times*, May 14, 2004. http://articles.economictimes.indiatimes.com/2004-05-14/news/27 416319_1_reform-process-nda-core-issue.

———. "$5-Trillion Economy Goal: PM Modi Calls Doubters 'Professional Pessimists.'" *Economic Times*, July 6, 2019. https://economictimes.indiatimes.com/news /politics-and-nation/5-trillion-economy-goal-pm-modi-calls-doubters-profes sional-pessimists/videoshow/70104393.cms.

———. "Here's What Makes Narendra Modi the Best Salesman India Has Ever Had." *Economic Times*, May 29, 2017. https://economictimes.indiatimes.com/news /politics-and-nation/heres-what-makes-narendra-modi-the-best-salesman-india -can-ever-have/articleshow/58895081.cms.

———. "India Inc Rallies behind Anna Hazare in the Anti-Corruption Movement." *Economic Times*, April 19, 2011. https://economictimes.indiatimes.com/news/pol itics-and-nation/india-inc-rallies-behind-anna-hazare-in-the-anti-corruption -movement/articleshow/7922112.cms.

———. "Is the Job Scene in India Bad? Depends on How You See It, Says Govt." *Economic Times*, June 1, 2019. https://economictimes.indiatimes.com/jobs/indias -unemployment-rate-hit-6-1-in-2017-18/articleshow/69598640.cms?from=mdr.

———. "People Who Feel Unsafe in India Are Traitors, Should Be Bombed: BJP MLA." *Economic Times*, January 4, 2019. https://economictimes.indiatimes.com /news/politics-and-nation/people-who-feel-unsafe-in-india-are-traitors-should -be-bombed-bjp-mla/articleshow/67378122.cms?from=mdr.

———. "The Times of Tata." http://economictimes.indiatimes.com/photo.cms?msid =13216320.

Economist. "Can India Fly?" *Economist*, June 1, 2006. http://www.economist.com /node/7004433.

———. "Why India's Newspaper Business Is Booming." *Economist*, February 22, 2016. https://www.economist.com/the-economist-explains/2016/02/22/why-indias -newspaper-business-is-booming.

ENS Economic Bureau. "India Leaps 30 Places to 100th Rank in World Bank's 'Ease of Doing Business Index.'" *Indian Express*, October 31, 2017. http://indianexpress .com/article/business/business-others/world-bank-ease-of-doing- business-india -ranks-100-out-of-190-nations-arun-jaitley-modi-gst-4915978/.

Ernst & Young, *Ready, Set, Grow, Ernst Young Attractiveness Survey: India 2015.* Mumbai: EYGM Ltd., 2015. www.ey.com/Publication/vwLUAssets/ey-2015-india-at tractiveness-survey-ready-set-grow/$FILE/ey-2015-india-attractiveness-survey -ready-set-grow.pdf.

Fabian, Johannes. *Time and the Other: How Anthropology Makes Its Object.* New York: Columbia University Press, 1983.

Ferguson, James. *The Anti-Politics Machine: Development, Depoliticization, and Bureaucratic Power in Lesotho.* Minneapolis: University of Minnesota Press, 1994.

Fichte, J. G. *The Closed Commercial State.* Translated by Anthony Curtis Adler. Albany: State University of New York Press, 2013.

Financial Express Bureau. "Big Boost for Narendra Modi, GDP Growth Powers to 6.3 Pct in Q2, 5-Quarter Slide Reversed." *Financial Express*, December 1, 2017. https:// www.financialexpress.com/economy/big-boost-for-narendra-modi-gdp-growth -powers-to-6-3-pct-in-q2-5-quarter-slide-reversed/955041/.

Financial Times. "Davos Corporations Swallow Sharp Increase in Fees." *Financial Times*, February 15, 2015. https://www.ft.com/content/c1935338a47b-11e4-895900144 feab7de.

——. "India Regains Title of World's Fastest-Growing Major Economy." *Financial Times*, February 28, 2018. https://www.ft.com/content/cb5a4668-1c84-11e8-956a -43db76e69936.

FP Staff. "Jayalalithaa Convicted in Disproportionate Assets Case: How It All Began." *Firstpost*, February 14, 2017. https://www.firstpost.com/politics/jayalalithaa -convicted-in-disproportionate-assets-case-how-it-all-began-1992325.html.

Fukuyama, Francis. "The End of History?" *National Interest* (Summer 1989): 1–18.

——. *The End of History and the Last Man.* New York: Free Press, 1992.

——. *Identity: Contemporary Identity Politics and the Struggle for Recognition.* London: Profile Books, 2018.

Ghassem-Fachandi, Parvis. *Pogrom in Gujarat and Anti-Muslim Violence in India.* Princeton, NJ: Princeton University Press, 2012.

Ghose, Deborate. "Ease of Doing Business Ranking: India Breaks into Top 100 for First Time; All You Need to Know." *Firstpost*, November 1, 2017. https://www .firstpost.com/business/ease-of-doing-business-ranking-india-breaks-into-top -100-for-first-time-all-you-need-to-know-4186895.html.

Ghosh, Jayati. "India Shining, India Declining." *MacroScan: An Alternative Economics Webcentre*, February 5, 2004. http://www.macroscan.net/index.php?&view=article &aid=459.

Gilroy, P. *The Black Atlantic: Modernity and Double Consciousness.* Cambridge, MA: Harvard University Press, 1993.

Girard, Michel. "States, Diplomacy and Image Making: What Is New? Reflections on Current British and French Experiences." Paper presented at Image, State, and International Relations Conference, London School of Economics, June 24, 1999.

Gomez, Nicolas Wey. *The Tropics of Empire: Why Columbus Sailed South to the Indies.* Cambridge, MA: MIT Press, 2008.

Goodman, Peter S. "Davos Elite Fret about Inequality over Vintage Wine and Canapés." *New York Times*, January 18, 2017. https://www.nytimes.com/2017/01/18/business/dealbook/world-economic-forum-davos-backlash.html.

Gooptu, Nandini. "Neoliberal Subjectivity, Enterprise Culture and New Workplaces: Organised Retail and Shopping Malls in India." *Economic and Political Weekly* 44, no. 22 (2009): 45–54.

Goswami, Manu. *Producing India: From Colonial Economy to National Space.* Chicago: University of Chicago Press, 2008.

Government of India. "Cashless India." Accessed November 15, 2018. http://cashlessindia.gov.in.

———, Ministry of Commerce. "Performance Budget 2005–2006," p. 7. Accessed November 21, 2018. http://commerce.nic.in/publications/PB-2005-06-FINAL.pdf.

———, Ministry of Commerce and Industry. "India's Rank Rises to 100 in World Bank's Doing Business Report, 2018." Press Information Bureau, October 31, 2017. http://pib.nic.in/newsite/PrintRelease.aspx?relid=173116.

———, Ministry of Electronics & Information Technology. "Home: About Digital India: Introduction." Accessed September 10, 2018. http://www.digitalindia.gov.in/content/introduction.

———, Ministry of Finance. "India—Macro-Economic Summary: 1999–00 to 2013–14." Central Statistical Organisation, May 30 2014, http://planningcommission.gov.in/data/datatable/data_2312/DatabookDec2014%201. pdf.

———, Ministry of Home Affairs. "Availability of Amenities and Assets." Office of the Registrar General & Census Commissioner. *Census of India*, 2001. http://censusindia.gov.in/Census_And_You/availability_of_eminities_and_assets.aspx.

———, Ministry of Housing and Urban Affairs. "Swacch Survekshan—2017: Sanitation Rankings of Cities/Towns State/UT-Wise." Press Information Bureau, May 4, 2017. http://pib.nic.in/newsite/PrintRelease.aspx?relid=161527.

———, Ministry of Information and Broadcasting, Publicity Division. "The Flag of the Indian Union." *New India* 1–2 (August 1947).

———, Ministry of Tourism. "Atithi Devo Bhave Campaign" 2010.

———, Ministry of Tourism and Culture. *National Tourism Policy 2002.* Department of Tourism, accessed February 10, 2018. http://tourism.gov.in/tourism-policy.

———, Planning Commission. *Annual Plan: 2002–03.* Accessed February 18, 2018. http://planningcommission.nic.in/plans/annualplan/index.php?state=ap020_03cont.htm.

Goyal, Malini. "How Performance-Based Rankings Are Shaking Up the Rigid World of Government." *Economic Times*, January 28, 2018. https://economictimes

.indiatimes.com/news/economy/policy/how-performance-based-rankings-are -shaking-up-the-rigid-world-of- government/articleshow/62674879.cms.

Graan, Andrew. "Counterfeiting the Nation? Skopje 2014 and the Politics of Nation Branding in Macedonia." *Cultural Anthropology* 28, no. 1 (2013): 161–79.

The Great Exhibition: The Crystal Palace Exposition of 1851. New York: Random House, 1995. First published as *Art Journal Illustrated Catalogue of the Industry of All Nations*, 1851.

Greenslade, Roy. "City AM Takes a Revolutionary Step by Opening Website to Advertisers." *Guardian*, June 3, 2016. https://www.theguardian.com/media/green slade/2016/jun/03/city-am-takes-a-revolutionary-step-by-opening-website-to -advertisers.

Guha, Ramachandra. *Makers of Modern India.* Delhi: Penguin, 2010.

Gupta, Akhil. *Red Tape: Bureaucracy, Structural Violence, and Poverty in India.* Durham, NC: Duke University Press, 2014.

Gupta, Shekhar. "Corruption and the Caste Differential." *Business Standard*, December 23, 2017.

Habermas, Jürgen. *The Postnational Constellation: Political Essays.* Cambridge, MA: MIT Press, 2001.

Hansen, Thomas Blom. "Governance and State Mythologies in Mumbai." In *State of Imagination: Ethnographic Explorations of the Postcolonial State*, edited by Thomas Blom Hansen and Stepputat, 226–27. Durham, NC: Duke University Press, 2001.

———. *The Saffron Wave: Democracy and Hindu Nationalism in Modern India.* Princeton, NJ: Princeton University Press, 1999.

Hardt, Michael, and Antonio Negri. *Multitude: War and Democracy in the Age of Empire.* New York: Penguin Books, 2005.

Harper, Douglas. *Online Etymology Dictionary.* s.v. "corporation (n.)," accessed April 20, 2018. https://www.etymonline.com/word/corporation.

Harriss, John. "'Politics Is a Dirty River': But Is There a 'New Politics' of Civil Society? Perspectives from Global Cities of India and Latin America." London: LSE Research Online, 2005. http://eprints.lse.ac.uk/487/1/CCLSConferencePaper.pdf.

Harvey, David. *A Brief History of Neoliberalism.* New York: Oxford University Press, 2007.

Hebdige, D. *Cut 'n' Mix: Culture, Identity and Caribbean Music.* New York: Routledge, 1987.

Held, D., and A. McGrew, eds. *The Global Transformation Reader: An Introduction to the Globalization Debate.* Malden, MA: Polity, 2000.

Herder, Johann Gottfried. *Outlines of a Philosophy of the History of Man.* Translated by T. Churchill. London, 1803.

Herzog, Tamar. *Frontiers of Possession: Spain and Portugal in Europe and the Americas.* Cambridge, MA: Harvard University Press, 2015.

The Hindu. "Satyam Scandal: Who, What and When." *The Hindu*, April 9, 2015. http://www.thehindu.com/specials/timelines/satyam-scandal-who-what-and - when/article10818226.ece.

Hindustan Times. "ADB Downgrades India's GDP Growth Outlook to 7% for 2017–
18." *Hindustan Times,* September 26, 2017. https://www.hindustantimes.com/busi
ness-news/adb-lowers-india-s-gdp-growth-outlook-to-7-for-2017-18/story-nKox
1qp2Ay4LMoUswzrrEO.html.

HT Correspondent. "Pledge to Make India a Cashless Society: Highlights from PM
Modi's Mann Ki Baat." *Hindustan Times,* November 27, 2016. https://www.hindu
stantimes.com/india-news/live-pm-modi-speaks-on-demonetisation-cross-bor
der-ties-in-mann-ki-baat/story-QGFJfAYbderasrlGbov32N.html.

Hutchinson, John. *The Dynamics of Cultural Nationalism: The Gaelic Revival and the
Creation of the Irish Nation State.* London: Allen and Unwin, 1987.

Huzefa Husain. "India Poised Anthem (Hindi)." YouTube Video, January 17, 2007.
https://www.youtube.com/watch?v=MEFMJgbLRaM.

IANS. "In Aftermath of Demonetisation, India's GDP Growth Sees Sharp Fall to
5.7% in Q1 of 2017–18." *Huffington Post,* August 31, 2017. https://www.huffington
post.in/2017/08/31/indias-gdp-growth-sees-sharp-fall-to-5-7-in-q1_a_23192099/.

IBEF. "Brand India: At the Annual Meeting of the World Economic Meeting." Davos, January 27–30, 2013.

———. "India Davos." India Brand Equity Foundation, accessed October 2, 2018.
http://www.india-davos-blogs.ibef.org/India—-Innovates.

———. Six Decades of Innovation, Influence, Demonstration and Impact." International Finance Corporation report, accessed July 14, 2016. http://www.ifc.org/wps
/wcm/connect/CORP_EXT_Content/IFC_External_corporate_Site/About
+IFC_New/IFC+History.

Ilaih, Kancha. "Caste, Corruption and Romanticism." *The Hindu,* March 22, 2013.
https://www.thehindu.com/opinion/lead/caste-corruption-and-romanticism/ar
ticle4534892.ece.

IMF. *Article of Agreement.* Washington DC: International Monetary Fund, 2006.

Inden, Ronald. *Imagining India.* Oxford, UK: Blackwell, 1990.

India, J., and R. Rosaldo. "Introduction: A World in Motion." In *The Anthropology of
Globalization: A Reader,* 1–34. Malden, MA: Blackwell, 2002.

"India on Fire: India's Economy." *Economist* 382, no. 8514 (February 3, 2007): 77.

India Today. "Cat Finally Out of the Bag: Unemployment at 45-Year High, Government Defends Data." *India Today,* May 31, 2019. https://www.indiatoday.in
/business/story/india-unemployment-rate-6-1-per-cent-45-year-high-nsso-report
-1539580-2019-05-31.

———. "How 26/11 Mumbai Attack Happened in 2008: From First Eyewitness to
Kasab." *India Today,* November 26, 2017. https://www.indiatoday.in/india/story
/how-2611-mumbai-terror-attack-happened-in-2008-from-first-eyewitness-to
-kasab-1094473- 2017-11-26.

———. "Jaitley Praises GDP Rebound, Chidambaram Says Pause in Declining
Trend." *India Today,* November 30, 2017. https://www.indiatoday.in/india/story
/gdp-growth-bjp-congress-arun-jaitley-chidambaram-mamata-banerjee-1097647
-2017-11-30.

———. "Tata Tea Tetley Merger: The Cup that Cheered." *India Today*, August 7, 2000. https://www.indiatoday.in/magazine/cover-story/story/20091228-2000-tata -tea-tetley- merger-the-cup-that-cheered-741660-2009-12-25.

———. "25 Deaths in a Week: PM Modi's Demonetisation Drive Takes a Toll on Aam Aadmi." *India Today*, November 15, 2016. https://www.indiatoday.in/india /story/demonetisation-deaths-in-country-352059-2016-11-15.

Indian Express. "Think 'Young' for Better Growth: CII." *Indian Express*, March 11, 2004. http://archive.indianexpress.com/oldStory/42668/.

An Indian Official. "India as a World Power." *Foreign Affairs* (1949): 550.

Indian Subcontinent: Managing and Measuring Subcontinent. Delhi: India Brand Equity Foundation, 2009. https://www.ibef.org/download/India_IBEF_v0509.pdf.

Indiresan, P. V. "A Reality Check on India Shining." *Hindu*, May 8, 2004.

Indo-Asian News Service. "Film Celebrities Laud Modi's 'Masterstroke' of Demonetisation." *Business Standard*, November 9, 2016. https://www.business-standard .com/article/news-ians/film-celebrities-laud-modi-s-masterstroke-of-demoneti sation-116110900441_1.html.

———. "Stop Padmaavat or We'll Jump into Fire, Warn Hundreds of Rajput Women." *NDTV*, January 22, 2018. https://www.ndtv.com/india-news/women -draw-swords-threaten-jauhar-in-chittorgarh-to-protest-against-padmaavat-re lease-1802926.

Iyer, Sriram. "Beyond Numbers: A Slowing Economy Risks Turning India's Demographic Dividend into a Disaster." Quartz India, January 8, 2018. https://qz.com /1173792/as-gdp-growth-slows-indias-demographic-dividend-could-turn-into -disaster/.

Jaffrelot, Christophe. "The Caste Based Mosaic of Indian Politics." India seminar, seminar no. 633, 2012. http://www.india-seminar.com/2012/633/633_christophe_jaf frelot.htm.

———. "Communal Riots in Gujarat: The State at Risk?" Working paper no. 17, Heidelberg Papers in South Asian and Comparative Politics, July 2003. http:// archiv.ub.uni-heidelberg.de/volltextserver/4127/1/hpsacp17.pdf.

———. "Narendra Modi between Hindutava and Subnationalism: The Gujarat *asmita* of a Hindu Hriday Samrat." *India Review* 15, no. 2 (2016): 196–217.

———. "The Politics of the OBCs." In *Repressing Disadvantages: A Symposium on Reservations and the Private Sector*, edited by Gurpreet Mahajan. Seminar no. 549, 2005.

———. "'Why Should We Vote?': The Indian Middle Class and the Functioning of the World's Largest Democracy." In *Patterns of Middle Class Consumption in India and China*, edited by Christophe Jaffrelot and Peter van der Veer. Delhi: Sage, 2008.

Jain, Kajri. "The Handbag That Exploded: Mayawati's Monuments and the Aesthetics of Democracy in Post-Reform India." In *New Cultural Histories of India: Materiality and Practices*, edited by Partha Chatterjee, Tapati Guha-Thakurta, and Bodhisattava Kar. New Delhi: Oxford University Press, 2015.

Jeffrey, Robin. "Communication and Capitalism in India, 1750–2010." *South Asia: Journal of South Asian Studies* 25, no. 2 (2000): 61–75.

Kant, Amitabh. *Branding India: An Incredible Story.* Delhi: Harper Collins, 2009.

Kant, Krishna. "Households Put Two-Thirds of Their Savings in Houses, Gold." *Business Standard*, May 31, 2014. https://www.business-standard.com/article/economy -policy/households-put-two-thirds-of-their-savings-in-houses-gold-114053001457 _1.html.

Kantorowicz, Ernst H. *The King's Two Bodies: A Study in Medieval Political Theology.* Princeton, NJ: Princeton University Press, 2016.

Kanwal, Rahul. "RSS Views Now More Aligned with Modi's? Mohan Bhagwat Says Sangh Not Opposed to FDI, Liberalisation." *India Today*, November 2, 2013. https://www.indiatoday.in/india/story/rss-mohan-bhagwat-narendra-modi-fdi -bjp-216245-2013-11-02.

Kapur, Akash. "In India, Sometimes News Is Just a Product Placement." *New York Times*, May 7, 2010. https://www.nytimes.com/2010/05/08/world/asia/08iht-letter .html.

Kar, Sabyasachi, and Kunal Sen. *The Political Economy of India's Growth Episodes.* London: Palgrave Macmillan, 2016.

Karabell, Zachary. *The Leading Indicators: A Short History of the Numbers That Rule Our World.* New York, Simon and Schuster, 2014.

Katju, Manjari. *Vishwa Hindu Parishad and Indian Politics.* Delhi: Orient Blackswan, 2003.

Kaur, Ravinder. "Distinctive Citizenship: Refugees, Subjects and the Postcolonial State in India's Partition." *Cultural and Social History* 6, no. 4 (2009): 429–46.

———. "Good Times, Brought to You by Brand Modi." *Television and New Media* 16, no. 4 (2015): 323–30.

———. "India Inc. and Its Moral Discontents." *Economic and Political Weekly* 47, no. 20 (May 19, 2012): 40–45.

———. "Nation's Two Bodies: Rethinking the Idea of 'New' India and Its Other." *Third World Quarterly* 33, no. 4 (May 1, 2012): 603–21.

———. "Remains of Difference: New Imaginaries of Otherness in Post-Reform India." In *Interrogating India's Modernity: Democracy, Identity and Citizenship*, edited by Surinder Jodhka, 221–43. New Delhi: Oxford University Press, 2014.

———. "World as Commodity: Or, How the 'Third World' Became an 'Emerging Market,'" *Comparative Studies in South Asia, Africa and Middle East* 38, no. 2 (2018), 377–95.

———. "Writing History in a Paperless World: Archives of the Future." *History Workshop Journal* 79, no. 1 (2015): 242–53.

Kaur, Ravinder, and Thomas Blom Hansen. "Aesthetics of Arrival: Spectacle Capital, Novelty in Post-Reform India." *Identities, Global Studies in Culture and Power* 23 (2016): 265–75.

Kaur, Ravinder, K. Hart, and J. Comaroff. "Southern Futures: Thinking through

Emerging Markets." *Comparative Studies in South Asia, Africa and Middle East* 38, no. 2 (1999): 365–75.

Kaur, Ravinder, and Nandini Sundar. "Snakes and Ladders: Rethinking Social Mobility in Post-Reform India." *Contemporary South Asia* 24, no. 3 (2016): 229–41.

Kazmin, Amy. "Modi Personality Cult Dominates India Election." *Financial Times*, April 8, 2014. https://www.ft.com/content/96b8ca94-bedo-11e3-a1bf00144feabdco.

Khanduri, Ritu Gairola. *Caricaturing Culture in India: Cartoons and History in the Modern World*. Cambridge, UK: Cambridge University Press, 2014.

———. "Picturing India: Nation, Development and the Common Man." *Visual Anthropology* 25, no. 4 (July 2012): 303–23.

Khanna, Ajay. "The Year in Review." In *Annual Report 2005–06*, by IBEF. Accessed January 5, 2020. https://www.ibef.org/download/year_review.pdf.

Khilnani, Sunil. *The Idea of India*. Delhi: Penguin, 1997.

Kohli, A. *Poverty amid Plenty in the New India*. Cambridge, UK: Cambridge University Press, 2012.

Koselleck, Reinhardt. *Futures Past: On the Semantics of Historical Time*. Cambridge, MA: MIT Press, 2004.

Kothari, Rita, and Rupert Snell, eds. *Chutneyfying English: The Phenomenon of Hinglish*. New Delhi: Penguin, 2011.

Kotler, Philip, and Gertner, David. "Country and Brand, Product and Beyond: A Place Marketing and Brand Management Perspective." *Journal of Brand Management* 9, nos. 4–5 (2002): 250.

Kriegel, Lara. *Grand Designs: Labor, Empire, and the Museum in Victorian Culture*. Durham, NC: Duke University Press, 2008.

Kriplani, Manjeet. "Narendra Modi: India's Salesman-in-Chief." Quartz India, May 22, 2015. https://qz.com/410498/narendra-modi-indias-salesman-in-chief/.

Krishna, Sankara. "Number Fetish: Middle-Class India's Obsession with the GDP." *Globalizations* 12, no. 6 (2015): 859–71.

Kuncheria, C. J. "Mayawathi's Garland of Cash Kicks Up Political Storm." Reuters, March 16, 2010. https://in.reuters.com/article/idINIndia-46965320100316.

Laidlaw, James. "A Free Gift Makes No Friends." *The Journal of the Royal Anthropological Institute* 6, no. 4 (2000): 617–34.

Lander, Mark. "'India Everywhere' in the Alps." *New York Times*, January 26, 2006. http://www.nytimes.com/2006/01/26/business/worldbusiness/india-everywhere-in-the-alps.html.

Landes, Joan B. *Visualizing the Nation: Gender, Representation, and Revolution in Eighteenth-Century France*. Ithaca, NY: Cornell University Press, 2001.

Live Mint, "Arun Jaitley: Taking India to Top 50 in World Bank Doing Business Index Doable." *Live Mint*, November 1, 2017. https://www.livemint.com/Politics/UftqeUiYVYiOojLekhCWGJ/Arun-Jaitley-says-taking-India-among-top-50-in-ease-of-doing.html.

Lloyd, Edward. *The Law of Trade Marks: With Some Account of Its History and*

Development in the Decisions of the Courts of Law and Equity. London: Yates and Alexander, 1862.

Logue, Ann C. *Emerging Markets for Dummies*. Indianapolis: Wiley, 2011.

Long, Jeffery D. *Historical Dictionary of Hinduism*. Lanham, MD: Scarecrow Press, 2011.

Ludden, David. "Imperial Modernity: History and Global Inequity in Global Asia." *Third World Quarterly* 33, no. 4 (2012): 581–601.

MacFarquhar, Neil. "What's a Soccer Mom Anyway?" *New York Times*, October 20, 1996.

The Madrid Agreement Concerning the International Registration of Marks from 1891 to 1991. Geneva: International Bureau of Intellectual Property, 1991. https://www .wipo.int/edocs/pubdocs/en/marks/880/wipo_pub_880.pdf.

Majeed, Javed. "A Nation on the Move: The Indian Constitution, Life Writing, and Cosmopolitanism." *Life Writing* 13, no. 2 (2016): 237–53.

Malkki, Liisa. "National Geographic: The Rooting of Peoples and the Territorialization of National Identity among Scholars and Refugees." *Cultural Anthropology* 7, no. 1 (2012): 24–44.

Mandhana, Niharika. "A Conversation With: Sociologist Ashis Nandy." *New York Times*, January 30, 2013. https://india.blogs.nytimes.com/2013/01/30/a-conversa tion-with-sociologist-ashis-nandy/.

Marlow, Ian. "PM Narendra Modi Spent $1 Billion on Ads, Foreign Trips." *Live Mint*, December 15, 2018. https://www.livemint.com/Politics/aSDTIh5323Hho HWsnk6mPL/PM-Narendra-Modi-spent-1-billion-on-ads-foreign-trips.html.

Marx, Karl. *Capital: A Critique of Political Economy*. Vol. I. London, Penguin: 1990.

Masood, Ehsa. *The Great Invention: The Story of GDP and the Making and Unmaking of the Modern World*. New York: Pegasus Books, 2016.

Mazzarella, William. "Affect: What Is It Good For?" In *Enchantments of Modernity*, edited by Saurabh Dube, 210–309. London: Routledge, 2009.

———. *Censorium: Cinema and the Open Edge of Mass Publicity*. Durham, NC, Duke University Press, 2013.

———. *The Mana of Mass Society*. Chicago: University of Chicago Press, 2017.

———. "The Myth of the Multitude, or, Who's Afraid of the Crowd." *Critical Enquiry* 36 (2010): 697–727.

———. *Shoveling Smoke: Advertising and Globalization in Contemporary India*. Durham, NC: Duke University Press, 2003.

McCrindle, J. W. *Ancient India: As Described by Megastenes and Arrian*. London: Trubner, 1877.

McLuhan, Marshall. *Understanding Media: The Extensions of Man*. Cambridge, MA: MIT Press, 1964.

Meiu, George Paul, Jean Comaroff, and John Comaroff. Introduction to *Ethnicity, Inc. Revisited*. Bloomington: Indiana University Press, forthcoming.

Menon, Nivedita. "We Should Be There: The Left and the Anna Moment." *Firstpost*,

August 20, 2011. https://www.firstpost.com/politics/we-should-be-there-the-left -and-the-anna-moment-65356.html.

Miller, Michele, and Holly Buchanan. *The Soccer Mom Myth: Today's Female Consumer: Who She Really Is, Why She Really Buys.* Austin, TX: Wizard Academy Press, 2010.

Mirzoeff, Nicholas. *The Right to Look: A Counterhistory of Visuality.* Durham, NC: Duke University Press, 2011.

Mishra, Akshay. "Hindutva vs. Hinduism: Why I Am Proud to Be Pseudo-Secular." *Firstpost,* December 10, 2012. https://www.firstpost.com/politics/hindutva-vs -hinduism-why-i-am-proud-to-be-pseudo-secular-552399.html.

Mishra, Asit Ranjan. "World Bank Endorses Modi Government's Reform Credentials." *Live Mint,* November 1, 2017. https://www.livemint.com/Companies/icjVb gr3PteKYupZlzwOtN/India%20jumps%2   oto%20100th-spot-in-World-Banks -ease-of-doing-busi.html.

Mitchell, Timothy. "Fixing the Economy." *Cultural Studies* 12, no. 1 (1998): 82–101.

———. *Rule of Experts: Egypt, Tech-Politics, Modernity.* Berkeley: University of California Press, 2005.

Mitchell, W. J. T. *Iconology: Image, Text, Ideology.* Chicago: University of Chicago Press, 1986.

———. "Realism and the Digital Image." In *Critical Realism in Contemporary Art: Around Alan Sekula's Photography,* edited by J. Baetens and H. Van Gelder, 12–27. Leuven, BE: Leuven University Press, 2007.

Mobius, Mark. *The Little Black Book* (Singapore: Wiley, 2012).

Mohan, Rakesh. "The Growth Record of the Indian Economy 1950–2008: A Story of Sustained Savings and Investment." Reserve Bank of India, February 14, 2008. http://www.rbi.org.in/scripts/BS_SpeechesView.aspx?Id=379.

Munro, J. E. Crawford. *The Patents, Designs, and Trade Marks Act, 1883: With the Rules and Instructions.* London: Stevens and Sons, 1884.

Nagaraj, N. "Growth Rate of India's GDP, 1950–51 to 1987–88: Examination of Alternative Hypotheses." *Economic and Political Weekly* 25, no. 26 (1990): 1396–1403.

Nakassis, Constantine V. "Brand, Citationality, Performativity." *American Anthropologist* 114, no. 4 (2012): 624–38.

———. "Brands and Their Surfeits." *Cultural Anthropology* 28, no. 1 (2013): 111–26.

Narayanan, C. K. Saji. "Why Fear a Hindu Rashtra?" *Outlook India,* May 7, 2018. https://www.outlookindia.com/magazine/story/why-fear-a-hindu-rashtra/300085.

Narayanan, Nayantara. "Five Ethical Problems That Plague Indian Journalism." *Scroll.in,* March 19, 2015. https://scroll.in/article/714570/five%20ethical%20prob lems-that-plague-indian-journalism.

Nath, Kamal. "India: The Paradigm Shift." Foreword to *Annual Report 2005–06,* by IBEF, accessed April 4, 2018. https://www.ibef.org/download/india_paradigm shift.pdf.

National Skill Development Corporation. "Organisation Profile." NSDC India, accessed April 24, 2018. http://www.nsdcindia.org/organisation-profile.

New York Times. "The New India Bill." May 19, 1858.

Nielsen Company. *Women of Tomorrow: A Study of Women around the World.* June 28, 2011. http://www.nielsen.com/us/en/insights/reports/2011/a-study-of-women-around -the-world.html.

Noorani, A. G. "India's Reaction to the International Concern over Gujarat." In *Gujarat: The Making of a Tragedy*, edited by Siddharth Varadarajn, 389–400. Delhi: Penguin, 2003.

North, Michael. *Novelty: A History of the New.* Chicago: University of Chicago Press, 2013.

Nye, Joseph. "Soft Power," *Foreign Policy*, no. 80 (1990): 153–71.

Oberoi, Harjot. *The Construction of Religious Boundaries.* Delhi: Oxford University Press, 1997.

Ohri, Raghav. "Robert Vadra Made Gains of Rs 50 Crore from a Land Deal in Haryana in 2008: Dhingra Panel." *Economic Times*, April 28, 2017. https://eco nomictimes.indiatimes.com/news/politics-and-nation/robert-vadra-made-gains -of-rs-50-crore-from-a-land-deal-in-haryana-in-2008-dhingra-panel/articleshow /58407295.cms.

Olins, Wally. *The Brand Handbook.* London: Thames and Hudson, 2008.

———. "Branding the Nation: The Historical Context." *Journal of Brand Management* 9, nos. 4–5 (2002): 242.

———. *Trading Identities; Why Countries and Companies Are Becoming More Alike.* London: The Foreign Policy Centre, 1999.

O'Neill, Jim. *The Growth Map: Economic Opportunity in the BRICs and Beyond.* New York: Penguin, 2011.

Orsini, Francesca. "Dil Mange More: Cultural Contexts of Hinglish in Contemporary India." *African Studies* 74, no. 2 (August 2015).

Osterhammel, Bayly. *The Transformation of the World: A Global History of the Nineteenth Century.* Princeton, NJ: Princeton University Press, 2014.

Padmanabhan, Mohan. "EPCs to Popularize India Brand Equity Fund." *Hindu Business Line*, June 17, 2000.

Pai, Sudha. *Dalit Assertion.* Delhi: Oxford University Press, 2013.

———. "Rise of Mayawati in Hindi Heartland Is a Remarkable Phenomenon." *Indian Express*, January 22, 2016. http://indianexpress.com/article/blogs /rise-of-mayawati-in-hindi-heartland-is-a-remarkable-phenomenon/.

Pande, Mrinal. "Hindi Media and an Unreal Discourse." *The Hindu*, November 18, 2009. https://www.thehindu.com/opinion/lead/Hindi-media-and-an-unreal-dis course/article16892944.ece.

Pande, Shamni. "Just in Times." *Business Today*, July 10, 2011. https://www.business today.in/magazine/cover-story/bennett-coleman-and-co-among-100-year-old-in dian-companies/story/16498.html.

Pandey, Tanushree. "Article 370 Gone, Investor Summit Planned in Jammu and Kashmir to Boost Industry and Healthcare." *India Today*, August 7, 2019. https:// www.indiatoday.in/india/story/article-370-gone-investor-summit-planned-j-k -boost-industry-healthcare-1578042-2019-08-07.

Papadopulos, N., and L. A. Heslop, eds. *Product and Country Images: Impact and Role in International Marketing*. Binghamton, NY: Haworth Press, 1993.

Parry, Jonathan. "The Gift, the Indian Gift and 'the Indian Gift.'" *Man, New Series* 21, no. 3 (1986): 453–73.

Payn, Howard. "Commanding Heights." Ch. 6, accessed July 20, 2016, https://www.pbs.org/wgbh/commandingheights/shared/minitextlo/tr_showo.html.

———. *The Merchandise Marks Act, 1887: With Special Reference to Importation Sections*. London: Stevens and Sons, 1888.

Penn, Mark J. *Microtrends: The Small Forces behind Tomorrow's Big Challenges*. New York: Twelve, 2007.

Perkins, Ryan. "A New *Pablik*: Abdul Halim Sharar, Volunteerism, and the Anjuman-e Dar-us-Salaam in Late Nineteenth Century India." *Modern Asian Studies* 49, no. 4 (2015): 1049–90.

Philips, Kavita. "Telling Histories of the Future: The Imaginaries of Indian Technoscience." *Identities: Global Journal of Power and Culture* 23, no. 3 (2016): 276–93.

Philipsen, Dirks. *The Little Big Number: How GDP Came to Rule the World and What to Do about It*. Princeton, NJ: Princeton University Press, 2015.

Pieterse, Jan Nederveen. *Global Melange: Globalization and Culture*. London: Rowman and Littlefield, 2003.

Pinney, Chris. *Photos of the Gods: The Printed and Political Struggle in India*. London: Reaktion Books, 2004.

Platts, John T. (John Thompson). *A Dictionary of Urdu, Classical Hindi, and English*. London: W. H. Allen, 1884.

Poland, Harry Bodkin. *Trade Marks: The Merchandise Marks Act, 1862*. London: John Crockford, 1862.

Polanyi, Karl. *The Great Transformation: The Political and Economic Origins of Our Time*. Boston: Beacon Press, 2001.

Prakash, Gyan. "Writing Post-Orientalist Histories of the Third World: Perspectives from Indian Historiography." *Comparative Studies in Society and History* 32, no. 2 (1990): 388.

Prashad, Vijay. *The Darker Nations: A People's History of the Third World*. New York: The New Press, 2007.

———. "No Entry for Modi." *Frontline* 22, no. 7 (March 12–25, 2005), https://frontline.thehindu.com/static/html/fl2207/stories/20050408003313100.htm.

Prothero, G. W. "First Charter to the East India Company, December 31, 1600." In *Select Statutes and after Constitutional Documents: Illustrative of the Reigns of Elizabeth and James I*. Oxford, UK: Clarendon Press, 1906.

PTI. "For the First Time in Their 120-Year-Old History, Mumbai's Dabbawalas to Take a Break for Anna Hazare." *Economic Times*, August 19, 2011. https://economictimes.indiatimes.com/news/politics-and-nation/for-the-first-time-in-their-120-year-old-history-mumbais-dabbawalas-to-take-a-break-for-anna-hazare/articleshow/9649340.cms.

———. "Possible for India to Be in Top 50 on Ease of Business Index: Jaitley." *The Hindu*, January 27, 2018. http://www.thehindu.com/business/possible-for-india-to-be-in-top-50-on-ease-of-business-index-jaitley/article22535396.ece.

Puri, Anjali. "Free from India?" *Outlook India*, August 18, 2008. https://www.outlook india.com/magazine/story/free-from-india/238163.

Purie, Aroon. "Davos 2006: India Showcases Contemporary Face at World Economic Forum." *India Today*, February 13, 2006. https://www.indiatoday.in/mag azine/cover-story/story/20060213-davos-2006-india-showcases-contemporary -face-at-world- economic-forum-785958-2006-02-13.

Raghavan, TCA Srinivasa. "The Economy beyond Numbers." *Open the Magazine*, March 23, 2018. http://www.openthemagazine.com/article/essay/the-economy-be yond-numbers.

Rai, Saritha. "India Just Crossed 1 Billion Mobile Subscribers Milestone and the Excitement's Just Beginning." *Forbes*, January 6, 2016. https://www.forbes.com/sites /saritharai/2016/01/06/india-just-crossed-1-billion-mobile-subscribers-milestone -and-the-excitements-just-beginning/.

Raj, Krishna. "Some Observations on Economic Growth in India over the Period 1952–53 to 1982–83." *Economic and Political Weekly* 19, no. 41 (October 13, 1984).

Rajagopal, Arvind. *Politics after Television: Hindu Nationalism and the Reshaping of the Public in India*. Cambridge, UK: Cambridge University Press, 2001.

Rajan, Rajeswari Sundar. "The Politics of Hindu 'Tolerance.'" *Boundary 2* 38, no. 3 (2011): 67–86.

Rajulapudi, Srinivas. "55-Year-Old A. P. Sugar Unit Closed." *The Hindu*, January 23, 2017. https://www.thehindu.com/todays-paper/tp-national/tp-andhrapradesh/55 -year-old-A.P.-sugar-unit-closed/article17080098.ece.

Ramaswamy, Sumathi. *The Goddess and Nation: Mapping Mother India*. Durham, NC: Duke University Press, 2010.

———. "Maps, Mother/Goddess, and Martyrdom in Modern India." *Journal of Asia Studies* 67, no. 3 (2008): 819–53.

Ramaswamy, Sumathi, and Martin Jay. "Introduction: The Work of Vision in the Age of European Empires." In *Empires of Vision: A Reader (Objects/Histories)*. Durham, NC: Duke University Press, 2014.

Ramesh, Randeep. "Newspaper Empires at War in India." *Guardian*, July 27, 2005. https://www.theguardian.com/media/2005/jul/27/pressandpublishing.business.

Rancière, Jacques. *Disagreement: Politics and Philosophy*. Translated by Julie Rose. Minneapolis: University of Minnesota Press, 1999.

———. *The Emancipated Spectator*. London: Verso, 2011.

Rankin, Jennifer. "Davos—A Complete Guide to the World Economic Forum." *Guardian*, January 21, 2015. https://www.theguardian.com/business/2015/jan/21 /-sp-davos-guide-world-economic-forum.

Ravindran, Shruti. "A Park for Maya Memsaab." *Indian Express*, January 9, 2011. http://indianexpress.com/article/news-archive/web/a-park-for-maya-memsaab/.

Reddy, B. Muralidhar. "It's Official: Modi Is BJP's Choice." *The Hindu*, September 13, 2013. https://www.thehindu.com/news/national/its-official-modi-is-bjps-choice /article5124375.ece.

Reddy, Y. V. "India's Foreign Exchange Reserves: Policy, Status and Issues." Reserve Bank of India, 2002, accessed June 25, 2014. http://rbidocs.rbi.org.in/rdocs/Bulle tin/PDFs/29869.pdf.

Renan, Ernest. "What Is a Nation?" [Qu'est-ce qu'une Nation?, 1882]. In *What Is a Nation? and Other Political Writings*, translated by M. F. N. Giglioli, 247–63. New York: Columbia University Press, 2018.

Reserve Bank of India. "Foreign Exchange Reserves." December 19, 2003. http://rbi docs.rbi.org.in/rdocs/Wss/PDFs/50084.pdf.

———. *Report on Foreign Exchange Reserves 2004–5 (Covering Period Up to March 2005)*. 2005, accessed June 25, 2014. http://rbidocs.rbi.org.in/rdocs/Publication Report/Pdfs/64264.pdf.

Richards, Thomas. *The Commodity Culture of Victorian England: Advertising and Spectacle 1851–1914*. Stanford, CA: Stanford University Press, 1990.

Robins, Nick. *The Corporation that Changed the World*. London: Pluto, 2006.

Rodrik, Dani, and Arvind Subramaniam. "From 'Hindu Growth' to Productivity Surge: The Mystery of the Indian Growth Transition." NBER working paper 10376, National Bureau of Economic Research, Cambridge, MA, 2004. https:// www.imf.org/external/pubs/ft/staffp/2004/00-00/rodrik.pdf.

Rosa, Hartmut. *Social Acceleration: A New Theory of Modernity*. New York: Columbia University Press, 2013.

Roy, Srirupa. "Being the Change: The Aam Aadmi Party and the Politics of the Extraordinary in Indian Democracy." *Economic and Political Weekly* 49, no. 15 (2014): 45–54.

———. *Beyond Belief: India and the Politics of Postcolonial Nationalism*. Durham, NC: Duke University Press, 2008.

Ruparelia, Sanjay, Sanjay Reddy, John Harris, and Stuart Corbridge, eds. *Understanding India's New Political Economy: A Great Transformation?* New York: Routledge, 2011.

Sachar Committee Report. *Social, Economic and Educational Status of Muslim Community in India*. New Delhi: Government of India, 2006. http://mhrd.gov.in/sites /upload_files/mhrd/files/sachar_comm.pdf.

Sainath, P. "The Feel Good Factory." *Frontline* 21, no. 5 (2004). http://www.frontline .in/static/html/fl2105/stories/20040312007800400.htm.

———. "Paid News Undermining Democracy: Press Council Report." *The Hindu*, April 21, 2010. http://www.thehindu.com/opinion/columns/sainath/Paid-news -undermining-democracy-Press-Council-report/article16371596.ece.

Salmon, Felix. "Davos's Status Levels." *Reuters*, January 19, 2012, http://blogs.reuters .com/felix-salmon/2012/01/19/davoss-status-levels/.

Sandel, Michael J. *What Money Can't Buy: The Moral Limits of Markets*. London: Penguin, 2013.

Sassen, Saskia. *Globalization and Its Discontents: Essays on the New Mobility of People and Money.* New York: New Press, 1999.

———. "Spatialities and Temporalities of the Global: Elements for a Theorization." *Public Culture* 12 (2000): 215–32.

———. *Territory, Authority, Rights: From Medieval to Global Assemblages.* Princeton, NJ: Princeton University Press, 2008.

Schneider's Davos. "Das Schneider's: Portrait." Accessed November 21, 2018. http://www.schneiders-davos.ch/schneiders/portrait.html.

Schwab, Klaus. *The Global Competitiveness Report 2017–18.* Geneva: World Economic Forum, 2017.

Sen, Tansen. "The Travel Records of Chinese Pilgrims Faxian, Xuanzang, and Yijing: Sources for Cross-Cultural Encounters between Ancient China and Ancient India." *Education about Asia* 11, no. 3 (April 2006): 24–33.

Sethi, Sunil. "Sunil Sethi: In Mayawati's 'Green Garden.'" *Business Standard*, January 20, 2013. http://www.business-standard.com/article/opinion/sunil sethi-in mayawati-s-green-garden-111102900057_1.html.

Shah, Alpa. *Behind the Indian Boom: Inequality and Resistance at the Heart of the Economic Growth.* Kolkata: Adivaani, 2017.

Shah, Rishi. "9–10% GDP Growth Is History for Indian Economy: Richard Iley, BNP Paribas." *Economic Times*, December 16, 2011. http://articles.economictimes.india times.com/2011-12-16/news/30525115_1_richard- iley-gdp-growth-growth-story.

Shani, Ornit. *Communalism, Caste and Hindu Nationalism: The Violence in Gujarat.* Cambridge, UK: Cambridge University Press, 2007.

Sharma, Mukul. "The Making of Anna Hazare. *Kafila Online*, April 4, 2011. https://kafila.online/2011/04/12/the-making-of-anna-hazare/.

Sharma, Sanam. "A True Hindu Is a Secular Hindu." *Huffington Post*, May 11, 2015. https://bit.ly/2sQaHxP.

Shetty, S. L. "Saving Behaviour in India in the 1980s: Some Lessons." *Economic and Political Weekly* 25, no. 11 (1990): 555–60.

Shimp, T. A., S. Saeed, and T. J. Madden. "Countries and Their Products: A Cognitive Structure Perspective." *Journal of the Academy of Marketing Science* 21, no. 4 (1993): 323–30.

Shryock, Andrew. "The New Jordanian Hospitality: House, Host and Guest in the Culture of Public Display." *Comparative Studies in Society and History* 46, no. 1 (2004): 35–62.

Shuchi, Vyas. "The Time Is Now." *Economic Times*, January 10, 2007.

Sidhartha. "India Is Replacing Red Tape with Red Carpet: PM Modi Tells CEOs at Davos." *Times of India*, January 23, 2018. https://timesofindia.indiatimes.com /business/international-business/india-is-replacing-red-tape-with-red-carpet-pm -modi-tells-ceos-at-davos/articleshow/62622556.cms.

Silverstein, Michael J., and Kate Sayre. "The Female Economy." *Harvard Business Review*, September 2009, 46–53.

Singh, Aditi. "Coal Scam Case: Former Jharkand CM Madhu Koda Convicted by

Special by CBI Court." *Live Mint*, December 13, 2017. https://www.livemint.com
/Politics/oIdl8xXT6qYR3pw8p4DBXM/Coal-scam%20case-Former-Jharkhand
-CM-Madhu-Koda-convicted-by.html.

Singh, Deepak. "Locating the Dislocated in Globalized India." In *Facing Globality:
Politics of Resistance, Relocation and Reinvention in India*, edited by Bhupinder Brar
and Pampa Mukherjee, 245–67. New Delhi: Oxford University Press, 2012.

Singh, Garima, and Basant Rawat. "Shourie Stings as Advani Shields Modi." *Telegraph* (Kolkata), September 28, 2003. https://www.telegraphindia.com/india
/shourie-stings-as-advani-shields-modi/cid/799320.

Singh, Jaswant. "India's Year of Living Stagnantly." *Project Syndicate*, January 25, 2012.
https://www.project-syndicate.org/commentary/india-s-year-of-living-stagnantly
?barrier=accesspaylog.

Singh, Upinder. *A History of Ancient and Early Medieval India*. Hoboken, NJ: Pearson Longman, 2008.

Sitapati, Vinay. *Half-Lion: How P. V. Narasimha Rao Transformed India*. Delhi: Viking, 2016.

Smith, Anthony D. *Early History of India, from 600 BC to the Muhemmadan Conquest, Including the Invasion of Alexander the Great*. Oxford, UK: Oxford University Press, 1924.

———. *The Nation Made Real: Art and National Identity in Western Europe, 1600–1850*.
Oxford, UK: Oxford University Press, 2013.

Smith, Vincent. *Oxford History of India*. Oxford, UK: Oxford University Press, 1919.

Sontag, Susan. *The Art of Revolution: 96 Posters from Cuba*. London: Pall Mall Press,
1970.

Sorkin, Andrew Ross. "A Hefty Price for Entry at Davos." Dealbook, *New York
Times*, January 24, 2011. https://dealbook.nytimes.com/2011/01/24/a-hefty-price
-for-entry-to-davos/.

Spear, Percival. *India, Pakistan and the West*. Oxford, UK: Oxford University Press,
1958.

Sreenivasan, Ramya. *The Many Lives of a Rajput Queen: Heroic Pasts in India, c. 1500–
1900*. Seattle: University of Washington Press, 2007.

Sridhar, V. "More Sops for the Elite." *Frontline* 21, no. 2 (2004). http://www.frontline
.in/static/html/fl2103/stories/20040213001704100.htm.

Stern, Philip J. *The Company-State: Corporate Sovereignty and the Early Modern Foundations of the British Empire in India*. Oxford, UK: Oxford University Press, 2011.

Stiglitz, Joseph E. *Globalization and Its Discontents*. New York: Norton, 2003.

Stiglitz, Joseph, Amartya Sen, and Jean-Paul Fitoussi. *Mismeasuring Our Lives: Why
GDP Doesn't Add Up*. New York: New Press, 2010.

———. *Report by the Commission on the Measurement of Economic Performance and
Social Progress*. Paris, 2009. http://ec.europa.eu/eurostat/documents/118025/118123
/Fitoussi+Commission+report.

Strausi, Rachl Rickard. "East India Co Is Back, with Indian Owner." *Times of India*,

August 16, 2010. https://timesofindia.indiatimes.com/india/East-India-Co-is
-back-with-Indian-owner/articleshow/6316784.cms?.

Sud, Nikita. "Constructing and Contesting a Gujarati-Hindu Ethno-Religious Identity through Development Programmes." *Oxford Development Studies* 35, no. 2
(2007): 131–48.

Sur, Abha. *Dispersed Radiance: Caste, Gender and Modern Science in India.* New Delhi:
Navayana, 2011.

Taussig, Michael. *Defacement: Public Secrecy and the Labour of the Negative.* Stanford,
CA: Stanford University Press, 1999.

Templeton, Franklin. *States of Emergence: The Evolution of Emerging Markets Investing.*
New York: Franklin Templeton Investments, 2014.

Tewary, Amarnath. "What Is the Lowdown on the Fodder Scam." *The Hindu,* January 13, 2018. https://www.thehindu.com/news/national/what-is-the-lowdown-on
-the-fodder-scam/article22437730.ece.

Thakurta, Paranjoy Guha. "The Times, the Jains, and BCCL." *The Hoot,* November 11, 2012. http://www.thehoot.org/media-watch/media-business/the-times-the
-jains-and-bccl-6425.

Tharoor, Ishaan. "A Rally in Mumbai: Remember 26/11." *Time,* December 3, 2008.

Tharoor, Shashi. "Meanwhile: India's Cellphone Revolution—Opinion—International Herald Tribune." *New York Times,* February 2, 2007. https://www.nytimes
.com/2007/02/01/opinion/01iht-edtharoor.4431582.html.

———. *Why I Am a Hindu.* Delhi: Aleph, 2018.

Thorner, Daniel. *Investment in Empire: British Railway and Steam Shipping Enterprise
in India 1825–1849.* Philadelphia: University of Pennsylvania Press, 1950.

Times Music. "India vs. India—TOI ft. Amitabh Bachchan HQ." YouTube Video,
January 25, 2017. https://www.youtube.com/watch?v=XzJj-PL-kPs.

Times News Network. "Awareness Campaigns Draw Mixed Reactions from Electorate." *Times of India,* April 23, 2009. https://timesofindia.indiatimes.com/city/goa
/Awareness-campaigns-draw-mixed-reactions-from-electorate/articleshow/443
2171.cms.

———. "India against Corruption: 'This Is Our 2nd Freedom Struggle.'" *Economic Times,* April 7, 2011. https://economictimes.indiatimes.com/news/politics
-and-nation/india-against-corruption-this-is-our-2nd-freedom-struggle/article
show/7895496.cms.

———. "Medianet: Innovative Content, Integrated Offering." *Times of India,*
March 4, 2003. https://timesofindia.indiatimes.com/india/Medianet-Innovative
-content-integrated- offering/articleshow/39286961.cms.

———. "Times Now Masthead of the World." *Times of India,* June 26, 2005. https://
timesofindia.indiatimes.com/india/Times-now-Masthead-of-the-World/article
show/1152489.cms.

———. "Who Is Anna Hazare?" *Times of India,* August 18, 2011. https://timesof
india.indiatimes.com/india/Who-is-Anna-Hazare/articleshow/9644794.cms.

Times of India. "Citizens' Charter for Change." *Times of India*, January 7, 2007. Available on Press Reader.

———. "GDP Growth Slips to 4.3 in 2002." *Times of India*, June 30, 2003. https://timesofindia.indiatimes.com/business/india-business/GDP-growth-slips-to-4-3-in-2002-03/articleshow/52422.cms.

Timesofindia.com. "We are the Best." *Times of India*, April 2, 2004. https://timesofindia.indiatimes.com/nrs-2003/We-are-the-best/articleshow/596413.cms.

Tomasso, Bobbio. "Making Gujarat Vibrant: *Hindutva*, Development and the Rise of Subnationalism in India." *Third World Quarterly* 33, no. 4 (2012): 657–72.

"Towards Creating Brand India." *Financial Express*, February 15, 2003. http://www.financialexpress.com/archive/towards-creating-brand india/73145/.

Treanor, Jill. "Occupy Activists Attempt to Take Over Davos Debate." *Guardian*, January 27, 2012. https://www.theguardian.com/world/2012/jan/27/occupy-movement-davos-capitalism-debate.

Tribune India. "BJP Sweeps Out Congress from 3 States." May 12, 2003. http://www.tribuneindia.com/2003/20031205/main1.htm.

Tripathi, Ashish. "Mayawati's Statue 'Beheaded' in Lucknow, Police Call It Sacrilege." *Times of India*, July 26, 2012. https://timesofindia.indiatimes.com/city/lucknow/Mayawatis-statue-beheaded-in-Lucknow-police-call-it-sacrilege/articleshow/15161969.cms.

Truss, Lynn. *Eats, Shoots, and Leaves: The Zero Tolerance Approach to Punctuation.* New York: Gotham Books, 2004.

Tsing, Anna. "The Global Situation." *Cultural Anthropology* 15, no. 3 (2000): 327–60.

Twain, Mark. *Following the Equator: A Journey around the World.* Hartford, CT: American Publishing, 1898.

UDAAN—National Skill Development Corporation. "What Is Udaan?" Accessed August 2, 2018. http://nsdcudaan.com.

Ulmer, Alexandra, and Ahmed, Aftab. "Modi's War Chest Leaves India Election Rivals in the Dust." Reuters, May 1, 2019. https://www.reuters.com/article/india-election-spending-bjp-congress/modis-war-chest-leaves-india-election-rivals-in-the-dust-idUSKCN1S7390.

Unnikrishnan, Dinesh. "GDP Flop-Show: Manmohan Singh Has the Last Laugh in War of Words with Narendra Modi over Note Ban." *Firstpost*, June 2, 2017. https://www.firstpost.com/india/gdp-flop-show-manmohan-singh-has-the-last-laugh-in-war-of-words-with-narendra-modi-over-note-ban-3508625.html.

———. "Narendra Modi in Davos: IMF's 7.4% GDP Forecast Is a Gift to PM, but Why Are Foreigners More Optimistic about Growth than CSO?" *Firstpost*, January 23, 2018, http://www.firstpost.com/business/narendra-modi-in-davos-imfs-7-4-gdp-forecast-is-a-gift-to-pm-but-why-are-foreigners-more-optimistic-about-growth-than-cso-4315555.html.

———. "World Economic Forum 2018: Narendra Modi Can't Ask for a Better Marketplace than Davos to Pitch India as a Hot Ticket Item." *Firstpost*, January 23, 2018. http://www.firstpost.com/business/prime-minister-narendra-modi-cant-ask

-for-a-better-marketplace-than-davos-to-pitch-india-as-a-hot-ticket-item-4313817
.html.

Vanaik, Achin. "Rendezvous at Mumbai." *New Left Review* 26 (2004): 53–65.

Vanham, Peter. "How Rick Goings Went from Dirt Poor to the CEO of a \$2 Billion Company." CNBC, December 27, 2016. https://www.cnbc.com/2016/12/27/how
-rick-goings-went-from-dirt-poor-to-the-ceo-of-tupperware.html.

Varadarajan, Siddharth. "Chronicle of a Tragedy Foretold." In *Gujarat: The Making of a Tragedy*, edited by Siddharth Varadarajan, 1–44. Delhi: Penguin, 2003.

Virmani, Arvind. *Propelling India from Socialist Stagnation to Global Power*. Delhi: Academic Books, 2006.

Waldman, Amy. "Sizzling Economy Revitalizes India." *New York Times*, October 20, 2003. http://www.nytimes.com/2003/10/20/international/asia/20INDI.html.

Wallerstein, Immanuel. "Entering Global Anarchy." *New Left Review* (July–August 2003): 27–35.

———. "New Revolts against the System." *New Left Review* 18 (November–December 2002): 29–39. https://newleftreview.org/II/18/immanuel-wallerstein-new-revolts
-against-the-system.

———. "Structural Crises." *New Left Review* (March–April 2010): 133–42.

Wark, McKenzie. *The Spectacle of Disintegration: Situationist Passages of the 20th Century*. London: Verso, 2013.

Washington Post. "The Times Of India's Business Strategy Start the Presses." *Washington Post*, July 2, 2015. https://www.washingtonpost.com/business/the-times-of
-indias-business-strategy-start-the-presses/2015/07/02/52d5e670-1c50-11e5-ab92
-c75ae6ab94b5_story.html?utm_term=.ca55ae2dd495.

Webb, Walter Prescott. *The Great Frontier*. Austin: University of Texas Press, 1951.

Weforum. "About: Our Mission." World Economic Forum, accessed March 20, 2017. https://www.weforum.org/about/world-economic-forum.

———. "Our Members and Partners." World Economic Forum, accessed August 2, 2018. www.weforum.org/members.

Weinraub, Bernard. "Economic Crisis Forcing Once Self-Reliant India to Seek Aid." *New York Times*, June 29, 1991.

Williams, Ernest Edwin. *Made In Germany*. London: William Heinemann, 1896.

Withnall, Adam. "How Modi Government Uses Ad Spending to 'Reward or Punish' Indian Media." *Independent*, July 7, 2019. https://www.independent.co.uk/news
/world/asia/india-modi-government-media-ad-spending-newspapers-press-free
dom-a8990451.html.

Witsoe, Jeffrey. 2011. "Corruption as Power: Caste and the Political Imagination of the Postcolonial State." *American Ethnologist* 38, no. 1 (2011): 73–85.

Women in Global Science and Technology. "National Assessments on Gender Equality in the Knowledge Society, Country Results: India." 2013, accessed July 14, 2014. http://wisat.org/wp-content/uploads/National_Scorecard_India.pdf.

Woolridge, Adrian. "The Visible Hand." *Economist*, January 21, 2012. http://www
.economist.com/node/21542931.

World Bank Group. *Doing Business 2018: Reforming to Create Jobs.* Washington, DC: The World Bank, 2018. http://www.doingbusiness.org/~/media/WBG/Doing Business/Documents/Annual- Reports/English/DB2018-Full-Report.pdf.

Zakaria, Fareed. "India Rising." *Newsweek India*, March 5, 2006. http://europe.news week.com/india-rising-106259?rm=eu.

Zanane, Anant. "Mayawathi's Elephant Statues: Could Be a 40,000 Crore Scam, Says Akhilesh Yadav." *NDTV*, May 15, 2012. https://www.ndtv.com/india-news /mayawatis-elephant-statues-could-be-a-40-000-crore-scam-says-akhilesh-ya dav-482599.

Page numbers in italic indicate material in figures.

brand new nation, 8–11, 21; anxieties regarding, 192; branding versus nation building, 10, 35; Brand Modi, 248; as business enterprise, 8–9; competition in branding, 270n91; demanding love and devotion, 19–20, 27; dichotomies within, 245; and hypernationalist cultural politics, 10, 251; and investments, 246; joining identity economy and politics, 14; joining of nation and state, 13; joining publicity and populism, 14; makers of, 34–37; and neoliberalism, 263; Olins on branding, 267n68; and performance rankings, 82; and popular politics, 15; and populist politics, 254; and production of hope, 255; and propaganda, 17; with superpower aspirations, 41, 253–54; as unique eternal person, 18; what is being sold, 271n99
Brazil, 4, 6. *See also* BRICS
bribery and kickbacks, 234–35, 298n83, 301n99
BRICS (Brazil, Russia, India, China, South Africa), 4–5, 65, 72, 147, 271n98
Britain Is Great campaign, 176
British East India Company, 46, 59, 184–85, 265nn45
Brosius, Christiane, 124
Buck-Morss, Susan, 261n9
Bull, John, 226
business loans, 60, 144, 272n21

Cameron, David, *173*, 176
"Can India Fly?" (*Economist*), 211–12, 219, 221
Capella, Martianus, 56
capitalism: and Brand Modi, 187–88; and cultural nationalism, 245–46, 248, 253; versus free markets, globalization, 251; and identity politics, 252–53; as modern, 210; Oath campaign "I Swear" advertisements, 195, *196*, 223,

223; refashioning itself, 251; state appropriation of, 191; tied to growth, 4–5, 11, 74, 82–84, 151, 154. *See also* neoliberalism
capitalization of nation-state, 8–9, 13–15, 18, 54, 257
Capital Markets, 65
captains of industry, 42, 46, 163, 168, *181*, 184–86, 243
"care," corporate brand value of, 211
Cashless India, 188, 292n62
cashless society pledge, 188, 190
caste politics, 47; 1990s Mandal politics, 234; affirmative action and, 199, 240; and antipolitics, 269n87; corruption of upper-caste politicians, 89, 299nn85, 301n99; Dalit symbols in parks, museums, 235–36; and election success, 219, 234–35; government employment reservations, 234; and Lever's Pappu character, 233–34, 237, 298n83; Madhu Koda as "brilliantly corrupt," 300n97; performance taking precedence over, 183; upper castes as "casteless," 236–37
"cell phone revolution," 229
Central Statistical Organisation, 78
chained India metaphor, 211–12
Chakrabarty, Dipesh, 160–61, 167, 178, 293n70
Chalo Dilli campaign, 218
Chandragupta Maurya, 56, 280n9
Chatterjee, Partha, 114, 235
Chatterjee, Ramanand, 203–4
Chawla, Juhi, 210
Chidambaram, P., 60
China: ancient descriptions of India, 93–94, 280n9; as BRICS country, 4–5, 65, 72, 271n98; as economic engine, 211–12, 229; India compared, contrasted with, 61, 77–78, 85, 87, 162–63, 168; known for cheap goods, 25; population size, 69

Chopra, Shaili (SC), 180, 182–83, 299n84
"Citizen's Charter," 215–16, *217*
Clinton, Bill, 67, 136
Cohn, Bernard, 98
Columbus, Christopher, 54–59, *55*, 268n75, 271n4
Comaroff, John and Jean, 20
commercial enclosures, 8, 20, 29, 31–32, 34, 268n76
commodities, commodification: of cultural nationalism, 18–19; drawing forth the future, 15–16; economic and noneconomic, 43; of emerging and preemerging nations, 70–71; and Hinduism, 113–14; of India, 7, 52–53, 57, 59–61, 83, 89–90, 94; at India Adda, 158–59, 171, 174–75, 190; of information, 208; of land, 30–32; Merchandise Marks Act (1887), 25–26, 28; of "nation brands," 1, 21, 29, 37, 271n99; as rediscovery, 53–54, 57, 69; as remixing history, 89–90; and spectacle, 154–55; of Taj Mahal, 108, 119; by World Bank, 79; and world exhibitions, 24, 265nn48–49. *See also* Brand India
Commonwealth Games scam, 182, 290n32
Communist Party of India, 151
competitive federalism, 15
Confederation of Indian Industries (CII), 60, 162
Congress Party, 156; *Aam Aadmi ko kya mila* campaign, 126, 149, 151, 200; and BJP, 248; capitalist reform project, 246; losing proreform image, 153; opposing India Shining, 149–51, 156; and "reforms with a human face," 187; and Sonia Gandhi, 186; use of online mobilization, 229
Constitution of India, 216
consumption: and GDP, 78; micro-targeting, 136; middle-class, 158, 209;

national rankings by, 30; new narrative of, 102, 107–10, 119, 129, 135; women driving, 138
COO (country-of-origin) effect, 28
Cook, Eli, 75
corporate-style, 36, 168
corporation(s), 264n42, 265n45; as artificial person, 23; British East India Company, 46, 59, 184–85, 265nn45; IFC loans to, 65; investment in public interest, 196–97; measuring performance of, 75; media revenues from advertising, 207; and nationalism, 20; online campaigns by, 45; promoting cashless economy, 190; and rebranding, 22; and WEF, 164
corporatized state power, 187
corporeal contracts, 222, 225
corruption, fighting against: Aam aadmi (common man, investor-citizen), 156, 186, 195, 231; antipolitics, 35, 186, 269n87; "awards" for corrupt politicians, 230; Delhi 2011 movement, 156, 185–86, 230; India Against Corruption movement, 152; media attention on, 182; "netashopping" for politicans, 230; Oath campaign "I Swear" advertisements, 195, *196*, 223, *223*
country, WEF definition of, 29
"cricket mom," 138–39
crowds versus mob versus multitude, 198
cultural nationalism, 18, 48, 246–48
cultural politics, 47, 90–91, 109, 245, 251, 254
culture of commerce, 2, 20, 30, 159
customs duties and policies, 145–46

da Gama, Vasco, 57, 59
Dalits, 219, 234–36, 254, 286n51, 298n83, 300n97
DANIDA (Danish Development Aid Agency), 68
Davos annual WEF meetings, 1–2, 7–8,

foreign investments, 38, 65, 73, 75, 152–53, 171, 174
Foucault, Michel, 270n88
"free from India" gated communities, 209–10
free press as "sacred duty," 203
free trade: aid-for-trade principles, 68; Modi and, 7, 24, 31, 34, 83; nineteenth-century era, 7, 24, 31, 34, 83, 266n53; World Bank as arbiter of, 81
frontier, 31; of capitalism, 9; frontier markets, 70–71; rights to tied to labor, development, 31, 64; third world as, 54
Fukuyama, Francis, 250–52

Gandhi, Mahatma, 233, 238, 269n87
Gandhi, Sonia, 186
gate-crashing, 41–42
gated communities, 209–10
GDP (Gross Domestic Product), 73–78
Ghosh, Jayati, 124
global elite: and Brand India, 64; at Davos, 7, 41–43, 47, 158; new members of, 40; promoting "new" India, 115, 163; widening gap with rest of society, 250–51
global investment, 1–5, 51, 58, 175
globalization: adda redesigned for, 190, 293n70; avoiding "capitalism" label, 251; and "culture gardens," 253; "end of history" versus "brand new nation," 11–13, 34, 252; of Hindu aesthetics, 254; of India as business brand, 61; Pappu Raj appealing to, 231–32; as reterritorialization, 253; scholarship on, 262n11
"globalization 3.0," 262n13
Godrej, Adi, 180–81
Goings, Rick, 175–76
great spectacle, 11, 15–17, 244
Gujarat, 153, 247–48, 303n8
Gulzar (musician), 215

Hannover Messe, 63
Hansen, Thomas Blom, 269n87, 292n61
Happening Hyderabad campaign, 218
"Happy Anniversary?" (*Economist*), 51–52
Hazare, Anna, 111, 237–38, 241, 302nn109
HDFC (Housing Development Finance Corporation), 65, 189
Herder, Johann Gottfried, 18, 264n28
Hindu civilizational culture, 46, 89–92, 109–10, 113
Hinduism, 110, 113, 117, 282n53, 283n64
Hindu nationalism, 98, 241, 248. *See also* Modi, Narendra
Hindu rate of growth, 76, 92, 276n79
Hindutva, 119, 245, 283n64
Hinglish, 231–32
Hobsbawm, Eric, 22
hospitality: determining merit for, 173–74; India Adda as performance of, 43–44, 168, 171, 173–74, 178; in Make in India Lounge, 192; in tourism, 290n32–33
human collective, 198
hypericons, 125–26, 284n11
hypernationalism, 10, 14, 16–18, 241, 251–53

IBEF (India Brand Equity Foundation), 60–62, *159*, 162, 191, 272–73n21, 273n25
Ibn Battuta, 94
identity economy, 14, 245, 252
identity politics, 13–14, 245, 250, 252–53
IFC (International Finance Corporation), 65
illiberal democracy, 250–51
"illusion of premediated existence," 263n21
image-world, 221–22
Incredible India campaign, *103*, *107*, 107–8, *108*; auto rickshaw as symbol,

Lightning Source UK Ltd.
Milton Keynes UK
UKHW010827260620
365611UK00003B/324